Archibald Lampman

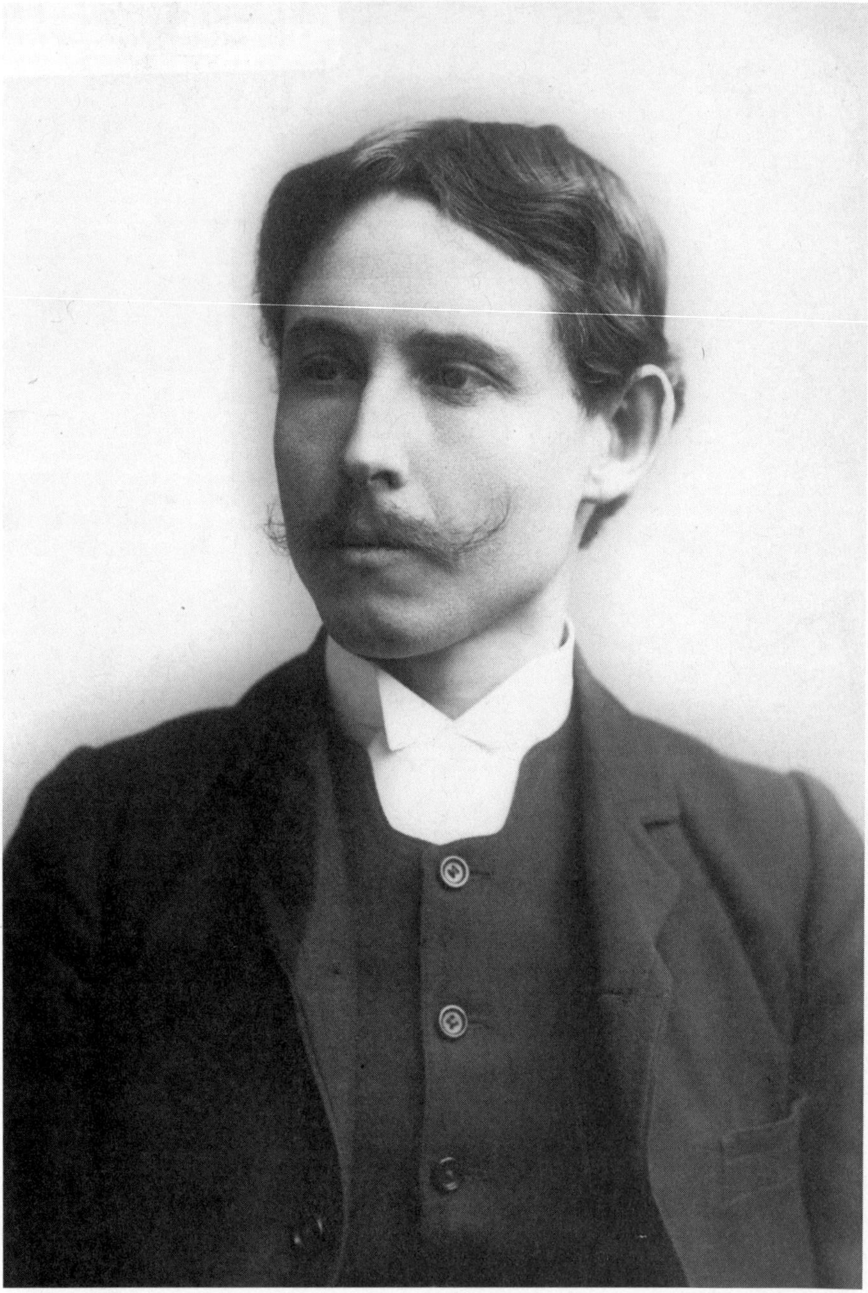

ARCHIBALD LAMPMAN

Memory, Nature, Progress

Eric Ball

McGill-Queen's University Press
Montreal & Kingston • London • Ithaca

© McGill-Queen's University Press 2013

ISBN 978-0-7735-4115-3 (cloth)
ISBN 978-0-7735-4160-3 (paper)
ISBN 978-0-7735-8860-8 (ePDF)
ISBN 978-0-7735-8861-5 (ePUB)

Legal deposit third quarter 2013
Bibliothèque nationale du Québec

Printed in Canada on acid-free paper that is 100% ancient forest free (100% post-consumer recycled), processed chlorine free

This book has been published with the help of a grant from the Canadian Federation for the Humanities and Social Sciences, through the Awards to Scholarly Publications Program, using funds provided by the Social Sciences and Humanities Research Council of Canada.

McGill-Queen's University Press acknowledges the support of the Canada Council for the Arts for our publishing program. We also acknowledge the financial support of the Government of Canada through the Canada Book Fund for our publishing activities.

Library and Archives Canada Cataloguing in Publication

Ball, Eric, 1951–, author
Archibald Lampman : memory, nature, progress / Eric Ball.

Includes bibliographical references and index.
Issued in print and electronic formats.
ISBN 978-0-7735-4115-3 (bound).–ISBN 978-0-7735-4160-3 (pbk.).–
ISBN 978-0-7735-8860-8 (ePDF).–ISBN 978-0-7735-8861-5 (ePUB)

1. Lampman, Archibald, 1861–1899 – Criticism and interpretation.
I. Title.

PS8473.A44Z698 2013   C811'.4   C2013-903271-1
C2013-903721-7

Frontispiece: Archibald Lampman, circa 1890
Reproduced by permission of Special Collections and Rare Books, Simon Fraser University

To Florence

So many happy memories

such good times

and so much still to do

Contents

Preface / ix
Introduction / 3

MEMORY *Alchemy in the Imagination*

1 The Workings of Memory / 27
2 Winter and Memory / 41

NATURE *The Full Furnace*

3 Beauty in Nature: Theory and Poetic Practice / 59
4 Discovering the Wilderness / 85
5 Heat and Cold: An Inclusive Vision / 97
6 *Lyrics of Earth*: Genesis, Design, Meaning / 123
7 Later Nature Poems / 162

PROGRESS *Through Lapse and Strife*

8 Ideas of Progress / 197
9 Poems of Progress / 218
10 Heroic Visionaries of Future Progress / 266

Appendix A / 289
Appendix B / 294
Notes / 297
Bibliography / 339
Index / 353

Preface

The origins of this study go back to a day when I was standing on a wharf in the tourist and shopping area known as Historic Properties in Halifax, Nova Scotia, with a book in my hand. I had moved east from southern Ontario to begin doctoral studies at Dalhousie University, and now I was seeing the sights. Having found my way into a delightful bookstore called A Pair of Trindles, I spotted among slim poetry books a substantial-looking volume entitled *The Poems of Archibald Lampman (including At the Long Sault)*, its wine-red cover matching, as I later discovered, the cover of Lampman's first published collection, *Among the Millet*. On an impulse I bought the book, and now here I was, listening to the lapping of the water, not realizing how that simple purchase would affect my life in the years to come.

I already knew who Lampman was. As an undergraduate at the University of Waterloo, and later in Robin Mathews's graduate seminar on Canadian poetry at Carleton University, I had become acquainted with his best-known poems – mostly those included in Malcolm Ross's New Canadian Library anthology *Poets of the Confederation*. (Dr Ross would become my second reader, and M.G. Parks my supervisor, for my dissertation on Lampman at Dalhousie.) There was in Lampman, I knew, a mystical response to nature, a focus on the Canadian scene, and a politically radical side to his writing. But there was more, much more, to find out – about Lampman, about poetry, and about Canada.

One of my greatest pleasures in doing the research both for my dissertation and, many years later, for this book, has been in connection with the archaeological aspect – reading old newspapers and magazines and manuscript materials and trying to ferret out the truth of things from a time long past. It was wonderful, one spring, to be sitting at a table beside a large window in the Special Collections Reading Room (no longer there) of Library and Archives Canada and looking down at the fast-flowing brown water of the Ottawa River carrying big rolling chunks of ice downstream, and then, in the silence of the archive, redirecting my attention to the pencilled script in one of Lampman's notebooks. I remember how thrilling it was – how moving – to turn a page and find the original holograph text of the poem "Heat." The writing was unusually small, cramped, and faint – barely visible – and my strong impression was that this was an on-the-spot composition. The glare of the sun that day, more than a century before, seemed to seep from between the now-familiar lines of the poem coming into being before my eyes.

In the course of producing this study, I have received help of many kinds from many quarters. I have had the good fortune to work for an institution that does not require of its faculty, but does support, academic research. My thanks therefore go to Langara College for granting me two six-month "educational leaves," fully funded, and two additional "renewal leaves for excellence." These leaves were vital to both research and writing, since to carry out either task with any degree of cohesiveness requires unbroken stretches of time. And thanks especially, in this regard, to Paul Headrick, who, as chair of the English Department, supported my initial application for a paid leave and since then has taken an abiding interest in my project. In addition, I would like to thank D.M.R. Bentley, general editor of Canadian Poetry Press, for encouraging my scholarly activities and for granting me permission to reprint here, in modified form, passages from my two-part article "Life 'Only Sweet': The Significance of the Sequence in *Lyrics of Earth*," originally published in the journal *Canadian Poetry: Studies, Documents, Reviews*. And to Eric L. Swanick, head of Special Collections and Rare Books at Simon Fraser University, and his predecessors in that position, I extend my thanks for graciously facilitating my research and for permission to include, from their collection, the portrait of Lampman that serves as the frontispiece to this volume.

I am hugely grateful to McGill-Queen's University Press for the combined friendliness and professionalism they unfailingly showed me throughout the process of vetting, editing, and producing this book. My thanks in particular go to Kyla Madden for opening the door, to Donald H. Akenson for setting me straight, and to Joan Harcourt, Mary-Lynne Ascough, and Mark Abley for steering me through. And to these names I would like to add that of my most thorough and helpful copy-editor, Grace Seybold, who was a pleasure to work with. To my peer reviewers, too, I wish to offer my thanks. I very much appreciate the careful attention they gave to my manuscript; I benefited enormously from their corrections and suggestions. I am grateful as well to Karen Evans, librarian with the Anglican Church of Canada, for conveying to me her thoughts on "high" and "low" Anglicanism in nineteenth-century Canada and other church-related matters; to Pamela J. Matz, of Widener Library of the Harvard University College Library, for furnishing me with copies of publications related to the death and funeral of William Dawson LeSueur; to Mike Childerstone, racing team leader with the Wey Kayak Club in Surrey, England, for defining the terms "hare" and "hound" in connection with canoe and kayak races; and to Derek Boles, blogger on the Heritage Toronto website, for providing information about the various incarnations of Union Station. And to those others in various libraries and institutes who have helped me, but whose names escape me now, my apologies and my thanks.

I would also like to acknowledge, with gratitude, that this book has been published with the help of a grant from the Canadian Federation for the Humanities and Social Sciences, through the Awards to Scholarly Publications Program, using funds provided by the Social Sciences and Humanities Research Council of Canada.

Finally, to my family and friends for being patient and interested and encouraging during the writing of this book, and especially to Florence Roy for her insights, her critiques, and her everlasting good cheer and upbeat support – my heartfelt thanks.

Archibald Lampman

Introduction

Born in Morpeth, Ontario, on 17 November 1861 and a resident of Ottawa all his adult life, Archibald Lampman would not live to see the fireworks go off above the government buildings to usher in the brave new century. He died of heart disease complicated by pneumonia on 10 February 1899, leaving a wife and two children (a third had died in infancy). In that short life, inspired by the beauty of nature in all its multiple manifestations and by the cause of progressive social change, he had created a body of work that garnered him a lasting reputation as a poet of high distinction – and distinctively Canadian.

A brief catalogue of critical assessments will show the incremental steps by which this reputation has been solidified over the decades from his time to our own. Shortly after the publication of his first book, *Among the Millet*, in 1888, Lampman was heralded in the United States by William Dean Howells, who stated that "his fame can only await the knowledge of work very uncommon in any time"; in Canada by E.W. Thomson, who offered high praise of "this most observant, most exact and most sympathetic of interpreters" of life and nature; and in England by an unnamed reviewer, who, while careful not to overstate the case, found "there is so much in [the book] of truth, simplicity, vivacity, and of something that fairly deserves the name of passion, that it is very pleasant and sometimes even impressive reading, almost from beginning to end."[1]

Although detractors have not been lacking, later criticism would for the most part corroborate the early reviewers. In 1929, biographer Carl Y. Connor stated that Lampman had become "recognized as Canada's best writer of nature verse, and perhaps the finest poet she had yet inspired."[2] Two decades later, both the high valuation of Lampman and his importance within the Canadian context were again emphasized by E.K. Brown, who, in an article marking the fiftieth anniversary of Lampman's death, described that event as "the most grievous loss our poetry has ever sustained." Brown was emphasizing the lost potential eventuated by Lampman's early death, but as he made clear in another passage, his estimate of achievement was that "[t]o this day no one has captured as Lampman did the beauty of the Canadian landscape, the march of the seasons in their astonishing extremes, the passing of day and night, land and water, storm and stillness, the fields at the city's edge and the untrodden wilds."[3] Forty years later still, in the introduction to his selected edition of Lampman, Michael Gnarowski offered this summation: "critical opinion has placed him in the front rank of Canadian poetry, and first among the writers of the nineteenth century."[4] And this view has held, with Tracy Ware observing in the year 2000 that Lampman's "style in his best work is so precise and so effective that its virtues are undeniable," criticism having shown "that such poems as 'Heat,' 'Among the Timothy,' 'Morning on the Lièvres,' 'The City of the End of Things,' and many of the sonnets are still among the best written in Canada."[5]

Running through the critical literature like the second strand of a double helix, however, and somewhat offsetting the high praise, is a persistent focus on the perceived derivativeness of much of Lampman's writing. A representative example may be found in the person of Roy Daniells, who in the *Literary History of Canada* (1965) relates that "Lampman has ... erected, though on narrow foundations, a small poetic edifice securely his own and the excellence of his best work is conditional upon its not attempting anything beyond these narrow limits." Beyond these narrow limits, Lampman's derivativeness – his "willing dependence on the Romantics and the Victorians for the tools of his trade and many of the materials of his craft" – is his downfall.[6] According to the writers who take this view, Lampman's acknowledged achievement is limited to poems emanating from a "small, pure stream" of uncontaminated inspiration, or, as Daniells puts it, punning on Lampman's name, "At the centre of his being there burned a small clear flame."[7] It must be said, however, that there is little agreement over which poems constitute the valued core of Lampman's output and that if everyone's choices were combined in one list, the critically approved corpus would expand considerably.

Here I wish to make two observations on the subject of literary influence. The first is that borrowing from literary antecedents, consciously or otherwise, is so widespread as to be almost universal among writers, not excluding undisputed masters (Shakespeare and Milton come to mind, as does Bob Dylan). As Alberto Manguel, challenging the usual perspective on this issue, has observed, "I find it moving that no literary text is utterly original, no literary text is completely unique, that it stems from previous texts, built on quotations and misquotations, on the vocabularies fashioned by others and transformed through imagination and use."[8] Without some degree of literary larceny, the world would lack many of the great works it treasures. Having said that, I acknowledge – this is the second point – that it is part of the critic's task to take note of literary precedents, not only to determine, since no work is "utterly original," the relative originality of a literary text, but also to show connections and establish pedigree. If Milton's Sonnet 23 ("Methought I saw my late espousèd saint") is derived in part from Walter Raleigh, as it is, or if Matthew Arnold's "A Dream" borrows from both Keats and Milton, as it does, or if the opening lines of T.S. Eliot's "The Waste Land" indicate a debt to Archibald Lampman, as, in chapter 1, I suggest they do, then it is well and of lasting interest to note the connection. The echo traced may detract very little or not at all from the impact and artistic success of the later poem, and indeed it is clear that, without the appropriation, the poem would not exist to give pleasure to those who have enjoyed it, in its present form. Or the echo may reveal a fatal lack of originality in the offending work. Whichever the result, such patterns of influence are of central importance in determining the values as well as the merits of a work of literature.

Certainly this issue must come to the fore in the present case, for rivalling Lampman's love of nature was his deep affection for the writers he admired, and it is fair to say he rooted in their words as much as in forests and fields for inspiration. Connor quotes a letter, since lost, that Lampman wrote to a college friend during his early days in Ottawa. "I have the long evenings to myself," he reports, "and invariably fall adreaming, which always ends in the shooting of a new subject across my brain." The nature of the dreaming is made clear in another passage: "I have been dreaming a great deal lately, sitting in the evenings with my pipe between my teeth, in an armchair, Matthew [Arnold] and Swinburne at my elbow and Shelley on my knee." On yet another occasion, lamenting the inhibiting effect of "self-distrust" on the creative imagination, he confesses, "I am in the barren wilderness at present. The only thing to do is to read and study myself back again."[9]

Books were consistently Lampman's solace and inspiration. Having taken a degree in classics, he had an abiding affection for the classical Greek writers and maintained an active interest in them all his life. During his final illness, Connor relates, "[e]very day he continued to read a little Greek, a page or two before breakfast," finding it "a great deal easier than he found Browning."[10] In addition, he loved the writers of the Romantic and Victorian traditions, especially Wordsworth, Keats, Arnold, and Tennyson, and more selectively the writers of other periods and traditions, among them Milton and – as I will demonstrate – John Keble, high Anglican clergyman and author of a once hugely popular collection of devotional poems, *The Christian Year*. Lampman's ancestors on both sides of his family were United Empire Loyalists, and as his close friend and literary executor Duncan Campbell Scott wittily observed, "Lampman was loyal to the great traditions of English poetry."[11] To this list should also be added the name of Charles G.D. Roberts, the Canadian writer who inspired Lampman to take up poetry and to play his part in the creation of a national literature in the early 1880s. Lampman studied all these writers closely, learned his art from them, and often used their works as a kind of springboard to launch his own compositions.

Lampman also admired a number of American authors of his own time and earlier, most notably Poe, Emerson, and, as D.M.R. Bentley has demonstrated, essayists John Burroughs and Bradford Torrey.[12] The American authors, however, did not have the same formative influence on Lampman as did the English (and Canadian) writers, whose works he frequently praised and in some cases wrote about at length. Still, it is clear that he felt he had much in common with Emerson, Burroughs, and Torrey and read their natural-world descriptions with pleasure and a sense of common purpose. Stylistic and verbal echoes of Poe and Emerson can be traced in Lampman's poems, and some writers have identified Emerson in particular as an influence on Lampman's interpretation of nature.[13]

While it is useful to investigate the issue of influence, there is a related trend in Lampman criticism that I believe has contributed to a misrepresentation and an under-appreciation of his work. It is remarkable how much effort has been expended on fitting Lampman into the aesthetics of the schools and periods he drew upon or can be associated with, to the point that he is defined *in terms of* his influences and the associations that may exist between his writings and those of the related groups. The most prominent term in this regard is Romanticism. As a writer of nature poems, Lampman is defined as a Romantic – and then at times faulted for failing to live up to Romantic ideals. In relation to his social-political poems, he is defined as a Victorian. Weighing the effects of these two sources of influence, L.R. Early has argued that "in general, Lampman learned much from the Romantics that he put to good use, and much from the Victorians that he put to bad."[14] Even the "good use" is tempered, however, by the tension of the contrary influences affecting Lampman. "The English Romantics," Early reminds us, "generally valued passion as an aspect of imaginative strength, and they tended to stress the process rather than the final issue of our destiny," whereas "Lampman's didactic account of Pan [in his essay 'The Modern School of Poetry in England'] recalls the long decades of Victorian gravity that succeeded Keats's and Shelley's ecstatic evocations of myth."[15] Lampman may have found "fertile ground" in the "tradition of prophetic humanism" within Romanticism, but he fell short of his Romantic predecessors in the sense that "he lacked their drive towards an ultimate synthesis" and, as a result of being subject to "diverse impulses" and "uncertainties," developed "a fissured vision."[16] What then of his achievement? It lies, according to Early, in Lampman's reworking of statements and beliefs from the Romantic tradition in certain well-honed poems, and, paradoxically, in his break from Romanticism, which symbolically occurs towards the end of Lampman's "Winter-Store," where a vision of human suffering and yearning interrupts the speaker's contented thoughts of rural scenes. For Early this constitutes "an admission of the limitations of his central mode of poetry, the Romantic nature lyric."[17] Early concludes that through Lampman's efforts, along with those of Charles G.D. Roberts and Isabella Valancy Crawford, "the Romantic tradition became naturalized in Canada," and Lampman's best poems, according to Early, were written in this vein.[18] At the same time, since the Romantic nature lyric was by this time an outmoded form, Lampman's triumph was to abandon it, making his greatest poetic achievement a kind of non-achievement and making Lampman more a transitional figure – "a worthy and a necessary ancestor" – than an accomplished poet in his own right, despite high artistic success in a handful of individual poems.[19]

Early's identification of Lampman as a Romantic poet – Bentley's review of Early's monograph *Archibald Lampman* is titled "A Romantic Lampman"[20] – is reinforced by Ware, who applies the term to the Confederation poets in general in his anthology *A Northern Romanticism: Poets of the Confederation*, among other writings.[21] A variation on this theme is introduced by Les McLeod, who makes a case for the term "Post-Romantic," rejecting "Confederation poets" in part because it "implies no aesthetic method or credo, and certainly no relationship between the poetry and international artistic or intellectual currents."[22] Employing the prefix "Post-" to indicate that the Canadian poets have moved beyond their Romantic antecedents but nevertheless are to be understood in relation to them, McLeod identifies an irony whereby they incorporate into their writing the Romantic "pathetic fallacy" of unity with nature only to emphatically, if unconsciously, undercut that stance. Taking his cue from Northrop Frye, who detected in Canadian poetry "a tone of deep terror in regard to nature" stemming from "the vast unconsciousness of nature," McLeod argues that this "terror" is in fact to be valued because the desire for "union with nature" amounts to "a death wish," whereas "the simpl[e] assertion of the fact of self in the face of solitudinous nature is as affirmative as it is terrifying. It is the necessary Canadian prelude to the existential act."[23] On the basis of the historical associations within the group and the fact that, in the words of Archibald MacMechan, "[t]he national impress [was] upon them all," Bentley has opted for the very descriptor McLeod dismisses as inadequate: the Confederation poets.[24] Nevertheless, Bentley applauds his fellow critics for their use of the term 'Romantic.' Having quoted passages from Roberts and Lampman in praise of Keats and Wordsworth, he writes, "Such statements as these and, more important, the evidence of their poems confirm that, as L.R. Early, Les McLeod, Tracy Ware, and others have long-since demonstrated, much of the poetry of the Confederation group is well described by such terms as 'Canadian Post-Romanticism' (McLeod) and 'Northern Romanticism' (Ware)."[25]

An offshoot of the Romantic designation is the term 'poet-impressionist.' Following upon A.J.M. Smith, who suggests that Lampman's "descriptive method ... is that of impressionism,"[26] and Early, who makes reference to the "impressionistic method that generally shapes Lampman's nature poetry,"[27] Anne Compton sets out to show that Lampman's aesthetic values are those of the French impressionists, with their focus on, not objects, but the evanescent play of light upon objects. "Like the Impressionists," she claims, "Lampman lauds the adequacy of the ordinary and the sufficiency of sensation."[28] Compton's analysis leads to many adroit observations. "Winter Uplands," she suggests, "is a composition of rapid notations ('The frost,' 'The long white drift,' 'The rippled sheet of snow,' 'The far-off city,' and so forth, begin the lines: strokes of a scene sketched in)," adding, "Lampman's tendency to move rapidly from point to point parallels the quick, fluent strokes in Impressionist painting."[29] Or again, comparing the descriptive methods of Roberts and Lampman, she writes that "[w]hereas Roberts ... aimed to make 'familiar things divine,'" as announced in the prologue to his *Songs of the Common Day*, "Lampman celebrated the fleeting, and thus unfamiliar face, of familiar things."[30]

To paint Lampman as an impressionist, however, proves highly reductive. For one thing, how do Lampman's social-political poems fit into this construct? Compton dismisses these poems by quoting Ralph Gustafson to the effect that "Lampman was not cut out to be a socialist poet; he was a nature poet," and concluding, "Misguided or insufficiently informed, our estimate of Lampman's socialism remains suspended."[31] Then there are those of Lampman's poems that fail to support such claims as "The momentary impression is, for Lampman, the truth of things" and "Landscape for Archibald Lampman is really an account of light."[32] "Heat" and "Solitude," according to Compton, work well as illustrations of these precepts, although the prominence of sound imagery in both poems requires some nimble rationalizing (and "heat" itself is not visual). "In November" and "Comfort of the Fields," on the other hand, fall short, the former because "the sensations are subordinated to narrative or to myth" and the latter because "Lampman conflates the 'mist of light' with the mist of dreams."[33] It appears the "sufficiency of sensation" can stand as Lampman's credo only by way of banishing from the slopes of Parnassus all of his poetry concerned with the human condition and half his nature poems as well. Finally, there is the issue of origins. As Compton acknowledges, there is little evidence to show that Lampman knew anything about the impressionist painters or had ever seen an impressionist painting. She suggests that Lampman could have heard about impressionism from his friend and correspondent Hamlin Garland, who was "the chief proponent of Impressionism in America," or encountered it on trips to Boston in the 1890s, but gamely adds that "even if he didn't, he anticipated it."[34] (Several of the poems that Compton puts forward as prime examples of impressionism in Lampman's writing, in fact, were written in the 1880s, before Lampman became acquainted with Garland or visited Boston.)

Of the various critics Compton aligns herself with, the two that stand out as having articulated ideas noticeably similar to her own are Smith and Daniells. It is worth noting, however, that Daniells himself diverges in a subtle but significant way from Smith and reaches a conclusion that differs not only from Smith's but from Compton's as well. Having made the point that Lampman's descriptive method is "that of impressionism," Smith declares (in a statement that Compton quotes) that "[s]ensation rather than idea is what Lampman derives from landscape," and continues:

> A painter's poet, he sees "the maple full of little crimson knots" in spring, and in autumn, "low thickets gray and reddish ... stroked white with birch ... pale greenish stems half hid in dry gray leaves." In winter "a few bronzed cedars ... lean their blue shadows on the puckered snow." Details of shape and color, seen always in the light of a precise minute, and valued for their own sake alone, give a special significance to Lampman's portrayal of Canada.[35]

Smith makes here a strong case for the painterly qualities of Lampman's descriptions, and he notes, as does Compton, the importance of the moment of perception. Granted he does not mention what Compton calls the "ever-changeful light" that characterizes French impressionism, and his emphasis on "shape and color" implies a broader definition of impressionism than the one she discusses. Still, his take on Lampman's methodology is fundamentally in synch with hers.

Daniells picks up on Smith's highlighting of "sensation rather than idea," but settles on a different lineage. He writes, "Like Keats, who influenced [Lampman] more than any other of the great Romantics and Victorians, his was primarily a life of sensation," adding a few pages later, "The marked quality and indeed the saving grace of Lampman's sensation when confronted by the face of nature is that it does not issue in ideas."[36] This is once again the "sufficiency of sensation" referred to by Compton but seen in the context of Keatsian Romanticism rather than French impressionism.

So the question arises: which *-ism* should Lampman properly be associated with? If we say both, then the associations begin to lose their meaning. Certainly Compton regards them as mutually exclusive, asserting that "[w]hat has often been taken as a Romantic declaration – his contiguity to nature – results, in fact, from his impressionist aesthetic."[37] Given the uncomfortable fit of such terms as 'Romantic' and 'impressionist' as applied to Lampman, along with the confusion created by the contrary aesthetic identities, I would suggest that it does not serve Lampman well to be slotted into either category. It limits our appreciation. I do nevertheless agree with Compton as well as with Early that, in terms of his response to nature, Lampman anticipates the Canadian painters who *were* influenced by French impressionism,[38] and about one of their number I shall shortly have more to say.

The defining term employed by one additional group of critics is transcendentalism. Barrie Davies, for example, who sees Emerson as "probably the most congenial and important influence upon Lampman" with respect to religion and spirituality,[39] has argued that Lampman's writing on these central issues was in essence an expression of that philosophy.[40] Lampman's "Heat" is thus "a fine transcendental poem."[41] A similarly fine transcendental poem, according to Carl F. Klinck, is "The Frogs,"[42] a work that, with its borrowings from Keats and Tennyson, is more often interpreted as belonging to the English Romantic tradition.[43] Another critic, Richard Arnold, takes the view that Lampman *wishes* to emulate Emerson, tries to do so, especially in *Lyrics of Earth*, but ultimately gives up, becoming in essence a failed transcendentalist: "he cannot allow himself to become a fully-fledged transcendentalist because he sees in nature awful, threatening elements which Emerson obviously overlooked, and also because he cannot allow himself to look at reality through the same optimistic glasses worn by Emerson."[44] Like Early, Arnold points to the closing lines of "Winter-Store" as indicating a change in Lampman's thinking: "This poem, ending in all its inconclusiveness, is ultimately a rejection of Emersonian Transcendentalism."[45] Early's previously quoted observation was that "Winter-Store" marks Lampman's rejection of "the Romantic nature lyric." In the one case, Lampman has followed in the footsteps of Emerson, ultimately to reject that philosophy; in the other, it was Wordsworth and Keats he was tracking, with the same result. So again, who is right? Or are English Romanticism and American transcendentalism interchangeable? The extent to which, in American national consciousness, the term transcendentalism is attached to the school of Emerson, Thoreau, and their associates would suggest that to the Americans, at least, their own Romantics are a different breed.

In the spring of 1975 a three-day symposium on Lampman was held at the University of Ottawa, and most of the papers from this event, together with four contributions to a panel discussion on "Lampman's Achievement," were published in *The Lampman Symposium* (1976), edited by Lorraine McMullen. The members of the achievement panel, according to McMullen, presented their ideas "clearly and cogently,"[46] but as Bentley, who was also present, relates, the panel discussion featured some "hard-hitting comments" and "had its memorable moments." Bentley's recollections of "the colourful give and take of characters and ideas" and of "heated exchanges" at the symposium are indicative of the energy and enthusiasm that characterized Lampman studies at the time.[47] One of the contributors to the achievement panel was Robin Mathews, who in McMullen's understated account "reminded us of the importance of Lampman's Canadian milieu, especially the intellectual milieu, to his artistic expression."[48] An outspoken poet, critic, and social activist best known for the cross-country campaign that he and fellow panelist James Steele conducted in the 1960s to promote the hiring of Canadian academics in Canadian universities,[49] Mathews declared that "the foreign names plastered on Lampman's thought and expression are odious and inept, misleading and imprecise." On the subject of Lampman's achievement, he spoke as follows:

> He is of commanding importance to us, when we fully understand ourselves, because he took from the world what he needed in his thought – from the [classical] Greeks, from the English, from the writers of the U.S. – in a way which permitted him to address the major questions of the day, as he saw them, with a consciousness that was of his time, that was informed and relevant. But what is infinitely more important to the measure of his achievement is that he *lived* in the ideas of his own time *in this place*, structuring his thought from objects and experiences which are the furniture of our own lives.[50]

In his overview of the symposium, Bentley offers this comparatively sedate corroboration of Mathews's impassioned declaration:

> On Lampman's Canadian *milieu* and the poet's place in it all too little work has been done, but the essays in this volume provide many hints about the directions in which such work should proceed. There can be little doubt that, to borrow and redirect a sentence from James Steele's piece on "Lampman's Achievement," that [sic] the poet *will* seem "all the more remarkable when seen in the context of the social and ideological forces which were dominant in late Victorian Canada."[51]

Steele had argued that Lampman, far from being inextricably attached to ideologies of the past, anticipated the major concerns of modernism, including a "feeling of alienation" and "anxiety about the social implications of industrialization," which seemed surprising given the conservative values and optimistic beliefs of Lampman's society.[52] Bentley rejigs the fragment he quotes from Steele to emphasize that, as yet, Lampman's relation to his own cultural milieu remains unexplored.

Since the time of this symposium, some considerable exploring has been done. Bentley himself has investigated the effects of the exigencies of the dominant American publishing market on the compositional practices of Lampman and other early Canadian writers – part of the Canadian milieu – and has also examined the relationship between poetic forms and the settings of landscape writings in either a baseland or a hinterland environment, whereby, for example, a prairie setting generates open forms, while depictions of an occupied and cultivated landscape, as in many of Lampman's poems, lead to closed forms such as the sonnet.[53] And numerous writers have identified "evolutionary idealism" as a prominent ideology in late-nineteenth-century Canada. Les McLeod, for example, states that "Evolutionary Idealism is the philosophical background for the Post-Romantic experience of the self in nature." This background is "indigenous" in the sense that it draws on the influential writings of Scottish-born Canadian philosopher John Watson and others. McLeod's point, however, is that this idealism, like Romanticism, is subverted – "officially" extolled but subtly undermined – and ultimately abandoned by Lampman and his fellow Confederation poets in favour of "naturalism and a radical individualism," albeit, once again, unconsciously, since "the Post-Romantic poets were, at best, only dimly aware that their poems expressed the sort of realization I am suggesting they do."[54] Interested primarily in Lampman's interpretation of nature, McLeod does not examine the social-political poems in the light of evolutionary idealism, even though it is in these poems that Lampman's progressivism finds its clearest expression. Richard Arnold acknowledges the significance of what he calls "evolutionary meliorism" in Lampman's poetry, but he sees it as part of a shallow and untenably optimistic transcendentalism that, as already discussed, Lampman rejects "in order to look directly at the frightening realities of nature and human nature."[55] Early likewise takes note of Lampman's "meliorist visions" but only in the context of "one of the deepest rifts in his imagination: on the one hand, a strong attachment to an Arcadian vision of nature; on the other, a commitment to late nineteenth-century evolutionary idealism. The one is fundamentally emotional and retrospective, the other intellectual and progressive."[56]

The idea that Lampman's nature poems are at odds with his "meliorist visions" is challenged by James Doyle, who argues that Lampman's socialism is at the heart of an "ideological unity" in his work. Socialism

INTRODUCTION 15

provided Lampman with "a natural and practical vision of human life as it can and ought to be," one that ran through his nature poems and social-political poems alike: "All of Lampman's poetry ... is informed by this belief." In Doyle's analysis, however, the ideological context for Lampman's progressivism has little to do with his Canadian milieu. Rather, Doyle speaks of an "anarchistic individualism" in Lampman derived from such influences as Carlyle, Emerson, and Oscar Wilde.[57]

F.W. Watt, another of the few critics to evince an interest in Lampman's socialism, had earlier characterized Lampman as "the poet probably most inclined of any of the Group of the Sixties to social analysis, commentary, and protest." One manifestation of the "evolutionary optimism" of the period, according to Watt, was a belief on the part of the working classes in "an inevitable movement towards socialism, however unsympathetic the immediate climate." This was exemplified by one J. Connell, who in April of 1913 stated in the *Western Clarion*, party journal (1904–20) of the British Columbia–based Socialist Party of Canada, that "capitalist individualism seems firmly rooted and strongly knit, but the laws of nature are fighting on our side ... The time is coming when the waves of the evolutionary tide will break and roar far, very far above it."[58] This is recognizably a belief, or dream, that Lampman adopted and frequently incorporated into poems, and it also reflects the ideas about social progress emerging from the philosophical writings of Watson and others in Canada during the last quarter of the nineteenth century. Part three of the present study looks at Lampman's social-political poems in the context of the progressivism that was in the air at the time, including among Lampman's own circle of friends.

There is undeniable insight, admiration, affection, and not a little ingenuity to be found in recent Lampman criticism. Taken together, though, it presents the reader with a confusing picture of the poet's values and achievement. The various *-ism*s applied to his work have the effect of dislocating Lampman from his own centre of being and misrepresenting his poetic enterprise. He seems an amalgam of influences primarily from the Romantic and Victorian traditions or, at best, a transitional figure doing a favour for future generations by exhausting those traditions and paving the way for modernism. Even his vaunted Canadianism seems to amount to little more than local colour for imported ideology and poetic practice. In an attempt to pry him loose from the *-ism*s that have,

I believe, limited our appreciation of his poems, I endeavour in this study to see Lampman on his own terms. By this I mean, first, to view his work as an expression of his own personality, stemming from family background, life experiences, education, friendships, hardships – not so much to trace cause and effect as to infer the man from the work; and second, to highlight both the geographical and the cultural features of Lampman's environment and investigate how he responded artistically to *these* influences.

Accordingly I have identified three core themes that Lampman returned to repeatedly, charting, as does any serious writer, the map of his imaginative world: one, the workings of memory; two, the depiction of beauty in nature and its effects on the sympathetic observer; and three, the repudiation of capitalism and promotion of humanity's advancement toward social harmony and justice; or, in short, memory, nature, and progress. (I have omitted love as a separate category because it was not productive of Lampman's best work except where it comes up in conjunction with the other themes, in the context of which I do include it.) The second and third categories were obvious choices, since Lampman's poetic responses to scenes in nature are what he is rightfully most admired for, and since the social critique he offered in the context of his progressivist politics constitutes the first authentic poetry of social protest and advocacy in Canadian literature. The theme of memory is included because it reveals an attitude toward experience – a desire to escape the linear flow of time – that was fundamental to Lampman's psychology and helps to explain the ironic perspective that is central to his definition of beauty in nature.

These themes correspond to the three faces of time – past, present, and future – although involving, in each case, a different aspect of experience. Memory refers to one's own past as it exists in consciousness, and Lampman, it appears, was fascinated by the way in which mental images of the past, like works of art, can dwell in a pure state, cleansed of distracting or disturbing information that may have compromised the actual experience. Nature is the place of refuge where it is possible to lose oneself in contemplation or, put simply, to relax in the absence of pressures from the social arena and to feel alive to the moment. In Lampman's rendering, this experience is not confined to mild, bucolic scenes, but rather is possible in a wide range of natural-world conditions and settings. Lampman's all-embracing definition of beauty in nature, derived from the very landscapes he was depicting, is the most distinctive quality of his nature poems. Progress relates to the future of humankind. The idea Lampman explores is that by furthering the cause of social advancement one shares in something larger than oneself and becomes, through participation in the process of achieving the transformation, transformed. What these various responses to time have in common is a seeking after redemptive experience in relation to time, and in pursuing this quest, Lampman emerges as a poet of mystical predisposition whose one overriding aim was to find spiritual-like fulfillment within the physical realm of existence.[59]

But since these are the subjects of the chapters that follow, I will not belabour them here. Instead, in an effort to refresh the critical perspective, I will devote the remainder of this introduction to exploring how Lampman's writing advanced patterns that we recognize as characteristic of Canadian artistic expression, looking forward rather than backward. The purpose of this refocusing is to situate Lampman not at the tail end of old traditions but rather at the forefront of new ones, and I offer it in the same spirit as that in which James Steele propounds the view that Lampman anticipated the concerns of modernism and Les McLeod traces an irony by which Lampman and his contemporaries distanced themselves from the very Romantics they ostensibly emulated. Though I am not precisely in agreement with either scholar, I share with these and other critics the conviction that Lampman's poems have a quality that echoes forward in time, allowing readers today to find a resonance that can readily be applied to their own experience.

The distinctive and in some ways prototypical Canadianism of Lampman's poetry, I submit, is nowhere more apparent than in his embracing of the extremes of climate and terrain and the endless cycle of life and death within an all-inclusive and affirming philosophy of nature. The paradox according to which, in the memory poems, events that might have had negative elements can be experienced in consciousness after the fact as entirely positive resurfaces in a more poetically rich way in Lampman's nature poems. It provides them with a complexity that as a collection of mere descriptions, however accurate, they would not possess. The extremes within nature are severe, yet attractive; the harsh conditions have a beauty of their own. Lampman recognizes the essentially paradoxical quality of this response and presents it as such, the irony itself being the ideological cornerstone of certain of his best poems, such as "Heat," as well as constituting the underlying theme of the sequence of seasonal poems that make up his second collection, *Lyrics of Earth*.

In perceiving beauty in all manifestations of nature, and in focusing specifically on the annual cycle of seasons as the overriding image to embody the inclusive irony of this vision, Lampman anticipated the depiction of nature by iconic Canadian painter Tom Thomson, whose artistic catalogue of the seasons, inspired by much the same terrain, is in many ways the visual-arts equivalent of Lampman's word studies. Art critic Joan Murray has noted that Thomson admired the writings of several of the Confederation poets: Carman, Roberts, and Campbell.[60] Murray does not mention Lampman, and whether Thomson read him or not is impossible to say with certainty, although Thomson's patriotism and love of poetry, combined with the widespread availability of Lampman's *Poems* during Thomson's formative and active years, make it seem at least possible. What the evidence of their respective oeuvres reveals, however, is that, of all the Confederation poets, Lampman is the one whose work bears the closest resemblance to Thomson's in terms of subject and theme. In a recent article on Lampman in *(Cult)ure Magazine*, Brendan Blom calls Lampman "Canada's greatest nature poet – its literary Tom Thomson," and the parallels bear him out.[61]

That the cycle of seasons was as compelling an image for Thomson as it was for Lampman is supported by a statement by Charles C. Hill, coordinator of the Thomson exhibit that toured Canada in 2002–03. The show included a particular grouping of paintings in their seasonal sequence, meant to highlight this aspect of Thomson's experience of nature. Hill's comment, however, relates in general to the "sketches" or small on-site paintings that Thomson made during his various trips to the north:

> In his sketches one is able to follow the seasons' passing, from the late winter snow to the budding of spring, the skies of summer and changing of fall leaves from red to yellow to the first snows of winter. These were his prime subjects, a limited number of motifs endlessly repeated in constantly evolving perceptions. It is

his intense observation and sensitivity to the seasons' colours and lights that are the source of his contributions to Canadian art. He saw and was able to express what had not been caught with such accuracy and expression before.[62]

If the painting-specific language were changed to terminology that applied to poetry, this passage could serve as a statement of Lampman's poetic practice as well. Lampman thought of his poems in seasonal terms, as his titles indicate; he frequently arranged them according to the progression of the annual cycle, most notably in his *Lyrics of Earth*, which also goes from "late winter snow" through to "the first snows of winter," but includes as well the entirety of winter within its compass, which Thomson's annual departure from the north with the onset of winter did not allow; and Lampman, like Thomson, saw nature in its entirety as a source of spiritual-like comfort and inspiration.

A comparison of titles used by Lampman and Thomson is revealing of their shared fascination with, and desire to chronicle artistically, the annual cycle of nature:

LAMPMAN	THOMSON
After Rain	After the Storm
Autumn Maples	Autumn Colour
In the Pine Groves	In the Woods
The Lake in the Forest	Lake in Algonquin Park
The Woodcutter's Hut	Shack in the North Country
A Forest Path in Winter	Path Behind Mowat Lodge
A Thunderstorm	Stormy Sky
A March Day	Summer Day
In November	Chill November
Winter Evening	Autumn Evening
Winter-Break	Winter Thaw
Snow	Late Snow

It is true that titles referencing the annual cycle of seasons are commonplace among poets and painters of landscape, but the preponderance of such titles and the particulars of phrasing employed by both

Lampman and Thomson indicate that these two artists were drawn to similar phenomena within nature and had similarly catholic tastes, wishing to depict the full range of an ever-changing landscape.

The association with Thomson is a significant one, pointing to what might be termed an aesthetic born of contact with the terrain depicted. Thomson was strongly influenced by French impressionism as well as by the English arts and crafts movement, just as Lampman was by his Romantic and Victorian forebears, and both may have appreciated the aesthetic values shared by these various movements, such as the shift "back to nature"; but what more fundamentally unites Lampman and Thomson is a common response to the same physical surroundings. Both were entranced by the singular beauty of the northern wilderness (northern, that is, relative to the populated south along the border with the United States), and both embraced that landscape in its totality, consciously incorporating harsh and forbidding natural-world imagery within a vision that extolled the beauty of all. The stimulus of their shared environment proved as strong as, or stronger than, the work of the writers and painters they admired in determining the distinctive qualities of their work.

In his social-political writings, too, critiquing capitalism and advocating socialism, Lampman set the standard for the future, for in Canada, progressive thought of various stripes, from revolutionary red to Red Tory, has been present over the past century both on the fringes of society and in the midst of the body politic, although radicalism had not much of a footing yet in Lampman's day and virtually no place in the nation's literature.[63]

Within academia, Lampman's poems of social protest have met with a mixed response, valued by some for their literary quality and political outspokenness and dismissed by others as unconvincing and ineffectual, however representative of strongly held convictions.[64] To the extent that they have been aware of them, on the other hand, non-academic left-wing readers with a literary bent have consistently welcomed these poems as moving poetic declarations of political conviction and advocacy. A curious instance is recounted by Brown in a letter to Scott pertaining to the publication in 1943 of *At the Long Sault, and Other New Poems*, a collection of previously unpublished poems by Lampman, including three – "The Usurer," "Epitaph on a Rich Man," and "Liberty" – expressive of his radical politics. Brown quotes an unidentified "young communist" who sees Lampman as having an awareness of "the fundamentally loathesome [sic] and inhumane character of society" and describes him as having discovered in his retreat to nature "a personal solution for the horror he felt about human and social relationships; he found in nature what he missed in society."[65] Implicit in these observations is a recognition of Lampman's strong sympathy for society's disadvantaged and equally strong antipathy to the social conditions that created their misery, feelings that were consistent, not at odds, with the impetus behind his nature poems. Or again, in the mid-1950s, Lampman was one of four early Canadian poets from whom selections were chosen to make up a small anthology of poetry issued by New Frontiers, publishers of a Marxist-affiliated cultural magazine of the same name that ran from 1951 to 1956, dedicated to resisting American domination of Canadian culture and promoting indigenous culture within Canada. As James Doyle has observed, the fulfillment of this aim would require more than just "railing against the adversary," for "*New Frontiers* would have to reveal evidence of a distinctive and aesthetically valuable Canadian progressive cultural tradition."[66] The anthology, titled *The Stone, The Axe, The Sword and Other Canadian Poems*, was clearly intended to contribute to this purpose, and the inclusion of Lampman, along with Alexander McLachlan, Isabella Valancy Crawford, and Peter McArthur, indicates that he was regarded as part of this tradition.

But undoubtedly the most significant recognition in later years of Lampman's role in helping to establish a literature of social protest in Canada is to be found in statements by Milton Acorn, the country's premier poet of the literary left of the mid-to-late twentieth century. Despite differences in the styles and poetic personae of the two writers, Acorn saw in Lampman's poetics an earlier incarnation of his own. He had good reason. Both wrote closely observant, evocative nature verse, and did so without sentimentalizing nature.[67] As self-proclaimed socialists they shared a belief in "progress" – the advancement of humanity toward a future in which the disparities of capitalism would be replaced by a more equitable, socialist system – while at the same time regretting that the times in which they lived were corrupt and misguided: in Acorn's phrase, a "dark age."[68] As Chris Gudgeon relates in his biography *Out of This World: The Natural History of Milton Acorn*, Acorn "discovered Lampman's writing in the fifties and recognized in it a true literary antecedent to his own work ... Writers like Lampman and [Dorothy] Livesay helped him feel that he was part of something better, an ongoing Canadian socialist poetry tradition."[69] The point is reinforced by an anecdote provided by Joyce Wayne, editor and friend in his later years, in a memorial article written two years after Acorn's death on 20 August 1986. When Wayne provided Acorn with a copy of Lampman's obituary notice from the *Ottawa Evening Journal* (where, in contrast to the notices that appeared in other newspapers, his political views had been prominently featured), Acorn "read it aloud in a voice flowing with intimations of his own passing." According to Wayne, Lampman was "the poet with whom [Acorn] most closely identified."[70]

The link between Lampman and Acorn is evident in both the prominent themes in their writing and the choices they made with respect to form and content. Two statements by Acorn are particularly illuminating in this regard. In a quotation from the front pages of the 1978 reprint of his selected poems entitled *I've Tasted My Blood*, Acorn states, "I have called myself many things; but I guess the one that sticks is 'Revolutionary Poet' – that is revolutionary in the political sense, not the poetic sense."[71] This seems at first an odd claim, self-deprecating and admitting of limitation, not the colours one would want to fly, especially in an era when both traditionalism and revolutionary politics in poetry were less valued than theoretical-technical experimentation and political disillusionment. But seen differently, there is a boast in the statement: Acorn is not siding with those whose political apology for the status quo is camouflaged by harmless intellectual-aesthetic games; rather, he is with those who remain "conservative" in form but who challenge with content. This position applies well to Lampman, whose "loyalist" poetics and radical politics led him to excoriate the perpetrators of capitalist greed and governmental corruption in sonnets.

The second statement comes from Acorn's introduction to his *Jackpine Sonnets* (1977), a book that, by his own account, had been influenced by Lampman's sonnets.[72] "The history of poetry," he writes, "as that of any great art, is often presented as a history of destructions, each generation turning its claws against the last. For obvious reasons, we Canadians can't afford to take that attitude all too seriously."[73] Canada as a nation depends for its survival on continuum, with a connection to

INTRODUCTION 23

the past, and its poetry does the same: it may wish to, and in Acorn's opinion should, put forward a "revolutionary" message, but it must formulate contemporary expression without severing its ties to tradition. That Acorn saw his own poetry as continuing a tradition initiated in part by Lampman is suggested by the dedication in a small book he co-wrote with James Deahl: "To the memory of Archibald Lampman, 1861–1899 and Isabella Valancy Crawford, 1850–1887 in honour of the Canadian poetry they established."[74]

The point of this brief look at two channels of artistic expression that came after Lampman has been to show that qualities in Lampman's poetry anticipate the aesthetic values of the future as much as they reference those of the past. In the pages that follow, I concentrate on the substance and quality of the poems themselves, taking it as a given that to measure Lampman's achievement it is vital to understand his poetic vision, and that without a demonstration of artistic achievement, the contexts for the writing are of little importance. At the same time, I pay attention to those contexts – both the ways in which he responded to his own geographical surroundings and social milieu and the uses he made of literary precedents – so as to clarify lineage, determine kinds and degrees of originality, and define new directions. By focusing on the themes of memory, nature, and progress, I hope to show that Lampman is a writer who, from across the intervening century between his time and ours, speaks to us still of what it can mean to look back, look around, and look forward in this particular geopolitical space.

MEMORY

Alchemy in the Imagination

CHAPTER 1

The Workings of Memory

Lampman was a poet preoccupied with states of consciousness in relation to time.

In his nature poems he demonstrates what it means to be at peace with the here and now, either by "tuning out" other thoughts and focusing intently on the present scene or simply by relaxing and letting his mind wander freely. In his poems on social-political issues, he explores the effects of serving a cause that is greater than oneself – the progress of humanity toward a more enlightened state of being in the future. These two themes, nature and progress, have to do with seeking fulfillment in relation to the present (engaging perceptually with the natural world) and the future (working toward the anticipated goal of social transformation), respectively. They are the major themes of Lampman's oeuvre, explored in parts two and three of this study.

An additional theme that engaged Lampman's imagination persistently over many years is that of experience seen from a remote point of view, or, in the form in which it typically manifests, memory. Through the exercising of memory, it is possible to escape the limitations of mundane consciousness, since the experience of imaginatively reliving past events, always selectively, can be pure and complete in a way not normally possible when the events are occurring.

Taken together, Lampman's explorations of these three themes reveal an obsession with finding purpose and meaning beyond the level of mundane existence. "Too well we see," he said of the condition of humankind in the modern world, "The drop of life lost in eternity."[1] Life without a spiritual dimension remains unredeemed from its ephemerality and insignificance. Through the appreciation of beauty in nature, or dedication to the cause of social progress, or "divine remembrance,"[2] it was possible to discover the meaning that was lacking in the spiritual vacuity of a materialist and increasingly secular world.

One reason to investigate Lampman's treatment of the memory theme, then, is to demonstrate how, in relation to the past, his quest for permanence and significance played out artistically. Another reason is that many of Lampman's poems are records of particular encounters with natural-world subjects, honed and refined so as to capture the essence of the experience. These poems exist as embodied memory, written both as personal keepsakes and as things to be shared. Just as important, though, is the fact that through his interpretation of memory as a means of freeing experience of its negative components, Lampman articulates a paradox that complements his outlook on nature, within which the extremes of weather and terrain are often seen as the opposite of what they appear – "sweet" rather than "sharp." The paradox, in essence, is that while a past experience might have been tinged with negativity, and almost inevitably by complications or distractions, in memory it can exist in a pure or self-contained state, cleansed of that debris. Lampman sometimes takes this idea to an almost ludicrous extreme, apparently preferring images of reality to reality itself and giving the impression he finds it hard to exist in the present at all. More than anything else, it was Lampman's goal to redeem experience – to find meaning in being – and the memory poems help to illuminate this quest.

The lineage of the memory theme in Lampman's writing can be traced to Wordsworth's "I wandered lonely as a cloud" and "Lines Composed a Few Miles above Tintern Abbey" (known familiarly as "Tintern Abbey") through Matthew Arnold's "Resignation" and Charles G.D. Roberts's "Tantramar Revisited," the latter two poems being likewise indebted to Wordsworth. "Tantramar Revisited" was published in 1883 in the *Week*, the Canadian magazine in which Lampman's first publications also appeared, accepted by Roberts himself during his short-lived stint as editor.[3]

More than his precursors, though, Lampman seizes on the theme, finding it fertile ground for a writer who, as in the sonnet "Outlook," longs "Not to be conquered by these headlong days, / But to stand free." Where distractions from without and within may prevent one from living in the moment or even from thinking clearly, remembered events can be experienced in their wholeness and purity, free of the static that may have compromised the integrity of the experiences to start with, exactly like a work of art. Another and better solution is the kind of intense involvement in the present made possible by natural-world observation. The two experiences, however, prove not to be as dissimilar as they might seem. In both cases, all peripheral and distracting matters are forgotten or diminished as the experience of the moment, past or present, is heightened or rarefied, becoming "pure" as most consciousness is not. What the memory poems reveal is a cast of mind that is central to Lampman's psychology, evident in the desire to be either the removed observer of, or the alert participant in, experience; to be, in terms of consciousness, aware, either from the outside or the inside.

"April"

The first poem in Lampman's first book, apart from the titular "Among the Millet," is "April," a work that, with its echoes of "To Autumn," pays homage to Keats and even suggests a trans-Atlantic reawakening of the Keatsian spirit. Lampman once commented, "Keats has always had such a fascination for me and has so permeated my whole mental outfit that I have an idea that he has found a sort of faint reincarnation in me."[4] Thus the Keatsian apostrophe to Autumn – "Season of mists and mellow fruitfulness, / Close bosom friend of the maturing sun" – receives its echo – "Pale season, watcher in unvexed suspense, / Still priestess of the patient middle day." And following this, as if in reply to Keats's rhetorical question "Where are the songs of spring?"[5] Lampman offers his depiction of April, "Maid month of sunny peace and sober gray." Although Lampman will find, and find words for, more severe extremes of climate and terrain than are evident in the gardens of Keats's odes, he is for the moment happily at one with his Romantic predecessor, extending a symbolic hand of fellowship and offering solace for the English poet's melancholy by substituting vernal for autumnal imagery.

In his characterization of April as a Janus-like interval between more decisive realities, however, Lampman is announcing a theme that adherence to Keats would not require, but which would often resurface in his own poems. To explain the peculiar beauty of April, he draws the following analogy:

> As memory of pain, all past, is peace,
> And joy, dream-tasted, hath the deepest cheer,
> So art thou sweetest of all months that lease
> The twelve short spaces of the flying year.

For Lampman, April is the sweetest (and not the cruellest) month because symbolically it defines a confluence between, in T.S. Eliot's terminology, memory and desire, and partakes of both without being involved in either. (Eliot's terminology, interestingly, was also Lampman's in the sonnet "Ambition," and it is not impossible that Lampman's *Poems* was precisely where Eliot found the germ of his image of April in "The Waste Land.")[6] Anticipated joys are happier than those actually experienced, while past sufferings lose their sting. It is the second point that is relevant here. One reading is simply that pain, once finished, is no longer pain. Another implication, however, is that past experiences, even those which at the time were compromised by pain, can become transformed by means of memory in the same way that imaginings of the future can take on an idyllic cast. Thus, where March, in the language of the poem, might very well have been "vex[ed]" by "frozen fear," that month can now, in April, be seen in a positive light, just as, in the opposite temporal direction, the happiness of May might turn out to have been better in imagination than in the event. In April all things are possible, even retrospectively. For Lampman, indeed, all things are possible in retrospect throughout the year, but the irony of this perspective is most apparent in April, looking back on winter.

"Three Flower Petals"

In several other poems in *Among the Millet,* Lampman returns to the idea of memory as a transformative power. One early example, composed in 1883, is "Three Flower Petals," in which the speaker – Lampman on one of his country walks – recalls being charmed by the appearance and behaviour of a yellow-haired girl he noticed in the entranceway to a farmyard garden.[7] The poem is suffused with brightness and warmth radiating from its three central images – the summer sun, a sunflower that the girl is shyly hiding behind, and the girl's hair – and from the girl's laughter, referred to four times in twenty-four lines. The main conceit, however, is that the three petals of the sunflower that the girl gives to the speaker "for token" are transformed by him into the three stanzas of the poem, which will prompt memory in such a way

> That a tender dream of her face may rise,
>   And lighten me yet in another hour,
> Of her sunny hair and her beautiful eyes,
>   Laughing over the gold sunflower.

He has gained "Something to keep for a charm in my heart – / A little sweet girl in a garden gate." With the emphasis placed on what is "to keep," the role of memory and the imagination takes precedence over that of the senses. The garden gate, in this context, seems a kind of frame for the picture preserved. Thus Lampman sets the stage for several poems emphasizing the appreciation of experience after the fact.

"An Athenian Reverie"

Perhaps his fullest treatment of the theme is found in "An Athenian Reverie," a narrative poem set in classical Greece, composed in 1885 and first published in *Among the Millet* in 1888.[8] The narrator is a young man much concerned with the topic of marriage, who, in meditative blank verse, likes to ruminate over scenes he has observed in the past, a way of relating to the world that he believes would have to be sacrificed in married life. Early in the poem we find him reflecting joyously on his recent experiences:

> How many things
> Even in a little space both good and ill
> Have fallen on me, and yet in all of them
> The keen experience or the smooth remembrance
> Hath found some sweet.

Two points about the narrator's way of seeing the world are relevant here. First, he treasures both positive and negative experiences, finding each contains "some sweet." This somewhat strange paradox was already a familiar one to Lampman. It is expressed in "The Harvest of Time," an unpublished poem written in June 1883 – "Dark memories and fair ones meet, / And the burden of all is sweet; / Hope is not slain of sorrow"[9] – and, as we have seen, it comes up again in "April," completed in May 1884, where the "memory of pain, all past, is peace." Lampman is intrigued by the idea that an experience can, in consciousness, exist in a pure state, freed from or untroubled by any difficult or distracting or painful components by which it may have been accompanied when it occurred. Negative experiences blend with positive experiences in memory, and together they make up the "harvest of time," entirely positive.

Nor is Lampman alone in postulating the transformative powers of memory. The proverb "That which was bitter to endure, may be sweet to remember," collected in Thomas Fuller's *Gnomologia* in 1733, expresses the idea succinctly. Classical precursors appear in Burton Egbert Stevenson's *Home Book of Quotations*, among them "How sweet to remember the trouble that is past," attributed to Euripides, and "Things that were hard to bear are sweet to remember," from Seneca's *Hercules Furens*.[10]

British philosopher Mary Warnock, born in 1924 and still today contributing articles on moral philosophy to the website of the *Guardian* newspaper,[11] takes up the subject in her 1987 study entitled simply *Memory*. Having made the points that memory and personal identity are "inextricably linked" and that memory and imagination are "impossible to separate," she goes on to discuss the transformation of "memory into art," using, as her prime example, Wordsworth. Two types of memories are possible: those comprised of images and those consisting of knowledge. With her focus on the former, she explains that, because memory-images belong to the past, they are mourned: "The very fact that the cause precedes the effect, that the course of history cannot be reversed, nor time move backwards, may itself contribute to the sense of loss often so powerfully associated with the images of memory, both in life and in art." And this applies to all kinds of experiences, both negative and positive:

> Anything that is *over*, even though we may be thankful that it is, carries with it the possibility of yearning. We shall never *have* it again. It is a lost *possession*. No wonder that so many people believe that, if they could only preserve the past, whether in autobiography, by photographs, or by some other means, they would be happy. The past is a paradise from which we are necessarily excluded, and this is true even though, when it was present, it was less than paradisical. And so an image, if it is taken to be a memory-image, may convey a sense of joy, in the regaining of something thought to be lost for ever.[12]

Expanding on the allusion to Milton here (and in the subtitle of her chapter, "Paradise Regained"), Warnock later in the book characterizes memory as "a saviour," one that "is to save us from the otherwise inevitable destruction brought by death and time." Memory, together with the imagination, makes possible "the re-creation of life."[13] A somewhat similar view was developed by the French philosopher Henri Bergson (1859–1941), who, according to British philosopher Roger Scruton, saw memory as the means by which human beings could discover order and meaning in the ongoing flux of time. "Memory," as Scruton explains, "gives us direct access to the past, and also the power to discover its true order and intrinsic character. This true order is an order of meaning, and may be quite distinct from the order of events as recorded by the physicist."[14] For both Warnock and Bergson, memory provides access to the truth of experience, necessarily subjective, and Lampman would have had little difficulty sympathizing with their views.

The other significant factor in the passage quoted from "An Athenian Reverie" is the association of pleasure with both "keen experience" and "smooth remembrance." These are the two states of being that

Lampman values: intense involvement and serene detachment. In "An Athenian Reverie" (as in the memory poems in general) it is detachment that dominates, but not without some degree of struggle, as we see in the narrator's ruminations over the details of a wedding he has witnessed:

> How joyously
> These hours have gone with all their pictured scenes,
> A string of golden beads for memory
> To finger over in her moods, or stay
> The hunger of some wakeful hour like this,
> The flowers, the myrtles, the gay bridal train,
> The flutes and pensive voices, the white robes,
> The shower of sweetmeats, and the jovial feast,
> The bride cakes, and the teeming merriment,
> Most beautiful of all, most sweet to name,
> The good Lysippe with her down-cast eyes,
> Touched with soft fear, half scared at all the noise.

This metaphorical rosary of newly acquired memories gives pleasure now and will, the narrator predicts, be "sweet" to recite in the future, just as, in Wordsworth's "Tintern Abbey," the present scene is valued partly because in it "there is life and food / For future years."[15] As soon becomes apparent, however, the narrator's nocturnal "hunger" and admiration of the bride suggest a yearning for love, intensified as in imagination he follows the bride and groom into the bridal chamber. For Keats's famous "Cold pastoral!" is substituted the "warm eternity" of the couple's embrace.[16] The narrator imagines the newlyweds so intensely involved in the act of love that they are removed from all consciousness of time; or again, post-coital, peaceful in sleep under their "weight of happiness." As an alternative to heightened consciousness, even non-consciousness is preferable to a mental state dominated by the petty concerns and ambitions of the everyday world – the world that, in "An Athenian Reverie," is inhabited by "most men" for whom "life is but a common thing."

The pros and cons of marriage continue to preoccupy the narrator, reflecting a parallel debate within Lampman himself, now (at the time of writing this poem) engaged to Maud Emma Playter, whom he would marry after a courtship of some two years.[17] The narrator values the distance from which he can appreciate the "pictured scenes" of life, but is attracted by the "warm eternity" of love. The more he thinks about it, though, the more he favours independence over the "one all-pampering dream" of love which, he decides, usually "withers like those garlands at the door." He recalls the happy marriages of two friends, feels tempted, but then concludes that he must remain single:

> For life, this joyous, busy, ever-changing life,
> Is only dear to me with liberty,
> With space of earth for feet to travel in
> And space of mind for thought.

The narrator's enthusiasm for "life" is conveyed by the burgeoning first line, overcrowded with twelve syllables, followed by the even-paced regularity of the next three lines, where clear-headed resolution is set down. He loves life, but to enjoy it he must be free to roam, not tied down with family responsibilities.

Even more than the "wanderer's dream" of travel, though, it is the "space of mind" that captures the narrator's interest. Taking up the anti-materialist, anti-hedonist stance to which he would often return, Lampman has the narrator distance himself from those "whose worth is reckoned by the sum they buy / In gold, or power, or pleasure," who live to satisfy their baser instincts but who die without ever having "seen / The picture of their lives." People caught up with worldly concerns are "blind," the narrator continues, whereas those who remain aloof can see:

> Happy is he,
> Who, as a watcher, stands apart from life,
> From all life and his own, and thus from all,
> Each thought, each deed, and each hour's brief event,
> Draws the full beauty, sucks its meaning dry.
> For him this life shall be a tranquil joy.
> He shall be quiet and free. To him shall come
> No gnawing hunger for the coarser touch,
> No mad ambition with its fateful grasp;
> Sorrow itself shall sway him like a dream.

The mode of behaviour depicted here, the same as that of the artist removed from society, facilitates the appreciation of life as a substitute, ironically, for involvement. As Warnock observes with respect to memory, "Our separation from our past ... our ability to stand back from it without its making demands on us, is precisely what gives us peace and satisfaction in contemplating it."[18]

A similar idea is expressed in Lampman's sonnet "Outlook," the opening phrases of which were quoted earlier in this chapter.[19] "Outlook" takes as its theme the desirability of viewing experience from a removed point of view – the philosophical cornerstone of Lampman's memory poems – and so provides a concise gloss on the present passage. The octave sets out the speaker's desire for freedom from mental entrapment:

> Not to be conquered by these headlong days,
>   But to stand free: to keep the mind at brood
>   On life's deep meaning, nature's altitude
> Of loveliness, and time's mysterious ways;
> At every thought and deed to clear the haze
>   Out of our eyes, considering only this,
>   What man, what life, what love, what beauty is,
> This is to live, and win the final praise.

The phrase "headlong days" suggests the sweep of daily activities and preoccupations in which people become absorbed, at the cost of the deeper understanding that belongs to the watchful non-participant. The preferred ideal is to "stand free," but this is difficult to achieve since, as is made clear in the sestet, "strife, ill fortune and harsh human need / Beat down the soul." With fortitude, however, one can avoid being caught up in these aspects of mundane reality, and the reward makes the effort worthwhile:

>   yet, patience – there shall come
>   Many great voices from life's outer sea,
> Hours of strange triumph, and, when few men heed,
>   Murmurs and glimpses of eternity.[20]

The speaker yearns to hear the wisdom of "great voices" from beyond the realm of the familiar, that is, to gain insight into the mysteries of existence. Interestingly, there are other "great voices" audible here – those of Arnold and Milton, whose phrases are echoed. It is, however, to a different purpose that Lampman applies the familiar terms.

In valuing a removed perspective, Lampman's speaker recalls the poet in Arnold's "Resignation," who likes "to scan / Not his own course, but that of man," and in setting great store by "patience," he reprises Arnold's similar stance in his sonnet "To a Republican Friend, Continued."[21] It is interesting to note, however, that Lampman's "Outlook" moves in the opposite direction to Arnold's sonnet, from closed and restricted to open and receptive. Arnold's speaker, having thought about "what life is" (echoed by Lampman's "life's deep meaning" and "What man, what life, what love, what beauty is"), decides that "the high / Uno'erleap'd Mountains of Necessity" hem people in and leave little room to effect change. Not only that, but a deeply entrenched selfishness in human nature is unlikely to be vanquished by social upheaval. He opts to retract the sympathy with republicanism he had expressed in "To a Republican Friend, 1848."[22] Lampman's speaker, by contrast, insists that though the realities of everyday life – "strife, ill fortune and harsh human need" – make it difficult to focus on beauty and indulge in metaphysical speculation, perseverance will offer its rewards. The themes are different, but it is nevertheless revealing that Lampman's poem turns the emotional direction of its precursor on its head. Lampman's "patience" carries the opposite meaning of Arnold's: to persist in fighting against the forces that limit one's vision rather than to surrender to them. Both speakers, if they could speak, would say they were being realistic – but their definitions of realistic are at odds with each other. This difference presages another one, for in his political "outlook," it is clear that Lampman's sympathies lie with, not Arnold, but the republican friend.

An influence on both poems, meanwhile, is Milton, whose recommendation of patience in his well-known sonnet on his blindness ("When I consider how my light is spent")[23] recurs in "To a Republican Friend, Continued" as well as in "Outlook." In Lampman's sonnet, the "stand" of Milton's famous concluding line is echoed in the phrase "stand free" with reference to an attitude made possible by patience.

This connection is reinforced by a similarity of form and theme: both poems are Petrarchan sonnets about resisting the temptation to abandon resolve. A little more positive than Milton's "They also serve who only stand and wait," however, and less discouraging than the conclusion of Arnold's "To a Republican Friend, Continued" ("Nor will that day dawn at a human nod"), dismissing the possibility of social transformation in the foreseeable future, are the closing lines of Lampman's sonnet, anticipating "Murmurs and glimpses of eternity" – a modicum of divine illumination.

One additional theme that "An Athenian Reverie" explores is that of friendship, elaborated in the context of the narrator's relationship with his friend Euktemon, who in many respects seems a fictionalized portrait of Duncan Campbell Scott, created not long after the two men first met in 1885.[24] Partly, it is for this kind of human contact that the narrator values his independence and resists the lures of "gold," "power," and "pleasure" to which "most men" fall prey. As soon becomes apparent, however, even the most worthwhile of experiences are valued primarily as grist to the memory mill. Recalling his first meeting with Euktemon, the narrator thinks "how sweet / The memory of that long untroubled day" is, and he wonders whether any adversity could "Divest ... such memories of their sweet." In contrast to worldly pursuits, which are either fleeting or vain, remembered experiences are characterized by wholeness and permanence. "With what sharp lines," the narrator muses, "The shapes of things that even years have buried / Shine out upon the rapid memory, / Moving and warm like life." The past may be dead ("buried"), but in memory it lives, becoming (in consciousness) life-like. What the narrator is thinking of here is the parade of passers-by he observed from the side of a "busy road" between Mycenae and Corinth, symbolically the road of life. But if it is ironic that observation rather than participation inspired the memories that the narrator cherishes, then the irony is compounded by his recollection that, while observing the passing crowd, he was even then lost in thoughts of other times:

What pleasant memories, how many things
Rose up again before me, as I lay
Half stretched among the crushed anemones,
And watched them.

It seems the narrator is never where he is. But while consciousness may undermine the possibility of entering fully into the experience of the moment, memory will redeem the experience. The "dreaming" that Lampman refers to in many nature poems may be understood as signifying nothing more than the reflection made possible by resting in a natural-world setting and taking in – unconsciously – the beauty of the surroundings.

The idea that memory can provide the kind of full appreciation of experience that normal consciousness cannot persists in Lampman's thinking. In his 1896 essay "Happiness," he writes that "[i]t is in memory, the recollection of things adventitious or episodical, that our deepest and securest pleasures consist." The point is illustrated by a "parable" in which the poet and his friends, on a canoe trip, wander from lake to lake in quest of "gray trout." In the end their search is unsuccessful, but not fruitless: "we never found the gray trout. Not the gray trout, indeed; but how many other things were conferred upon us, things vital and beautiful, a store of inextinguishable reminiscence!" He mentions "the rare brown water," "the tingling forest air," "the passing of the loons above us," and concludes, "These and many other things we remembered afterward with luxurious joy, when the gray trout were no longer a care to us. So it is with happiness."

In the four reprinted versions of "Happiness" that followed the original publication in *Harper's New Monthly Magazine*, the essay ends on this positive note, with the final sentence, actually the beginning of a new paragraph, shifted to the end position of the previous one. In the original text, restored in *The Essays and Reviews of Archibald Lampman*, edited by D.M.R. Bentley, the essay closes with a much more muted affirmation:

> So it is with happiness. We spend long lives in the pursuit of objects which we seldom attain, but always before us are the glories of anticipation, and behind us the magical playhouse of memory. Let us therefore cultivate a mood of the utmost spiritual openness. Let us not be exacting with life, nor demand too much of the present hour. Let us be content if we lay up for ourselves treasures of fruitful memory; for there is an alchemy in the imagination which can brew pleasure out of the most unpromising material,

and gleams of a curious sunshine will some day fall even upon the recollection of our darkest miseries.[25]

Just as, in 1884, Lampman had proclaimed that "memory of pain, all past, is peace, / And joy, dream-tasted, hath the deepest cheer," so now, twelve years later, he extols the virtues of "the glories of anticipation" and "the magical playhouse of memory." The idea that even negative experiences can be transformed by memory – "Dark memories and fair ones meet, / And the burden of all is sweet" – is also returned to here in terms of the "alchemy" that distils ("brews") experience, eliminating the dross of suffering, so it can be treasured in purified form. And only Lampman, one suspects, could end an essay on happiness with the phrase "darkest miseries." In such statements, he is emphasizing his conviction that, because the present distracts from the present, so to speak, it is only from a removed point of view, as in memory, that one can fully appreciate experience in a way that, paradoxically, experience itself precludes.

An important exception to this construct is the effortless yet intense involvement of natural-world observation, recorded most *memorably*, perhaps, in "Heat." Although essentially different, however, the two kinds of experience are not without their points in common. In "Heat," for example, it is once again by a kind of alchemy, this time expressed in terms of metal-refinement, that the speaker's inner experience is transformed; and indeed it is again a "negative" experience – the oppressive heat of the poem's title – that becomes redemptive. What we find in "Heat," moreover, is that, with city demands no longer impinging on consciousness, the speaker's mind is free to wander (as in day-dreaming) and only in "intervals of dreams" attends to the present scene, just as the mind of the narrator in "An Athenian Reverie" reflects back while (not) watching the scene before him. The two experiences, reflecting and observing, may be seen as complementary sides of – to adapt the metaphor of alchemy – the same gold coin.

CHAPTER 2

Winter and Memory

So far in this discussion of the memory theme, I have omitted any consideration of seasonal poems, apart from "April," in order to show that Lampman's thinking on this subject is not tied to his interpretation of nature. It is the case, however, that in the context of the annual cycle of seasons – the most important image in Lampman's oeuvre – memory is often associated with winter. Typically the speaker sees winter, frigid and severe, as a time to dip into his "store" of memories garnered from the other seasons, or even from winter itself since winter has its own attractive qualities – the "silence, frost and beauty everywhere" of "Winter Uplands," for example. Poems that feature this aspect of Lampman's explorations of memory include "Winter-Thought," which sets out the theme; "Winter Hues Recalled," which shows both the active appreciation of winter's beauty and the recollection of it in (warm) tranquility; and "Winter-Store," a curiously complex piece, at once the best expression of the winter-memory theme and a poem whose unity and overall effectiveness have been compromised by Lampman's changes and additions to his original manuscript. As Barrie Davies has observed, "Winter-Store" is "not a complete success" because of Lampman's having tried "to say too much in it."[1] Following a consideration of these poems, the chapter will conclude with a brief consideration of one additional, non-seasonal memory poem: "The Child's Music Lesson."

"Winter-Thought"

In this sonnet, the speaker begins by placing himself, with the reader, squarely in the midst of a field of flowers, but with a surprise in store. Surrounded "on every side" by daisies, he hears their "whispering companies" and observes how the buttercups "swing and toss with all the airs that pass, / Yet seem so peaceful, so preoccupied" – descriptions that convey a sense of immediacy. As we soon discover, however, and as the title implies, the season is in fact winter and the flowers only imaginary. Still, the remembered images have a curative effect on the speaker's state of mind:

> Even to dream of them is to disown
>   The cold forlorn midwinter reveries,
> Lulled with the perfume of old hopes new-blown,
>   No longer dreams but dear realities.

By "dreaming" of them (remembering them), the speaker is lifted out of his gloomy mood and is returned to his summer thought patterns and even to a more youthful optimism – an instance of how, for Lampman, dreams are indeed real even while they are acknowledged dreams, since consciousness is what counts. But what of actual experience? The language of close observation throughout the octave suggests that the speaker's experience of the flowers when he actually saw them was one of immediacy. At line nine, however, the flowers are designated "the emblems of pure pleasures flown." The speaker is remembering them now, but even at the time of observation they evoked other memories.

The central conceit of the poem emerges as follows: not only do the flowers transport one's mind, but merely the memory of them ("Even to dream of them") does so; or, to reverse the emphasis, not only does the memory of the flowers transport one's mind (back to the flowers), but the flowers themselves, when seen, provoke memories. Thus the speaker, even while observing them, is, like the buttercups themselves, "thought-wrapped" and "preoccupied" – off somewhere else, perhaps communing with the speaker of the sonnet "In November," who, though inspired by a very different scene, is similarly "Wrapped round with thought, content to watch and dream." In "Winter-Thought," then, while primarily concerned with calling to mind and thus restoring to life an image of beauty from the past, Lampman reveals his awareness of the "otherness" that qualifies almost all human consciousness.

"Winter Hues Recalled"

Like "Winter-Thought," "Winter Hues Recalled" focuses on both experience and memory. Written in blank verse styled on Wordsworth's *The Prelude*,[2] the poem begins with a discursive preamble on the workings of that valued faculty that provides access to the "treasure of hours gone." The speaker defines two levels of consciousness, one that interferes with memory and another that facilitates it. On the "noisy surface" is the level of negative "effort" at which the busy routines of life prevent one from indulging in reflection. In "the silent unaccounted depth" of the mind, however, lies "the quiet garner-house of memory" where "All things that ever touched us are stored up, / Growing more mellow like sealed wine with age." Here again is the "alchemy" whereby past experiences are transformed, albeit with the metaphorical vehicle shifted from beer to wine. The memories are shy, however, and can only be conjured under conditions of calm:

> In moments when the heart is most at rest
> And least expectant, from the luminous doors,
> And sacred dwelling place of things unfeared,
> They issue forth, and we who never knew
> Till then how potent and how real they were,
> Take them, and wonder, and so bless the hour.

As the alchemy takes hold and the realities of "the heated strainage and the rush" of life fade into obscurity, the memories become "real," never properly valued until now. In memory comes the appreciation.

Following the theory, logically enough, comes an example. Twice removed from the experience being remembered, the speaker recalls that he recalled while "Passing from one remembrance to another" a memorable "moment" – a "miracle of colour and of beauty." As his description of the original experience makes clear, however, he wasn't always aware, at the time, of the images he was gathering for future enjoyment:

> An hour had passed above me; I had reached
> The loftiest level of the snow-piled fields,
> Clear-eyed, but unobservant, noting not
> That all the plain beneath me and the hills
> Took on a change of colour splendid, gradual,
> Leaving no spot the same; nor that the sun
> Now like a fiery torrent overflamed
> The great line of the west.

Here the speaker details all those aspects of the scene which, as it were, he failed to observe at the time, illustrating how one's memory is able to preserve those images which the senses take in but to which the mind, wandering elsewhere, remains oblivious.

The point about memory having been exemplified, the poem appears to have done its job. But just where we feel it could wrap up, it shifts into the passage that is poetically its most successful. Before returning home, the speaker reports, a "buried fence" made him a seat where its "topmost log just shouldered from the snow." No longer "Clear-eyed, but unobservant," he is now acutely aware of the landscape before him:

> I looked far out upon the snow-bound waste,
> The lifting hills and intersecting forests,
> The scarce marked courses of the buried streams,
> And as I looked lost memory of the frost,
> Transfixed with wonder, overborne with joy.
> I saw them in their silence and their beauty,
> Swept by the sunset's rapid hand of fire,
> Sudden, mysterious, every moment deepening
> To some new majesty of rose or flame.

The threefold repetition of vision verbs suggests the intensity of the speaker's involvement with the scene. Whereas earlier he had been oblivious to the beauty of his surroundings (which he would, nevertheless, later recall), he is now so caught up in the present as to lose awareness of the cold. The two experiences are similar to the extent that, with mind wandering or mind intensely focused, one is removed from everyday, uninspired consciousness. The rapturous tone of the final passage, however, suggests that the sharp awareness of actual observation occupies a sublimer plane than does the pleasure of remembering.

Toward the end of the poem, it is with the enthusiasm of proclaiming a revelation that the speaker declares simply of the hills, forests, and streams, "I saw them"; and his seeing is conveyed, not just by this assurance, but by the power of the descriptive language, detailing colour and quality of light, as in the following panorama:

> The whole broad west was like a molten sea
> Of crimson. In the north the light-lined hills
> Were veiled far off as with a mist of rose
> Wondrous and soft. Along the darkening east
> The gold of all the forests slowly changed
> To purple. In the valley far before me,
> Low sunk in sapphire shadows, from its hills,
> Softer and lovelier than an opening flower,
> Uprose a city with its sun-touched towers,
> A bunch of amethysts.

Overwhelmed by the beauty of the sunset, the speaker keeps shifting his gaze, pivoting to take in all four compass directions. So rich is the evocation of the scene that the passage comes close to disproving the thesis of the poem. The overriding argument, however, still holds. Past experiences can be relived through memory, and so, restored, redeemed. This is implicitly the argument of all artistic expression, but here made the thematic crux.

"Winter-Store"

A different perspective on memory is presented in "Winter-Store," a poem written mostly in the future tense, first published in Lampman's second book, *Lyrics of Earth*. Here the speaker is ostensibly not recalling but looking forward to recalling. Before coming to any conclusions about how "Winter-Store" relates to the other memory poems, however, it is important to consider the problematic compositional history of the poem. As previously noted, Lampman subjected "Winter-Store" to revisions that muddied his original conception. He dropped twenty-eight on-topic lines at the beginning and added stanzas at both the beginning and end. The new opening stanzas were a rearranged version of the poem "Vision," first published in the Toronto *Globe* in 1892,[3] lamenting the spiritual atrophy of contemporary humanity and urging upon "us" recognition of the threads that link us to a universe imbued with spiritual meaning. As Richard Arnold has demonstrated, the "Vision" stanzas show the influence of Emerson in Lampman's employment of phrases such as "the All" and "the Immensity," referring to God, not found elsewhere in the poem.[4] The stanzas added to the end reflect his empathetic view of human suffering and aspiration. These additions now frame the long middle section, consisting of first-person descriptions of countryside scenes that the speaker anticipates visiting and then recalling with pleasure.

If the changes Lampman made to his original text represent a lapse of judgment, it is an understandable one. In 1887, when it was first conceived, "Winter-Store" was concerned entirely with the quaintly practical idea of laying in imaginative provisions for the winter. The feeling was optimistic, tinged with melancholy at the inevitability of seasonal change. Over the next few years, Lampman's frustrations at not being able to find publishers for his various manuscripts grew. He became increasingly intolerant of the image of himself that his first book had created among readers – that of an untroubled nature-boy who delighted in fields and flowers – at a time when he had become much more focused on social and political issues. It took him four years – 1892–96 – to see *Lyrics of Earth* into print,[5] with many rejections intervening, and during the same period he tried unsuccessfully to interest publishers in at least three other collections, all of which contained poems that reflected his current preoccupations. In 1895 he complained to E.W. Thomson that he felt "forcibly held down" and "smothered."[6] With the impending publication of *Lyrics of Earth*, compiled years before and consisting entirely of nature poems, it seems likely that Lampman added the extra stanzas to "Winter-Store" to offset his readership's false sense of his values and beliefs, or, in short, out of desperation to be heard. By

1898 Lampman had arranged for the private publication of a new volume, *Alcyone*, containing a number of poems that reflected his social-political concerns. Before that book appeared, however, Lampman died, and Scott, as his literary executor, arranged for the publication of a limited edition of twelve copies, so as to leave the field free for the marketing of *Poems* a year later. Lampman never did succeed, in his own lifetime, in setting the record straight.

There is a limited sense in which the "Vision" stanzas can be seen as relevant to the central portion of "Winter-Store." The remedy for the spiritual malaise afflicting humanity is for people to open their eyes to the beauty and wonder of the universe:

Subtly conscious, all awake,
Let us clear our eyes and break
Through the cloudy chrysalis –
See the wonder as it is.

The connection to "Winter-Store" is that this recommendation of open-eyed receptivity will now be acted upon, for, as is soon made clear, the speaker's intention is to visit and absorb the beauty of various countryside scenes. His goal, however, is not to increase his awareness, for he is already aware; it is to gather countryside images – the raw materials of memory – for his store. As a prelude to a poem mainly concerned with this goal, the "Vision" stanzas function awkwardly, at best.

A case, though less direct, can also be made for the relevance of the additional stanzas at the end of "Winter-Store." At the close of the poem's central section, having now secured his store, the speaker is comforted by the thought that, in the coming "darker days" of winter, his imagination will not starve: "Safe within the sheltered mind / I shall feed on memory." Following this conclusion – the point at which, in two manuscript versions of the poem, both dating from 1889, the poem ends[7] – the second added segment introduces another "vision." In this case it is "a vision sad and high / Of the labouring world," essentially an evocation of humanity in all its variety, from lovers to mourners, who now, asleep in their beds, do not heed the poet's craft or art. The speaker is troubled by "a passion and a cry" that fills him with a "nameless hunger of the soul."

What Lampman has done here, according to L.R. Early, is perform "an astonishing volte-face" whereby he "relinquishes his belief in dreams and his inclination toward pastoral." Early sees "Winter-Store" as "the major poem of Lampman's second volume" not despite but because of this addition. In his view, "the speaker's awareness of human suffering impairs his appreciation of natural beauty, reversing his previous state of mind." Thus the closing stanzas amount to Lampman's expression of "the loss of a deep faith": "Specifically, it is an admission of the limitations of his central mode of poetry, the Romantic nature lyric. He became dissatisfied with the genre as he came to realize that the imagination is a human, not a natural phenomenon, and a mixed blessing with a darker side than his landscape poetry could express."[8] Early may be right in attributing to the addendum a kind of declaration on Lampman's part, signalling a shift toward a greater concentration on social-political themes, although not a repudiation, since Lampman did not give up on his philosophy of nature, as his wilderness sonnets from the late 1890s and "The Old House," written in 1898, will attest. Even allowing this relevance to the "labouring world" passage, however, it does not follow that it enhances the poem of which it now forms a part. As Early himself says, "'Winter-Store' is the kind of poem that yields its full meaning only in the light of its author's whole body of work, and perhaps only in the wider light of the tradition in which his poetry participates."[9] Because of their remoteness from the theme of memory, the added lines, whatever their intrinsic virtue, must be seen as broadening Lampman's poetic palette at the cost of compromising the integrity of the poem in which they are presented.

Let us now consider the poem without the fore and aft additions. In Lampman's "good copy" manuscript book version of "Winter-Store," neither the "Vision" stanzas nor those about the speaker's vision of the "labouring world" appear, but included at the beginning are the original on-topic lines referred to earlier.[10] This passage, expanded from twenty-eight to thirty lines and with some rearrangements and minor changes, was still in place when Lampman submitted his copy text to his publisher, Copeland and Day, in 1895. At this point, the extra stanzas at the beginning and end were also present.[11] Ultimately Lampman decided to cut the original opening lines (which were positioned after the

Winter and Memory

"Vision" stanzas), thus completing the complicated surgery that preceded the birth of "Winter-Store."

The deleted passage – the original opening – begins with a *carpe diem* declaration in which the speaker exhorts his fellows to enjoy with him the passing spectacle of the seasons:

> Ere the faltering year be gray,
> Brothers, let us seize the day.
> Month by month, before we know,
> Time with subtle fingers steals,
> And the seasons come and go,
> Treading on each other's heels,
> Spring blown about with golden gleams,
> Summer's languid weight of dreams,
> Then with silent step austere,
> Pacing in the sombre rear,
> Autumn's melancholy mood,
> Winter's whitened solitude.

The catalogue of seasons here suggests that Lampman's intent was to have the speaker and his friends explore the beauty of nature throughout the year. This plan is not consistent with the direction the poem actually goes, for the idea that takes shape is that the speaker will gather only summer images for winter contemplation, as is indicated further in this introductory passage where he asks rhetorically whether it will be his fate and that of his friends, once winter comes, to sit staring "at the frosted pane" and "Think how summer came and went, / And we dreamed and passed her by, / Without mark or memory?" As if in response to his own question, shifting into first-person singular, the speaker declares his intention not to waste "these blissful hours" but, in sensible, Canadian fashion, to make provision for the future:

> While light and leaf and blossom last,
> Ere the times of song be past
> I shall count each summer day
> As a treasure stored away.

Likely it was the inconsistency between the earlier seasonal references and the focus on summer here (and throughout the long descriptive portion of the poem) that prompted Lampman to omit the entire passage.

It appears, then, that two approaches to time were in Lampman's mind during the composition of "Winter-Store," one involving a plan to observe nature throughout the year and the other to do so specifically in the summer. The first approach complements the design of *Lyrics of Earth* itself, a book comprised of a chronological sequence of seasonal poems tracing the annual cycle from spring through winter – the realization of the speaker's stated plan in the excised opening. As is consistent with its winter focus, however, "Winter-Store" comes not at the beginning but rather at the end of the sequence, not counting a final "coda" poem, "The Sun Cup," which ended up in that position as a result of an error on the part of the publisher.[12] The lines referring to the four seasons from the original opening passage of "Winter-Store," with their future-tense verbs, can thus be seen as providing a kind of after-the-fact introduction to the sequence as a whole. The poem that "follows" the last winter poem is, after the introductory poem, the first spring poem. At the end of the sequence we look back on the poems tracing the seasons and at the same time forward to those same poems. The poems of the sequence are the "memories" that the speaker now has/will have as the cycle continues.

It is true that in "Winter-Store" Lampman abandoned the four-seasons plan in favour of the summer-for-winter plan. Something of the former, however, survives in his placement of "Winter-Store" at the end of a chronology of seasonal poems, since that placement implies that everything that has gone before makes up the speaker's collective "store" of memories.[13] Thus, in a complicated way that is not quite sorted out, summer represents the field of life when memories may be gathered, and winter represents the time of death – poetic emptiness – when the images of life will provide vital sustenance; at the same time, all the seasons offer their treasures which may then be enjoyed, as it were, outside of time. The focus on only one season in the descriptive portions of "Winter-Store," moreover, does not mean that the idea of cyclic return plays no part, but only that the cycle is presented in terms of summer scenes recurring each year. Indeed, the idea that the scenes depicted belong both to the past and to the future is made evident in the repeated use of generic rather than specific references to countryside locations in combination with precise descriptions.

Both the generic quality of the imagery, conveyed, for example, by plural nouns and typical rather than unique images, and the immediacy of the descriptive language, suggesting prior knowledge, are evident throughout the middle section of "Winter-Store," as here:

> I shall search in crannied hollows
> Where the sunlight scarcely follows,
> And the secret forest brook
> Murmurs, and from nook to nook
> For ever downward curls and cools,
> Frothing in the bouldered pools.

The speaker is looking forward to re-encountering what is obviously familiar territory. The idea that the anticipated scenes are based on past ones, combined with the idea that the purpose of the planned return visits is to gather memories to sustain future reflection, shows the extent to which, for Lampman, experience and memory are intertwined. Having seen, one can anticipate seeing, and even look forward to recalling what one will see.

As the imagined tour of countryside attractions progresses in the middle section of "Winter-Store," we pause to look down upon "some rough-coasted river" where both the mills and the river rapids are loud and where the "river-dogs" (men guiding the booms) are at work and weighted barges ply the water. Moving scenes in nature evidently need not be confined to the observation of woodland flowers. Such sightings of active industry on the river will also be part of the speaker's store. Other stops include "sun-hot hayfields," "quiet secluded bays," and a spot near certain "upland fences," a place to which, in "Winter Uplands," Lampman's last poem, his muse will return for a final visit. Attached to each of these locales are detailed descriptions of the anticipated/remembered scenes, such as "the jungled river meads" where a gentle breeze

> Stirs a whisper in the reeds,
> And wakes the crowded bull-rushes

> From their stately reveries,
> Flashing through their long-leaved hordes
> Like a brandishing of swords.

The language of such passages is freshly evocative, with the same descriptive powers at work as in "April" and "Winter Hues Recalled," but here less dependent on Romantic antecedents. The poetry offers a kind of rustic chamber music that repays close attention.

Toward the end of the middle section, lulled by the quiet catalogue of rural scenes and acclimatized to the summer setting, we are surprised to meet with a contrary indication of time: "What though autumn mornings now, / Winterward with glittering brow, / Stiffen in the silver grass." Time present, it turns out, is fall, raising the question of how this temporal setting sorts with the fact that the experiences referred to thus far in the poem have been imagined as happening in the summer, situated in the future. A simple explanation is that the verse-paragraph break that precedes the lines just quoted marks a significant passage of time (even though previous verse-paragraph breaks do not have that function) and that now the planned excursions have been accomplished. This indeed might literally have been true for Lampman, since the fall-setting part of the poem does not appear with the lines that were originally penned in the summer of 1887, but does appear with the draft of the poem dated 26 November 1889.[14] This explanation is plausible, but not quite satisfactory. Less obvious but more likely is that the planned excursions are taking place one by one as the poem proceeds, either imaginatively as the speaker recalls and anticipates, or in fact as, over the course of the summer, he follows through with his plans to "seize the day." By the end of this part of the poem, he can sift through his memories and feel "secure, / Conscious that my store is sure," and at the same time look forward to winter, when "Safe within the sheltered mind, / I shall feed on memory." This reading fits with the idea that "Winter-Store," coming at the end of *Lyrics of Earth*, is meant to suggest that the speaker is now well provisioned, with all his observations – the poems of the sequence – safely recorded. They will serve as memories to be enjoyed again in the absence of the experiences they describe as well as harbingers of future encounters during the next round of the seasonal cycle, which the future-tense verbs anticipate.

It is at this point that in the published version of the poem the tacked-on ending appears. The speaker now is situated on an imagined height from which he can see "the labouring world down there." The only reference to memory occurs in the context of a lament:

> In vain, in vain,
> I remember how of old
> I saw the ruddy race of men,
> Through the glittering world outrolled,
> A gay-smiling multitude,
> All immortal, all divine,
> Treading in a wreathèd line
> By a pathway through a wood.

In the earlier sections of "Winter-Store" there appears no hint of this ruddy race, so what the speaker is vainly remembering must be something else, as is consistent with the fact that the closing stanzas were written separately from the main part of the poem. The temporal setting, moreover, has switched from seasonal to diurnal. It is now nighttime, the city is asleep, and the speaker is troubled by "a passion and a cry" that vaguely express the desires and sorrows of the sleeping multitudes, which he cannot ignore. Undoubtedly this passage imparts disillusionment as well as recognition of the pathos of human aspiration and suffering. If Lampman ever thought, as he implies here that he did, that humanity was a jolly crew tramping through the woods, he no longer sees it that way. The idea that this passage signifies Lampman's departure from nature verse, however, seems not tenable, since what it immediately follows is a statement of faith in *memory* ("I shall feed on memory") and since Lampman continued to write poems about his experience in nature, including some of his best, right to the end of his life. It belongs somewhere, but not at the end of "Winter-Store," where it declaims its message in the wrong meeting hall – and where the meeting is already over.

Lampman clearly had great difficulties with the composition of "Winter-Store," in terms of both its internal workings and its relationship to the sequence in *Lyrics of Earth*. The result is a poem that must be judged as flawed, but which nevertheless provides insight into what was for Lampman an endlessly fascinating subject: namely, the redemptive power of memory (and poetry) in providing food for the soul in the form of experiences to be enjoyed, ironically, outside the realm of experience.

"The Child's Music Lesson"

Contrasting the complexities of "Winter-Store" is the relative simplicity of "The Child's Music Lesson," a poem in which the alchemy in the imagination performs its magic, but one which also makes clear the distancing effect that can limit the memory experience compared to that of conscious observation. In this poem, the speaker associates the musical ineptitude of a young pupil with the innocence of childhood, for which he feels nostalgic yearnings. "Nay," he reflects, "clear and smooth I would not have you go, / Soft little hands upon the curtained threshold set / Of this long life of labour, and unrestful fret." The speaker himself, having crossed that threshold, is familiar with what lies ahead for the youngster, and from his garden seat he can hear "the voices of hard life" as "the city strains with its eternal cry." The now-familiar remedy is at hand, however, since "My heart, a garden in a hidden place, / Is full of folded buds of memories." Inspired by the child's faltering notes, as by the daisies and buttercups in "Winter-Thought," the speaker finds these memory-buds unfold to offer comfort. He remembers his own childish efforts and, with them, the happy days of childhood. Significantly, those days were, in fact, not always so happy at the time. There were "Quick griefs, that made the tender bosom wild, / Short blinding gusts, that died in passionate tears," but now the "old time beauties" are "undefiled" and the burden of all is sweet: "Sweet life, with all its change, that now so happy seems, / With all its child-heart glories, and untutored dreams." The past is lamented, but through memory it can be recreated, untinged by the sorrows that may have marred it at the time, or, in Mary Warnock's Miltonic language, become paradise regained even if "less than paradisical" when first experienced.[15] The images recalled in "The Child's Music Lesson," however, remain hazy. They are "Quiet gliding ghosts" with which the speaker associates "No joy or aching pain; but only dim delight." The two experiences – memory and conscious observation – have in common the ability to remove the speaker from a gloomy awareness of the worries and difficulties of mundane existence. But the intensity of the more direct experience of conscious observation, such as the one presented in the final third of "Winter Hues Recalled," makes it distinct from its milder cousin.

Throughout his career, Lampman was fascinated by the issues of time, memory, and quality of consciousness. Under normal circumstances, when the mind lacks freedom to wander or "dream," there is life, but not an appreciation of life. A solution is for one to "stand free" – to be the observer and, by implication, the artist. One gathers memories and through them can appreciate experience in ways not possible when the remembered events took place. And one can sift out the essence of these past events so that, following the analogy of alchemy, the nuggets of joy emerge from the complicated dross of circumstances. The experiences remembered are similar to, and often form the substance of, poems. Memory, like art, is redemptive, discovering and preserving meaning in experience.

NATURE

The Full Furnace

CHAPTER 3

Beauty in Nature: Theory and Poetic Practice

In 1883, after graduating with a B.A. in classics from Trinity College, Toronto, and following a short-lived career as schoolmaster in Orangeville, Ontario, Lampman arrived in Ottawa. With the help of Archibald Campbell, a college friend whose father, Sir Alexander Campbell, was postmaster general of Canada, he had secured an appointment as a clerk in the Post Office department, where he remained employed for the rest of his life.[1] Lampman frequently complained about the drudgery of this job, the low pay, and the time restrictions it imposed on him, but there were advantages to his situation. He had no after-hours tasks to attend to. He was able to conduct much of his correspondence from his office (using departmental stationery), and he could always walk to work, with benefit to his poetic avocation. As Scott observes, his poems "were principally composed as he walked ... to and from his ordinary employment" as well as on location in the countryside or pacing the floor of his study at home.[2] When possibilities arose of achieving a position with greater responsibilities, such as a professorship at Cornell University, he resisted.[3] Still, he grumbled.

From the start, however, Lampman was enamoured of Ottawa for its geographical setting and climate. He loved the city, not for its eminence as a commercial centre or seat of government, but for its atmosphere "borne upon the breath of the prevailing northwest wind, an intellectual elixir, an oxygenic essence thrown off by immeasurable tracts of pine-clad mountain and crystal lake." It was the nearness of the north that appealed to him. In Scott's words, "He was on the borders of the wild nature that he loved."[4] The city may not have become, as he predicted it would, "the Florence of Canada, if not of America," home to a New World renaissance of literature and art, but for him it provided stimulus and inspiration.[5] Of all factors, it was this location that had the strongest and most lasting impact on Lampman's writing over the sixteen years of his residence there.

Characteristic of this region were the qualities that have helped to establish a deep-seated notion within the Canadian imagination of the natural world as possessed of pristine beauty but at the same time characterized by extremes of climate and terrain – Tom Marshall's "harsh and lovely land."[6] It was in this context that Lampman's concept of beauty in nature took shape. He discovered the word, as it were, in Keats, whose famous lines – "'Beauty is truth, truth beauty' – that is all / Ye know on earth, and all ye need to know"[7] – were never far from his consciousness. It was the local countryside and, close by, the woods and waterways of the Ottawa Valley and Gatineau Hills, however, that defined beauty, with the result that the extremes were part of the definition. They figure prominently in his poetry, together with the great variety of image and mood within nature, from lowly and obscure to grand and spectacular, and from breezy and light-hearted to melancholy and austere, as it was present before him. What emerges is a poetry that embraces the changes, extols the extremes, and sees beauty as permeating all. The last point is key. Since the contemplation of beauty in nature gives rise to a spiritual-like uplift – a transformation of consciousness that produces, by times, simple comfort and profound regeneration – and since beauty pervades nature, it follows that such transformation can be experienced in any natural-world location and at any time of year. The answer to spiritual yearning is thus always within reach, just as, in most religions, the divine is ever-present, requiring only acceptance on the part of the seeker of salvation.

Throughout his career, Lampman returned to these ideas in various writings: poems and prose works that treat of beauty and nature in the abstract; poems that explicitly or implicitly delineate the actual experience of communion with nature; and works – individual poems and groupings such as the sequence of poems in *Lyrics of Earth* – that represent the cycle of seasons. Implied by the shifting year that these poems all variously map are the realities of change: birth, growth, decline, and death. In theme and especially in imagery, all have a place in Lampman's portrayal of nature. The "negative" imagery has prompted some commentators to find in the poet a surprising ambivalence toward nature, betraying unconscious fears or, if deliberate, creating "tension" in a poem between its surface meaning and its "undercurrents." The alternative view presented in this study is that where the "negative" images occur, it is by virtue of an inclusive irony that they do not make the picture any less ideal for being real, but rather support a definition of natural-world beauty expanded beyond nature's milder manifestations. This irony, I will argue, is central to Lampman's outlook and serves as the crux of several of his best poems, including "Heat" and the sonnet "In November." In such works, Lampman demonstrates his inclusive attitude by finding in apparently unpleasant circumstances, not contradiction, but confirmation of his affirmative stance, just as, in his memory poems, he finds joy, not sorrow, in the recollection of experiences that involved discomfort at the time.

First, however, it is important to observe how, in poetry and prose, Lampman employs the word "beauty" and, from his usage, to gather a meaning that can then be applied to poems in which, though beauty is present, the abstract notion remains implicit. The word appears in the last line of his last poem, written less than two weeks before he died: "And silence, frost and beauty everywhere."[8] Here it is one in a series of three, with the other two components being concrete nouns, giving beauty, by association, a tangible quality. It is featured as well in many other poems, but nowhere more centrally than in the sonnet "Beauty," where the titular subject is depicted as "the lost goal, the unsought cure" of human misery, defined figuratively in relation to goodness and truth as "the perfect ring / That circles and includes the other two." Lampman thus makes beauty the first among equals in his characterization of the tripartite classical ideal.[9]

In a number of philosophical sonnets from early in his career, the words "beauty" and, frequently, "nature," which is the seat of beauty, are generalized terms. A good illustration is "An Old Lesson from the Fields," where the "we" of the poem, representing humanity in the contemporary world, are depicted as having cut themselves off from a life in tune with nature, and where the speaker, in an apostrophe to the light, the sky, the earth, and "ye, tall lilies," laments the lost potential: "What power and beauty life indeed might yield, / Could we but cast away its conscious stress, / Simple of heart becoming even as you." The same note is struck in "Sight," "A Prayer," and "On the Companionship with Nature." In these sonnets, human beings are seen as having become preoccupied with worldly concerns and, in the process, alienated from nature. In biblical phraseology, they are wayward, weak, blind, and in need of redemption.

The antidote for the "could we but" malaise, like all religious cures, is near at hand. Human beings gain beauty and strength – these are frequently coupled – simply by opening their eyes to beauty in nature and letting the natural world seep into their consciousness through the senses, as in "Freedom" and "Among the Timothy," discussed below. If nature were to prove capricious, displaying beauty only sometimes, then the god of Lampman's universe would be something like those of the classical Greeks he so greatly admired. In his philosophical outlook, however, Lampman was more Christian than pagan, and his god, though sometimes harsh in aspect, does not betray the faithful. And like those religious thinkers who have had to struggle to justify the ways of God to man, Lampman exerts himself to show that, for all the extremes one encounters in the natural world, beauty remains a constant.

In his prose writings, too, Lampman explores these same ideas, focusing on the qualities of beauty in nature and the effects of natural-world observation on the mind of the sympathetic observer. For a year and a half in 1892–93, Lampman, Scott, and fellow poet Wilfred Campbell conducted a column in the Toronto *Globe* entitled "At the Mermaid Inn," consisting of short, casual essays on a wide range of topics – to literary scholars, a gold mine of information on the writers themselves and their engagement with the issues of the day. In a contribution directly relevant to this discussion, Lampman elaborates on the pleasures enjoyed by the "pure loafer" of countryside rambles:

> The happiest man is he who has cultivated to the utmost the sense of beauty. The man who is able at all times to find perfect and prolonged satisfaction in the contemplation of a tree, a field, a

flower, or a "spear of grass," can never be bored save by his fellow creatures. For him life is full of variety; every moment comes to him laden with some unique enjoyment, every hour is crowded with a multitude of fleeting but exquisite impressions. If health and a reasonable destiny attend him he cannot be otherwise than happy; pessimism for him is impossible. The beautiful is everywhere about us. As a matter of fact, there is nothing fashioned by nature herself that is not beautiful, either in itself or in its relation to its surroundings. You do not need to go to the Rocky Mountains or the Yosemite Valley in order to find the beautiful; it is in the next field; it is at your feet. Wherever there is earth and any live or growing thing not perverted by the hand of man, there is a study in beauty that one cannot exhaust.[10]

Touched on here, in the breezy, forthright style that Lampman adopted for the *Globe* column, and with a friendly nod to Walt Whitman,[11] are three key points relevant to his poetic creed: that the appreciation of beauty leads to happiness, that beauty in nature is characterized by "variety," and that nature (except where it has been "perverted by the hand of man") is entirely beautiful.

This last point – that beauty is pervasive in nature – comes up again in the essay "Poetic Interpretation" where Lampman compares the effects of various images from nature on the consciousness ("soul") of the receptive individual:

Every phenomenon in life, every emotion and every thought produces a distinct impression of its own upon the soul of the poetic observer. The impression produced by a Mayday sunrise is very different from that produced by an October sunset. The feeling left upon the soul by the contemplation of a full-blown rose is not the same as the sense which it gathers from the beauty of a bunch of sedge. The latter is perhaps not less beautiful than the former, but the essence of its beauty is different.[12]

The idea that "there is nothing fashioned by nature herself that is not beautiful" is here expressed in terms of seasonal change and variety within nature. The quality of beauty may change with the shifting of the diurnal and seasonal cycles, and with the substituting of one image for another, but the extent to which beauty is present in nature remains unaltered over time.

In these two passages, Lampman would appear to be drawing upon Emerson, who famously wrote, "To the attentive eye, each moment of the year has its own beauty, and in the same field, it beholds, every hour, a picture which was never seen before, and which shall never be seen again," adding a few pages later, "A leaf, a sun-beam, a landscape, the ocean, make an analogous impression on the mind. What is common to them all, – that perfectness and harmony, is beauty. Therefore the standard of beauty is the entire circuit of natural forms ... Nothing is quite beautiful alone: nothing but is beautiful in the whole. A single object is only so far beautiful as it suggests this universal grace."[13] Like Emerson, Lampman notes the fleeting quality of the impressions one can derive from nature, and their uniqueness. As well, he seems to incorporate the idea that "[n]othing is quite beautiful alone" when he states that "there is nothing fashioned by nature herself that is not beautiful, either in itself or in its relation to its surroundings," although clearly allowing that an object in nature may be beautiful "in itself." Lampman, however, is seldom drawn toward the abstraction whereby "the standard of beauty is the entire circuit of natural forms." Neither does he choose to follow, if we judge by the bulk of his writing, the tendency in Emerson toward neo-Platonic conceptualizations or, in other words, transcendentalism, as where Emerson states: "But beauty in nature is not ultimate. It is the herald of inward and eternal beauty, and is not alone a solid and satisfactory good. It must therefore stand as a part and not as yet the last or highest expression of the final cause of Nature."[14] It is evident that for Lampman, in poem after poem, beauty in nature is ultimate.

Another possible source for Lampman's observations in the passages quoted above, as Bentley has shown, is prominent Victorian critic and Oxford professor of poetry John Campbell Shairp, who stated in a similar discussion: "Any real object, vividly apprehended ... will awaken in an intelligent and emotional being a response which is the beginning of poetry. The depth and breadth and volume of that response will, of course, be proportioned to the nobility of the object which evokes it, and to the

Beauty in Nature 65

responsive capacity of the mind to which it makes its appeal."[15] Once again, however, it is the contrast between the two commentaries that is most revealing, for whereas Shairp dwells on the shifting magnitude of one's response to particular images, depending in part on the "nobility" of those images, Lampman's point is that beauty in nature, and therefore one's response, does *not* vary in magnitude. A similar distinction can be drawn between Lampman and Shairp in relation to another passage cited by Bentley. To exemplify what constitutes inspiration in nature, Shairp adduces "a beautiful sunrise, or a gorgeous sunset, or the starry heavens on a cloudless night."[16] Lampman too refers to a sunrise and sunset, as well as to "a full-blown rose" and "a bunch of sedge." In Shairp's case, the images are all sublime. By contrasting "a Mayday sunrise" with "an October sunset" and by including the other pair of contrasting images, Lampman downplays the sublime, allowing for the inspirational potential of imagery more melancholy (the October sunset) or pedestrian (the bunch of sedge). Lampman may well have read and admired Shairp, but he resisted the sentimentalism that seems inherent in Shairp's views on the poetic process. The presence of two possible sources, moreover, suggests that Lampman concurred with neither, but rather, to quote again the words of Robin Mathews, "he took from the world what he needed in his thought – from the [classical] Greeks, from the English, from the writers of the U.S. – in a way which permitted him to address the major questions of the day, as he saw them, with a consciousness that was of his time, that was informed and relevant."

For Lampman, because beauty in nature is ever-present, even though its "essence" in various objects may be different, the potential for the transformation of consciousness derived from the appreciation of beauty in nature is not limited or circumscribed, but always available, contact with nature (at any time of day or year) being the only requisite. This philosophy may seem innocuous enough, but in the context of the geographical setting in which it took shape – a region of climactic and topographical extremes – it becomes more robust, and its poetic expression more rewarding. There is nothing remarkable, and no irony, in perceiving beauty and finding inspiration in the gentle or the sublime manifestations of nature. Lampman's reach is more inclusive: The strategy he employs in some of his best poems of natural-world observation is precisely to surprise the reader with the irony of an unlikely point of focus, and it is the convincing power of the unexpectedness that gives such poems their unique flavour.

"Freedom" and "Among the Timothy"

In his philosophical sonnets Lampman depicts humanity's alienation from nature and notes the contrast between the human condition as it is and as it could be, as expressed, for example, in the closing lines of "Sight":

> Yet if we could but lift our earthward eyes
>   To see, and open our dull ears to hear,
>   Then should the wonder of this world draw near
> And life's innumerable harmonies.

The phrasing "if we could but" makes it seem as though the act were beyond the ability of human beings to perform, but as it turns out, to lift one's eyes, one need only (but receptively) lift one's eyes. In "Freedom" and "Among the Timothy," this solution is acted upon, demonstrating the ease with which the seemingly impossible transformation can be effected and a natural-world redemption achieved. Both deal explicitly with the process by which the consciousness of the receptive individual is transformed by exposure to beauty in nature, affording insights that can be carried over into poems in which the same kind of experience remains implicit. At the same time, the two poems are a study in contrast in terms of style and tone, demonstrating the different moods in which Lampman could delineate the positive benefits of contact with nature. They also illustrate the ways in which Lampman sometimes borrowed from literary models, in each case using source material as a kind of "culture" from which to create a poem that, in the end, finds a thematic direction and a poetic diction distinctively its own. In these poems, we seem to be witnessing Lampman as he shifts from library to countryside, at first remembering and echoing the poetry he had just been reading and gradually becoming absorbed by his surroundings.

Beauty in Nature

The "we" of "Freedom" – not humanity in general, as in the philosophical sonnets, but the speaker and his like-minded friends – abandon the city and make their way through fields, swamps, and meadowlands, past fences and woods, to "the hills," conceived as the symbolic pinnacle of the alternative world of nature. The city, housing the infernal "furnace of care," is a place where materialism, greed, and conflict reign and even "beauty is lying"; the earth, on the other hand, is personified as the "broad strong mother," an image embodying Lampman's favoured combination of beauty and strength: "Mother of all things beautiful, blameless, / Mother of hopes that her strength makes tameless."

Following the group's departure, the central part of the poem (stanzas four to ten) describes the journey. The gradual curative effect of nature is brought to bear on the trekkers as they pass through various scenes, closely observed by the speaker – a grassy plot, for example,

> Where the restless bobolink loiters and woos
>   Down in the hollows and over the swells,
> Dropping in and out of the shadows,
> Sprinkling his music about the meadows,
>   Whistles and little checks and coos,
>   And the tinkle of glassy bells.

Here Lampman's artistry reinforces the sense of the words. The onomatopoeia of the repeated *ink* sound and of "whistles," "checks," and "coos," combined with the synesthetic "Sprinkling his music," as if the bird's song were a kind of aural confetti, does just what such devices are meant to do: make the imagery, through the poetry, seem to live. The effect is enhanced by the shortening of the first two feet of the third line, creating brief delays in imitation of the irregular flitting of the bird among the shadows, while the absence of the expected fourth foot in the sixth line (present in all other stanzas) sustains for a moment, in the quiet of the meadow, the sound described as "the tinkle of glassy bells."

Not all the imagery in the poem is as prettily described, or as pretty, as this. There are places where "spiders weave" and "gray snakes hide" – not conventionally idyllic images. In addition, the hikers pass a kingfisher poised in the air, ready to dive for a kill, and later make their way

"Into the dim woods full of the tombs / Of the dead trees soft in their sepulchres." Such images, according to one school of thought, are examples of the aforementioned "negative" side of Lampman's vision of nature,[17] introducing an irony that would, if true, compromise the idea that "there is nothing fashioned by nature herself that is not beautiful, either in itself or in its relation to its surroundings." The more challenging irony, and the one consistent with his stated views, is that the affirmation and the realism are complementary. Death is part of nature, and Lampman weaves its images into his tapestry without disturbing the overriding beauty of all the scenes described. As the speaker and his companions, having reached their destination, "gaze on the face of our mother, / Earth in the health and the strength of her peace," it is not a compromised happiness they feel, but rather an unmitigated joy based on their appreciation of nature as it is, spiders and snakes notwithstanding.

Referred to by one critic as Lampman's "Swinburnian piece,"[18] "Freedom" does indeed show the influence of that once-prominent Victorian, with whose works he was familiar. In terms of both its rollicking dactylic metre and especially its "mother" imagery, Lampman's account of where the hikers are heading –

> Into the arms of our mother we come,
>   Our broad strong mother, the innocent earth,
> Mother of all things beautiful, blameless,
> Mother of hopes that her strength makes tameless

– and his declaration in the final stanza – "Here we shall commune with her and no other; / Care and the battle of life shall cease" – recall passages from Swinburne's "The Triumph of Time" where the speaker announces his resolve to return to the sea in the aftermath of spurned love, most notably the following:

> I will go back to the great sweet mother,
>   Mother and lover of men, the sea.
> I will go down to her, I and none other,
>   Close with her, kiss her and mix her with me;
> Cling to her, strive with her, hold her fast:

> O fair white mother, in days long past
> Born without sister, born without brother,
> Set free my soul as thy soul is free.[19]

Whether consciously or not, Lampman has clearly borrowed, in addition to phraseology and metrics, the image of the adored elemental mother from Swinburne. At the same time, he has redefined the figure, identifying her with the earth instead of the sea, making her life-affirming rather than vaguely threatening, and characterizing her as the epitome of innocence rather than the focus of erotic desire.

The poem has numerous qualities that reflect its more immediate inspiration and the preoccupations of its author. In terms of its delineation of the theme of escaping the city, traversing the landscape, and experiencing regeneration by means of the journey, "Freedom" is characteristically Lampman – and characteristically Canadian in the sense that a retreat to the countryside or wilderness for its restorative effects is a recognizable Canadian pattern, attested to by the abundance of camps, cottages, and wilderness parks in all regions of the country. The striding rhythmic energy of the poem is well suited to its depiction of the hikers' jaunt across the landscape. From the beginning, a momentum is established that propels the poem, for all its pausing to appreciate scenes along the way, forward to its destination. The use of the present tense from the beginning through the penultimate stanza creates an impression of immediacy, while the "shall" in the final stanza – "Here we shall commune with her and no other" – looks joyously onto the future. Realistically, the trekkers will have to return home. With no return mentioned, however, the effect of the closing lines is to elevate the hikers' tramp to the level of archetypal journey from spiritual emptiness to enlightenment – and there make an end.

Consistent with the idea that "Freedom" depicts a symbolic journey, one that could stand for many, is the typicality of the events described. As in "Winter-Store," the scenes mentioned, though clearly familiar to the speaker, are representative rather than actual. Hence there is an accumulation of plural nouns – "swamps," "meadow lands," "fences," "robins" – as well as a general use of such terms as "the city," "the earth," and "the whole world." In places, the generalizing combines awkwardly with the presentation of particular images. In the account of the kingfisher "Watching a spot by the edge of the streams," for example, the plural "streams" is distracting, drawing the reader away from the particular image rather than toward it. But despite its flaws, "Freedom" is a highly successful poem – an energetic *tour de force*, blending closely observed imagery with a purposeful movement forward and upward, culminating in the triumphant arrival at the symbolic holy temple of the natural world. Written in June of 1887, it shows Lampman – soon to be married and working up to the publication of his first book the following year – in the early stages of his poetic maturity, happily denouncing capitalism and confidently expressing his love of nature and belief in its restorative powers.

"Among the Timothy," completed on 5 August 1885, almost two years earlier, is a striking instance of, on the one hand, heavy borrowing from literary precedents, and on the other, success in extending and transforming the appropriated material to produce a poem of impressive power and originality. In contrast with "Freedom," it describes the experience of contact with nature, leading to a restored sense of emotional-psychological well-being, in intimate terms.[20] Its observations are not typical but rather reflect the speaker's solitary encounter with a rural scene on a particular hot summer's afternoon. In this sense it anticipates "Heat," written two years later, as well as, less directly, many other poems that highlight the effects of natural-world observation on the receptive individual. In certain respects an apprentice work, it stands nevertheless as a vital reference point in terms of the meaning of contact with nature, providing the clearest articulation of that experience to be found in Lampman's oeuvre, an experience which, in later poems, is often conveyed simply through the descriptive language.

Structurally, "Among the Timothy" can be divided into three sections: one that sets out the speaker's need of comfort for an "aching mood" occasioned by the stresses of city life (stanzas two, three, and four), another that depicts his immediate surroundings (stanzas five, six, and seven), and a third that describes the salutary results of prolonged exposure to, and observation of, the natural world as manifest before him (stanzas one, eight, and nine). The effect of beginning *in medias res*, with the speaker already present in the scene, is to make the countryside setting the imaginative centre of the poem, not the destination, and to

Beauty in Nature

undercut any suspense or feeling of urgency. An atmosphere of peace pervades the poem, even while the first full section, following stanza one, recalls the disquiet that led to the quest for comfort and renewal.

The imaginative centre has as its midpoint a "circle clean and gray" that a mower has left around a tree stump by which the speaker now reclines. As Michael Gnarowski has pointed out, in the original published version of "Among the Timothy" (in *Among the Millet*), it is a reaper rather than a mower who has unwittingly created this resting place for the speaker, but since the poem mentions a scythe (used by mowers) rather than a sickle (used by reapers), Scott changed the word to "mower" in *Poems*.[21] Lampman's use of "reaper," however, is significant because it matches his primary source: Matthew Arnold's "The Scholar-Gipsy." In this poem, as in "Among the Timothy," the speaker – on a hot summer afternoon – has found a spot in the countryside that a reaper has cleared, suitable for observation and rumination, and in stanza two sets out his plan:

> Here, where the reaper was at work of late –
>   In this high field's dark corner, where he leaves
>   His coat, his basket, and his earthen cruse,
>   And in the sun all morning binds the sheaves,
>   Then here, at noon, comes back his stores to use –
>   Here will I sit and wait.

In the following stanza he adds, "Screen'd is this nook o'er the high, half-reap'd field, / And here till sun-down, shepherd! will I be.[22] The parallel passage in "Among the Timothy" – the opening stanza – reads as follows (with Lampman's original "reaper" enclosed in brackets):

> Long hours ago, while yet the morn was blithe,
>   Nor sharp athirst had drunk the beaded dew,
>   A [reaper] came, and swung his gleaming scythe
>   Around this stump, and, shearing slowly, drew
>   Far round among the clover, ripe for hay,
>   A circle clean and gray;
>   And here among the scented swathes that gleam,

>   Mixed with dead daisies, it is sweet to lie
>   And watch the grass and the few-clouded sky,
>   Nor think but only dream.

The imagery, setting, and characterization of the speaker are all derived from Arnold, but combined with these are features that are Lampman's own: the more natural language; the introduction of the recently sheared "dead daisies" into the scene, without compromising its idyllic atmosphere; the image of what has been variously called "a magic circle" and "sacred circle" within which the speaker's transformation of consciousness occurs;[23] and the simple but pregnant concluding phrase. Also evident are traces of a secondary influence, that of Keats, both in phrasing – "Nor sharp athirst had drunk the beaded dew" – and verse form (Lampman's stanza is similar to that of "Ode to a Nightingale" as well as to that of "The Scholar-Gipsy"). Arnold's poem was also influenced by Keats.[24] It is safe to say that, without "The Scholar-Gipsy," there could be no "Among the Timothy" as we know it; and without Keats's odes, neither poem would exist in its present form.

Recalling his unhappiness in the city, the speaker reflects that "those high moods ... that sometimes made / My heart a heaven, opening like a flower" – in an earlier draft, "My heart a home of bright imaginings"[25] – "Were all gone lifeless now." The mental straightjacket of city life had become overpowering, preventing even poetry's escape. Like the depressed speaker of Shakespeare's Sonnet 29, who is "With what I most enjoy contented least,"[26] Lampman's speaker notes that he was "weary most of song." Flights of fancy would not suffice to brighten his mood. Stronger medicine was needed in the form of actual contact with nature, and so, having found his place of refuge, he resolves he will no longer devote his thinking to "barren search and toil that beareth nought,"

>   But let it go, as one that hath no skill,
>   To take what shape it will,
>   An ant slow-burrowing in the earthy gloom,
>   A spider bathing in the dew at morn,
>   Or a brown bee in wayward fancy borne
>   From hidden bloom to bloom.

The speaker will release his consciousness so that, like the simplest of creatures, alive to the moment, it can pursue its own course rather than persist in the negative thought patterns that, under the influence of contemporary life in the city, seemed dominant. He will rest his brain, "Nor think but only dream." For human beings, of course, it is not possible not to think. It is possible, however, to relax, and the result of mentally unclenching is that one's thoughts can wander freely, sometimes noticing, without trying to, one's surroundings, and sometimes focusing on other things, but all the while, because of the absence of the "conscious stress" referred to in "An Old Lesson from the Fields," remaining receptive to the beauty of the immediate environment.

Following his resolve, with respect to his thinking, to "let it go," the speaker shifts into a purely descriptive mode, with metaphorical language predominating. He observes in "the rocking grass" the breezes that lightly sway the higher blossoms

> And scarcely heed the daisies that, endowed
> > With stems so short they cannot see, up-bear
> > Their innocent sweet eyes distressed, and stare
> > > Like children in a crowd.

Later his wandering consciousness lights upon "a pale poplar" that "stands / With glimmering leaves that, when the wind comes, beat / Together like innumerable small hands." The references to children in these passages – a third instance depicts the breezes as the "Soft-footed children of the gipsy wind" – reinforce the quality of innocence that characterizes the rural scene, matching the portrayal of "the innocent earth" in "Freedom."

Often singled out for special praise because of their aptness of metaphor and felicity of expression,[27] such passages support the theme of the poem by conveying perception. The objects described come sharply and pleasingly into focus: with the speaker, we see the short-stemmed daisies untouched by the wind and hear the applause of the leaves. But what of the fact that the eyes of the children in Lampman's simile are "distressed"? Does this not compromise the idyllic quality of the scene? My answer is that the metaphorical vehicle is offered in the spirit of a charming, sentimental, almost Rockwellian picture. The emphasis, however, is on the tenor so that, through the image of the upward-turned faces of the children and their frustratingly small stature, we see the daisies and catch the precise effect of the breeze. We are not meant to grieve because the children's view is blocked, but rather to delight in our mental picture of the flowers. These passages demonstrate the effectiveness of the antidote to the spiritual malaise identified in the poems that lament humanity's alienation from nature. The yearning aspiration of "Yet if we could but lift our earthward eyes / To see, and open our dull ears to hear" is answered by the evident seeing and hearing reflected in the descriptive language and confirmed by the speaker's simple statement in the closing stanza: "I feel and hear and with quiet eyes behold." As with religion, all that is required is to avail oneself of the solution. That such opportunities are not seized upon by humanity in general stands as Lampman's version of a recalcitrance on the part of human beings, almost a determination to remain unenlightened, with which religion has long been familiar.

It is the case, however, that images such as those of the dead daisies and the distressed children are seen by some critics as tinged with strong negativity. Barrie Davies, for example, interprets the daisy-destroying mower as "death," suggesting that with his arrival comes "a total destruction of the natural order."[28] In a similar vein, Bentley, with reference to both the stump that the speaker has found in his "circle clean and gray" and the "dead daisies," argues that the speaker "has sought out in nature a locale whose attributes are those of his own [initial] dead and uncreative condition."[29] Brian Trehearne agrees, finding the image of "dead daises" suggestive of "morbidity," while that of the unhappy children gives rise to "troubling resonances."[30] For Trehearne, however, this is merely a starting point. In the first case, he argues, Lampman's syntax – "And here among the scented swathes that gleam, / Mixed with dead daisies, it is sweet to lie" – allows for the possibility that for the speaker it is "sweet" to lie with death – hence the "morbidity" (even though "Mixed" is awkward if referring to a human being lying "among the scented swathes" that contain the flower clippings: the person would not be "mixed" with the daisies).[31] In the second, the image of "children in a crowd" recalls "the jingle of the throng" in the city in such a way that the emotions "remain distinctly negative: the daisies 'cannot

Beauty in Nature

see,' their 'innocent sweet eyes [are] distressed,' and these qualities make them like the urban 'children.' In that collocation one glimpses perhaps the later socialist Lampman."[32]

The context for these observations is Trehearne's analysis of what he sees as the complex psychology underlying "Among the Timothy," whereby the apparently positive passages of the poem are undercut by negative implications and vice versa. In the passages that describe the speaker's supposedly negative mental state in the city, for example, Trehearne finds vibrant poetry featuring rhythmic variations and skilfully handled alliteration and other devices, belying or complicating the speaker's claim that his poetic inspiration had failed him.[33] The many verbal echoes in the poem, moreover, indicate that the positive and negative passages in which the recurring words appear are each pulled in the direction of their opposite. There is a relationship of "reciprocity" between them. The occurrence of the word "blind" in the phrases "blind gray streets" (negative) and "breezes, blithe as they are blind" (positive), for example, connects the two passages with the result that each carries something of its meaning to the other.[34] The argument is that, influenced by nineteenth-century associationist psychology, "Among the Timothy" is concerned with states of mind, and that these are not as absolute as the traditional negative-to-positive reading of the poem would suggest. The poem offers us an "enactment of a creative psychology that moves, not from negative to positive as on a thread, but haphazardly between those two extremes, never so approximating one condition that its contrary is lost to the record."[35] At the same time, Trehearne relates, it does move in a generally positive direction toward a reconciliation of conflicting states of mind. The reconciliation is evident, for example, in the phrase "flower and blade" in the list of objects imbued with sunlight at the end of the poem. The word "blade" recalls the sharp edge of the scythe used by the mower, personifying death, to cut clover, referred to in the opening stanza; now, however, those images are in harmony: "'flower and blade' (literally, of course, a blade of grass) are no longer antagonists, as they [were] when the mower's scythe [was] in action."[36]

Trehearne's reading would have us accept that Lampman had designed a brilliantly elaborate puzzle, according to which a naive speaker may believe that if he says he was weary, he really was, and if he says he is relieved, he really is, but the poet, by means of strategically employed metric variations, alliteration, echoic associations, and suggestive metaphors, undercuts these beliefs. Thus the stanzas of close observation in the middle of the poem, rightly seen, are characterized by a "multiplicity of consciousness," a "confusion of subject and objects," and "undercurrents of fear and longing" of which the speaker is unaware, and are the better for it. As Trehearne explains, "That these implications are more or less opaque to the persona only enriches the poem's rendition of psychological process: represented so deftly, he need not perceive in himself all that is made plain to us by Lampman's genius."[37]

While it is intriguing to think that Lampman might have indeed constructed such a complex, self-reflexive text, it seems doubtful that, even if he were capable of doing so, he would have wanted to. Instead, he did something equally ambitious: he mapped out in personal terms the process by which a countryside meditation can have a curative effect on the mind of the person who seeks that benefit. This does not deny "Among the Timothy" its subtleties of language and image. It simply means that these are deployed in the service of advancing the less complicated theme of natural-world restoration. And the references to death are not inconsistent with this aim; they support it. The depiction of personified breezes that wish "to taste of every purple-fringèd head / Before the bloom is dead," for example, underscores the importance of valuing the ephemeral and being alive to the present moment. The poem thus complements, rather than quarrels with, a poem like "Freedom," where the movement is clearly from corruption to purification, notwithstanding that poem's realistic references to a living forest.

The final two stanzas of "Among the Timothy," which return to the overview introduced in stanza one, describe in summary terms the restorative effect of observing the nearby environment while resting within the fortuitously prepared circle among the timothy. As "hour by hour" the speaker loiters, to "wind and sun and peaceful sound laid bare," his mood slowly changes. He becomes "quite fashioned to forget" the "aching dim discomfort of the brain" that afflicted him earlier. He attains, in other words, a condition exactly the opposite of that of the city dwellers who, in "Freedom," are depicted as being alienated from "our mother," the earth – people "Whose hearts in the furnace of care have forgotten / For ever the scent and the hue of her lands." A healing forgetfulness has replaced the forgetfulness that gives rise to the disease.

Repeating the phrase ("hour by hour") that emphasizes the protracted quality of the experience, the speaker concludes:

> And hour by hour, the ever-journeying sun,
>   In gold and shadow spun,
> Into mine eyes and blood, and through the dim
>   Green glimmering forest of the grass shines down,
> Till flower and blade, and every cranny brown,
>   And I are soaked with him.

Here the sun – the celestial disk that echoes the "circle clean and gray" of the opening lines of the poem – is the power that permeates all of nature, even "every cranny brown." Donne-like in its intensity, it is almost as if this quiet climax of the poem, religious in tone yet sensual and intimate, suffused with colour and light, were the answer to the prayer of the Holy Sonnets: "for I, / Except you enthrall me, never shall be free, / Nor ever chaste, except you ravish me."[38] It is not the "I" alone, though, that is affected. Lampman's "And I" is part of a list, making the speaker just one more object in nature, and the position of the phrase at the beginning of the final line, tucked in after the rhyming word "brown" and followed by the inclusive "are," is so unobtrusive as to make the speaker almost invisible. The effect is reinforced by the positioning of the speaker intimately close to the minutiae he describes, perceiving the grass as a "green glimmering forest," as if from the point of view of an ant. The grass, the earth, the speaker – all are subject to the overwhelming and purifying energy of the sun.

It is not often that Lampman offers a gloss on his own poems. His self-criticism seldom goes beyond "a good thing" or "one of the best things I have ever offered to any publication" or, at times, "hopeless rubbish."[39] In a letter to Hamlin Garland, however, he explains his intentions in "Among the Timothy" in a way that illuminates his aim in presenting natural-world description. Garland, who advocated descriptive realism of the kind also admired by William Dean Howells – accurate and unsentimental – had come across Lampman's "Heat" (most likely in Howells's review of *Among the Millet*, where it was quoted in its entirety) and had written him praising the poem, initiating a correspondence that lasted ten years.[40] Lampman responded by sending Garland a copy of *Among the Millet* and, in an accompanying letter, deflecting Garland's praise of "Heat" and drawing attention to his other poems: "I hope that the body of my work may not disappoint you, or cause you to abate the good opinion which you have based upon a single piece. The contents of my book are very varied, but those that are devoted to natural description are certainly the best, and Mr. Howells without doubt picked out the strongest pieces."[41] These remarks, while graciously agreeable, reveal an impatience on Lampman's part with people's admiration for what he referred to elsewhere as his "nature-work, as they call it."[42]

As it turned out, Garland did have reservations about Lampman's other poems. As James Doyle has pointed out, "Like many late nineteenth-century exponents of the realist doctrine, Garland was of two minds about the kind of lyric poetry in which Lampman specialized, stressing the interaction between nature and the poetic sensibility."[43] In his response to Garland's criticisms (contained in a letter that has not survived), Lampman attempts to resist the confining strictures of critical definition:

> I have read your last letter with deep interest. I understand your point of view perfectly, but I cannot say that I quite agree with it. I think a great deal of latitude should be allowed the poet in his methods, the only absolute requisites being beauty and truth. I confess that my design for instance in writing "Among the Timothy" was not in the first place to describe a landscape but to describe the effect of a few hours spent among the summer fields on a mind in a troubled or despondent condition. The description of the landscape was really an accessory [in] my plan.[44]

Here Lampman carefully distinguishes his own approach from that of the realists of the Howells-Garland school. Important to him is his belief in the restorative quality of nature, which fits into a larger belief system about contact with beauty, morally upright behaviour, and human progress. He wishes to devote his creative efforts to all of these concerns. It therefore does not sit right with him to be admired solely for the descriptive realism and local colour in his poems.

This view of his work would prove persistent, however. As the writer of one obituary notice expressed it, "Himself he put little into his poetry. It is purely objective. Neither did the world of men, enchained in materialism and distracted by aspiration, afford him subjects for interpretation."[45] It seems very likely that, as increasingly he was praised – and sometimes faulted – for the "purely objective" descriptive realism of his nature poems, Lampman felt determined to concentrate more directly on the human side of his poetic palette. This side was present in *Among the Millet*, but seemed to go unnoticed. It could not go unnoticed in *Alcyone*, the proofs of which Lampman had just completed correcting when he died, but that book would never be released to a wider audience except in the larger compass of *Poems*.

"The Frogs"

A third poem from *Among the Millet* that treats the theme of regeneration through contact with nature is the sequence of five sonnets collectively titled "The Frogs." Like "Freedom," this poem concerns a group of people – "we" – who together benefit from their attentiveness to the natural world, but like "Among the Timothy" it has a single focal point, which in "Among the Timothy" is the immediate environs of the cleared circle and in "The Frogs" is the "piping" of the title creatures. Written in May of 1887, this poem was influenced by Keats in terms of diction as well as theme and, to a lesser extent, by Tennyson's "The Lotos-Eaters."[46] What distinguishes "The Frogs" from its English predecessors is its focus on the quality and meaning of contact with nature, together with Lampman's employment of a deliberately non-poetic central image, that of the frogs, to show how inspiration may be found in the most unlikely of sources.

The Keatsian precursors of "The Frogs" are "Ode on a Grecian Urn" and "Ode to a Nightingale." In these poems, Keats examines the ironic contrast between human conceptions of permanence and the fleeting quality of experience. As David Perkins has pointed out, the tension between these conceptions is central to Keats's achievement: "The strength of [Keats's odes] is that they give complete and powerful expression to the natural human longing for a better world, a more perfect love, a lasting intensity of happiness, and yet they also remain faithful to the critical intelligence that forces us to acknowledge that dreams are only dreams and that in the sole world we know values are tragically in conflict."[47] In their acknowledgment that "dreams are only dreams," the Keats poems convey the pathos of human aspiration, even while, as works of art themselves, they lend permanence of a sort to the transitory images they embody.

In the opening sonnet of "The Frogs," the "Quaint uncouth dreamers" of the title are described as

Sweet murmurers of everlasting rest,
  For whom glad days have ever yet to run,
  And moments are as aeons, and the sun
But ever sunken half-way toward the west.

As John Ower has suggested, the image of the sun suspended in mid-descent "recalls [Tennyson's] lotos-land where 'it seemèd always afternoon,' where 'The charmèd sunset linger'd low adown / In the red West.'"[48] But it is also clear that both passages echo Keats's "Ode on a Grecian Urn," where the lovers are frozen in time on the verge of a kiss and the leaves on the nearby boughs will not fall "nor ever bid the spring adieu."[49] The difference between Lampman's poem and its precedents is that, in the former, the song of the frogs communicates the "inmost dream" of the spirit of nature "Ever at rest beneath life's change and stir." Although Keats's ode has a garden-style natural-world setting, it is not about nature. Lampman, by contrast, adapting a Wordsworthian philosophical outlook to a Keatsian sensibility, proposes that, amid the flux, there exists within nature the permanence of the ever-present moment with which human beings can connect by means of attentiveness to the beauty of nature. It is this paradoxical idea that the poem sets out to explore.

For Keats, the notion of timelessness is a trick of art or of the imagination. For Lampman, it has more to do with a state of consciousness. Because "moments are as aeons" for the frogs, they may be said to dwell, in terms of their froggy consciousness, in the eternity of the present; and human beings who hear them – that is, who "open [their] dull ears" to become receptive to beauty in nature – share in their enlightened state of being. It is just such a state of mind, attuned to the eternal now, that mystics over the ages have sought to attain. It is perhaps part of the meaning of the deity's self-identification in Exodus: "I AM." And a similar idea has been expressed by the philosopher Ludwig Wittgenstein, who, speculating on the meaning of death in *Tractatus Logico-Philosophicus*, postulates that "[i]f we take eternity to mean not infinite temporal duration but timelessness, then eternal life belongs to those who live in the present."[50] In this sense, the appreciation of beauty in nature offers a kind of salvation in the form of transient participation in the everlasting now.

In the middle three sonnets of "The Frogs," the depiction of the eternal presence within nature is reinforced, not contradicted, by the numerous references to time passing. The temporal setting is early spring, but the earth, once again characterized as "the mother," is imagined as musing on the future – "on life, and what the hours might be, / When love should ripen to maturity." The hours pass from noon through night to dawn, the days also pass, and connecting all is the pervasive and persistent piping of the frogs – that familiar, non-stop canticle that in swampy locations fills the spring air – described in such elevated terms as to prompt one contemporary critic to ask, "Who ever before thought there was so much sentiment connected with that little, neglected, abused, serio-comic animal – the frog?"[51] Their voices "high and solemn," they dream "beyond the night and day"; they watch "with fathomless eyes"; and with the first light of dawn they are heard "with soft throats unaltered in [their] dream." The idea that gradually emerges is that, although time passes, it is only each successive moment of existence that has meaning. The frogs' piping speaks of the constant presence of the eternal in which all mortal life (potentially) participates. With this established, it is possible for both the growth and decline of living things to be acknowledged without a ripple of concern. "And ever as ye piped," the speaker recalls, apostrophizing the frogs,

> The great buds swelled; among the pensive woods
> The spirits of first flowers awoke and flung

>   From buried faces the close-fitting hoods,
>   And listened to your piping till they fell,
>   The frail spring-beauty with her perfumed bell,
>   The wind-flower, and the spotted adder-tongue.

The short-lived existence of the early flowers – lovingly named by the speaker – is not lamented because it is the eternity of the moment, not the brevity of mortality, that matters. While alive, the flowers "listened" to the piping of the frogs. Attuned to the wonder of present existence, they achieved their humble apotheosis.

In the closing sonnet of "The Frogs," as in the final section of "Among the Timothy," the speaker re-introduces the human element and describes the effect the frogs' piping has upon those who have been attentive. Just as the flowers "listened," the speaker recalls that "we heard you," with the result that the dissonant sounds of urban "discord" grew "faint and far away." Whereas those who, in the city, see nature only distantly, as if through the wrong end of a telescope, and as a result of their alienation remain subject to the "roar" of a troubled existence, those who open themselves to nature's beauty – who hear the voices of the frogs – succeed in reversing those perceptual relations. The "realities" of human suffering resulting from, for example, consciousness of mortality, are not so much conquered as rendered irrelevant. They exist, but having receded into the distance, they pose no threat.

The final six lines offer a subtly phrased and complex summation of the effects of the trance-like experience outlined earlier in the poem:

>   Morning and noon and midnight exquisitely,
>   Rapt with your voices, this alone we knew,
>   Cities might change and fall, and men might die,
>   Secure were we, content to dream with you
>   That change and pain are shadows faint and fleet,
>   And dreams are real, and life is only sweet.[52]

In terms of style and strategy, Lampman is returning here to the Keatsian odes that have partly inspired the poem. His conclusion, though, is altogether different, in keeping with his natural-world focus. In "Ode to a Nightingale," after the nightingale suddenly flies off and the spell of identification is broken, the speaker wonders at the quality of his experience: "Was it a vision, or a waking dream? / Fled is that music ... Do I wake or sleep?"[53] Lampman reiterates the word "dream" and, like Keats, ponders the significance of recognizing two different states of consciousness. But while Keats's questions allow at least for the possibility that, in Perkins's words, "dreams are only dreams," Lampman's conclusion is emphatically that "dreams are real." To be sure, this is the case only in the sense that the speaker and his friends "dream" it to be so, but the qualification, rather than compromising the point, subtly strengthens it, since it is only for the person inspired by an appreciation of beauty in nature, alive to the moment, that the redemptive declaration applies, and since it goes without saying that for the person unattuned to the eternal present, *not* living, as Early puts it, "in another dimension,"[54] dreams are mere illusions and time conquers all.

In the closing lines of "Ode on a Grecian Urn," the image on the urn is imagined as communicating to the generations of the living its aphoristic insight, to which the speaker appends his own conclusion: "'Beauty is truth, truth beauty,' – that is all / Ye know on earth, and all ye need to know." Both here and at the end of "The Frogs," an approved-of limitation on understanding is introduced: the listeners in "The Frogs" are "content to dream" something, while the people addressed in "Ode on a Grecian Urn" are informed that the beauty-truth equation is "all [they] need." By focusing on the effects of natural-world observation instead of aesthetic perception, however, Lampman's conclusion departs from that of Keats. To those who are focused on beauty in nature, it suggests, happiness comes ("life is only sweet"), and what normally seems mere fantasy is, properly seen, the way things really are. As for loss and suffering, it is specifically to emphasize the immunity of the "we" of the poem to the negative influence of thoughts of "change and pain" that the reassurances at the end of "The Frogs" are juxtaposed with an acknowledgment of mutability. It may be true that all life is ephemeral, but for those who are alive to the moment, there is only the present, the eternal now. Ephemerality is of no consequence.

In all three of these poems, written in his early to middle twenties, we see Lampman taking poetic ideas from works by those writers he most admired and then adapting them to his own purposes. In each case, his poem finds a direction quite distinct from those of the literary sources that inspired it. Lampman appears at this stage to be working out his ideas in relation to his Romantic and Victorian predecessors on the one hand and his own environment and experience on the other. And this – the fact that the ideas are being worked out – is perhaps why in these poems Lampman offers his clearest delineation of the process by which natural-world observation has a curative effect on the receptive individual. These poems thus provide an excellent gloss on those subsequent poems in which the same ideas are present, but not spelled out so clearly – poems in which the speaker may "hear" and "see," but the significance of the hearing and seeing remains implicit, or nearly so. Among these more purely descriptive poems are Lampman's finest poems in the nature idiom, those upon which his reputation for sharpness of observation and subtlety of expression rests.

CHAPTER 4

Discovering the Wilderness

In his introduction to *Lyrics of Earth: Sonnets and Ballads*, the Lampman selection he edited in 1925, Scott makes reference to a canoe trip taken by the two friends in the spring of 1886 on the River Lièvre in the Gatineau Hills.[1] This was Lampman's first foray into a wilderness environment. Two of the three poems that, according to Scott, derive from this experience – "Morning on the Lièvre" and "A Dawn on the Lièvre" – stand out, by their finely realized evocations of place, as heralding the productive encounter between artist and favoured subject. These poems are largely descriptive and reflect the travellers' actual observations. The third poem, "Between the Rapids," depicts imaginary canoeists passing a rural community with which the speaker has past connections. Perhaps Lampman and Scott observed farms on their way up the river, prompting this nostalgic narrative, which has romantic appeal but lacks the originality of the other two poems. Lampman would, after this initiation, continue to treat the fields and woods of the Ottawa area as subjects for poetic interpretation, with eminent success, but the wilderness – that is, the relatively unpopulated and undeveloped forest regions of northern Ontario and Quebec – had now established itself as his imaginative centre of gravity.

"Between the Rapids"

In Lampman's day, "Between the Rapids" was one of his most popular poems. Scott praised it for its blend of native landscape and human emotions; Charles G.D. Roberts exclaimed, "How I envy you that!"; a reviewer of *Among the Millet* in the London *Spectator*, noting the successful evocation of Canadian scenery in the poem, called it "the piece which has ... given us most pleasure"; Canadian novelist and journalist Agnes Maule Machar, writing under the sobriquet "Fidelis," found it highly evocative of place and "altogether delightful"; and Clarence Edmund Stedman included it as one of five Lampman selections in his influential *A Victorian Anthology* (1895).[2] This poem, however, has not worn well. Admired a hundred years ago for its local colour, it has since been criticized for its derivative style and theme – curiously invisible, or acceptable, to Lampman's contemporaries, but anathema to later generations.

The poem weaves a fiction of canoeists who journey past an old haunt filled with emotional significance, evoking, as Scott remarks, "a touch of the romance of the old voyageurs."[3] As in Wordsworth's "Tintern Abbey," the time that has elapsed is five years, and as in Roberts's own "Tantramar Revisited," the speaker, gazing from a distance, wonders about the changes that might have taken place in his absence.[4] In his appreciation of the poem, Scott notes that the *Spectator* reviewer compared it "with discrimination, I think," to Arthur Hugh Clough's "Les Vaches" (identified by its alternate title, "Ite domum saturae, venit Hesperus"), which relates a similar story, but told from the point of view of one who remains behind rather than those who have left their rural home.[5] The opening statement of Clough's poem, "The skies have sunk," seems echoed by Lampman's equivalent, "The point is turned," and in both cases a question is raised about whether the woman left behind may find or have found another "mate." An implied French-language setting, moreover, is a feature of both poems, reinforced by the use of French names.

Other possible precursors, as Bentley has shown, include Thomas Moore's "Canadian Boat Song" and Rossetti's translation of François Villon's "The Ballad of Dead Ladies."[6] The main influence, however, was Clough's friend Matthew Arnold, whose "A Dream" depicts sailors (rather than canoeists) sailing past a "plank-built cottage" (rather than a "white log cottage"), remembering, yearning, and then being carried on by the current of what now seems "the river of Life."[7] Arnold's poem, notwithstanding its own indebtedness to Keats and to Milton,[8] succeeds as a poignant evocation of yearning toward the past, and toward a lost ideal. Lampman's re-enactment, with its "sigh for Jeanne" and "sob for Virginie," is a successful transplant, but a transplant nonetheless. It shows Lampman doing what critics have often said of him in general: building the local scene into Old World templates.

By contrast, the other two poems inspired by the Gatineau canoe trip seem shaped by their subject matter in terms of image, style, and structure, as if the scenes themselves were insistent of expression to match their novelty. Symbolically, with their morning freshness, these poems mark a new beginning for Lampman and for Canadian poetry – an authentic response to wilderness.

"Morning on the Lièvre"

In "Morning on the Lièvre,"[9] the speaker does not offer an account of arriving at the inspirational locale, and if he was seeking "comfort for an aching mood," as in "Among the Timothy," he does not say so. Instead, he depicts from the outset the scene itself, implying with word and image the receptive seeing and hearing extolled and explained in "Among the Timothy."

The poem begins with a pair of canoeists (not yet identified as such) immersed in their surroundings, attentive and alert. A bird provides nature's version of a morning song as the two companions take in the scene:

> Far above us where a jay
> Screams his matins to the day,
> Capped with gold and amethyst,
> Like a vapour from the forge
> Of a giant somewhere hid,
> Out of hearing of the clang
> Of his hammer, skirts of mist

> Slowly up the woody gorge
> Lift and hang.

The harmony of the opening rhyming couplet is jarred by the dissonant juxtaposition of the churchy "matins" and the woodsy "screams," undercutting any suggestion of mild and gentle nature, while the massive presence of the colossal smith evokes a sense of wonderment, as in a fairytale. It is Lampman's handling of sentence structure, however, that stands out as the most distinctive feature of this passage. The buildup of seemingly unrelated sub-images preceding the main statement forces us to train our senses on the objects described, without fully comprehending, so that our appreciation of the qualities of things precedes our understanding of what is taking place. Something is "Capped with gold and amethyst"; something is like "a vapour" produced in the forge of a giant. The absence of a central point of focus makes us pause over the images themselves. The rhymes, meanwhile, after the initial couplet, become irregular, preventing us from taking aesthetic refuge in a predictable pattern of decorative sound. As far as standard comprehension goes, we are in the woods. Finally the subject, "skirts of mist," appears in line seven, and two lines later the compound verb, "Lift and hang"; having paused to watch, we can now move on.

The technique of syntactic delay is used twice more in this poem, in combination with other poetic devices, indicating a deliberate plan. The second instance is in stanza two, where the presence of the canoeists on a river is alluded to for the first time and where the speaker, attentive to sights and sounds, describes the scene:

> ... and the dip
> Of the paddles scarcely breaks,
> With the little silvery drip
> Of the water as it shakes
> From the blades, the crystal deep
> Of the silence of the morn,
> Of the forest yet asleep.

The separation of verb and object has the effect of expanding a pocket of relative silence as we attend to the small sound of the dripping water before learning what the dip "scarcely breaks," the sense of quiet being reinforced by the contrast between the tiny "drip" and the vastness of the "crystal deep." The rhymes, meanwhile, have become more regular, following an *abab* pattern, with the exception of two rhyming couplets toward the end of the stanza. A peaceful calm pervades the atmosphere as the canoeists proceed on their way. Finally, in stanza three, consisting of a single compound-complex sentence spread over nineteen lines, the subject – "seven ducks" – does not appear until line nine, while the second of the two main verbs is held back until line fifteen. Our attention is focused first on the reedy place at the side of the river from which the ducks "With a splashy rustle rise" and then on the ducks themselves – the sound they make is an onomatopoeic "swivelling whistle" – before, at the word "go," they are propelled forward, quickly disappearing "behind a rocky spur, / Just ahead." With that last word, the canoeists are drawn further down the river, and we are left to contemplate the significance of an experience to which no meaning has been overtly attached. The rhymes in this part of the poem are once again irregular, as befits the fact that the ducks have disturbed the scene with their ruckus.

In addition to sentence structure and rhyme patterns, there is one further aspect of design that contributes to this poem's remarkably successful marriage of form and content. The trochaic metre, with masculine endings throughout, creates a seven-syllable unit – just about the duration of a paddle's stroke and return, with a slight break at the end for a pause before the next stroke. Interspersed are occasional two-beat, three-syllable lines, for shorter strokes and longer pauses. The rhythm of the action depicted and the rhythm of the artistic representation are in synch.

A final point about this poem relates to the quality of its imagery – a mix of the fanciful and the realistic – and, with respect to the latter, the occurrence of images that have been seen by some commentators as offsetting the idyllic quality of the scene. The sense of nature as a realm of marvels established by the evocation of the mysterious giant in stanza one is reinforced with admirable simplicity at the beginning of stanza two, where we see the canoeists on the river for the first time: "Softly as a cloud we go, / Sky above and sky below, / Down the river." The phrase "as a cloud" may be a borrowing from Wordsworth ("I wandered lonely as a cloud"),[10] but not the conceit. Lampman's notion is that, with the sky reflected in the glassy water, the canoeists have the sensation they are floating through the air, simultaneously right-side-up and upside-down.[11] They are under nature's spell. The picture drawn is otherworldly, magical, only the other world is nature. At the same time, the smooth surface of the river is a realistic image, and indeed the imagery throughout is charged with a naturalness that makes clear it is not fairyland but forest land the paddlers are exploring. As already noted, the jay "screams" its morning song, and later we are presented with muskrats that "peer and sneak / In around the sunken wrecks / Of a tree that swept the skies / Long ago."

In critical writings on this poem, we encounter again the persistent idea that there lurks in such passages, in Munro Beattie's phrase, "an ominous cross-current of suggestion," as if, despite himself, Lampman were after all ambivalent in his attitude toward the natural world.[12] The proponents of this view seem to regard the perceived negativity as a virtue, lending depth and complexity to an otherwise simplistic portrayal of nature, boringly affirmative. In my reading, Lampman's subtlety is of a different sort, his evident aim being to celebrate nature in all its manifestations and at the same time to represent it realistically – to have it both ways. Dead trees – seen everywhere in forests – appear frequently in his poems, strengthening the verisimilitude of his depiction. If their presence is interpreted as compromising his positive outlook, then the conclusion we must reach is that Lampman thinks well of nature, except where nature is harsh or where there are indications of decay or death – or mischief (one critic finds it disturbing that the muskrats "sneak").[13] Much more in tune with Lampman's sensibilities is the idea that nature is valued for what it is. Part of the reason for including the dead trees is to show that they do *not* disturb. The strength of Lampman's affirmation derives from the inclusiveness of a portrayal which pointedly does not dodge or deny the implications of the constant flux within nature, but rather embraces them. It is noteworthy that in his National Film Board movie *Morning on the Lièvre*, filmed on location in 1961, the centenary of Lampman's birth, David Bairstow presents the landscape as sometimes rugged and dramatic, but hauntingly beautiful throughout.[14]

"A Dawn on the Lièvre"

The formal design of "Morning on the Lièvre" is unique among Lampman's poems. Though he would often return to trochaic metre, and would again employ irregular rhymes and stanza lengths as well as unconventional syntax, he never again combined these features within the compass of a single poem. Tied to the specifics of subject and setting, they did not lend themselves to repetition. In the sonnet, by contrast, he found a congenial vehicle that he could often revisit.

Lampman's approach to the sonnet can be gathered from two comments he makes on the subject. In his essay "Happiness," arguing that it is in people's interest to "accept the limitations of life," he offers the following analogy: "Thus the poet, when he might give to the impulse of expression the freest and wildest liberty, chooses for his own pride and pleasure to confine himself within the difficult bounds of the sonnet. The form is finite and severe, but it is his glory to prove that the spirit within may be gracious and infinite."[15] Aligning himself with those many poets who enjoy the challenge of the sonnet form, Lampman emphasizes the paradox of infinitude within narrow limits and of easy ("gracious") expression despite restriction. And certainly one of Lampman's great strengths was his ability to write in a natural idiom within the strictures of traditional forms. As Bernard Muddiman comments in an early appreciation, Lampman's verse is to be valued in part "for its calm nonchalance and unruffled flow of thought."[16] The opening stanza of "Among the Timothy," compared with the stanza from Arnold's "The Scholar-Gipsy" on which it is modelled, provides a good example of his skill in this respect.

In the second passage, loosening somewhat the bars of constraint, he claims to have "no very profound respect for rules and regulations,"[17] and this is evident in his handling of the sonnet structure. Although he employed both the Petrarchan and Shakespearian versions, and claimed in a letter to Carman that "one form or the other will immediately occur to the writer as applicable to the picture he has in mind, he can hardly define why,"[18] he typically produced a hybrid, preserving the two-part octave-sestet design of the former but incorporating more rhymes than traditionally prescribed in the octave and frequently introducing a rhyming couplet somewhere in the sestet. Finding in the sonnet form a suitable length and structure to contain his poetic ideas, along with a flexibility that permitted each poem to find its own way, Lampman produced in excess of one hundred and fifty sonnets, and these have been more consistently admired than any other category of his poems.[19]

"A Dawn on the Lièvre," the third poem from the 1886 camping trip with Scott, is a sonnet of this hybrid variety. The subject is similar to that of "Morning on the Lièvre," but the mood is entirely different – dynamic rather than tranquil. This is a dawn that one has to hang on to one's seat to experience. The effect is like that of a painting in which the boldness of line and colour gives movement and energy to what might otherwise be a placid landscape.

Setting the scene for the "action" to come, the poem begins with the two canoeists, both strong paddlers, hard at it. As if giving an oral account of their adventure and wanting to impart to his audience the drama of the experience, the speaker recalls their early start in an anecdotal style:

> Up the dark-valleyed river stroke by stroke
>   We drove the water from the rustling blade;
>   And when the night was almost gone we made
> The Oxbow bend; and there the dawn awoke.

The canoeists appear to be racing through the night toward an encounter with the dawn at a predetermined place, specifically named, where the spectacle will be the most impressive. The quick succession of three declarative statements, in contrast to the numerous qualifying phrases of "Morning on the Lièvre," suggests an urgency. Then comes the dawn:

> Full on the shrouded night-charged river broke
>   The sun, down the long mountain valley rolled,
>   A sudden swinging avalanche of gold,
> Through mists that sprang and reeled aside like smoke.

There is kinetic energy in this description as well as close observation: the advancing sunlight resembles an avalanche in the sense that the movement is visible. We witness the power of nature and the spectacular drama of the transformation from dark to light.

Dazzled, the canoeists adopt a stance of worshipful awe as, in the sestet, they watch the mountain come into being in the light:

> And lo! before us, toward the east upborne,
>   Packed with curled forest, bunched and topped with pine,
>   Brow beyond brow, drawn deep with shade and shine,
>   The mount; upon whose golden sunward side,
> Still threaded with the melting mist, the morn
>   Sat like some glowing conqueror satisfied.

What was moments before shrouded in darkness now stands revealed in its monumental size and incredible beauty, reaching high and back, its topography articulated with the alliteratively marked chiaroscuro contrast of "shade and shine." On the heels of this description, the final clause seems justified: the day has overwhelmed the night, now dominating the scene, as does the sun in "Among the Timothy," but here with less serenity, more dynamism.

Two literary parallels are worth noting in connection with "A Dawn on the Lièvre," the first an instance of most likely unconscious imitation and the second either unconscious borrowing or simply a coincidence of common method and purpose. Since both sources are contemporary and Canadian, they suggest a reorienting of the imagination on Lampman's part away from the Romantics and Victorians and toward the Canadian milieu, literary and topographical.

In the subject-verb reversal of "broke / The sun," Lampman's phrasing echoes a syntactic mannerism of Charles G.D. Roberts, whose constructions "as spreads the blind / Pale grain" from "The Sower" and "Lumbers the wain" from "The Potato Harvest" are similar. As well, Lampman's description of mists "that sprang and reeled aside like smoke" recalls Roberts's "and day fades out like smoke," also from "The Potato Harvest."[20] I do not mean to imply that either the syntax of the first examples or the simile "like smoke" is unique to Roberts, although the latter, applied to dusk, is perhaps so. The fact that the Roberts poems, both sonnets, were written just prior to Lampman's canoe trip and published that same year,[21] however, together with the fact that the two possible echoes occur in the same poem, makes the connection seem viable.

What the evidence of Lampman's critical writings suggests is that he read Roberts closely and followed his career with abiding interest. He provides a detailed assessment of Roberts in his lecture "Two Canadian Poets," faulting him for a lack of delicacy and spontaneity in some poems, but praising him roundly for his artistry, the "broad and full-vowelled flow" of his diction, and his ability to invest with meaning "a bit of vivid landscape description," along with other qualities.[22] As well, Lampman makes Roberts his subject in two contributions to "At the Mermaid Inn" and mentions him in a third.[23] Neither Scott nor Campbell writes of Roberts in "At the Mermaid Inn." It is not surprising, then, that aspects of Roberts's style should have rubbed off on Lampman, nor that, in composing a nature-focused sonnet in 1886 or later,[24] Lampman should have had Roberts's landscape sonnets prominent in his mind. It could be that Lampman was deliberately incorporating something of the descriptive method Roberts used in his depictions of rural New Brunswick – a method simply flagged by the specific echoes I have mentioned – as a way of furthering a poetic mapping of the nation. At any rate, the echoes stand as examples of the flattery of imitation, revealing perhaps better than his sometimes lukewarm critical assessments his admiration for the writer whom he regarded as "the founder of a school" and "the originator of a new era in our poetic activity," and whom he credited with having set the standard for a new Canadian literature.[25]

The second parallel relates to Isabella Valancy Crawford's well-known depiction of daybreak in a wilderness setting, "The Dark Stag." The similarity of theme and (in part) method, supported by publication dates, suggests that Crawford's poem could have influenced Lampman's, even though the two works differ in obvious ways. Whether or not a relationship of influence existed, a comparison of the poems is illuminating in showing the similar ways in which Lampman and Crawford responded to the same subject, and then, with similarities established, the distinctive qualities of their respective poems.

In the closing simile of "A Dawn on the Lièvre," the evocation of the "conqueror" introduces into the poem a mythopoeic dimension. A natural phenomenon – the sunrise – is described in mythic terms in order to suggest the colossal magnificence of the scene. A similar device, interpreting the same theme, is employed by Crawford in "The Dark Stag," a poem in which the supplanting of the night by the day is vividly imagined as the defeat of the fleeing stag by "the hunter, Sun."[26] The time frame, too, is the same, beginning with pre-dawn and ending with the triumphant victory of day. One difference is that in "The Dark Stag" there are no observers; the depiction is objective. Lampman's canoeists are an important presence in his poem, which is as much concerned with perception as with events perceived. In addition, Crawford's *mise en scène* is more elaborate, as all of nature is involved in the chase and aboriginal imagery serves both to animate the natural-world description and to emphasize the wilderness setting. The hunter wears moccasins and shoots arrows – shafts of sunlight. The red leaves of the sumach (the time of year is fall) are "council-fires," and birds, winds, and fish are all in league with the sun. Over seven stanzas, remarkably, the complicated metaphorical construct holds together as the hunt unfolds. In Lampman's sonnet, by contrast, the invasion of sunlight is sweeping and abrupt. A further difference, one that can perhaps be attributed to authorial gender, relates to the representation of emotion. In Crawford's poem, the title creature – and the figure last mentioned in the poem – is strongly sympathetic. Its antlers silhouetted against the antagonistic pale blue of the pre-dawn sky create an image of pathos. Its dark and mysterious male presence is appealing. The stag, moreover, is mated with "a snow-white doe" – the moon – and the triumph of the sun over both, even though it is the victory of life, is muted by our sorrow for their lost love. In "The Dark Stag," there is tragedy as well as triumph, whereas in "A Dawn on the Lièvre" we experience no grieving or sense of loss. The colour that predominates at the end of "The Dark Stag" is blood red; in "A Dawn on the Lièvre," it is gold.

The initial publication of "The Dark Stag" in the *Toronto Evening Telegram* on 28 November 1883[27] makes it possible that Lampman was familiar with the poem at the time of writing "A Dawn on the Lièvre." But he may not have known the poem. Crawford published her first and only (non-posthumous) volume, *Old Spookses' Pass, Malcolm's Katie, and Other Poems,* in 1884, but the book did not include "The Dark Stag," and it was not until 1893 that the subject of Crawford's poetry came up in the correspondence between Lampman and Thomson.[28]

Nevertheless, it is noteworthy that, confronted with the same subject matter, both writers felt the need to extend the bounds of natural-world description in the direction of mythic constructs, perceiving darkness and dawn as adversaries in epic contention (albeit with predetermined results). A sunrise in the wilderness demanded metaphors of power to match its high drama of colour and light.

In the poems from the River Lièvre canoe trip it is evident that Lampman had discovered his poetic terrain. His life would afford him only a handful of wilderness adventures, and certainly he would continue to be enamoured of the countryside closer to hand – he had not yet written "Heat" – but just as the painter Tom Thomson would do some twenty-five years later, he would feel drawn to this region as the source of his happiest inspiration for the rest of his life, and treasure it in memory. Even the river that flowed southeastward past his city, apostrophized in "To the Ottawa," would come "Laden with sound from far-off northern glens / Where winds and craggy cataracts complain," reminding him of that place of uncontaminated, rugged beauty. Among the poems that are direct responses to the wilderness are "An Ode to the Hills," "The Lake in the Forest," and a group of sonnets written on another canoe trip, this one to the Lake Temagami region in 1896. In the meantime, there were the rural surroundings of the Ottawa area. "The wild scenery of the forest is beautiful," he wrote in 1892, "and not less lovely in another way are the fields of our forefathers, mellowed by long years and the patient and affectionate usage of men."[29] Here he is thinking of orchards, most likely those of his own ancestral background in the Niagara and Lake Erie regions, celebrated in poems such as "Among the Orchards" and especially *The Story of an Affinity*, his poetic attempt to set his world to rights. But the Ottawa Valley, too, could boast well-cultivated farms amid hills of forest and rock, and a gathering of poems from this environment, among them Lampman's finest creations, are the subject of chapter 5.

CHAPTER 5

Heat and Cold: An Inclusive Vision

Lampman believed that, through memory, experience is transformed so that even negative occurrences can be seen in a positive light, owing to the workings of "an alchemy in the imagination which can brew pleasure out of the most unpromising material."[1] At first this idea seems merely delusional, but if it is understood to mean that, from a removed perspective, one can clarify experience, then it appears much more in tune with the way in which, as we reflect, we process information. In retrospect, we can appreciate the positive aspects of events that may have seemed compromised, or that were obscured, at the time.

It was not only in the context of memory that Lampman discovered a sense of ironic reversal. Indeed, the more one reads him, the more one recognizes the mindset of a contrarian, prone to finding that the truth of a phenomenon, or else his own experience of it, is just the opposite of what one might expect. Altogether characteristic, for example, is his semi-serious suggestion in a "Mermaid Inn" essay that, contrary to the popular truism that genius is a form of madness, "men of the world are the real madmen." People could just as easily make *this* claim, he declares, "with all the best of the argument in their favour."[2] In another contribution he relates that, while many people see the poet as an impractical dreamer and the businessman as sensible and down to earth, "[i]t is a curious thing to reflect that the very reverse is the fact." In view of Lampman's attachment to the "dream" experience and frequently asserted self-definition as "dreamer," there is a double irony in his insistence that it is the businessman who, accumulating wealth, "spends his whole life in the pursuit of a dream," whereas the poet is clear-sighted and "attaches himself to no dream."[3] But then, for Lampman, frogs are divine choristers, and the dreams they inspire, real.

The idea that beauty in nature persists over time despite seasonal change, together with the complementary idea that beauty resides in nature even when, without seasonal change, conditions are extreme or a scene is not conventionally picturesque, becomes increasingly central to Lampman's outlook as his vision of nature evolves. To illustrate these ideas, I have chosen six poems that together depict beauty in nature as reverberating and ricocheting around the seasonal compass. Since these poems have discrete temporal settings, and since the idea of the persistence of beauty in nature is best established by comparison, I will examine them in pairs: the two sonnets "Solitude" and "A January Morning," "Heat" and the sonnet "In November," and more briefly, "April" and "In October." The chapter will then conclude with a discussion of a poem that over the years has met with amusement and puzzlement, but has not been appreciated for the clear insight it offers into Lampman's ironic perspective: "The Dog."

"Solitude" and "A January Morning"

As sonnets that convey meaningful engagement with the scene, "Solitude" and "A January Morning" display Lampman's descriptive powers at their most evocative. They illustrate what is perhaps his greatest achievement: the conveying of both the object perceived and the perceiving of it, without comment, so that the poem becomes a very close analogue of the experience, allowing us to understand directly by imaginatively taking part. A common experience in reading literature is that an event takes place against a setting and what we respond to most powerfully is that background setting – the evocation of time and place. In poems such as "Solitude" and "A January Morning," the setting, along with the sense of being there, is the event. As a consequence, these poems are about almost nothing, yet it could be argued that they are about the only thing that matters – conscious engagement in the world of the here and now. In addition, they serve as examples of Lampman's skilful handling of the sonnet form and his ability to mould it to his own purposes.

"Solitude" begins with a simple declaration: "How still it is here in the woods." The only rhetorical flourish here is the emphatic *how*-plus-adjective construction, suggesting something remarkable. With this deft stroke, Lampman locates the poem at the centre of his own imaginative universe and, at the same time, without preliminaries, transports the reader to that archetypal focal point of Canadian consciousness, the forest, the place outside the garrison, once feared but now desired. The words convey, moreover, a sense of wonder. It is as if we have just entered a cathedral and noted the singular atmosphere before observing the particular qualities of the space. Yet despite the reverential tone, the language is not precious, but prosaic. This quality is complemented by the metre, which is irregular, as any attempt to read those eight words with iambic stress will quickly confirm. Instead, we hear a more natural pattern of stress, which might be scanned as follows:

/ / ˘ ˘ / ˘ ˘ /

How still it is here in the woods.

A spondee followed by two anapaests, bearing little resemblance to the underlying pattern (made clear later in the poem), results in a dressed-down version of the statement. Our attention is drawn away from the poem as stylized construct and toward the subject matter. Thus the poem becomes almost invisible, a facilitating lens.

With the general atmosphere established, the speaker goes on to make a series of observations, noting the trees and the spaces between them, then a brook, and finally, in the sestet, a succession of bird sounds. This is a natural sequence of perception: first an overall impression, then the specifics of the nearby surroundings, and then, as time passes, the occasional sounds that intrude upon the prevailing stillness. The syntax, meanwhile, remains simple, with clauses unfolding in a straightforward fashion from subject to verb to qualifier or object: "The trees / Stand motionless," "The air / Hangs quiet," "a hawk screams," "a woodpecker startles the stillness," "I hear." Again, the plainness keeps the focus on nature and away from art.

The "unartistic" quality of this sonnet is reinforced by Lampman's skilful structuring of lines, deployment of rhymes, and handling of the sonnet form. The caesura that occurs after the opening statement is echoed by two equally strong pauses in lines three and eleven. These breaks suggest silent observation, followed, in each case, by a noting of some new feature of the scene. By interrupting the lineal flow, they support the naturalism of the poem: they occur when they occur, not when a line or section ends. The complementary device is enjambment, and Lampman uses it repeatedly – for example, in the first three line endings: "trees / Stand motionless," "did not dare / To stir," and "air / Hangs quiet." Of the sonnet's fourteen lines, only five are clearly end-stopped, and only three of these with periods, including the end of the octave and the end of the poem. The end rhymes are thus downplayed – passed over – with the result that, although we hear them, we hear them distantly. Like the still trees, they do not "break the spell."

This effectiveness of this technique, combined with several other sound devices, is evident in the second half of the octave:

> Even this little brook, that runs at ease,
>   Whispering and gurgling in its knotted bed,
> Seems but to deepen, with its curling thread
> Of sound, the shadowy sun-pierced silences.

The enjambment at the end of the third line here carries the sound of the brook into the next line, illustrating how it weaves its way through the air, as if tracing a small meandering path within the larger silence, and at the same time it de-emphasizes the end rhyme, since the pause occurs at "sound" rather than at "thread." In the last line, the use of a rhyme that is both slant, as a result of the shift in the vowel sound from *eez* to *əz*, and lightened, with the final syllable unstressed, has a similarly quieting effect, one that is especially felicitous occurring at the word "silences." Combined with the onomatopoeia of "Whispering and gurgling" and the synaesthesia involved in presenting a visible sound and silence pierced with sunlight, these devices contribute to the poem's remarkably successful evocation of place and of perceptual experience. One need not have recourse to aesthetic theory to find a standard by which Lampman's achievement in this poem may be measured. Instead, exactly right choices of word and image, simplicity of expression, a rare facility with figurative language and formal structure, and a deeply sympathetic response to the particulars of the scene will suffice.

Like "A Dawn on the Lièvre," "Solitude" is a Petrarchan sonnet in which the first rhyme is extended through the octave, but the second is dropped in favour of a third in lines six and seven. Both poems employ three rhymes in the sestet, although in different arrangements. This variation of the form – a frequent choice of Lampman's – lends itself ideally to the content of this particular piece. The initial observations are contained in the first four lines, which form a unit. As the brook enters the perceptual field in the second set of four lines, a new rhyme is introduced. A pause then occurs between octave and sestet, after which the intermittent bird sounds are noted. We are not told that the speaker lingers; we experience the prolongation by the structuring of the poem, the stopping and starting, the listening and waiting. The poem ends, not with a wrapping up or a departure, but with the "five pure notes" of a "dreamy whitethroat" (the whitethroated sparrow) drifting off, their fading sound matched by the light rhyme of the unstressed closing syllable of "pensively," matching "tree." As do the hikers at the end of "Freedom," the speaker experiences heightened awareness attained through sensory involvement with the scene, and the conclusion of the poem leaves him there, in a woodsy state of grace.

As we turn from summer to winter, shifting from the sun-dappled environs of "Solitude" to the frigid world of "A January Morning," we might expect a change in attitude on the part of the speaker, in the sense that people talk about good and bad weather. What we find instead is a remarkable similarity. This poem – another Petrarchan sonnet with an extra rhyme in the second half of the octave and with yet another arrangement of the three rhymes in the sestet – also begins by noting the stillness of the scene, but with a particular rather than a general observation: "The glittering roofs are still with frost; each worn / Black chimney builds into the quiet sky / Its curling pile to crumble silently." While the imagery is entirely different, the emphasis on stillness and silence is the same as in "Solitude," and the techniques of lineation are also much the same. In place of the trees and the still air "quiet as spaces in a marble frieze," we have the frozen roofs – not warm enough to be dripping – and the smoke from the chimneys. The contrast between the substantiality implied by "builds," "pile," and "crumble," creating expectations of loud sound, and the noiselessness with which the smoky structures dissolve in the air, lends a magical quality to the image, while simultaneously painting a word picture with admirable precision. The passage resembles a musical crescendo that builds mightily only to resolve in a delicate dispersal of notes.

In terms of metrics, the opening statement ("The glittering roofs are still with frost") is closer to the sonnet standard than its equivalent in "Solitude," the only variation being the extra syllable in the second foot, adding sparkle to "glittering," but the second line varies the pattern, once again infusing a naturalness into the expression:

Black chimney builds into the quiet sky

As well, the enjambed line endings ("each worn / Black chimney" and "the quiet sky / Its curling pile") serve to tone down the end rhymes, and a lightened rhyme reinforces the content: as the tower of smoke, instead of crashing down, evaporates, the expected rhyme is quieter, with the final syllable of *silently* only faintly echoing *sky*.

These opening images are followed, as in "Solitude," with further observations of the surroundings, although this time the vista is broader. Looking beyond the houses to the western horizon, the speaker sees "on the edge of morn" – blending time and place – the "slender misty city towers" reflecting the rose of the sunrise against the "pallid blue" of the western sky; and turning, notes the clouds, resembling "fleeces dull as horn," nestled against the distant northern hills. Then, after the pause between octave and sestet, his attention is caught by loud sounds coming from the opposite direction:

And here behind me come the woodmen's sleighs
With shouts and clamorous squeakings; might and main
Up the steep slope the horses stamp and strain,
Urged on by hoarse-tongued drivers – cheeks ablaze,
Iced beards and frozen eyelids – team by team,
With frost-fringed flanks, and nostrils jetting steam.

As the language of close observation makes clear, the new arrivals, who seem like visitors from a painting by Cornelius Krieghoff, do not so much disturb the speaker's meditation as give him something new to contemplate. They are the equivalent of the birds whose calling and tapping become the focus of attention in the sestet of "Solitude."

That the noise-makers on this occasion are of his own species makes it clear that Lampman does not draw an arbitrary line between nature and human beings. In several nature-focused poems he presents the speaker in company with other people, and in many more incorporates a human presence (besides his own) without disturbing the overall positive portrayal of landscape, as where, in "Across the Pea-Fields," "A little old brown woman on her knees / Searches the deep hot grass for strawberries." In such poems, instead of artistically shutting the door to human intrusion upon the sacrosanct precincts of his retreat, he demonstrates a willingness, perhaps a desire, to populate his ideal place – countryside or wilderness – with fellow sojourners, who, in terms of identity, are almost always the workers of farm or forest that one would find in such environments. On this score, one of the similarities between Lampman and Tom Thomson comes into focus, since for Thomson, too, the human presence within the landscape was not repugnant, even though, like Lampman, he fled the city and sought to capture, in relatively uninhabited regions, the multifaceted beauty of nature.

"Heat" and "In November"

The parallels between "Solitude" and "A January Morning" – the same mood, the same descriptive technique, the same structure – suggest that similar conditions at opposite times of year could give rise to a similar response, despite the contrast of mild ("Solitude") and severe ("A January Morning") weather, supporting the idea that, for Lampman, beauty in nature, like love in Shakespeare's Sonnet 116, does not alter "when it alteration finds,"[4] but persists over time – that is, throughout the changing seasons. Neither poem, however, explicitly states this point. It is the cold-weather poem that might be expected to do so, but "A January Morning" does not deviate from its descriptive method and is none the worse for that consistency. In my second pairing, on the other hand, both poems not only capture but also articulate the ironic reversal whereby uninviting scenes prove captivating and restorative.

Of all Lampman's poems, the one that best captures this irony is "Heat," the most frequently anthologized and analyzed of all Lampman's works. As Scott remarks in another context, "There will always be one or two poems in the works of every writer which will seem to epitomize the character and aim of his genius."[5] In Lampman's case, both critical acclaim and popular consensus point to "Heat." At the same time, this poem is regarded as one of Lampman's most enigmatic productions, primarily in relation to the last of its six stanzas. The ending becomes less puzzling, however, when seen in the context of Lampman's attitude to nature, informed by the ironic perspective that I have suggested is central to his outlook.

In "Heat," as in "Among the Timothy," the speaker has found a suitable countryside resting place from which to view his surroundings – in this case a roadside field. The temporal setting is also the same: a hot mid-summer day with the sun at its zenith. Whereas the perspective in "Among the Timothy" is limited to the nearby grass and flowers, though, in "Heat," from where he sits, the speaker can see both near and far, making it a vaster world within which he is situated at the symbolic hub: "From plains that reel to southward, dim, / The road runs by me white and bare." These lines evoke landscape on a grand scale, with the road linking the more immediate setting to the entire geographical region. There is, in addition, a dynamic quality to the description. The image of "plains that reel" sets the landscape in motion, giving a "heady" feel to the passage, as does the similar language in "A Dawn on the Lièvre," where reference is made to a "swinging avalanche" of sunlight and to mists that "reeled aside." The descriptions later in "Heat" of the "revolving" song of a thrush and of grasshoppers that "spin" their sound into one's ear reinforce this dynamism, as if the peaceful environs of the rural setting shared certain properties with a midway of Ferris wheels and carousels.

But for all its complexities of image and language, this poem is single-minded in its purpose, which is to describe the effects, on the observer and his surroundings, of a particular kind of day, with its one overriding feature. Thus the mild dizziness that certain of its images convey can

Heat and Cold

be understood as a function of the weather, just as the distortion whereby the road "seems to swim / Beyond, and melt into the glare" captures an effect of light under the prevailing conditions. In this passage, matching style to content, Lampman executes a simple but effective manoeuvre of lineation. With an inward squinting of the eyes, we follow the road to where it blurs, and our visual reaching is echoed by the enjambment that extends the phrase past the end of the line with the very word that means *further*.

As he continues to observe the road in the second half of the first stanza, the speaker's attention is caught by movement. His eye closes in on a (presumably horse-drawn) wagon, with a man walking at its side, and the effect of this image is to reinforce the sense of heat and stillness that dominates the scene:

Upward half-way, or it may be
   Nearer the summit, slowly steals
A hay-cart, moving dustily
   With idly clacking wheels.

The descriptors – "dustily" and "idly clacking" – are evocative of sight and sound, while the self-correcting re-assessment has the effect of strengthening verisimilitude: we observe the speaker making a change to get it right, and as we adjust our own picture, we are, by implication, looking more closely, seeing more accurately. Next the wagoner (another example of the human presence incorporated into Lampman's natural-world descriptions) comes into focus, described, in a lazy-sounding phrase, as "slouching slowly at his ease" – we do not blame him – and then our eyes shift back to the vehicle:

This wagon on the height above,
   From sky to sky on either hand,
Is the sole thing that seems to move
   In all the heat-held land.

Evidently time has passed, as the wagon has now reached the crest of the hill. Its position returns the speaker to the larger vista, and the stillness of all else in the perceptible world is emphasized by the one exception, just as, in "Solitude," the sound of the brook "seems but to deepen" the silence.

The fact that the speaker does not explicitly account for the passing of time, but only implies it with the shifting location of the wagon, suggests that he is simply recording things as they appear at the moment of perception – a nice illustration of how an awareness of the eternal present takes place in the context of the temporal: the time is always now. As it happens, in the manuscript notebook in which the poem was first set down, the second half of stanza two, where the wagon has moved, appears for the first time after stanza five, as part of a second draft of stanza two.[6] It would seem that, in the real world of Lampman's composition rather than the imaginative world of the poem, more time has elapsed than the position of these lines in stanza two would suggest. In other words, the wagon has had ample time to reach the hilltop, and as he looks at it again, Lampman is simply describing in the present tense what he sees. It is likely that Lampman attached the later wagon lines to the earlier ones simply to cluster the wagon references and to avoid upsetting the momentum later in the poem. Nevertheless, the shifting of the passage to its final position, preceding, as it were, earlier events, indicates a compositional equivalent of the swirling quality of the poem itself, involving a detachment from the strict realities of linear time.

In stanzas three, four, and five, specific details of observation are included, all contributing to the single idea of a hot, still atmosphere. In a passage that echoes the ending of "Among the Timothy," with its Donne-like intensity, "the sun / Soaks in the grass and hath his will." The power of the sun is overwhelming. The various flowers are motionless; not the slightest breeze is visible on the surface of a brook; the waterbugs seek the shade of a bridge; and the cows in a nearby field are lying down and "waiting for the heat to pass." In stanza four, a sound intruding on the silence is brought to life by the vibrancy of the descriptive language:

> From somewhere on the slope near by
>   Into the pale depth of the noon
> A wandering thrush slides leisurely
>   His thin revolving tune.

Heat and Cold

The strongly visual representation of an aural phenomenon allows us to hear the song uniquely, while the image of a deep place into which the circling sound disappears gives a hallucinatory feel to the passage. A sense of the profound is implied by "pale depth"; we are close to the essence of things.

Both the passing of time and something of the meaning of the word "dream" are touched on in the opening lines of the penultimate stanza:

> In intervals of dreams I hear
>   The cricket from the droughty ground;
> The grasshoppers spin into mine ear
>   A small innumerable sound.

In this passage, "dreams" can be understood in the normal sense of daydreams. At rest in the natural world, the speaker is able to relax and let his mind wander, and as it wanders, now and then – during "intervals of dreams" – he is returned to particular aspects of the present scene. (The word "of" indicates intervals that interrupt, rather than facilitate, the dreams.) He does not attend constantly to the cricket or the grasshoppers, but the sounds are continuously there, creating the conducive atmosphere, and when his mind comes back to them, he hears them. If nature is a tonic to Lampman, it is so partly because it lets him be.

In the last four lines of the same stanza there is an almost cinematic effect as a series of observations is put forward, one per line, with line-ending colons linking the pictures, as if each similarly timed image blurred in a glare of light, vanishing to reveal the next image, with mounting intensity:

> I lift mine eyes sometimes to gaze:
>   The burning sky-line blinds my sight:
> The woods far off are blue with haze:
>   The hills are drenched in light.

The end-stopped lines imitate the short duration of the periodic observations before the speaker lowers his eyes, unable to look for more than a moment into the "burning" light.

At this point the poem has reached a sort of climax, although not a release. The conditions (internal and external) are at their most intense. In terms of poetic strategy, it is the same point as, in certain of Shakespeare's sonnets, the impossibility of solving a painful dilemma is most apparent: "Or what strong hand can hold his swift foot back? / Or who his spoil of beauty can forbid? / O, none, unless ..." Lampman's hot day does not require a solution, as does the loss of all beauty to the destructive power of personified time, but a reversal similar to Shakespeare's "miracle" in Sonnet 65 – "That in black ink my love may still shine bright"[7] – is about to be presented. In Shakespeare's sonnet it is of course ironic that in the darkness of the "black ink" with which the poem is written the beauty of the speaker's beloved will glow, and a similar irony is at the heart of Lampman's poem. Throughout the stanzas leading up to this point of greatest intensity, Lampman has evoked, with consummate skill, the conditions of an oppressively hot and windless summer day at the height of a protracted noon. The wagoner moves in slow motion, the cows lie resting, and even the water-bugs are not immune; the light is blinding, and the temperature dizzy-making. Only mad dogs and Englishmen (and farmers with hay to transport) would remain out of doors; anyone else would seek the shelter of a well-insulated room with the curtains drawn. But deprived of the benefit of Noël Coward's satire, the speaker has a different response:

> And yet to me not this or that
>   Is always sharp or always sweet;
> In the sloped shadow of my hat
>   I lean at rest, and drain the heat;
> Nay more, I think some blessèd power
>   Hath brought me wandering idly here:
> In the full furnace of this hour
>   My thoughts grow keen and clear.

These lines, especially the first two, have given rise to numerous far-reaching interpretations,[8] but their meaning is perhaps not so very obscure. The heat is overbearing, but to the speaker ("And yet to me") what might normally be perceived as "sharp" or "sweet" is sometimes not so. That is, in the sharpness – Lampman's initial choice for "sharp" was "bitter"[9] – sometimes lurks the sweet, and vice versa. In this case, the heat of the day, despite its extremity, need not be seen as negative ("sharp"). For one thing, the speaker is able to obtain relief by resting and protecting his eyes in the shade of his hat. What makes him happy, however, is not merely that he can relax in this countryside setting and reduce his discomfort. On the contrary ("Nay more"), he feels he has been blessed with the richer experience of heightened awareness, the transformation being described metaphorically in terms of metal refinement.[10] As gold is distilled from dross in a furnace fire, the speaker's consciousness has been purified by his experience of nature subject to the influence of midsummer heat. This metaphor has its roots in metaphysical tradition.

A parallel with, and possible source for, Lampman's metaphor can be found in *The Christian Year*, a collection of devotional poems by the English poet and founding member of the Tractarian or Oxford Movement within the Anglican Church, John Keble (1792–1866). Keble's influence on Lampman is evident in other poems as well, including "Sapphics" and "To the Prophetic Soul," discussed elsewhere in this study. A brief account of Keble's role in ecclesiastical controversies and of the publication history of *The Christian Year* will help to show how Keble could have become part of Lampman's knowledge base. What emerges is the story of a book that rose to almost unprecedented heights of fame, only to crumble silently into oblivion like the smoke of the winter chimneys in Lampman's "A January Morning."

On 14 July 1833, Keble delivered at Oxford University his famous sermon "National Apostasy," regarded by John Henry Newman, another prominent Tractarian, as marking the beginning of a movement that sought the restoration of a more "Catholic" version of the Anglican Church and led to many defections to the Roman Catholic Church, the most famous being that of Newman himself in 1845.[11] Keble remained staunchly "High Church" Anglican, believing the Anglican Church, like the Roman Catholic Church, to be one branch of the one true Catholic Church with historical ties to the original Church Fathers, but at the same time rejecting certain tenets of Roman Catholicism, including the infallibility of the pope, the doctrine of transubstantiation, and the belief in the literal, physical Real Presence of the blood and body of Christ in the Eucharist.[12]

It was not for his central role in the Oxford Movement, however, that Keble's name became virtually a household word throughout English Christendom in the nineteenth century. In 1827, six years prior to giving his history-making sermon, Keble had published *The Christian Year*, a small book of hymn-like poems attached to particular days of worship in the annual liturgical cycle of "seasons" – for example, the Third Sunday in Lent and the Fourth Sunday after Trinity. The book succeeded far beyond Keble's expectations, selling, over the next half century, an average of 10,000 copies annually. In Keble's lifetime it ran to ninety-five editions, and by the time its copyright expired in 1873 that number had risen to one hundred and forty.[13] As a source of spiritual comfort for a readership "disconcerted by the Evolutionists," it was rivalled only by Tennyson's *In Memoriam*.[14] John Campbell Shairp, though a Presbyterian and a Scot, was of the view that the Oxford Movement, which in the years following 1833 generated a great many publications, had left to the Anglican Church "two permanent monuments of genius," namely, Newman's sermons and *The Christian Year*.[15] After his death, Keble was honoured by the establishing of Keble College at Oxford, which opened in 1870.[16] In the twentieth century, however, the popularity of *The Christian Year* quickly waned for the same reason it had flourished in the previous century: it was overtly Christian and tied to church traditions and practices. Keble's book is a remarkable example of how perceived greatness in a work of literature is tied to cultural preoccupations and needs.

As a student at Trinity College, Lampman would have known of Keble, and it may be that he had some sympathy with the Oxford Movement. George Whitaker, the provost and professor of divinity at Trinity College from 1852 until 1881, was known to have moderate High Church leanings,[17] and shortly after Lampman's graduation in 1882, chairs were established at Trinity in the names of Keble and Tractarian luminary Edward Bouverie Pusey.[18] Thus Lampman was educated in an environment that, in contrast to most areas served by the Anglican Church in nineteenth-century Canada, was to some degree Anglo-Catholic in its orientation. In his sonnet "To an Ultra Protestant," originally titled merely "To a Protestant,"[19] the speaker advises the addressee to stop fretting about Catholicism, with its "monkish rod" and "holy wizardry" – the tone is anti-Catholic – since that religion and all its prac-

Heat and Cold

tices will vanish with the advance of "thought and liberty." In the sestet, however, he somewhat turns the tables. The Protestant's "forms and dogmas," too, and the "narrow, joyless, ungenerous path" of that brand of Christianity will disappear in the same sweep of progress. Essentially this poem is anti-*creed*, anticipating with relish the end of formal Christianity. Its strategy, though, is specifically to take issue with the Protestant's railing against Catholicism and hence, indirectly, to defend Catholicism or at least put it on an equal footing with Protestantism. To this can be added the evidence of a poem Lampman wrote to French Canadian poet Louis Fréchette, seeking a kind of poetic rapprochement between Catholic Quebec and Protestant Ontario. "I cannot love thy faith," Lampman announces, since for him are "other ways" (unspecified), but he avows that he loves Fréchette himself for his passionate love of his own people and religion, and affirms the two writers' "common bond / Of song and country" – poetry and Canada.[20] And finally there is Lampman's letter to Thomson concerning the relationship between human suffering and "the success of Christianity" in which Lampman quotes the famous lines "Lead kindly light / Amid the encircling gloom" by Newman, who in 1879 had become a Catholic cardinal, commenting, "Newman hit it exactly."[21] Lampman distances himself from Christianity and especially from churchgoing in this letter, but his attitude to Newman seems entirely respectful.

As for *The Christian Year*, it is likely that Lampman became familiar with the book while growing up in an Anglican household with a father who was a minister. Lampman Senior would probably not have been High Church, since it was the Low Church that predominated in most areas served by the Anglican Church in Canada and there is no evidence to suggest he was an exception,[22] but the appeal of Keble's book was not at all limited to the High Church constituency. As John R. Griffin points out, "*The Christian Year* was a collection of the most elevated sentiments belonging to the common experience of Christians."[23] It has been described, moreover, as a "family book" to be "read round the fireside."[24] With reference to Lampman's boyhood, Connor paints the following picture of the living quarters of the family's Cobourg house in the 1870s: "Behind the parlor and the hall ... was the living room. It was a square room, large enough for a whole family to draw round the table in the centre or to sit in front of the plain old fireplace." It is not hard to imagine that in this environment selections from *The Christian Year* were read aloud by Lampman's father, who, as Connor relates, had himself "been writing poems all his life,"[25] and to whose memory Lampman dedicated *Alcyone*, acknowledging his father as the person "who first instructed me in the art of verse."

If Lampman did become acquainted with Keble's poems in early life, he would have enjoyed their frequent descriptions of scenes in nature at various times of year; in later years, Keble's paradoxical interpretations of nature would have appealed to him as well. In Keble's poem for the First Sunday after the Epiphany,[26] a willow tree in April is pictured sprouting red buds "ere winter blasts are fled." Bad weather ensues, but the willow merely "droops awhile," waiting out the storm, and then "when showers and breezes hail her, / Wears again her willing smile." From this the speaker draws a moral:

> Thus I learn Contentment's power
> From the slighted willow bower,
> Ready to give thanks and live
> On the least that Heaven may give.

One's faith should not be shaken by adversity. A similar perspective is evident in the poem that bears more directly on "Heat." Keble presents in the poem for the Twenty-Third Sunday after Trinity[27] an image of humankind, earthbound, envying the breezes, birds, clouds, fish, and shooting stars in their respective elements: "Who would but follow, might he break his chain?" Through the sacrifice of Christ, of course, human beings *will* break the chain of earthly existence; "But first," says the speaker, addressing humanity, "by many a stern and fiery blast / The world's rude furnace must thy blood refine." The parallel to Lampman's closing lines in "Heat" is evident in both idea and language: "In the full furnace of this hour / My thoughts grow keen and clear." In each case, a seeming negativity has a purifying effect, freeing some vital aspect of self – one's consciousness (Lampman) or one's essential self or perhaps passionate nature (Keble) – from contrary influences, and the metaphorical vehicle by which this paradox is expressed is the same.

Informing Keble's conceit, and perhaps lying in the backgrounds of both poems, is the familiar biblical passage best known from Handel's

Messiah in which the metaphorical language, signifying the power of God, is similar: "for he is like a refiner's fire," to which in the source text is added, "he shall sit as a refiner and purifier of silver: and he shall purify the sons of Levi, and purge them as gold and silver, that they may offer unto the Lord an offering in righteousness" (Malachi 2:2–3).[28] In Lampman's poem, it is not God but the all-powerful sun that has this cleansing effect, but the notion of purification is the same. To have such a positive response to stifling heat, Lampman himself implies, is ironic, but the point of the closing stanza, and the point of the whole poem, is precisely to show that the obvious or conventional response is not the meaningful one.[29] (The point is not, as one notable critic has argued, and others have repeated, that the antitheses in the poem – for example, hot ["heat-held land"] and cold ["cool gloom"] – are ultimately reconciled; this is to confuse poetic means with thematic ends.)[30] Most people, Lampman felt, found the game of whist enjoyable; he detested it.[31] Most people might be expected to experience the conditions described in "Heat" as enervating; for Lampman they were the mysterious means of a natural-world redemption.

As the parallels to the excerpts from Keble and to the Old Testament suggest, the paradoxical view of nature that "Heat" exemplifies may be understood in part as Lampman's adaptation of his Christian heritage to his philosophy of nature,[32] and here again a comparison with *The Christian Year* is illuminating. In his poem for the Twentieth Sunday after Trinity,[33] uniting a Romantic love of nature with his Christian theology, Keble suggests that wild and remote locations such as high mountains and powerful rivers are the places best suited to religious meditation, for here one might find an analogue for "the voice of God within" contending with "care and sin" for one's soul. The voice of God (who speaks in the third person), quoted over three stanzas, concludes with an expression of Keble's version of the Christian paradox:

"And as this landscape broad – earth, sea, and sky,
    "All centres in thine eye,
"So all God does, if rightly understood,
    "Shall work thy final good."

Using one miracle to explain another, the voice asserts that all aspects of experience in a God-created world – including of course those that might seem not to qualify, since this is the strength of the paradox – are beneficial. Lampman shares with Keble this paradoxically positive and all-inclusive world view, even while he grounds his own version, not in Christian theology, but in the consciousness-transforming experience of contact with nature itself. Faintly audible in the background of "Heat," if my conjecture is correct, is the voice of Lampman's father reading Keble by the firesides of his youth.

As a postscript to this discussion of "Heat," the controversial history of one line is worth mentioning in the context of poetic originality and influence. Briefly, Lampman's phrase "A small innumerable sound," descriptive of the chirping of grasshoppers, was accidentally plagiarized by Bliss Carman, who in his "The Eavesdropper" described maple leaves as rustling "With small innumerable sound." After the fact had been drawn to his attention by a friend (and mentioned, as well, in the literary column of a newspaper), Carman wrote to Lampman acknowledging the error. In subsequent publications of the offending poem he substituted an alternative line.[34]

Wilfred Campbell, meanwhile, angered by what he perceived as a slight, had ignited a "war among the poets" that took the form of articles and letters appearing in various Canadian newspapers over a period of a year and a half on the subject of "log rolling" (writers promoting each other for mutual benefit) and plagiarism.[35] The American journalist Joseph Dana Miller had written an article on Canadian poetry in which he largely dismissed Campbell while lavishing praise on his contemporaries, especially Carman. In this article, he had declared that the Canadian writers under discussion were "not mere echoes" of earlier writers, and so Campbell, focusing on, in his words, "the lion of the article," set out to show that Bliss Carman was "perhaps the most flagrant imitator on this continent."[36]

In a subsequent contribution to the ensuing debate, Miller attempted to bolster the case for Carman by arguing that Lampman's phrase itself was not without its precedents: "Even in the instance which The World thinks the most striking – 'with small innumerable sound' – which Carman is thought to have appropriated from Lampman, the evidence is far from conclusive. The resemblance is in the word 'innumerable,' and it therefore remains to be asked if Lampman

Heat and Cold

did not get it from Tennyson, where it occurs; and if Tennyson did not get it from Homer, who speaks of the 'innumerable ripple.'"[37] Since Lampman's phrase, minus the initial article, was fully reproduced in Carman's poem, Miller's assertion that "the evidence is far from conclusive" lacks credibility. In a letter to the Toronto *Globe*, Carman himself, likely in an effort to defuse this kind of defence, admitted to his "unconscious (or, better, subconscious) appropriation" of the phrase.[38] Still, Miller's point about the use of the word "innumerable" by other writers was well taken. It occurs repeatedly in Tennyson, with "sated with the innumerable rose" from *The Princess* being perhaps the closest in construction to Lampman's phrase, as well as in, not Homer, as it turns out, but Aeschylus, whose *Prometheus Bound* includes a reference to – in one English translation – "the innumerable ripple of the ocean's waves."[39] Listed in the *Oxford English Dictionary* (1989), moreover, are over a dozen historical instances of the word used in combination with singular nouns, dating from 1340, the last of which, indeed, is Lampman's, though attributed only to *Harper's New Monthly Magazine*, where it was quoted in a review.

Not mentioned by Miller nor listed by Oxford, however, is the instance that most closely resembles Lampman's. In Book 3 of *Paradise Lost*, the Son declares that heaven and earth will praise God "with th' innumerable sound / Of hymns and sacred songs."[40] In Carman's line, curiously, Milton's "with" is restored. Milton could have drawn on any number of precedents, such as Spenser's "An innumerable flight / Of harmfulle fowles," cited by Oxford.[41] A plausible lineage emerges: "the innumerable ripple" (Aeschylus), "An innumerable flight" (Spenser), "with th' innumerable sound" (Milton), "A small innumerable sound" (Lampman), "With small innumerable sound" (Carman).

Situations like this give rise to inevitable questions about poetic inspiration and originality, but do not always point to satisfactory answers. The majority of participants in the Campbell-Carman fracas take the view that a certain amount of poetic thievery might be forgivable, depending on how well the new writer puts the appropriated phrases to use. More than one writer makes the point that Carman's lines – never word-for-word copies, except in the one case – are better than those of his alleged sources. Judged by these standards, Carman's "With small innumerable sound" had to be amended, as Carman himself readily acknowledged. Lampman's phrase, on the other hand, expanding Milton's with the addition of the reductive "small," seems reconstituted and fully integrated into its new context. A case could even be made that Lampman is referencing Milton in a meaningful way. Since "Heat" has a decidedly religious tone, and since the conditions described in the poem are at once oppressive (because of the heat) and inspirational, an allusion to Milton's description of hymns in praise of a severe, yet just and merciful, God is not out of place. The vocalizings of Lampman's frogs, we know, resonate with spiritual meaning, and it could be that his grasshoppers, too, give voice to a spiritual presence in nature. Finally, it is interesting to note that in his analysis of "Heat," Barrie Davies seems to sniff but not quite locate this connection. Lampman's grasshoppers, it will be recalled, "spin" their sound into the speaker's ear. "The singing of the grasshoppers," Davies writes, "suggests the creative possibilities for the artist of nature, the circle image, and the unity in multiplicity. The sound is 'innumerable.' The line, 'I lift mine eyes sometimes to gaze,' with its Biblical overtones, brings to mind both the loss of physical sight and corresponding growth of spiritual illumination as in the poetry of Milton."[42] No sooner does Davies quote the key word in what is either a borrowing from or an allusion to Milton than, detecting a religious tone in the next line (and presumably thinking as well of the line that follows – "The burning skyline blinds my sight"), he thinks of Milton! It seems clear that, beyond the echo of a distinctive phrase, the ghost of Milton is lurking in the precincts of "Heat."

A poem in which the conditions within nature are the opposite of those in "Heat," even while the speaker's response is almost identical, is the sonnet "In November." As in its summer counterpart, an observer's attention is caught by a particular landscape, only now the time of day is dusk rather than noon, the time of year late autumn rather than midsummer, the central image snow rather than sun, the weather stormy rather than still, and the predominating feeling one of cold rather than heat.

In the opening lines, the speaker, already present in the scene, takes stock of his surroundings: "The hills and leafless forests slowly yield / To the thick-driving snow. A little while / And night shall darken down." Using the same techniques of simple language and caesural pauses as were evident in "Solitude" and "A January Morning" to give a plain-spoken, non-poetic feel to the verse, Lampman quickly establishes the salient features of the scene: bare trees, heavy wind-blown snow already building up on the ground, and approaching dark. From where he rests, the speaker can see the "woodmen's carts go by" as "homeward wheeled" they abandon the bleak landscape. The one exception (apart from the speaker) is the "last ploughman" who "follows still his row, / Turning black furrows through the whitening field." His lone presence emphasizes by contrast the emptiness of the scene, while the blackness of the freshly turned soil, briefly exposed, perfectly sets off the blanketed quality of everything else. The general impression created by the falling snow, the gathering darkness, and the homebound workers is one of a forbidding world of the out-of-doors from which human beings would do well to retreat. Rather than join the "woodmen," however, the speaker (*not* made of wood) remains behind, observing his surroundings. Unprepossessing images such as that of "thin fading stubbles" hold his attention. Seemingly subject to magnetic properties that operate in reverse of the norm, he is attracted rather than repelled by the scene.

In the first three-and-a-half lines of the sestet, the impression of an inhospitable landscape is reinforced:

> Far off the village lamps begin to gleam,
>   Fast drives the snow, and no man comes this way;
>   The hills grow wintry white, and bleak winds moan
>   About the naked uplands.

The light and warmth suggested by the distant village lamps contrast the dark and cold of the speaker's more immediate surroundings. The "naked uplands," buffeted by audible winds and driving snow, seem, again, inhospitable to a meditative sojourn. Even the words of the poem have been infiltrated by the wind, as the "oh" sound resonates throughout: "slowly," "snow" (three times), "go," "homeward," "golden," "sowed," "follows," "row," "furrows," "no," "grow," "moan," and "alone." This repetition of sound makes the wind seem a constant presence, pervasive and unrelenting. All the signals, deliberately built up in the poem, indicate that it is time to go home.

Having established, through image and sound, a sense of the harsh and forbidding quality of the scene, the speaker in the closing lines confides his own reaction: "I alone / Am neither sad, nor shelterless, nor gray, / Wrapped round with thought, content to watch and dream." It would be reasonable, he implies, to feel unhappy and uncomfortable, vulnerable, perhaps fearful, but like the speaker in "Heat," he has a different response. Indeed, the simple rationale offered in "Heat" seems equally applicable here: "And yet to me not this or that / Is always sharp or always sweet." Although the prevailing conditions are once again "sharp," the speaker finds in the scene an unexpected sweetness. Under its influence, he is able to let his mind wander, and so to become impervious to or unconcerned about the cold: his thoughts protect him. Of this location, too, it could be said that "some blessèd power" has brought the speaker "wandering idly here," for ironically there is a beauty in the chill November uplands, just as there is a beauty in the landscape subject to the intense heat of a stifling midsummer noon. The extreme conditions, moreover, are the substance of that beauty, as the detailing of specifics throughout both poems makes clear. Lampman has sometimes been thought of as the poet of springtime or as the poet of autumn. He is, in fact, the poet of all seasons, but it is noteworthy that, according to Scott, his two favourite times of year were August, "the month of intense heat," and January, "the month of intense cold."[43] He loved the extremes.

"April" and "In October"

A brief consideration of two additional poems from *Among the Millet*, "April" and "In October," will serve to reinforce the point that common links exist between the speakers' responses to nature in poems depicting contrasting scenes, set at opposite points on the cycle of seasons. In the former, to be sure, the prevailing atmosphere is one of cheery good spirits, as is evident in stanza three:

> The gray song-sparrows full of spring have sung
> Their clear thin silvery tunes in leafless trees;
> The robin hops, and whistles, and among
> The silver-tasseled poplars the brown bees
> Murmur faint dreams of summer harvestries.

The lighthearted optimism of these lines contrasts sharply with the grievous tone of "In October" where the red of the sunset is "dolorous," both the "wet winds" and the "wet woods moan," and the very pines are reduced to serving as "priests of storm."

In both cases, however, the speaker finds solace in the beauty of the natural world, albeit the solace of two different moods. In "April," having "wandered with unwearied feet, / All the long sweetness of an April day," he succeeds in making his "spirit free / With the blind working of unanxious spring," while in "In October" he sits upon a "naked stone" and, having sent his "heart out to the ashen lands," feels "Not torn with pain of any lurid hue, / But only still and very gray and dreary, / Sweet sombre lands, like you." Whether near in time to the vernal or the autumnal equinox, the speaker identifies with nature and has a positive response. That this is so in the more surprising case of "In October" is due not so much to any hint of spring's return, but rather to the presence of a soothing, though melancholy, beauty in nature.[44] Thus, while the "sweetness of an April day" may be vastly different from the sweetness of "sombre lands" in bleak October, yet both are sweet, just as, to draw an analogy, the seasons of Christmas and Easter are equally holy in the Christian calendar. In this sense, the beauty of the natural world is a constant, even while the face of nature is altered over time.

It is interesting to note that the rationale used in "In October" to explain the positive effect of the melancholy scene on the speaker is somewhat at odds with what we find in the sonnet "In November." In the latter poem, although the conditions are bleak, the speaker, "Wrapped round with thought," is "Neither sad nor shelterless nor gray," while in the former, more literally, he draws his "coat closer" with "numbèd hands" and is, like the landscape, "gray and dreary." So in the one poem he is sad and "gray," and in the other he is *not* sad and "gray." Of the two poems, "In October," completed in October 1884,[45] is the earlier, as its indebtedness to Keats – "What balmèd breaths of dreamland spicery, / What visions of soft laughter and light sadness" – and to Poe – "The dry dead leaves flit by with thin weird tunes, / Like failing murmurs of some conquered creed, / Graven in mystic markings with strange runes" – would suggest. It could be that Lampman was working out the exact nature of the paradox that makes a bleak scene pleasing at the same time as he was finding his own poetic voice, the later poem representing his final stance on this issue. On the other hand, the response of identification, of taking on the mood that the natural world seems possessed of, as in "In October," is also characteristic of many later poems. Another explanation is that the precise terms of the rationale are rather secondary to the fact of an ironic reversal. Whether the speaker, gray or not gray, draws his coat against the cold, or his thoughts, whether he slips over the line to metaphor or not, makes surprisingly little difference to the emotions generated by the two poems. In each case we imagine a solitary individual choosing to linger in a setting despite inhospitable conditions, and we experience vicariously the same shiver and sense of warmth within and cold without.

The two poems, however, are not artistic equals. While "In October" shows Lampman responding powerfully to his environment and highlights both his skill with metaphor and the realism of his depiction of the natural world, as in the image of rustling leaves whose sound resembles "So many low soft masses for the dying / Sweet leaves that live no more," overall the poem is not fully mature. "In November," on the other hand, with its strong contrasts, economy of expression, and vivid evocation of the scene, shows Lampman in full possession of his art. Its sensibility, as E.K. Brown has suggested, is a "highly personal one," and indeed, with its stubborn adherence to a contrary view of things, evoking what Brown calls the "strange, moving beauty" of the bleak landscape,[46] it deserves recognition for uniquely capturing an experience so recognizable and characteristic of Canada's forbidding yet appealing northern clime.

"The Dog"

The ironic sensibility at the heart of poems such as "Heat" and "In November" was one that Lampman also liked to express more casually, as his comments about fun (the game of whist) not being fun, and dreams not being dreams, attest. This same sensibility is evident in the closing poem of *Among the Millet*, entitled plainly "The Dog," in which the reviewer of *Among the Millet* in the London *Spectator* found "sufficient evidence that Mr. Lampman has a true eye and a true sense of humour."[47] In this sonnet Lampman once again employs his favourite version of the Petrarchan form: an octave with the first rhyme preserved throughout, but with the second giving way to a third in lines six and seven, and with three rhymes in the sestet. In this case, though, as rarely elsewhere, he incorporates feminine endings – six out of eight in the octave – partly to suggest the inelegant look of the dog and partly to inject the humour that, perhaps because of their trail-off effect, feminine rhymes can elicit. The question to consider in relation to this sonnet is whether or not it explores a serious theme – and I will argue that it does – despite, or through, its comic content and design.

At the outset, the speaker and his friends are amused by the ludicrous "conceit" of the title creature, which seems laughable in view of his physical attributes – his "short ears close together" and especially his "queer feet / Planted irregularly." "Grotesque!" they exclaim, after which they playfully tease the dog, who seems not to enjoy their kibitzing, but puts up with it. Following this – with no feminine endings – comes the sestet:

> Then flung we balls, and out and clear away,
>   Up the white slope, across the crusted snow,
> To where a broken fence stands in the way,
>   Against the sky-line, a mere row of pegs,
> Quicker than thought we saw him flash and go,
>   A straight mad scuttling of four crookèd legs.

Almost miraculously, the dog manifests as supreme example of his kind in terms of speed, traversing in a flash the ground between the observers and the far-off fence that, diminished by distance, appears "a mere row of pegs." Astonished at this performance, the speaker and his friends have suddenly a new respect for the dog. As in other sonnets employing the same strategy, presenting strong evidence on one side of the scales only to tip the balance in the sestet, Lampman savours the irony, which in this case, to mix high with low, is something akin to a fulfillment of the biblical prophecy: "the crooked shall be made straight."[48]

It is with the same happy sense of hidden truths revealed that in another sonnet, "After the Shower," the speaker delights in the fact that, of all flowers, it is the "small, dainty violet, pure and white, / That holds by magic in its twisted face / The heart of all the perfumes of the wood."

The unorthodox sensibility evident in these examples does not go unnoticed by Connor, who observes that in certain poems – he names "The Frogs," "Heat," and "The Dog" – "there were indications that [Lampman] was not entirely in the thrall of the conventional in treatment or viewpoint."[49] In a contemporary review, Agnes Maule Machar goes further, but from a critical point of view. She objects to both "The Frogs" and "The Dog" on the basis of "insufficient theme." In "The Frogs," she suggests, "[t]he occasion seems too slight to hang on it so much thought," while the subject of "The Dog" strikes her as "unworthy of a sonnet."[50] Bentley, who has written about this poem on several occasions, agrees fundamentally with Machar, dubbing "The Dog" "a mongrel about a mongrel" and, as such, a violation of Lampman's own sense of decorum, but allows that the incongruous blend of form and content is "appropriate" because of the comic intent.[51] What Connor's understated commendation and Machar's criticism point to is a boldness on Lampman's part that, in his own time, challenged the reader with unusual perspectives. From Lampman's point of view, the poet, though solitary, was not lonely because he could see, where others could not, "hidden faces."[52] This ability to see beyond the superficial, or to see differently, lies at the heart of his interpretation of nature. The mild and fair are beautiful, but so are the harsh and extreme. The inclusive irony by which this is possible, present in various poems that focus on individual times of year, is also central to Lampman's purpose in his second collection of poems, *Lyrics of Earth*.

CHAPTER 6

Lyrics of Earth: *Genesis, Design, Meaning*

I

Over the years and months leading up to the publication of *Among the Millet*, Lampman was gradually evolving his perspective on nature. As the number of nature poems expanded, the most characteristic feature to emerge was the catholicity of his vision, embracing a broad range of seasonal settings and climatic conditions. Gradually this inclusiveness began to take hold as a conscious philosophy, giving rise to poems such as "Heat" and the sonnet "In November," where the benefits of natural-world observation in unlikely settings or under inhospitable conditions are extolled and the irony made explicit. In the wake of the success of *Among the Millet* in 1889 and the early 1890s, Lampman sought to explore these ideas further. The most important outcome of his efforts was his second volume of poems, *Lyrics of Earth*, a collection that traces the cycle of seasons from early spring through winter.

The genesis of *Lyrics of Earth* can be traced in Lampman's correspondence over a four-and-a-half-year period, from the fall of 1891 to the spring of 1896 – but not without the most careful scrutiny of the relevant letters. Lampman was working on several manuscripts during this period, and it is sometimes difficult to determine the one to which a passing reference in a letter refers. Linking certain key statements to the collections to which they pertain, however, is critical to establishing an accurate record of how this book came into being, and it is in this context that I must take issue with one small but significant point put forward by the critic who was the first to investigate the significance of *Lyrics of Earth* as a gathering of related poems.

In 1976, D.M.R. Bentley published a "working text" edition of *Lyrics of Earth*, providing in his introduction much useful documentary information about, among other things, the difficulties Lampman experienced in trying to find a publisher for his second collection of poems, even after the considerable success of his first volume. In the course of analyzing one particular letter from Lampman to Thomson, Bentley concludes – mistakenly, as I will argue – that several non-nature poems were originally slated for inclusion in the volume that was to become *Lyrics of Earth* and were left out only as a result of Thomson's recommendation that they be omitted.[1] In my reading of *Lyrics of Earth*, the sequence of poems conveys Lampman's belief that beauty in nature persists over time and throughout the vicissitudes of seasonal change, thus complementing his expressions of that belief elsewhere. The idea that the sequence originated with Thomson, or that *Lyrics of Earth* would have included non-nature poems without Thomson's involvement, casts doubt on this conclusion. And it is this view of things, supported by Bentley's analysis, that has begun to take hold in Canadian letters. Biographer John Coldwell Adams states, "Relying upon Thomson's advice in preparing *Lyrics of Earth*, Lampman selected and arranged his poems to follow the sequence of the seasons from spring to winter," adding, "Lampman had great confidence in his friend's opinion, and indeed the seasonal pattern gives the collection greater uniformity than *Among the Millet*."[2] As it happens, what the evidence shows, when carefully sifted, is that the sequence was part of the design of this volume from the beginning – long before Thomson's involvement – and remained so throughout its lengthy evolution, even while the precise makeup of the collection was altered over time as individual poems were dropped and added and the order of poems was changed. An examination of the relevant passages from the Lampman-Thomson correspondence, together with manuscript evidence, will help to establish the provenance of the book.

Lampman first mentions his plan to publish a second volume of poems in a letter to Thomson dated 28 October 1891: "I think if I can ever get a certain other poem or sequence of poems I am working at finished I shall try what steps can be taken towards getting out another book – not yet for some months however."[3] The phrase "poem or sequence of poems" suggests a closely integrated sequence, and indeed a number of poems that Lampman had recently completed, or would soon complete, seem conceived in the spirit of just such a sequence. Three poems with month titles – "In May," "June," and "September" – and one with a seasonal title – "By an Autumn Stream" – were all written the previous year.[4] As well, five poems written between May 1890 and April 1892 all begin with phrases that, while not formulaic, suggest a kind of guided tour of the annual cycle. The titles, composition dates, and opening lines are as follows:

"The Meadow" (May 1890)
  – "Here when the cloudless April days begin"
"September" (October 1890)
  – "Now hath the summer reached her golden close"
"The Return of the Year" (May 1891)
  – "Again the warm bare earth, the noon"
"By an Autumn Stream" (November 1891)
  – "Now overhead"
"April in the Hills" (April 1892)
  – "To-day the world is wide and fair"

The "here" and "now" references in the opening lines of these poems suggest that they were written for inclusion in an interconnected series of seasonal poems, and the compositional time frame fits. Moreover, two titles that Lampman considered for this early version of the book – "Pictures and Meditations" and "A Gift of the Sun" – are consistent with the idea of a sequence of poems following the seasons.[5] If it is indeed true that his original idea was to produce a closely integrated sequence, however, he must have relaxed his plan somewhat, since the sequence in *Lyrics of Earth* includes a number of seasonal poems that were written earlier, likely before the idea of tracing the annual cycle had occurred to him, as well as later, in both cases without the phrases, such as "Now overhead," that would suggest an ongoing single work. The design had shifted in the direction of a looser sequence of seasonal poems.

In late October of 1892, Lampman sent his manuscript to Houghton Mifflin. Buoyed by the praise that *Among the Millet* had received, and pleased with his recent productions, he was optimistic of success. Long delays ensued until, on 10 February 1893, he complained to Thomson, "I have had no decision from Houghton Mifflin & Co. yet. If they decline my book, after keeping me four months in suspense, I shall swear indeed." A postscript to this letter reads, "I have just heard from H.M & Co. They decline my book."[6] It was soon thereafter that Lampman assembled the first version of the collection of non-nature poems that would ultimately become *Alcyone*. As he explains in a letter to H.E. Scudder, a reader for Houghton Mifflin who had tried to advance his cause, "This new collection contains nothing that is in the book I submitted last year, and I have made it up as far as I could with reference to the publisher['s] criticism, that 'the appeal was not to the general lover of poetry but to lovers of poetry of the descriptive and reflective order.'"[7] From these comments, it is clear that the collection Lampman compiled in 1892 did indeed consist entirely of nature poems, arranged, in all likelihood, to follow the sequence of the seasons, as Lampman's phrase "poem or sequence of poems" would suggest.

Over the next twenty-seven months, from February 1893 to May 1895, the "poem or sequence of poems" collection was rejected by three more publishers: Scribner's, Roberts Brothers, and Stone and Kimball.[8] Disheartened, Lampman sent his manuscript to Thomson on 30 May 1895, presumably in response to an offer to promote his cause with Copeland and Day of Boston, a publisher with whom Thomson had some influence. "If you are good enough to take the trouble," writes a despondent Lampman, "you may make whatever selection you choose and I shall be content."[9] Thomson's reply is not extant. In two subsequent letters, however, Lampman responds to various suggestions that Thomson had put forward to him. Bentley assumes that both these letters refer to the collection Lampman sent Thomson on 30 May 1895. Since one of the letters, dated 29 August 1895, indicates that Thomson had recommended the omission of three non-nature poems from the collection they were in, and since these poems do not appear in *Lyrics of Earth* (although in his letter Lampman states that he will retain, not omit, the poems), Bentley concludes that Lampman must have removed them in response to Thomson's recommendation and therefore that, without Thomson's involvement, *Lyrics of Earth* would not have been what it is, a sequence of nature poems following the seasons.[10] As Bentley puts it, "*Lyrics of Earth* differs, not only from *Among the Millet*, but also from *Alcyone* in being an attempt by Lampman *and* Thomson to organize an entire volume of poems as if it were in itself one extended poem."[11]

Ten days before he sent Thomson the manuscript of the collection that would become *Lyrics of Earth*, Lampman had sent him another manuscript – the one he had written Scudder about. He says to Thomson, "I am sending you a collection of poems I have just had stitched together. If you think there would be any use in submitting them to Crowell & Co. please do so." This collection, Lampman adds, "has my latest outpourings in it – some things you have not seen."[12] The three non-nature poems that Lampman mentions in his 29 August 1895 letter to Thomson – "Chione," "Vivia Perpetua," and "Ingvi and Alf" – were written in October 1894, December 1894, and March 1895, respectively. Thus they qualify as relatively recent productions. Then there is the fact that, in the manuscript book "Miscellaneous Poems," Lampman has written out lists of the contents of three proposed volumes of poetry: "A Century of Sonnets," "Afoot with the Year," and "The Land of Pallas, and Other Poems."[13] The last of these lists, representing an early version of *Alcyone*, includes the titles of all three of the poems under discussion, two of which are retained in *Alcyone* itself; only "Ingvi and Alf" did not make the final cut. This early version of *Alcyone*, not *Lyrics of Earth*, is clearly the subject of the letter in which Lampman responds to Thomson's recommendation that the three non-nature poems be dropped.

There is no reason to doubt, then, that the early version of *Lyrics of Earth* Lampman sent Thomson on 30 May 1895 contained only nature poems, since the only poems discussed in the extant correspondence that fail to qualify were not, after all, intended for inclusion in that volume. The question remains, however, as to how much influence Thomson had on the specific contents and arrangement of the final version of *Lyrics of Earth*, given that Lampman had handed him what Bentley calls a "carte blanche" to make whatever selection he wished from the manuscript Lampman was sending him.[14]

In his letter of 6 June 1895, Lampman's response indicates that the changes Thomson made to the manuscript were considerable, including the possibility that the title phrase itself came from Thomson: "Your alterations in the arrangement of the book are I think very good ones. I am a poor hand at composing and naming a book." In the remainder of the letter, however, Lampman refers to only two omissions and one shift of location. He agrees to leave out "An Ode to the Hills" and "A Midwinter Phantasy," but says he will retain the opening eight stanzas of "Successors of Pan" (later titled "Favorites of Pan"), which Thomson had recommended dropping. (As discussed in chapter 2, Lampman at some point removed lines from near the beginning of "Winter-Store," and it is possible that he did so on Thomson's recommendation.) He further accepts with enthusiasm Thomson's idea of shifting "The Sweetness of Life" to the beginning of the collection: "Your notion of putting 'The Sweetness of Life' first is an excellent one. It would never have occurred to me.'"[15]

The list of the contents of the second of Lampman's three planned volumes, "Afoot with the Year" (see Appendix B), designed, as its title suggests, to follow the sequence of seasons from spring through winter, is consistent with this information. Indeed, twenty-eight of the twenty-nine poems that make up *Lyrics of Earth* were to appear in "Afoot with the Year," the one omission being "Refuge," for which "Distance" was substituted. Also to be included in "Afoot with the Year," in addition to "An Ode to the Hills" and "A Midwinter Phantasy," were "After Snow" and "A Snowshoer's Halt," poems not mentioned in the correspondence. The ordering of two pairs of adjacent poems – "Godspeed to the Snow" and "April in the Hills," and "Favorites of Pan" and "The Meadow" – was in each case the reverse of what it became in *Lyrics of Earth*. "The Sweetness of Life," which Thomson advised Lampman to put first, was to appear as poem number sixteen in "Afoot with the Year," while "An Ode to the Hills" was poem number one. Finally, "The Sun Cup," which appears at the end of the sequence in *Lyrics of Earth* only because Lampman had it reinserted into the manuscript at the last minute after it had been "somehow" dropped, was to be poem number nine in "Afoot with the Year."[16] With the letter of 6 June 1895 and the list of the contents of "Afoot with the Year" matching in every detail, it is clear that this collection is the one under discussion in that letter and further that Lampman's original vision for *Lyrics of Earth* remained intact.

At the same time, the contents of "Afoot with the Year" cannot have been identical with those of the earliest version of the collection that would become *Lyrics of Earth*. By 9 November 1892 Lampman had consigned his original compilation to Houghton Mifflin. At least three of the poems included in the list of the contents of "Afoot with the Year" were written after that date.[17] It is difficult to say with certainty when the changes to this early version yielding "Afoot with the Year" were made, but an educated guess is possible. After the manuscript was rejected by Houghton Mifflin in the winter of 1893, Lampman sent it first to Scribner's and then to Roberts Brothers. By 18 April 1893 it had been rejected by the one, and by 5 July 1893, by the other. At this point there occurs a hiatus in his efforts to publish the collection. He considered having it published in Toronto, the advantage being that he could "at any rate do it there without paying for it," but there is no evidence to show that he followed through with this plan.[18] Then, on 26 February 1894, Bliss Carman, serving as literary adviser to the newly formed American firm Stone and Kimball, wrote to him suggesting that he send a manuscript there.[19] Lampman's response was favourable, and by 25 April 1894 he had furnished Stone and Kimball with a manuscript. It seems probable, then, that after Roberts Brothers returned the manuscript in the summer of 1893, Lampman put it aside for a time, and then, with his interest rekindled by Carman, revised it before submitting it to Stone and Kimball, that is, in the spring of 1894.

To summarize, what Lampman's correspondence, together with the holograph lists of the contents of "Afoot with the Year" and "The Land of Pallas, and Other Poems," tells us is that the sequence in *Lyrics of Earth* originated with Lampman in 1891; that the sequence remained a feature of the collection even while its precise makeup was altered over a period of four-and-a-half years as it passed through at least two distinct versions before taking its final form as *Lyrics of Earth*; and that Thomson's contribution, while significant, was limited to the following: the removal of two to four poems; the shifting of "The Sweetness of Life" to the beginning of the sequence, where it replaced "An Ode to the Hills"; and possibly the switching of the order of two pairs of adjacent poems, the excising of lines from near the beginning of "Winter-Store," and – a major bestowal, if true – the naming of the book. Lampman, it appears, had the final word on all modifications to his manuscript.

II

From the publishing history of *Lyrics of Earth*, we turn now to the design of the book, crucial to the meaning of the collection as a whole.

The idea of compiling nature poems to mirror the changing seasons throughout the year appealed strongly to Lampman. Not only did he maintain this design throughout the long evolution of *Lyrics of Earth*, but he also arranged a group of forty-six nature sonnets in a similar sequence in his unpublished collection of one hundred sonnets, titled "A Century of Sonnets," the contents of which he copied out in the manuscript book "Miscellaneous Poems."[20] Even the twelve nature sonnets that he ultimately included in *Alcyone* "to make a variety" are presented in that same order, from spring through winter, though distributed throughout the volume, so that the wonder of the seasonal procession weaves its way through the collection, as if to suggest that, even while the disturbing prospects of "the city of the end of things" lurk, wars rage, and the prophet-preacher of peace, order, and good human relations is scorned, the redemptive power of nature is ever present, always at hand.[21]

There are numerous precedents for this kind of seasonal sequence. As Bentley (assuming the sequence in *Lyrics of Earth* to be the result of a collaboration between Lampman and Thomson) states, "Of [the many models available to them] Lampman and Thomson doubtless knew James Thomson's *The Seasons*, William Morris' *The Earthly Paradise*, and, perhaps (in view of Lampman's life-long enthusiasm for Keats), Edmund Spenser's *The Shephearde's Calender*."[22] The precedent that bears the closest resemblance to *Lyrics of Earth*, however, is Keble's *The Christian Year*. Beginning with Christmas in keeping with its Christian theme, this book traces the liturgical "seasons" through the year, making use of scenes from nature throughout, and unlike the other works mentioned, it is comprised of short lyrics written in a variety of forms. Keble's sensibility, moreover, is similar to Lampman's in that he recognizes the harsher aspects of nature while affirming the goodness or rightness of all. As John R. Griffin says of Keble's use of nature in *The Christian Year*, "All of created Nature – its beauties and its terrors – were analogues of God's power and mercy," and as he comments again, the simplicity of Keble's scriptural mysticism is grounded in the belief "that, in spite of evil and the general decay of the world, there is a provident God who rules the world."[23] A similarly paradoxical world view is evident in Lampman's nature poems, except that for Lampman it is not the presence of a benign God that is evident everywhere but simply the beauty of a spiritually imbued natural world.

Lampman's purpose in compiling the sequence in *Lyrics of Earth*, I contend, is to show the pervasiveness of beauty in nature, imaged in terms of the annual cycle, and at the same time to convey, where conditions are harsh, the irony by which this positive outlook is upheld. The irony is the same as that of "Heat" and "In November," where severe natural conditions are viewed in a positive light, in contrast to what those poems imply would be the conventional response. At the level of imagery, we have seen it in references to dead leaves, dead trees "soft in their sepulchres," and flowers that, despite the brevity of their lives, are characterized as participating in the eternity of the everlasting present – all presented in the context of beauty in nature.[24] It is only by inference, however, that pairings of independent poems and patterns of imagery can be seen as supporting the idea that Lampman saw the cycle of seasons itself as a single, unifying entity, perpetual as a circle, to which people could turn at any time of year for comfort and inspiration. In *Lyrics of Earth*, we have a single work which conveys that idea. Since this book is made up of separate, individual poems, with each one representing one particular point of the cycle, however, it follows that no one poem conveys the meaning of the whole. (Three partial exceptions are discussed below.) How, then, to ascertain its larger significance? One answer is that the internal evidence makes the case: the poems depict particular manifestations of nature that, taken together, make an implicit statement about the larger cycle of which they form the component parts. In addition, there is the external evidence of two poems – "The Lesson of the Trees" and "The Old House" – that depict the changing seasons and at the same time make the point that nature's beauty is manifest throughout the year. These poems function as micro images of *Lyrics of Earth*, articulating ideas that implicitly inform the sequence it comprises.

Written circa 1891 and first published in January 1894,[25] "The Lesson of the Trees" dates from the period when the sequence in *Lyrics of Earth* – conceived in 1891, assembled in 1892, and dispatched to various publishers over the next several years – was prominent in Lampman's mind. Because this short poem is not included in *Poems*, I quote it in its entirety:

> The tall trees stand without fear, without pain,
>   Though summers gather their gold and go;
> For life is a thing to be lived; it is gain;
>   In the bounty of June or the winter's snow;
> They are earth's, they are God's, and whatever may be,
> They stand, as *we* ought to do, straight and free.[26]

Here Lampman returns to the familiar "we" of the philosophical nature sonnets "Sight" and "An Old Lesson from the Fields," where the first-person plural designates a wayward humanity that has lost touch with nature. As in those poems, it is here recommended that people emulate in human terms the purity and strength of nature. In this case, though, it is specifically the trees that "we" are meant to be like, within the framework of a simple analogy: as things change in our lives, we should remain positive, just as (in the speaker's conception) the trees do in the face of change within nature, conveyed in terms of the contrasting images of summer and winter. The point is not that, for the trees, the shifting seasons do not bring trials. By mentioning the absence of "fear" and "pain" in the imagined experience of the trees, the speaker suggests that there might be cause for having those responses. Instead of performing some arboraceous equivalent of cringing at the fact of change, however, the trees stand "straight and free" throughout the year, aloof from despair.

In part, the speaker of this hortatory poem is recommending endurance, but there is more, since life is "gain" even in the absence of summer's "bounty" – or perhaps winter offers a different kind of bounty. Certainly Lampman loved the Canadian winter. "The northern winters of Europe," he declared, "are seasons of terror and gloom; our winters are seasons of glittering splendour and incomparable richness of colour."[27] The statement that "life is a thing to be lived" in both summer and winter implies that one can respond to the beauty of the season, can enjoy the present, throughout the year – that is, always. Thus, even though "the bounty of June" and "the winter's snow" may be, in terms of the poem's moral dimension, analogues of good fortune and adversity, which must be accepted with equal grace, these images also suggest that the positive value of nature is an absolute, unchanging with change. Summer is pleasant (except on scorching days such as the one described in "Heat"); winter is severe; but beauty may be found in both.

A resemblance in terms of both theme and device suggests that part of Lampman's inspiration for "The Lesson of the Trees" was Tennyson's short lyric "The Oak," published in *Demeter, and Other Poems* in 1889, just two years before Lampman wrote his poem.[28] Stylistically different in that it comprises three five-line stanzas, with each line consisting of a single amphimacer or metric foot following a stressed-unstressed-stressed pattern, Tennyson's poem is similar in that it depicts the tree of the title as being equal to the changes that the seasons bring and thus able to serve as a model of how to "Live thy life." As in "The Lesson of the Trees," the speaker mentions the "gold" of the trees, although this is the gold of both spring buds and autumn leaves, whereas for Lampman it is only the latter. At the end of the poem, the oak, though bereft of leaves, remains impressive, an image of "Naked strength." "The Oak" is a mini–*tour de force*, an example of Tennyson's lyric gift at its best. With its tight structure, compact expression ("Summer-rich"), and metric design perfectly suited to its content – the stressed outer syllables enclose the trunk of the poem like tough bark – it seems gnarled and sturdy. Stephen Fry has called it a "*shaped* poem ... inasmuch as its layout suggests its subject."[29] "The Lesson of the Trees" is a slighter and much less rigorous production, more simply drawn. But it is Lampman's reworking of the theme and central image of "The Oak" that is relevant here. Both poems are concerned with how one should confront change, and both employ trees as exemplars, but whereas "The Oak" maps out the "seasons" of a single life in linear time, "The Lesson of the Trees" extols the positive qualities of both summer and winter in a continuing cycle. "The Oak" is about aging; "The Lesson of the Trees" is about finding the benefits in life, "whatever may be."

The theme of "The Old House," completed on 18 March 1898, less than a year before Lampman died, and first published in *Poems* (and never reprinted), is essentially the same as that of "The Lesson of the Trees." Its methods, however, are entirely different. For one thing, it does not exhort. With its faint medievalism, its overriding symbolism, and its unusual, almost ethereal serenity, it combines features in a way that is unusual for Lampman – and yet it explains, retrospectively, his philosophy of nature and understanding of the relationship between mortality and eternity, life and nature, in the clearest terms. It is Lampman's philosophical swan song, written, one feels, not to convince, but – in the spirit of "if you could write just one poem" – simply to express a deeply held conviction, a known truth.

The poem consists of six complexly patterned stanzas of sixteen lines each, trochaic in metre, with five-foot lines except for line six (four feet), lines eleven to fourteen (a song-like interlude of four two-foot lines), and line fifteen (six feet). There are, in addition, variations, as where six-foot lines and four-foot lines substitute for five-foot lines. The stanza form, then, is elaborate, yet not adhered to strictly, indicative perhaps of a new easiness of style that, had he lived, Lampman might have pursued.

Structurally, the four central stanzas depict the house – symbolically the centre of human habitation within nature – in each of the four seasons, framed by one stanza each of introduction and conclusion in which, as if from outside the cycle of seasons, the location of the house, its ideal quality of life, and its eventual demise are described. Thus the natural world of cyclic time is seen to exist within the human world of linear time, reflecting the idea that people's experience of the eternal takes place within the linear and finite duration of mortal life. The house is "a home of friendly pilgrimage," a sanctuary within the natural world where people can seek refuge and know the joy of being alive until, as is acknowledged with equanimity at the end, "All be past, work and play." As in "The Frogs," death does not have power to disturb because, within the precincts of the old house, one dwells (for the moment) in the eternal present.

Besides the simple yet philosophically challenging blend of time and eternity that is inherent in its structure, the most striking feature of the poem is the combining of realistic observations of natural-world phenomena with fanciful descriptions of the permanent denizens of the mythical house: "The master and his noble company." The natural-world observations, on their own, resemble those of any number of Lampman's nature-focused poems. Gazing "along the level west," the speaker notices "lines / Of pencilled hills and slender pines"; in the spring stanza, he notes where "about the arbours and the eaves / Sparrows[,] busy with their nesting, meet" – only the arbours and eaves are those of the imaginary house. Another example is the passage in stanza five where, for the first time, he makes direct reference to his own experience:

> Often in the winter nights I see
>   One or two great stars, that seem to pry
> Just above the roof-edge, wonderfully
>   Hard and sparkling in the bitter sky.

This could easily be a passage from a winter sonnet, but again, the "roof-edge" here belongs to the mythic house, and as the stanza progresses, we find we are wandering the grounds of the castle-like building, within which "Kindly lips / Bend and smile" and "the magic of the dance illumes / The dreamy faces in the festal rooms." In no other poem does Lampman so closely interweave descriptive naturalism with whimsical imaginings, although efforts in the same direction may be found in such poems as "Inter Vias" and "A Vision of April." The association of the real with the ideal suggests, in symbolic terms, the emotional-psychological effects of the appreciation of natural-world beauty. Nature, we know, is a refuge, a place where, in another poem, the speaker feels wrapped by his thoughts and content to dream. In this poem we are given images for the dream-world state of being.

Two points about the four-stanza middle section of the poem, representing the four seasons, are relevant here because of how closely these stanzas parallel the sequence in *Lyrics of Earth*. First, the beauty of each season is evoked in terms narrower than what would be needed to encompass the entire three months. Autumn, for example, is represented by "the golden long October days," while "the winter nights" are allowed to stand for their season, with the focus falling even more narrowly on specific images, such as stars just visible beyond the roof edge and "icicles that beam like pearl" in the moonlight. By presenting specifics rather than a general overview, Lampman conveys an impression of actual perception. Each season allows for a myriad of observations; the ones included epitomize rather than fully describe the beauty of the season in question. The same method is followed in *Lyrics of Earth*, where individual poems show in specific terms the potential for meaningful contact with nature in the seasons to which they belong. The restorative power of nature operates through involvement with particulars, not in the abstract.

The second parallel to *Lyrics of Earth* has to do with the "guided tour" quality of the narrative. Just as poems in *Lyrics of Earth* are introduced with phrases such as "Here when the cloudless April days begin" and "Now hath the summer reached her golden close," the first of the seasonal stanzas of "The Old House" begins, "When the angel of the springtime broods / O'er the dead leaves and the vanished snow," and the second, "Summer comes." The technique is not used in a formulaic way. The autumn stanza, for example, begins without reference to the season: "All the golden long October days." As in the larger sequence of *Lyrics of Earth*, however, a sense of leading the reader through the seasonal cycle is well established, making it clear that central to the purpose of each work is the desire to say something *about* the seasons.

The qualities associated with the old house are beauty, love, and happiness, for as we hear at the beginning:

> To its ways
>   Love belongs;
> All its days
>   Are but songs

and at the end:

> Softly round it, light of hand like sleep,
>   Beauty grows upon its stones with age:
> Love, its only master, keeps the hall,
>   The surest-sceptered lord of all.

Contact with nature, then, at any time of year ("All its days / Are but songs") will make possible the kind of fulfillment that these words evoke, for the old house is restorative.

This is the locale that Lampman has visited in many different moods throughout his career. The speaker of "April" ventured out to see the new signs of life in its precincts. The speaker of "Heat" came for a visit on a stifling day – the kind of day to which "The Old House" also alludes, "When the too great sun forgets his power, / And the fainting leaves desire the night." And the speaker of "Winter Uplands," Lampman's valedictory sonnet, will stop by its walls to admire one last time the "Hard and sparkling" stars, described now as "jets of silver from the violet dome, / So wonderful, so many and so near." The old house is, again, the mythic human abode within nature, the place of dream where one can always find comfort and inspiration. It is "Open-doored" and beloved by all. In a sense it is life itself – but life lived in the context of the appreciation of beauty, which makes its magic possible.

"The Old House," finally, is notable for the unruffled serenity with which the fact of mortality is introduced. The poem includes characteristic references to "dead leaves" and a "dreaming garden, / Pavèd all with red and russet leaves." Even the mythic life of the house is presented in the context of natural decay as "among the faded stalks and ruined roses / The easy master of the house reposes." Neither are the references to death confined to the trees and bushes of its natural surroundings. In the closing stanza, the speaker gives the following account of the ultimate fate of the house:

> So the old house for its day shall flourish,
>   Till the twilight and the dark descend,
> And the heart within shall cease to nourish,
>   Ending as all mortal things must end;
>   Till at last,
>   Some dark day,
>   All be past,
>   Work and play;
> And forsaken, deaf to every wind that blows,
> The rooms fall silent and the shutters close.

It is tempting to think that, on some level, what Lampman had in mind with his central image was a symbol of the human body, which contains within it the means of feeling love, knowing joy, and constructing images of the ideal life that contact with nature inspires in one's imagination. Thus "roofed with brown" in the opening line refers, a bit restrictively, to hair, the windows with their shutters are eyes, and the heart is – the heart. The rooms are the chambers of consciousness. According to this reading, it is the individual who dies at the end. The very physical descriptions of the house throughout the poem – its walls ornamented with creepers, for example, against which the sunlight beats – would seem to disqualify this interpretation, although the suggestion is not entirely erased. Another possibility is that, as the life of each individual comes to an end, the house for that person "dies"; and still another is that the end of the poem anticipates, although without much evident remorse, the end of all human life. The exact sense in which the house will die remains obscure. What is clear is that the ideal life of the house and, more literally, the joy of natural-world observation are not compromised by the inevitable end of the house. The experience of the eternal is a function of temporal existence.

In both "The Lesson of the Trees" and "The Old House," Lampman expresses his belief that nature in its entirety, and nature as it really is, is replete with beauty. This belief is conveyed specifically in terms of seasonal change and, in "The Old House," largely through the handling of structure. Because of the close parallels that exist between these poems and *Lyrics of Earth*, the inference may be drawn that Lampman's purpose in assembling the sequence of poems in that collection was to impart the same idea – that the quality of beauty may change with the shifting of seasons, but the presence of beauty in nature remains unaltered over time – but to do so implicitly since, in a collection of separate poems with individual points of focus, there is no poem that explicitly offers a summary statement. In "The Old House" we are told that "All its days / Are but songs." Similarly, all the days of the year – Lampman's image of nature as a whole – possess their own quality of beauty. In some cases, this may be a melancholy or tragic beauty, but even so, as rewarding in its way as its cheerier counterparts. As Lampman puts it in the winter stanza of "The Old House," the sky is "bitter," but set in that sky are the stars, "wonderfully / Hard and sparkling," to delight the observer.

But whereas the variety in nature is conveyed in brief compass in "The Lesson of the Trees" and "The Old House," in *Lyrics of Earth* it is much more richly represented. Within this volume are to be found some of Lampman's most evocative, moody, and original depictions of nature. Taken together, they are his testimony of love for the natural world.

III

Although as an assemblage of individual nature poems, *Lyrics of Earth* does not include a statement of general purpose, there are three partial exceptions in the form of poems that have a specific temporal setting but nevertheless comment on life and nature in more general terms. The following discussion of the contents of *Lyrics of Earth* will include a consideration of these poems – one at the beginning because of its role as the introductory piece, and the other two later; an examination of images and motifs that recur throughout the volume; a comparative analysis of two poems, "After Rain" and "By an Autumn Stream," that together illustrate Lampman's purposes in the sequence as a whole; and an evaluation of "The Sun Cup" as the terminal poem. My aim is to show the variety of responses to nature in the collection and at the same time to highlight the irony by which, as in "Heat" and the sonnet "In November," the harsher seasons are seen to possess a beauty of their own. The presence of beauty throughout the year supports the implicit argument of the book, namely, that beauty is pervasive in nature and therefore that the potential for the spiritual restoration derived from the contemplation of beauty in nature is as ongoing and everlasting as the turning of the seasons themselves. Because "Winter-Store," the closing poem of the sequence (not counting "The Sun Cup") has been discussed at length in chapter 2 in the context of memory, it is omitted from the present overview of the sequence in *Lyrics of Earth*.

"The Sweetness of Life"

Although "The Sweetness of Life" was not originally intended to serve as the opening poem of *Lyrics of Earth* – in "Afoot with the Year" it was to be poem number sixteen, among the summer poems – it functions well as an introduction to the sequence. The original choice, "An Ode to the Hills," is more wide-ranging in terms of seasons and climactic conditions, but its central image makes it too narrow. The hills, rather than all of nature, are the focus of that poem. "The Sweetness of Life," on the other hand, though narrower in terms of its temporal setting, has a broader, more inclusive scope, as where the speaker states, "I stretched my hands to the meadow, / To the bird, the beast, the tree," and where it refers, not to a particular experience, but to "life." As well, "The Sweetness of Life" has a quality of lyric celebration that the more ambitious "An Ode to the Hills" does not possess, and perhaps this lightness appealed to Lampman. Then there is the poem's title, a kind of nominal reiteration of the closing statement of "The Frogs": "life is only sweet." This is a challenging, and exactly suitable, claim to put forward at the front of a collection that will affirm the beauty of all nature by taking the reader on a guided tour of the seasons, examining its harsh as well as its mild manifestations. As Lampman explored his surroundings throughout the year, he repeatedly found that joy and comfort were to be experienced in nature regardless of, or even because of, its extremes. In *Lyrics of Earth*, he makes his most ambitious attempt to convey this idea through a collection of poems which together constitute his image of nature – the cycle of seasons whose beauty, though always changing, is never lost.

A question that arises in response to the notion that life is "only sweet" is whether the fact of mortality should be ignored and, if not, then how it should be dealt with. In "The Frogs" and "The Old House" it is not ignored: consciousness of mortality is seen as having no compromising effect on the happiness of those able to respond fully to life in the present. In "The Sweetness of Life," the same position is established over the course of a fanciful dialogue between the speaker and nature, one that is modelled stylistically on certain poems by Tennyson but reflects Lampman's own view of mortality in relation to the eternal in a way that seems puzzling even to him (in the person of the speaker).

Addressing the various natural objects he sees around him on a hot, bright midsummer's day, the speaker asks, "Why are ye all so happy?" Nature responds:

"We are born, we are reared, and we linger
   A various space and die;
We dream, and are bright and happy,
   But we cannot answer why."

Despite being aware of their own mortality, the respondents here – an anthropomorphized meadow and trellis display of roses – remain untroubled and aloof. They know they will die, but are happy regardless. In similar fashion, the speaker realizes that, even though the conditions of life are the same for him, his dream remains unimpeded and his happiness intact. We see this in the closing stanza of the poem where, having received nature's enigmatic reply, he directs his question to himself, conceived as "a ghost" that "the while / Stood from me." The answer provided by the speaker's "self," spoken with a "slow and curious smile," is essentially the same as nature's:

"Thou art born as the flowers, and wilt linger
   Thine own short space and die;
Thou dream'st and art strangely happy,
   But thou canst not answer why."

As L.R. Early has pointed out, the speaker's understanding here echoes that of the psalmist: "As for man, his days are as grass: as a flower of the field, so he flourisheth. For the wind passeth over it, and it is gone; and the place thereof shall know it no more" (Psalms 103:15–16). Given the religious parallel, it is difficult to see why Early regards the speaker's "self" in "The Sweetness of Life" as "a subversive figure in [Lampman's] realm of dreams," disturbing the speaker's reverie with "self-consciousness" and "awareness of mortality."[30] What the overall joyous tones of the poem suggest is that for the person in tune with nature and alive to the moment there exists mysteriously ("we know not why") a happiness that awareness of mortality is powerless to disturb. Such a person sees death, however "real," as distant and unthreatening, and can say with the speaker of Lampman's "Amor Vitae," "I care no jot for death." It is not just because the shadow of death is obscured by the bright light of present happiness, however, that the mutability of all life can be blithely acknowledged in poems such as "The Sweetness of Life." It is also because the happiness of which the poem is a celebration is, and must be, a function of life, time-bound and mortal. At the heart of Lampman's world view is an earth-bound metaphysics whereby time and physicality are the only means by which redemptive experience may be known.

While such ideas are perhaps modern, "The Sweetness of Life" is nevertheless Victorian in its sensibilities, as is evident in its echoes of Tennyson. In the "Come into the garden, Maud" lyric at the end of Part I of Tennyson's *Maud*, the speaker addresses a lily and a rose, and later in the same lyric the flowers are imagined as responding to the speaker's thoughts: "The red rose cries, 'She is near, she is near;' / And the white rose weeps, 'She is late.'"[31] Lampman, too, has talking flowers. In terms of phrasing, a passage from another Tennyson poem, "The Voice and the Peak" –

> Hast thou no voice, O Peak,
>   That standest high above all?
> "I am the voice of the Peak,
>   I roar and rave for I fall"[32]

– finds a close echo in Lampman's

> What sayst thou, O meadow,
>   That stretchest so wide, so far,
> That none can say how many
>   Thy misty marguerites are?

It is difficult to know whether such patterning was simply unconscious, the result of Lampman's immersion in the work of the poets he admired, or conscious and deliberate, a way to build on and extend a poetic track. In support of the second view is Lampman's own analysis – part of a "Mermaid Inn" column on Arthur Waugh's 1892 biographical study of Tennyson – of how Tennyson himself was influenced by, and then influenced, other writers:

> In one of his most interesting chapters [Waugh] shows how Tennyson not only concentrated in himself the widely differing artis-

tic impulses of his immediate predecessors, but disbursed again from himself the germs of the peculiar qualities of the poets who rose after him. Keats, Wordsworth, Shelley, and Byron[,] each of them contributed something to his style, while Rossetti, Swinburne, Morris, Patmore, and others followed out impulses which rayed forth from the larger master's work like so many beams of variously coloured light.[33]

Lampman seems to delight in the ways in which poetry provides the "germs" for other poetry. He would agree with Alberto Manguel who, in a passage quoted in the introduction to this study, speaks positively of how a work of literature connects to antecedents, employing "quotations and misquotations" that are then "transformed through imagination and use."

Certainly it is the case that, despite the borrowings from Tennyson, Lampman's poem has its own distinctive qualities. The setting is convincingly authentic; the "sun-blanched wall" and "black-shadowed trellis" seem not literary but real. As well, the content of the dialogue between speaker and surrounding objects on the subject of happiness bears Lampman's stamp. And the central idea that the speaker's "self" belongs as much to the present as do the rose and the shadow is a characteristic conceit. As a final note, it is an interesting comment on imitation and authenticity that Thomson, on whose recommendation Lampman shifted the poem to the front of his collection, always regarded "The Sweetness of Life" as the "most lovely and *Archieish* of all in the big book [*Poems*]."[34]

Recurring Images and Motifs in *Lyrics of Earth*

While "The Sweetness of Life" does not reference the four seasons, it announces in simple terms the theme of the book – that life (for those who are receptive to nature's beauty throughout the year) brings joy, fosters happiness, is sweet. Lampman's adherence to this view does not stem from naivety or insensitivity to the sad poignancy of passing time and loss. In "June," the loss of early spring is lamented – "Gone are the wind-flower and the adder-tongue / And the sad drooping bellwort, and no more / The snowy trilliums crowd the forest's floor" – while in "September" we learn with sorrow that "soon, too soon" the scene of beauty before us will be changed. It stems, rather, from nature's answer to change. What we invariably find is that a future season makes up for the loss of the one that is slipping away or, more commonly, that the present season compensates for those that are gone.[35] Thus, in "June," summer "Lets in the torrent of the later bloom, / Haytime, and harvest, and the after mirth, / The slow soft rain, the rushing thunder plume" while the several poems that follow "September" reveal an intimate attachment to the fall and winter scenes that matches the feelings of connection recounted in the earlier poems associated with milder conditions. In short, there are notes of sorrow and fear struck at various points in the sequence, but the beauty of nature during all seasons provides the solace to assuage these feelings.

In pursuing his "sweetness of life" theme, Lampman's strategy seems to have been to infuse as much variety as possible into the collection, as if to test the strength of the main idea. He incorporates a wide range of forms and poetic strategies, with few duplications. Only five stanza structures are repeated – four once and a fifth twice – in a collection of twenty-nine poems. Broadly descriptive evocations of landscape are intermixed with more narrowly focused lyrics, and time orientations range from past to present to the complicated mix of future, present, and past in "Winter-Store." This highly varied poetic terrain reinforces the idea that beauty in nature has many faces. At the same time, reaching forward and backward are recurring images, responses, and ways of seeing that contribute to the unity of the collection. Imagery of the supernatural, for example, is evident throughout, beginning with the reference to "immortal days" in "April in the Hills" and carrying through to the description of the wine of sunlight which fills the earth's cup and "makes it divine" in "The Sun Cup." Such phrases as "An hour of blessedness," echoing "Heat," and a "moment's golden reverie" are typical.[36] These references do not signify any kind of orthodox theology on Lampman's part, but rather indicate by way of analogy the spiritual quality to be found in the natural-world environment.

In one case, "Cloud-Break," the spell of enchantment is lamentably brief. The sun shines out from between wind-blown clouds, seeming like "some god" who "Looks forth and is gone," transforming the landscape. This is the kind of meteorological phenomenon that draws the attention of even the most unpoetic witnesses, who may experience vague metaphysical yearnings or imagine themselves in the presence of a supernatural power. In the first three stanzas of "Cloud-Break," no such witnesses are mentioned. In the closing quatrain, however, while emphasizing the short-lived quality of the "immortal days," the speaker introduces a plural but otherwise unspecified group of observers:

Only a moment! – and then
The chill and the shadow decline
On the eyes of rejuvenate men
That were wide and divine.

It is as if all people within range of the phenomenon stop for a moment, experience briefly a sense of connection with the eternal, and then, the phenomenon having passed, carry on with their activities in the mundane world.

It might seem to some readers that this final stanza, with its broader compass, constitutes an awkward add-on to "Cloud-Break," like a philosophical afterthought. And these lines do indeed appear to have had a separate relevance for Lampman, who inscribed them in a pocket-sized manuscript book in which he kept records of finished poems.[37] There is, however, a structural unity within which the ending is integral to the poem, which consists of four stanzas of four, eight, eight, and four lines respectively. The brevity of the sunburst is referred to in both the opening and closing stanzas. Between them, the longer stanzas describe the landscape bathed in the warm light. The scene is by a river, and the speaker is suddenly aware of colour and smell. He receives "a whiff" from the "blossoming shore" opposite; he notices islands "kindled with gold / And russet and emerald dye"; he sees where "a vapour of azure distills / Like a breath on the opaline green." These close observations implicitly convey the experience of involvement with the scene. The opening and closing stanzas are like the two walls of cloud through which the sun shines, while the middle stanzas are the glory that is briefly revealed.

Also sounding a supernatural note in *Lyrics of Earth* are the numerous references to "magic." In "June," the thrush "Tunes magically his music of fine dreams" and a "golden magic" remains in the aftermath of the speaker's imagined glimpse of a personified embodiment of the month. The sunbursts featured in "Cloud-Break" and "The Bird and the Hour" are described in similar terms. Although the wonderment suggested by the word "magic" is evident throughout *Lyrics of Earth*, the word itself is confined to the spring and summer sections of the sequence. The one exception is "Winter-Store," where it occurs in the phrase "magic pageantry" in the second of the three added-on preliminary stanzas, discussed in chapter 2. These stanzas, however, have no seasonal setting, and the long middle section of "Winter-Store" deals with the speaker's anticipated summertime rambles. Thus, the "magic" retains its spring-summer seasonal setting.

Another kind of supernatural imagery, or a close relative, is present in the recurring evocations of the mythic past. The most prominent instance of this motif is the threefold appearance of the wood god Pan in "The Return of the Year," "Favorites of Pan," and "June," in the spring section of the sequence. In the first of these, the "warm bare earth" and other signs of spring seem to invoke the "vanished youth" of the world. The gods themselves may have disappeared, but for "one short hour" the listener will detect the residual evidence of their presence and be reassured that "Pan is at his piping still." This poem is followed appropriately by "Favorites of Pan," where, in faux-mythic fashion, the speaker explains how Pan, before being displaced by a "mightier hand," infused the throats of the frogs with his song, with the result that those who attend to the frogs' music will be "renewed" and rediscover "the eternal mood / Wherein the world was made." It is consistent with Lampman's ironic sense of beauty that the frogs' croaking is once again rendered as divine music, just as, in "The Meadow," even the squawking of crows creates "a pleasant din," whereas church organs are described in "Life and Nature" as "moaning shrill." Nature's least likely representatives are reverenced, while a conventional source of comfort from the world of orthodox religion is deemed morbid and objectionable.

The third appearance of Pan occurs in the climactic close of "June," following descriptions of both the daytime and nighttime charms of that month. Imbued with the spirit of the season, the speaker has a vision of all the figures of "antique beauty" that he associates with spring, including – in what now seems "the Arcadian valley" – "Psyche, the white-limbed goddess," fleeing: "Down the bright sward and through the reeds she ran, / Urged by the mountain echoes, at her heels / The hot-blown cheeks and trampling feet of Pan." The resurgence of life in the spring put Lampman in mind of a mythic golden age, as his numerous sightings of gods and goddesses in another valley, the Ottawa Valley, attest.

As the seasons progress, other forms of "antique beauty" come into play. In "The Moon-Path," a summer poem, the speaker is drawn into an "old-world spell," under the influence of which he sees various figures from the mythic past, including "monsters of the elder world," "Giants and demi-gods," and shapes "whose marble lips yet pour / The murmur of an antique tongue." These gods and demons make him feel part of the "eternity" within which they dwell. In this poem and others, including "June," it is notable that nighttime images form part of the inclusive vision of nature that *Lyrics of Earth* embodies. Lampman seems as happy figuring the moon as "The mother with her brood of stars" in "The Return of the Year" as he does characterizing the earth as the "mighty mother" in "Comfort of the Fields."

Not as lighthearted as the ringing of "fairy tambours" in "In May," and in some ways more challenging, but also more rewarding, is the spectacle of "hermit folk" that a patch of "mulleins long since dead" evokes for the speaker in "In November." Here Lampman invents the myth: the anchorites were surprised by death at their compline prayer, and now they remain, shrivelled and thin, haggard and austere, as they were left. There is a macabre element to this story, with its dead plants being compared to dead people. Is Lampman's point, then, to make us turn away from a side of nature too depressing for rewarding contemplation? I suggest it is no such thing. Rather, it is to capture the particular beauty of a time of year and a scene which, though "sombre," is enchanting. And this is what the poem is about – this particular quality of beauty. Transfixed, the speaker lingers. His sense of belonging, of relating, is stirred. Once again, as in "In October," his "heart goes out to the ashen lands," and once again those lands are "sweet." In the "hermit folk" (the metaphorical vehicle), we are meant to see the mulleins (the tenor), dry and swaying in the wind. "There was no sound about the wood," we are told, "Save the wind's secret stir." The wind, the mulleins, and the chill all conspire to produce a feeling of close connection with the autumn scene, and the effect is heightened by the sudden shining out of the sun, whose "thin light" dispenses "A semblance of weird joy, or less, / A sort of spectral happiness." The speaker is entranced. He does not wish to exaggerate ("or less"), but wants to capture the subdued thrill of his experience. As W.J. Keith, who regards "In November" as Lampman's "best poem," has remarked, in this passage "we share with the poet his insistence on finding the right words for a complex experience (one of the chief functions of poetry, we might say, is to do just this)."[38] As in this poem's earlier namesake, the sonnet "In November," the speaker's "thoughts" protect him from the cold "like a cloak," and in the closing lines he describes the awakening of "something in my blood": "A nameless and unnatural cheer, / A pleasure secret and austere." The word "unnatural" here suggests that the speaker's reaction violates the norms of human responses to scenes in nature. In tune with the "secret" wind, at one with the "austere" mullein plants, experiencing perhaps the deathly qualities of the season, but still alive, he attains a quiet triumph – not the happiness of spring renewal in the reconstituted vales of Arcadia, but happiness nonetheless.

The sunburst is a phenomenon that recurs throughout *Lyrics of Earth*, producing in the receptive observer a shift of consciousness to match the sudden illumination of the landscape. It is the pivotal event in "In November," nudging the speaker into a minor-key ecstasy, and it is the focus of "Cloud-Break," where it transforms the landscape, causing meadows to be "greening, as if / They never were green before." We find it also in "Favorites of Pan," where it represents metaphorically the "unnamed delight" that the sound of Pan's music once brought to the "tired listener's ear," resembling a "magic fire" from "Paradise, / That rent the cloud with golden gleam apart"; and in "By an Autumn Stream," where it is the final descriptive detail that precedes a cryptic summation of the prevailing mood in nature, discussed below. However, it is in "The Bird and the Hour" that the phenomenon is most exquisitely rendered. This short lyric, written in an open form without stanzas, with irregular rhymes and irregular line lengths, was a particular favourite of Lampman's, who felt that his longer descriptive poems, such as "Comfort of the Fields," were sometimes marred by a tedious catalogue-like quality.[39]

Of "The Bird and the Hour," alternately titled "The Hermit Thrush," he wrote Thomson, serving as an editor with the *Youth's Companion* at the time, "Your Y.C. readers have gone below zero in my estimation since they rejected the 'Hermit Thrush', which was one of the best things I have ever offered to any publication. They must be a set of block heads."[40] Over a number of years, Lampman and Scott jointly produced printed sheets of poems, one poem each, to serve as greeting cards for their friends at Christmas. As if to show his scorn for the *Youth's Companion*, Lampman chose "The Hermit Thrush" as his selection for 1894,[41] and included the poem, of course, in *Lyrics of Earth*.

In "The Bird and the Hour," the sunburst does not suddenly appear to alter the speaker's experience, as in "In November," but is the main focus throughout. In language that recalls "Heat" and "A Dawn on the Lièvre," the sun here "floods the valley with gold – a torrent of gold," while a cloud glows "molten and bright." The scene is that of a sunset sky, with cloud outlined in luminous aureole, and light spilling over the entire landscape, pictured from a vantage point that takes in sky, hill, and valley. Observing the spectacle, the speaker is amazed, but also dismayed, to think that a radiance so glorious must be of such short duration: "And soon the hill, and the valley and all, / With a quiet fall, / Shall be gathered into the night." The adjective "quiet" reinforces the sense of awe, since it seems incredible that such a vast transformation could be carried out, not only quickly, but in silence. The image of a "quiet fall" recalls the towers of smoke in "A January Morning" that "crumble silently." In this case, though, the speaker is looking ahead. His thoughts have distracted him from the scene as he anticipates the imminent change. It is at this point that the call of the ethereal "hermit" catches his attention:

> And yet a moment more,
>   Out of the silent wood,
> As if from the closing door
> Of another world and another lovelier mood,
>   Hear'st thou the hermit pour –
>   So sweet! so magical! –
> His golden music, ghostly beautiful.

Just as, in terms of consciousness, he abandons the vision, thinking about the transience of beauty instead of remarking the landscape, the bird song offers the speaker a reprieve: "a moment more." He is once again alive to the present, called back by the music which seems a voice from some heavenly realm of beauty.

The feeling that predominates in "The Bird and the Hour," not described but implied by language and tone – "ghostly beautiful" – is the summertime equivalent of the "spectral happiness" that pervades the scene in "In November." In both cases, sunlight, combined with other sensory input, produces a natural-world epiphany. Thus two similar scenes, set at different times of year, give rise to a sense of connection with the eternal, which may be defined abstractly as full immersion in the present, a function, in each case, of sensory contact with natural-world phenomena. Such an explanation, however, seems not quite right. The strength of these poems is that the experiences recounted, mysterious to the author, remain so in the poetic record. In "The Bird and the Hour," the focus stays on the descriptive details, and it is the speaker's lyric cry – "So sweet! so magical!" – that conveys his joyous response; in "In November," the speaker does describe his feeling, but obscurely, referring only to his "pleasure secret and austere." These poems capture an experience – perceptual and emotional – and it is experientially that they convey their meaning to the sympathetic reader.

Recurring features in *Lyrics of Earth*, then, include evocations of the supernatural, allusions to the mythic past, and transformative images of sunbursts. The most frequently occurring feature, however, and the one that unites the poems more than any other, is the repeated narrative account of the speaker's identification with the natural-world setting in which he is immersed. In spring, here represented by "April in the Hills," "the world is wide and fair," the woods are alive with birdsong, and the speaker responds in kind:

> I feel the tumult of new birth;
> I waken with the wakening earth;
> I match the bluebird in her mirth;
>   And wild with wind and sun,
> A treasurer of immortal days,
> I roam the glorious world with praise,

The hillsides and the woodland ways,
    Till earth and I are one.

The short declarations bespeak exuberance, and the verse form, with its multiple rhymes and short, end-stopped lines, reflects that mood. In summer, the speaker's attentiveness to his surroundings is again rewarded by a sense of full identification with what he observes, as in "Comfort of the Fields," where roaming "in idleness and sober mirth, / Through summer airs and summer lands," he drains the "comfort of wide fields unto tired eyes," becoming "filled" with the beauty of the season. In the fall, a sombre mood prevails, and the speaker's mood corresponds, as where a "thin light" of the sunburst casts its spell over the landscape, including "every plant and tree," and the speaker becomes subject to the same "spectral happiness" that pervades the scene: "And I, too, standing idly there, / With muffled hands in the chill air, / Felt the warm glow." The melancholy of poems such as "In November" may suggest a dread of the coming season, yet winter brings its consolations, as in "Snow," one of Lampman's most successful blendings of descriptive language and lyric feeling, where the building snow gradually obliterates the landscape, creating "silence everywhere," temporarily broken by the sounds of a passing farmer's sleigh, a dog barking, and a "call / To cattle, sharply peeled," and then once more pervading the scene:

The world seems shrouded far away;
    Its noises sleep, and I,
As secret as yon buried stream,
    Plod dumbly on, and dream.

The familiar "and I" serves to link the speaker with the world around him; his "noises sleep," as do those of the external environment, as "dumbly" (not telling) he plods. And clearly the snow is no enemy to the "dream" experience in this poem, any more than in the sonnet "In November," where the speaker lingers "content to watch and dream."[42] The combination of its winter setting and ethereal moodiness is perhaps what recommended "Snow" to singer-songwriter and harpist Loreena McKennitt, whose haunting musical setting evokes eloquently the spirit of its muted joy.[43]

"After Rain" and "By an Autumn Stream"

In chapter 5, a comparison of "Heat" and the sonnet "In November" served to demonstrate the consistency with which Lampman depicted the effects of natural-world observation under very different seasonal conditions. Similar comparisons can be made between poems on different points of the seasonal compass in *Lyrics of Earth*. Some cross-seasonal parallels have already been noted, as between "The Bird and the Hour" and "In November." To demonstrate the point more fully, I have chosen as representative examples "After Rain" and "By an Autumn Stream," poems that furnish us with a telling combination of contrasting moods and similar states of involvement with the present scene.

Set in late spring or early summer, "After Rain" describes, first, a three-day rainfall, with "columns" of rain moving in "sullen packs" across the landscape and raindrops "drumming on the roof" all night, followed by a clearing of the weather on the fourth day, when "all the world was flecked and strewn / With shadows from a fleecy sky." The metaphorical shift from wolves ("packs") to sheep ("fleecy") effectively captures the transformation from stormy to clear. The idea is not, however, that the storm is "bad" and the sunny weather "good." At both stages, the speaker was attuned to the beauty of nature as it presented itself. He observed the rain throughout the storm "till ear and sense were full," and then, with its passing, responded sympathetically to the change:

> Then, too, on me that loved so well
> The world, despairing in her blight,
> Uplifted with her least delight,
> On me, as on the earth, there fell
> New happiness of mirth and might;
>   I strode the valleys pied and still;
>   I climbed upon the breezy hill.

The speaker is "despairing" and becomes "Uplifted" in the sense that, viewing a comedy, the audience feels sorrow at the lovers' estrangement and happiness at their reconciliation; but the entire play is a delight. In this respect, nature is like art: it is all a revelation, all beauty, all an escape. Thus the speaker recalls that, having observed mountains, river, and plain, he felt a oneness with them; and having heard a chorus of birdsong, he identified with the birds as well: "And as I went I sang with them."

Throughout the poem, a dynamism prevails. The columns of rain have "flying fringes," windows are "rattled" by the rain, rushing water is heard to "gurgle in the creaking eaves," and after the storm's passing, birds sing and fly, haymakers are "forth and gone," and even the newly visible river is described as "unfurled," as if it had been rolled up during the rain. The ringing *abbabcc* rhyme scheme, the four-foot lines (all the same) and striding iambic metre, and the preponderance of short statements (twenty-one independent clauses over forty-two lines, as opposed to ten over thirty-six in "By an Autumn Stream") all make for a lively poetic experience.

In "By an Autumn Stream" that expansiveness is gone; the time frame is narrower, and the focus much more intimate. Here the speaker describes, in the present tense, only the sights and sounds he detects from his vantage point beside a cul-de-sac of pooling water over a period of perhaps an hour. "Flickering light," he observes ambiguously, "Come the last of the leaves down borne." The time of year is late fall, as the poem's position between "In November" and "Snowbirds" would indicate. Sensitive to the absence of summer's vigour and sap, he notes how "patches of pale white corn / In the wind complain" and

> Withered and thinned,
> The sentinel mullein looms,
> With the pale gray shadowy plumes
> Of the goldenrod.

Slightly less dolorous are the "bunches of beautiful berries" on the "bittersweet" (woody nightshade) that hangs from above, and the snowbirds that appear and disappear "Like fringes of spray / That vanish and gleam on the gray / Field of the sea." Mostly, though, the mood of the poem is one of sadness. Even the sunlight that appears for a moment at the speaker's feet is described as "a sad silvery sheet, / Utterly still." Nevertheless, the speaker's response is not to resist or abandon the landscape but, again, to identify with nature as he finds it. He dwells with tenderness, even with yearning, on the landscape confronting him, seeking to capture the essence of its melancholy beauty.

In the closing stanza of "By an Autumn Stream," the human element, implied throughout by the close observation, is overtly introduced for the first time:

> All things that be
> Seem plunged into silence, distraught,
> By some stern, some necessitous thought:
> It wraps and enthralls
> Marsh, meadow, and forest; and falls
> Also on me.

By including himself in his list of objects subject to the influence of the prevailing conditions, the speaker repeats the pattern exhibited in "After Rain." He even uses the same vocabulary – "and falls / Also on me" recalls "On me, as on the earth, there fell" – to express the same idea. But because the speaker is so empathetic with the "world," "despairing in her blight, / Uplifted with her least delight," his response is, emotionally, the opposite of his response in "After Rain." It is as if this poem were part of the slow movement of a symphony, and the composer, interpreting the landscape, had written strains of sorrow and perhaps foreboding into the music, making it no less beautiful for that. At the same time, a kind of northern fortitude has been built into the piece. The terms "stern" and "necessitous" imply that the changes taking place in nature must be borne. "The tall trees stand without fear, without pain, / Though summers gather their gold and go," we are informed in "The Lesson of the Trees," and so "ought" we to do. Subject to the same "stern" precept as the outer world appears to be, and responsive, as well, to the peculiar beauty of the season, the speaker in "By an Autumn Stream" reacts in a way that is consistent with this exhortation. Nature is always to be valued, and the presentation here of a consciousness as much permeated by the thin light of November as, in "Among the Timothy," its summertime equivalent is "soaked" by the intense energy of the sun, highlights a recognition of the virtue of both.

The differences of mood in "After Rain" and "By an Autumn Stream" – crucial to the point that, despite changes in the face of nature, beauty persists – are evident in Lampman's handling of form as well as content. The short lines, consistent line lengths, energetic iambic metre, and proximate rhymes of "After Rain" have already been mentioned. In "By an Autumn Stream," the variations in line lengths (lines one, four, and six of each stanza have two beats while the remaining lines have three) and in metre (the pattern is anapaestic, but with many exceptions) create a slow-moving rhythm that is appropriate to the meditative stillness of the scene. In terms of metrical variation, the second-to-last line of the final stanza provides a good illustration of how verse form and meaning intersect. According to the underlying anapaestic metre of the poem, the word "marsh" should be unstressed –

˘ ´ ˘ ˘ ´ ˘ ˘ ´

Marsh, meadow, and forest; and falls

– but normal speech requires that it receive emphasis:

´ ´ ˘ ˘ ´ ˘ ˘ ´

Marsh, meadow, and forest; and falls.

The gravity exuded by the greater-than-expected mass of "marsh" has the effect of holding our attention as we pause to look more closely at the autumn panorama. It reinforces the impression of a brooding stillness that the words themselves convey. Equally supportive of mood and atmosphere is the *abbcca* rhyme scheme: the separation of the *a* rhymes emphasizes the quiet of the day into which a sound intrudes only now and then, while the inner rhymes suggest the closer, more intimate harmonies of the scene. Finally, even though the stanzas of both poems, without exception, comprise single sentences, those of "After Rain" consist largely of coordinated or juxtaposed shorter declarations, producing a cumulative effect of high energy, while those of "By an Autumn Stream" are mostly complex, slow-building descriptions of a cluster of related images, separated (at the stanza breaks) by silence.

The close attention to form in these two poems is consistent with Lampman's practice of crafting a poem so as to reflect in the aural qualities of the verse the particular mood of the scene. Lampman describes this practice in his essay "Poetic Interpretation." Elaborating on his statement about the variety of equally beautiful impressions produced by "a Mayday sunrise," "an October sunset," "a full-blown rose," and "a bunch of sedge," he states:

> The poet's reproduction of any impression must be effected not by a vivid picture only, or by a merely accurate description, but also by such a subtle arrangement of word and phrase, such a marshalling of verbal sound, as may exactly arouse, through the listening ear, the strange stirring of the soul, involved in every beautiful emotion, which we feel to be akin to the effect of music. If the poet should undertake to reproduce the impression of the summer sunrise, the October sunset, the rose, and the bunch of sedge, not only must the pictures be different, but the tones must be different too.[44]

The "tones" of "After Rain" and "By an Autumn Stream" are decidedly different, even while the thematic content, involving identification with nature, is the same, and both poems may be said to convey a "beautiful emotion," largely owing to the "subtle arrangement of word and phrase" and "marshalling of verbal sound" brought to bear on the content in each case.

What these two poems illustrate is Lampman's attempt in *Lyrics of Earth* to craft poems in such a way as to capture the full range of moods he encountered in nature. To employ "merely accurate description" would be to map the seasons, but not to convey the emotional quality of the landscape or the "strange stirring of the soul" that each scene inspires in the sympathetic observer. This is perhaps why, as a lyricist, Lampman was never satisfied with the approbation he received for the descriptive accuracy in his poems. No "merely accurate description" would support the kind of emotional involvement on the part of the observer that is so fundamental to his depiction of, not just nature, but the human response to nature. What was needed instead was the blend of descriptive accuracy and emotional energy that we find in a poem such as "Heat." In *Lyrics of Earth*, he sought to express that larger purpose in the context of the annual cycle in order to demonstrate that each aspect of nature possesses what he calls in "Poetic Interpretation" a "peculiar harmony" that distinguishes it from all other aspects and at the same time connects it, by virtue of participating in nature's beauty overall, to its counterparts in the round of seasons.

"Forest Moods" and "Life and Nature"

It now remains to comment briefly on "Forest Moods" and "Life and Nature," poems that, like "The Sweetness of Life," make reference to the theme of the collection as a whole even while they occupy the seasonal positions that match their specific temporal settings, and then to conclude with a consideration of "The Sun Cup" in relation to its position at the end of the sequence.

"Forest Moods," it will be recalled, was one of three poems in *Lyrics of Earth* written in 1893, too late to be included in the original compilation of the sequence. Possibly it was inserted later because of its particular relevance to the book as a whole. Certainly it was written at a time when Lampman's creative energy was focused on his second collection. A springtime poem, it nevertheless expresses Lampman's inclusive vision of natural-world beauty, though not in terms of the seasons or the passing of time.

In a forest setting, the speaker takes note of the variety of birds and flowers around him. The "moods" with which he associates his subjects vary, but his response remains consistently affirmative. The songs of some birds seem nostalgic, while those of others express what he interprets as a gleeful contentment with "the present and here." To the speaker, however, "all the notes of their throats are true." His attitude to the flowers is the same. Although "the pale wood-daffodil covers her face, / Agloom with the doom of a sorrowful race," he is able to say of the flowers in general that "every leaf of their sheaf is fair." The fanciful metaphorical constructs imply opposite moods. But despite the superficially "negative" or "positive" qualities that the flowers possess metaphorically, their rightness and beauty are what comes through. They are as they should be. In the same vein, Lampman can say of his beloved in another poem, "Or whether sad or joyous be her hours, / Yet ever is she good and ever fair."[45] Emotionally, there can be happiness or sadness, just as, in nature, there can be mild or bleak, but overriding these variations is a larger beauty (related, in the case of the love poem, to goodness as well as beauty) that embraces all. The speaker in "Forest Moods" delights in making just such a paradoxical affirmation. It is the point of the poem.

As the title *Lyrics of Earth* implies, the book is meant to have a lyrical, rather than philosophical or didactic, feel. A poem that stands out as one of Lampman's most successful lyrics, song-like in its simplicity, yet succinctly captures his philosophic outlook on nature, is "Life and Nature." Written in September of 1889, when Lampman was first formulating his ideas for the collection, the poem makes the claim, familiar enough in nature poetry, that nature, not orthodox religion, is the true source of spiritual fulfillment, but does so with such naivety that we are won over by the feeling, just as, in a love song, the pronouncements may not be new, but the simple words and melody work their magic regardless.

Having listened one Sunday to the "solemn singing" emanating from churches, the speaker is grieved by the mournful evidence of human suffering: "'O Life! O Life!' I kept saying, / And the very word seemed sad." He flees the gloom-infected urban arena, passing through the symbolic city gates that divide the world of affliction from that of regeneration. Now, in the countryside, he is "Afar from the bell-ringing." The metre in the poem is rising – a mix of iambic and anapaestic – with alternating feminine and masculine line endings. If the rhyme at "bell-ringing," positioned as a masculine ending, is not wrenched – if the final syllable is not unnaturally stressed – then the effect will be pleasingly naive and will suggest, moreover, the fading of the unhappy sound as the speaker distances himself from its source. Safe in "the depth and the bloom of the meadows," he reclines "on the earth's quiet breast." He listens to the birds, and the transformation is complete:

> Blue, blue was the heaven above me,
>   And the earth green at my feet;
> "O Life! O Life!" I kept saying,
>   And the very word seemed sweet.

The repetitions, the exclamations, and the all-inclusiveness of this passage impart the pure happiness that attends the reversal. As Ralph Gustafson has remarked with reference to this stanza, "The Canadian landscape became a joy almost painfully extreme to Lampman's sensitive spirit."[46]

A literary legend has grown around the placement of a brass plaque in Lampman's memory in St Margaret's Church, Vanier, near Ottawa, inscribed with those last two lines. The source of the anonymously donated tablet, the story goes, was Katherine Waddell, the Post Office department co-worker Lampman had a close friendship with, and nursed a frustrated love for, in the mid-1890s. It seems more likely, however, that the tablet was donated by a group of Lampman's Ottawa friends.[47] Whatever the truth, the lines are well chosen, reflecting the observer in a mood of keenest attachment to the natural world.

"The Sun Cup"

Following "Winter-Store," *Lyrics of Earth* concludes with "The Sun Cup," a short lyric depicting the close of day and coming on of night. Although this poem has no obvious seasonal setting, it evidently is a spring poem. In "Afoot with the Year," it was to be poem number nine, near the beginning of the sequence. When Lampman discovered it had been omitted from the proofs of *Lyrics of Earth*, he wrote to his publisher requesting its reinstatement: "I find that one short poem has been omitted somehow from the M.S.S. I enclose a copy of it. It comes between 'In May' and 'Life and Nature,' but if it is inconvenient to insert it there it would do just as well at the end. I would like to have these verses put in."[48] The first impression one gets from this letter is that Lampman's concern about the overall design of *Lyrics of Earth* was overridden by his desire to have the poem included. Would he have been just as willing, though, to have "In May" or "September" added on at the end? Probably not. It seems likely, therefore, that with its lack of a clear seasonal association, "The Sun Cup" made in Lampman's judgment a suitable end piece or, as Bentley has suggested, a pleasing "coda" to the collection.[49]

It is not hard to see why Lampman concluded that "The Sun Cup" "would do just as well at the end." The main conceit is that, with each day, Apollo fills his cup, the earth, with divine essence, "the vintage of gold and of light," and at sunset, with "a long last look of his eye," drains his cup and closes its lid. Bereft of light, the world becomes "Empty and hollow and dim" – but not quite. Just as earlier in the sequence the loss of one moment's experience is compensated for by the advent of another, with the night comes a form of recompense, for the "slow-turning luminous lid" of the cup is revealed as "Its cover of darkness and stars, / Wrought once by Hephaestus of old / With violet and vastness and gold." The splendour of the night sky has replaced the radiance of the day, reconfirming the point made, for example, in "June" and "The Moon-Path" that the nocturnal world forms part of nature's panoply of beauty: it has its own "gold." The references to classical gods, moreover, echo the earlier evocations of a mythic past that the beauty of nature inspires. Indeed, the odd mix of archaic verb formations – "filleth," "draineth," "setteth" – with modern ones – "fills," "drains," "lifts" – creates an impression of the two worlds intersecting.

This notion of compensation, however, is secondary to the main point, articulated in the opening line of the poem: "The earth is the cup of the sun." As attractive as the night might be, the chief wonder of the world is the potent power of the sun, the "warm, strong wine" that the sun god pours every morning and drains every night. At this level of meaning, the typical day referred to symbolizes life, and nighttime, death, implying in the context of the sequence as a whole that life, each day, is our source of redemption, under the influence of which death – acknowledged in "The Sun Cup" without morbidity – need not be feared. This is similar to the relation between time and timelessness presented at the end of "The Old House," where we learn that the house is destined to flourish only "for its day." In both cases, the effect of acknowledging the transience of existence is not to undermine the speaker's happiness but to reinforce the idea that through life comes one's spiritual fulfillment, however brief, and to suggest, perhaps, that with death comes a final release as individuality is supplanted by the timelessness of non-being.

Beginning with a poem that expresses a belief in ";the sweetness of life" notwithstanding that "we linger / A various space and die," and ending with a poem in which both the beauty and the brevity of life are affirmed, *Lyrics of Earth* is Lampman's testament to the glory of earthly existence, as experienced by one who is receptive to the beauty of nature in all its moods. The overriding image of nature is the annual cycle of seasons, and the implication of the structure is that the comfort, happiness, and redemptive change derived from close contact with nature are always available, if not always sought. As long as it lasts – that is, until "the end of things" – the cycle will continue. The poems about snow at the end of the sequence should thus be seen as anticipating, at the beginning, "Godspeed to the Snow" and "April in the Hills." Each individual encounter with nature is unique by virtue of its specific temporal and spatial relations; but in cyclical rather than linear time, the poems of a given season all belong together, even if based on experiences that took place during different calendar years. In Lampman's case, it was literally true that the poems representing one year in *Lyrics of Earth* were written over a period of more than a decade.[50]

Put abstractly, the means to redemption is always available, just as in "The Old House" the house itself is a home of friendly pilgrimage, and the beauty of nature a fact of life, throughout the year. This is the underlying theme of *Lyrics of Earth*. In the poems themselves, however, this idea remains secondary to the celebration of actual scenes, in which the close and intense appreciation of nature is its own reward. The goal of the poems is to bring the scenes alive: to make them live artistically. If he knew that future readers were to delight at the return of the sun in "After Rain," smile at the image of Pan pursuing Psyche in "June," or shiver at the sudden appearance of the thin sunlight in "In November," then the poet, one suspects, would feel amply compensated for the labour of translating the perceptual and emotional experience of nature into words.

CHAPTER 7

Later Nature Poems

What the nature poems examined so far reveal is that central to Lampman's depiction of nature, and fundamental to the meaning of the sequence in *Lyrics of Earth*, is the simple idea that nature is pervaded by beauty despite change, along with the complementary notion that the restorative effects of contact with nature can be experienced throughout the annual cycle. In presenting these ideas, Lampman does not downplay or disguise the severity of extreme conditions. The strength of his "And yet to me" at the end of "Heat" depends precisely on the success with which the oppressive heat of the day has been captured in the preceding stanzas.

At first these ideas seemed a happy discovery. The speaker in "Heat" takes evident pleasure in finding in the furnace-like conditions a purifying, cleansing quality. As time went by, however, and hardships mounted in the form of marital difficulties, frustrated love, guilt, money problems, rejections by publishers, and the death of an infant son, it became more of a challenge for Lampman to affirm the virtue of scenes giving rise to physical discomfiture or in which death and decay were predominant. The hostile conditions seemed emblematic of his own pain. This challenge is analogous to that of the religious believer who must be reconciled to the human condition and be strong in the face of personal tragedy. Life's difficulties test one's faith. In a small group of nature poems written in the 1890s, among them "Sapphics," "Earth – the Stoic," and "An Ode to the Hills," this kind of struggle is evident. Then, toward the end of the decade, and of Lampman's life, the strain abates. We see the change in "The Lake in the Forest," in a small group of wilderness sonnets, and in "Winter Uplands," written less than two weeks before he died. The harsh world of the out-of-doors and the approach of night, because of their beauty, now comfort the speaker, with no effort of strength required to reap that benefit.

"Sapphics"

In "Sapphics," Lampman attempts a marriage of his own lexicon and philosophy of nature with the classical form referred to in the title, and to judge by the uniformly positive critical response, the post-nuptial life of the poem has been a happy one.[1] Lampman's handling of the four-line stanza, English renderings of which he would have been familiar with from Swinburne and others, is particularly successful. The "falling" metre, trochaic but with a requisite medial ripple ("beautifully sad") in the first three lines, and with the ripple repeated in the shortened fourth line ("Full of foreboding"), with feminine endings throughout, is ideally suited to the melancholy theme. Lampman's rendition, as he himself boasted, is "musical."[2] Based on its shifts in focus, the poem may be divided into three sections consisting of the first three, the next two, and the final two stanzas.[3]

In section one, following the familiar strategy of depicting at the outset an apparently hopeless situation only to turn it around, the speaker evokes a melancholy vision of an autumn landscape. "Clothed in splendour, beautifully sad and silent," the personified season is "full of divine remembrance, / Full of foreboding" – nostalgic for the vitality of spring and summer, and fearful of death. The forecast that follows is resonant with pathos:

Soon the maples, soon will the glowing birches,
Stripped of all that summer and love had dowered them,
Dream, sad-limbed, beholding their pomp and treasure
    Ruthlessly scattered.

Inevitably, time will advance and the trees be left naked, bereft of all of life's gifts. Characterized as brides of summer, they now have reason for despair. Their reaction, however, introduced at the beginning of stanza three by Lampman's favourite conjunction, is not despairing: "Yet they quail not." Despite the "wind and iron" of winter, the trees will remain not only "silent and uncomplaining," but "beautiful still and gracious, / Gravely enduring." They will evince the strength that Lampman admires, and will display, as well, a winter beauty.

In section two, the speaker applies this lesson (as in "The Lesson of the Trees") to himself. Like the trees, he has been "plundered" and left "naked" by "changes." His resolve, introduced with another "yet," is to emulate what he sees in nature:

> Yet will I keep my spirit
> Clear and valiant, brother to these my noble
> Elms and maples, utterly grave and fearless,
> > Grandly ungrieving.

This response to nature is perhaps just one or two steps removed from what we find in poems such as "Among the Timothy" and "By an Autumn Stream," where the "I" of the poem becomes one more object within a landscape that is subject to the influence of prevailing conditions. The difference is that, now, effort is required to bring the desired state into being. The speaker does not recommend this effort; he simply puts it into practice. As G.H. Unwin has observed, "by turning [the moral] inward upon himself the writer avoids the effect of preaching, a practice altogether foreign to his character."[4] Poems such as "Avarice" and "To an Ultra Protestant" might call into question Unwin's final point, and indeed Lampman was judged in his own time to be a "didactic" writer.[5] But in relation to "Sapphics" (and almost all his writing on nature) Unwin's main observation holds.

An early critic, John Logan, finds in these stanzas a uniqueness of thought and expression that he classifies as distinctly Canadian. Nature is valued for more than just its sensual beauty: "Lampman's attitude to nature is not the attitude of an impressionistic portrait-painter, but of one for whom physical loveliness is supremely a spiritual revealment." In addition Lampman depicts a recognizably local terrain and shows the salubrious influence of that landscape on "the mind and heart and moral imagination" of the sympathetic observer. These qualities, combined with a "humanizing" of nature, the establishing of a "mutual bond" between humankind and nature (the speaker is "brother" to the trees), and the expression of the human wish to emulate nature, are characteristically Canadian, borne of the exposure of Celtic sensibilities to the rugged New World terrain.[6] The qualities referred to may not be, and Logan does not say they are, uniquely Canadian. In "Sapphics" we again hear echoes of the "Naked strength" of Tennyson's oak. It is true, however, that the notion of a moral order derived in part from exposure to nature is prevalent in Canadian thought and artistic expression. It is common to the point of cliché to regard the images of rocks and trees in paintings by the Group of Seven, for example, as symbolizing the strength and endurance required to survive, and embodying, in a harsh climate, a rugged beauty. In this context, Logan's observations are illuminating and all the more valuable for the fact that they offer a perspective on the Canadianism of Lampman's interpretation of nature otherwise missing from the critical literature.

On one point, however, a different genesis can be traced, for the characterization of the trees as "uncomplaining" and "ungrieving" again recalls John Keble's poem for the Twenty-Third Sunday after Trinity, from *The Christian Year*. In this poem, also set in autumn, the falling leaves are an image of content. Despite having no prospect of "a second spring" – Christian salvation – they seem unperturbed, "calm," and "ask no more," and thus highlight by ironic contrast the spiritual failings of humankind:

> Man's portion is to die and rise again –
>   Yet he complains, while these unmurmuring part
> With their sweet lives, as pure from sin and stain,
>   As his when Eden held his virgin heart.

In "Sapphics," a similar idea is expressed, based on a different foundation. Life is a blessing, offering its own salvation in the present, and since this, as the poem implies, is enough, people would do well to emulate the uncomplaining trees. Lampman accepts Keble's moral, but not his theology. For Keble, there is no cause to complain because there is everlasting life; for Lampman, despite no assurance of everlasting life, there is no cause to complain. "Sapphics" provides a fascinating example of Lampman's blending of disparate ideologies – Christian and classical – into a philosophy the truth of which was evident to him in the autumnal beauty of the trees themselves.

The final section of "Sapphics," stanzas six and seven, provides a serene account of the brevity – and the beauty – of all life, reiterating in muted tones the philosophy of "The Sweetness of Life" in the context of the greater struggle to which the autumn scene gives rise:

> Brief the span is, counting the years of mortals,
> Strange and sad; it passes, and then the bright earth,
> Careless mother, gleaming with gold and azure,
>   Lovely with blossoms –
>
> Shining white anemones, mixed with roses,
> Daisies mild-eyed, grasses and honeyed clover –
> You and me, and all of us, met and equal,
>   Softly shall cover.

Employing faux-Sapphic diction to good effect,[7] the speaker here acknowledges the conditions of life and gives voice to an attitude of acceptance. Still, he cannot refrain from pausing to reflect back on the now-lost flourishing summer landscape, lengthening the poem by one stanza with his yearning remembrance. If the descriptive phrases had been omitted, this might have been the result:

> Brief the span is, counting the years of mortals,
> Strange and sad; it passes, and then the bright earth,
> Careless mother, all of us, met and equal,
>   Softly shall cover.

In terms of idea, nothing is missing. The list of natural-world images, however, builds feeling into the passage. It is hard to let go. The close of the poem is thus a mixture of sadness and comfort – sadness at the passing of each individual life, and comfort at the thought of the larger life, that of the "bright earth," which buries the dead but unlike the "mortals" is everlasting. The speaker's gentle tone implies that this is the way things must be.

"Stoic and Hedonist" and "Earth – the Stoic"

A word that Lampman does not employ in "Sapphics," but that applies to the ethos of that poem, is stoicism.[8] This concept, signifying in its simplest sense strength and endurance in the face of adversity, was prominent in his mind in the mid-1890s, as the burdens of experience weighed heavily on his thinking. For Lampman, the challenge was to resist the demons that plagued him – depression, frustration, and, as he would say, pessimism – and to find his way back to the life-affirming stance more natural to his character and consistent with his aesthetic. The sonnets "Stoic and Hedonist" and "Earth – the Stoic" provide a partial record of this struggle.

In "Stoic and Hedonist," a Shakespearian sonnet, the hedonists, oddly, are cast as "dreamers" subject to "luminous reveries" and as consumers of "knowledge" and manipulators of the truth, while the stoics are unworldly and accepting, finding only "Strength and self-rule" to be "sweet." The phrase "self-rule" implies an overpowering of one's egocentric feelings and desires. The poem addresses the hedonists, and while it stops short of making an absolute judgment, it sees their instability as they "smile and frown" in their unenlightened way as a fundamental flaw. Possessed of curiosity and even "grace of heart" – undefined, but seemingly positive – they are weak and amorphous at their core. Interestingly, the hedonists are foregrounded in the poem, luxuriating in a "perfumed atmosphere" of self-indulgence within the immediate purview of the speaker, whereas the stoics, whom the hedonists observe with "biting sneer," are pictured in the distance, passing "with stately tread," unconcerned about whether their path is strewn "With bitter herb or blossoming rose." The positioning implies the dominance of the hedonists in the world of the poem and the relative obscurity of the stoics. The degree of prominence is exactly the opposite of their merit. The hedonists come across as all appetite and no discipline, whereas the stoics are possessed of a crucial virtue, extolled in the closing couplet as "life's acme, and its key – / The stoic's grander portion – Dignity." The speaker does not characterize himself as belonging to either group. Nevertheless, he admires the stoics and, we can infer, would learn from them the ability to meet the vicissitudes of life with equanimity.

In terms of artistry, this poem is weakened by its unoriginal epithets – the hedonists' art is "Subtle and shining as the ringèd snake" – and by the blandness of its diction, as where there is "one thing" that the hedonists lack, "The thing that is life's acme, and its key." It is marred, as well, by its self-righteous tone, which is different from forthrightness. At the same time, it is valuable in conveying Lampman's strongly felt dislike of pleasure-seeking acquisitiveness, on the one hand, and his admiration for stoic endurance, on the other. Indeed, the flaws might be seen as casualties of the intensity of feeling that prompted the poem.

Quite a different case is "Earth – the Stoic," a sonnet that effectively encapsulates the ideas about nature and the emulation of nature found in "Sapphics," expressed with strong feeling balanced by constraint. "Sapphics" is built around the opposition between the negative response that the autumn landscape would appear to invite and the impervious strength that the trees, as the speaker interprets them, do in fact exhibit. In "Earth – the Stoic," this contrast is fitted neatly into the two-part Petrarchan structure. As in "The Sun Cup," the earth is "a goblet," now – in mid-winter – "empty of delight" and filled with "that other draught of death and night / And loss, and iron bitterness." The carrying over of the list into the next line, when "death and night" might have sufficed, along with the repeated "and," emphasizes the speaker's distraught state of mind. On the positive side, in the description of landscape that completes the octave, the speaker seemingly cannot help but notice how the clouds above the snow-covered "upland rifts" are "heaping grandly on the hills." Still, up to this point the picture is bleak.

The change in direction, occurring again on the pivot of the conjunction most compatible with irony, takes place at the beginning of the sestet where the speaker addresses the earth directly as in a prayer: "Yet thou complainest not, O steadfast Earth, / Beautiful mother with thy stoic fields." Moved by what he sees as the enduring strength of nature, the speaker now portrays the earth as god-like exemplar. The tone is worshipful as he broadens the perspective to encompass the life of the planet from the time of its astro-chemical origins:

> In all the ages since thy fiery birth
>   Deep in thine own wide heart thou findest still
> Whatever comforts and whatever shields,
>   And plannest also for us the same sheer will.

The phrase "sheer will" is difficult to interpret, but "sheer" implies absolute and "will" suggests determination. The earth moves forward through its seasons. Warmth and vitality are replaced with snow and a landscape "empty" of vegetation. Nevertheless, the earth discovers within itself both consolation and protection, providing a model of how salvation might be achieved: conformity (in human terms) to the code by which nature, as in "Sapphics," remains "Grandly ungrieving." The word "plannest" could imply either necessity or a moral imperative, but since the comparison around which the poem is built implies a moral, the conclusion must be that it is up to humanity to choose to follow the example of all creation.

It is notable that the imagery of "Earth – the Stoic," composed in February 1893, closely resembles that of the sonnet "In November," written five years before. The "upland rifts ... gleaming white with snow" of "Earth – the Stoic" recall the "naked uplands" of "In November," where "The hills grow wintry white" in "the thick-driving snow." In "Earth – the Stoic," "The north wind pipes" and "the forest groans below"; in "In November," "Fast drives the snow" and "bleak winds moan." The strategy in both cases is to present the strongest possible picture of a forbidding winter landscape, only to counter the expectations with a contrary response in the closing lines of the poem. But whereas in "In November" the speaker at the end follows his own inclination, "content to watch and dream," in "Earth – the Stoic," overcome by the barrenness of the landscape (and perhaps, like Lampman himself, inwardly troubled), the speaker must draw from nature a moral, learning to find, as the earth seems to do, "Whatever comforts and whatever shields."

"An Ode to the Hills" and "The Lake in the Forest"

Two longer poems in which Lampman once again apostrophizes nature as a god-like power are "An Ode to the Hills" and "The Lake in the Forest." These ambitious productions both reflect changes in his handling of the theme of nature in the 1890s, even while, as separate works, they contrast each other in terms of style and mood. The settings are predominantly wilderness rather than countryside; the scope is wide-ranging, shifting from one time and place to another, rather than localized; and the content combines realistic description with philosophical reflection. These poems show *and* tell. In "An Ode to the Hills," completed on 11 August 1893, half a year after "Earth – the Stoic," the vastness of time is once again introduced, extending back not quite to the "fiery birth" of the planet but to the geological origins of the hills, and nature is again cast in the role of exemplar with its enduring strength and inscrutable silence. "The Lake in the Forest," composed in September of 1897,[9] six months before "The Old House," has some of the serenity of this later poem. Lampman is worshipful still, but no longer self-reproachful, having found, perhaps, the philosophical outlook so painfully absent in the grieving opening lines of "Earth – the Stoic." Finally, both poems are centrally concerned with the same inclusive vision of nature's beauty that underlies the sequence in *Lyrics of Earth*. It is as if, having consolidated his own understanding, he was desirous of articulating it within the compass of single poems.

"An Ode to the Hills" includes two allusive passages in the first two stanzas, the first helping to establish a religious context for the poem and the second serving to draw a parallel to, and at the same time define a departure from, a literary precedent. The opening words, "Aeons ago ye were, / Before," echo Milton's apostrophe to light in Book 3 of *Paradise Lost* – "Before the sun, / Before the heavens thou wert" – and create, in combination with the poem's epigraph from Psalm 121 – "I will lift up mine eyes [un]to the hills, from whence cometh my help" – a twofold religious invocation, setting the tone for the characterization of the hills to follow.[10] The speaker then contrasts the relative timelessness of the hills with the short lifespans of great cities. He anticipates the complete destruction and disappearance of present-day cities and, as if to lend credence to this dire prediction, observes in stanza two that past civilizations have

Later Nature Poems

indeed been blotted out while the hills themselves have lasted, "firm-set, secure, / Like Treasure in the hardness of God's palm." Images of cities "sunk in nameless ruin" and "names once writ in stone," now "vanished in the dust and void of time," put us immediately in mind of Shelley's "Ozymandias."[11] In contrast to Shelley's desert, however, the landscape surviving the human creations in "An Ode to the Hills" is infused with a spiritual energy, for the hills mysteriously "endure / By virtue of an old slow-ripening word." Louis Dudek has suggested that this poem reveals Lampman to have been "an evolutionist."[12] The idea that Lampman accepted the science-based concept of the earth evolving over vast stretches of time ("aeons") is supported by his application of Milton's (mythic) notion of creation to the (geologic) formation of the hills.[13] At the same time, the reference to an evolving "word," linking biblical origins[14] with those of geological time, suggests a religiosity associated with the process. Lampman's attention is on the survival of nature more than the destruction of the symbols of human power, and any pathos generated by the images of lost empires is offset by his glorification of the power and splendour of the hills.

The middle section of the poem, stanzas three to seven, illustrates first the strength and then the beauty of the hills. Storms armed with "whirlwinds dipped in midnight at the core" – dark and unfeeling – combined with torrential downpours are pictured as gouging wounds into forest and rock and filling the "hollow gorges" with "clash and roar":

> Around your barren heads and granite steeps
> Tempestuous gray battalions of the rain
> Charge and recharge, across the plateaued floors,
> Drenching the serried pines; and the hail sweeps
> Your pitiless scaurs.

This recalls Lampman's sonnet "A Thunderstorm," where, following a hush in the atmosphere, a sudden "wild white flash" of lightning unleashes the storm and "Column on column comes the drenching rain." In "An Ode to the Hills," though, the columns of rain have become battalions as the elements mount their assault on the hills, which stand firm and, like the trees in "Sapphics," "quail not." The word "pitiless" seems an odd choice. In this part of the poem, no other reference is made to any feelings or actions that could be associated with the hills, which are merely the recipients of the attack. Lampman appears to be using the word as a transferred epithet from "hail": the crags are shown no pity by the storms.

The rain and hail are not the only aggressors, as is made clear by the catalogue of further assaults on the "person" of the hills in stanza four:

> The long midsummer heat
> Chars the thin leafage of your rocks in fire:
> Autumn with windy robe and ruinous feet
> On your wide forests wreaks his fell desire,
> Heaping in barbarous wreck
> The treasure of your sweet and prosperous days;
> And lastly the grim tyrant, at whose beck
> Channels are turned to stone and tempests wheel,
> On brow and breast and shining shoulder lays
> His hand of steel.

The meteorological extremes of three seasons are included here, cast as massive beings striding the hills and pursuing their destructive ends; and if the rains of the previous stanza are to be associated with the spring, then the entire annual round – a cycle of devastation – emerges as the focus. In terms of style, the verse unfolds with an unobtrusive naturalness. Few syntactic contrivances distract from the picture being evoked. There appear to be no fillers: each line, each image, seems integral to the scene. And the language suitably reflects the content, as where the hand of the "grim tyrant" winter, whose powers enable him to transform the very elements,[15] touches the body of the personified hills with menacing purpose. The passage is disquieting partly because of the unhurried "lays" and partly because of the ease with which the final phrase fits so tidily into the four-syllable template of the closing line of the stanza. The stanza form is a variation of those found in Keats's "Ode to a Nightingale" and Arnold's modification in "The Scholar-Gypsy" and "Thyrsis," incorporating a single three-foot line mid-stream among the regular pentameter lines, as all three of those poems do, but introducing a three-foot line at the beginning and finishing more sharply with the two-foot line just illustrated. Like "Ode to a Nightingale," but unlike the Arnold poems, Lampman's ode avoids adjacent rhymes.

In stanza five, Lampman introduces a redirection in thought similar to the turn in the sonnet "Earth – the Stoic" ("Yet thou complainest not"), and similar as well to the ironic shift in the closing stanza of "Heat": "And yet to me not this or that / Is always sharp or always sweet." Even the language is similar as Lampman employs the same simple hinge phrase to signal the ironic reversal:

And yet not harsh alone,
Nor wild, nor bitter, are your destinies,
O fair and sweet, for all your heart of stone,
Who gather beauty round your Titan knees,
As the lens gathers light.

For all the meteorological extremes to which they are subject, the hills are intensely beautiful, and again a positive outlook triumphs, for their beauty endures. It may manifest in the most delicate and ephemeral of life forms, such as the "soft maianthemums" (a flowering plant preferring moist soil and shade) mentioned later in the poem, but still this beauty proves pervasive and indestructible, as its survival of the elemental onslaught attests.

Following the tender, romantic, almost erotic praise of the hills in the passage just quoted, the speaker concentrates on the visual qualities of the scene. Still apostrophizing the hills, he notes the effects of light on "your splendid brows" at sunrise and sunset and at noon when the sun "folds you in his might" – an image of the full power of the sun overwhelming, or embracing, the earth. Looking more closely, he observes the obscure flowers and birds of the wild, among them the "lily-breathing slender pyrolas" that "Distil their hearts for you" – the "for you" suggesting that the very lives of these flora and fauna constitute a kind of worship. Then we have the "fierce things of the wild" – eagle, loon, wildcat, and fox – that "Find shelter in your tenantless rocks," safely remote from "the ominous noises of mankind." The speaker in this part of the poem emerges as having much in common with his countryside cousin in "Among the Timothy," concerned with escaping, as in the earlier poem, "The blind gray streets, the jingle of the throng," absorbed by natural-world minutiae, and in awe of the overriding dominance of the sun. Now, however, the locale has shifted, as Lampman, following up on poems such as "Morning on the Lièvre," extends his reach to encompass the wilderness within the range of his poetry – and Canadian poetry – with image, language, and tone evoking setting in a realistic and convincing way.

The closing section of "An Ode to the Hills," beginning quaintly with the syllogistic term "therefore," offers two conclusions, both based on the only argument that the preceding stanzas have made, which is that the "destinies" of the hills, despite severe conditions, are "not harsh alone, / Nor wild, nor bitter," as superficially they are, but also, and more profoundly, since this is the uncovered truth serving as the crux of the poem, "fair and sweet." Conclusion one – stanzas eight and nine – is that (because the hills are what they are) two types of people, the poet and the "worn philosopher," seek out the "bare peaks and radiant loneliness" as an escape from the "ever-thickening press" of city life to rediscover true purposes through contact with nature. Able to "breathe once more / The wind of the Eternal," and with their senses made receptive to beauty, they gain "new courage and a second prime" – benefits, perhaps, that will enable them to work for the betterment of humankind upon their return. Conclusion two – stanzas ten and eleven – is that the speaker himself may "some day" follow in their footsteps and, like a traveller to some wilderness-style Innisfree, "make my dwelling in your changeless heart" where "in some quiet glade" he will carry out a further purpose: "I'll build a blameless altar to the dear / And kindly gods who guard your haunts so well / From hurt or fear." All the evidence, we gather – including, ironically, the earlier depiction of the hills ravaged by the elements – supports the idea that the hills are an ideal place to seek refuge and spiritual sustenance. Although besieged by wind and rain, they are not in their "heart of stone" adversely affected by the assaults. Instead they are, by implication, proved by them, standing strong in the face of the recurring barrage. The raging storms experienced in nature are altogether preferable to the "fierce hands and fraudful lips" that characterize the city. The speaker's final prayer will be, he anticipates, still addressing the hills, for the "gods" to make his spirit the equivalent of the hills in outer show ("bountiful, divine, and fair") and "inwardly" to make him "strong like you." Almost inevitably, the abstract language falls short of precisely defining the desired state of being, but unmistakable is the wish to emulate the two qualities most central to Lampman's concept of nature: beauty and strength.

"An Ode to the Hills" brings together various aspects of Lampman's depiction of nature. The extremes are there, as is the unambiguous affirmation. His ironic sense of things being other than what they seem is prominent. Also present is nature in two related roles: as sanctuary from a society mired in oppression and greed, and as progenitor of the restoration needed, for example, by those who choose to do battle for social change. If it lacks the descriptive-lyrical simplicity of "Heat" or the sonnet "In November," it possesses, like the world of nature it describes, a more large-scale grandeur, and it successfully merges metaphysical philosophy with richly descriptive writing. On a personal level, at a time when Lampman was subject to feelings of self-reproach, it presents nature as possessing the very quality he felt he lacked, inner strength, and as being serenely free of the very quality that plagued him, desire, for the hills are, as he wished he could be, "passionless" and "immutably glad."

It was perhaps for these reasons that Lampman had "a special liking" for the poem. He sent an autograph copy to his sister Isabelle Voorhis, who took an ongoing interest in his writing. He planned to position it as the opening poem of the sequence in *Lyrics of Earth*, and after replacing it in that collection with the more suitable "The Sweetness of Life," included it in *Alcyone*. On 23 June 1897, he read the poem to a meeting of the literary section of the Royal Society of Canada.[16] There is no evidence to suggest how the reading was received, but the response may well have been favourable, for within three months Lampman had completed another poem on a similar design, "The Lake in the Forest." In this poem, however, a freer, less strenuous style indicates a serenity lacking in the earlier work.

Like its predecessor, "The Lake in the Forest" employs a variation of Keats's "Ode to a Nightingale" stanza, but with two shortened (three-foot) lines and with a much more sonorous rhyme scheme (*abbacdcdee*), including two pairs of proximate rhymes, than in the earlier poem. Another feature in common with "An Ode to the Hills" is the presentation of the poem as an extended apostrophe or prayer, in this case directed toward Manitou, alternatively identified as the "Spirit," "Maker,"

"Master," and "Worker unconfined" – altogether, the spiritual presence in nature as well as its creator. Whether derived from Longfellow, who in his popular *The Song of Hiawatha* refers to the aboriginal deity variously as "Gitche Manito," "Spirit," and "the Master of Life,"[17] from Isabella Valancy Crawford, who in *Malcolm's Katie* employs the terms "Manitou" and "the Great Worker" for the same purpose,[18] or from any number of other sources, this vocabulary serves Lampman's purposes well. It conveys a religious feeling while keeping the focus on the natural world. The choice of the Algonquian term Manitou is especially apt, since it is a New World wilderness scene that the poem depicts and Lampman is attempting to set that scene in a timeless, yet localized, context. With the various terms used interchangeably and applied to separate specific aspects of setting, as where Manitou is the "Spirit of the snow," we see that the spirit is immanent in all of nature or, perhaps more accurately, that nature and the spirit are one and the same. One passage in particular strongly supports such an equation. Two "when" clauses, descriptive of, first, the reflection of moonlight on the water, and second, the "yells and demon laughter of the loon," are followed by a "then" clause: "Then art thou present, Spirit, wild as they." To see and hear these things is to experience the presence of the divine.

As in "An Ode to the Hills," we are presented with a procession of times, seasons, and images, framed by stanzas with a more general focus, the closing stanza evoking explicitly the presence of the speaker (in "The Lake in the Forest" this evocation echoes stanza one). The slightly skewed tracing of diurnal and annual patterns in the middle section – night, morning, noon, sunset; spring, fall, snow, and silence – makes for a pleasing asymmetry and spontaneous-seeming randomness. Each example is seen as being imbued with the spirit and thus as contributing one more instance to the ever-expanding vision of nature as a whole, replete with beauty. If just this *idea* were the goal, then a much shorter and less impressive poem might be the result. Instead, each manifestation of nature is caught with language that reflects concentrated, sympathetic observation and reflection, as in this description of the mists of morning –

> Belated broods of spectres break and fly,
>   And cringe, and curl away –

> Thin mists – the ferns of midnight, and her bines –
> That vanish tangled in the topmost pines

– or this of a scene at the opposite time of day:

> This hollow of the forest brims with fire,
>   And piling high to westward builds a pyre
> Of sombre spruces and black pines that stand,
> Ragged, and grim, and eaten through with gold.

The goal in these passages, as in all of Lampman's best writing on natural-world subjects, is to recreate the scene, allowing nature itself to be its own best argument by showcasing imagery with little in common with the conventionally scenic or picturesque.

Central to Lampman's representation of nature are the extremes of climate and condition, and "The Lake in the Forest" is no exception. The burning trees at sunset are one example; another, less metaphorical, is the noonday heat in stanza four, affecting some lazy fish and a group of deer that strangely seem like fugitives from Shakespeare's forest of Arden:

> O Master of the noon; the dusky bass
>   Lurk in the chambers of the rocks – the deep
>   Cool crypts of amber brown and dark – and sleep,
> Dim-shadowed, waiting for the day to pass.
> The shy red deer come down by crooked paths,
>   Whom countless flies assail,
> And splash and wallow in the sandy baths,
>   And cry to thee to veil
> Thine eye's exceeding brightness and strike dead
> The hot cicada singing overhead.

As the behaviour of the lurking bass and unhappy deer suggests, the noonday heat is thick and oppressive. Even without a voice declaring "And yet to me," however, it is clear that there is a beauty to the scene that enchants the speaker, for all the realism of the flies. Similarly, at the opposite point of the seasonal cycle, "the hissing winds that plunge and blow," "The frost that hath its way," and the ice that "roars beneath the winter moon" all serve to augment the picture of winter's beauty. The "spirit" is present in these scenes as well. At the same time, something new for Lampman is the playfulness that would have the deer pleading with the spirit to dim the sun and kill that noisy insect. There is an easiness and confidence in Lampman's writing during this period that contrasts markedly with the struggles reflected in his poems of a few years before.

Matching the lightness of manner is the simplicity of the conception in "The Lake in the Forest," in contrast to the relative complexity of "An Ode to the Hills." In the earlier poem, the speaker addresses the hills, pictured as enduring the climactic assaults of all seasons, and invokes "the gods" as their protectors: observer, object, prevailing conditions, and overseeing supernatural power. In "The Lake in the Forest," the speaker addresses the spirit and the natural world as one, the logic being that, where nature is manifest, the spirit is present. He does not implore the gods for assistance, and if the trees and hills are meant to be emulated, this idea remains implicit. As witness to the beauty of the wilderness, the speaker simply records what he has observed at various times of day and of year, affirming all. With their mutual employment of direct address and their shared religious tone, both poems are psalm-like, but "An Ode to the Hills" is a beseeching prayer, whereas "The Lake in the Forest" is a hymn of praise. It may be that in the fall "the blighting power" strips the trees "and all their rustling braveries / In urns and earthen caskets lays away," but compensating, the spirit prepares and looks after its "children," the plants, "Whose secret buds in woolly folds abide, / And the fur thickens on the fox's hide." All is well.

"The Lake in the Forest" constitutes a kind of summing-up on Lampman's part. For one thing, it reiterates his positive response to seasonal change in a harsh climate. But it is also retrospective in a more personal way. As Early, who regards this poem as one of Lampman's finest productions and "a culmination of his talent," has observed, "by far the greater number of its echoes direct us to his own earlier work."[19] Among the many self-referencing passages are the evocations of the sleepy bass that rest in shadows "waiting for the day to pass," resembling the cows that, in the shadows of elm trees, "Lie waiting for the heat to pass" in

"Heat"; the "shouting woodmen" of the springtime, recalling the occupants of "the woodmen's sleighs" who "With shouts and clamorous squeakings" break the silence in "A January Morning," and who, in "September," gather in "clamorous gangs" before setting out for winter tree-cutting; the frogs that "ever, night or noon," provide the accompaniment as "The rivers swell," as do, with a slight variation, their predecessors in "The Frogs" – "And ever as ye piped, on every tree / The great buds swelled"; and the trees that "make revel for an hour" in the autumn wind, harking back to where, in "A Fantasy," one of Lampman's earliest published poems, we find, "Haste, wind, make revel for a day and night!"[20] As these examples show, in terms of idea, image, and vocabulary, Lampman was reflecting on his various encounters with nature throughout the years, revisiting them as he speaks of doing, and anticipates doing, in "Winter-Store," only now his own phrases serve to evoke the scenes encountered in seasons past and the remembering takes place within the context of a new poem.

At the same time, "The Lake in the Forest" also looks forward to the poem I referred to earlier as Lampman's philosophical swan song, "The Old House," written half a year later. In this poem, all four seasons are systematically evoked in the four middle stanzas, demonstrating the pervasiveness of beauty within nature. In "The Lake in the Forest," the evocation of seasons, times of day, and specific natural-world phenomena, with beauty manifest in all, serves the same purpose. Even more striking is the strangely serene attitude toward mortality presented in both works. "The Old House" anticipates in its closing lines a time when "All be past, / Work and play" and when "deaf to every wind that blows, / The rooms fall silent and the shutters close." In the face of this acknowledgment of mortality, the mood remains untroubled, as if the thought of death can have no bearing on the joys of being alert to the present moment as one participates in the beauty of each season as it passes. In "The Lake in the Forest," the world of linear as opposed to cyclical time is introduced in the closing stanza by means of references to humanity. First we have the aboriginal hunter with "light and sinewy frame," the natural human inhabitant of the wilderness. Then, with the focus returning to the first person "I" from stanza one, the speaker fits himself into the scene:

> O Manitou, before the mists are drawn,
>   The dewy webs unspun,
> While yet the smiling pines are soft with dawn,
>   My forehead greets the sun;
> With lifted heart and hands I take my place
> And feel thy living presence face to face.[21]

The main idea here is simply that the speaker, wishing to connect with the spirit at this moment of new beginnings, with its ethereal beauty, does so: "I take my place." But there is also an odd sense of finality as, at the dawn of a new day, the speaker "greets the sun," as if about to merge with his surroundings, and the merging permanent. The *carpe diem* quality of the time references ("before" and "While yet"), implying urgency or desire, reinforces this idea. The quoted lines invite this reading but do not insist upon it. Either way, the conclusion of the poem marks a joyous union of the speaker with the source of all earthly power, the sun, met in this case not at high noon, the time of deepest infusion, but at dawn, the time of renewal.

Wilderness Sonnets

In light of Lampman's personal circumstances, it is not surprising that in "The Lake in the Forest" and "The Old House" a note of doom, although not of gloom, is noticeable. These poems were written in September of 1897 and March of 1898, respectively. By January of 1898, Lampman was severely ill with a weakened heart, and bedridden. As he wrote to Thomson on 17 February 1898, "It appears that I have been cultivating a serious organic heart trouble for a long time without knowing, and during the past year it has been making great progress. Last winter I began to notice that any vigorous exertion caused me pain and unusual exhaustion, but I did not bother much about it."[22] Even though his earlier letters give no indication that he knew he was ill, this comment suggests that, at the time of writing "The Lake in the Forest," he was on some level aware of his condition.

Beginnings and endings were merging, however, for as John Coldwell Adams has pointed out, it was "almost nine months to the day" after a canoe trip Lampman took with Scott in September of 1897 to Lake Achigan that Maud gave birth to the couple's third child, Archibald Otto, born 21 June 1898.[23] One poem that dates from this trip is "The Lake in the Forest"; another is "An Invitation to the Woods,"[24] a lighthearted piece of doggerel (Lampman's word), which concludes:

> Oh! the triumph of the hound!
> Oh! the joy,
> When the rapid spins you round
> Like a toy!
> When you race with birch and paddle,
> And the stern-sheet for a saddle,
> You shall feel yourself as sound
> As a boy.[25]

Despite the increasingly worrisome state of his health, Lampman felt rejuvenated by this trip, as both poems attest. This feeling, at least in terms of his physical health, would not last, but the sense of contentment and emotional well-being that made such responses possible was apparently not to be shaken.

Among the poems of Lampman's final years that incorporate the wilderness as both setting and subject, and that reflect this same positive feeling, is a group of sonnets dating from two additional canoe trips, one before and one after the Lake Achigan trip. The first was a holiday expedition that Lampman embarked on with two brothers-in-law in the late summer or early fall of 1896 to the Temagami region of north-eastern Ontario. The travellers encountered various others along the way, including a fire ranger named David Maclaren who was, according to Connor, "one of the most famous woodsmen in Canada"; a professor from Yale with two students; and a number of local aboriginal people. They experienced storms, made numerous difficult portages, and had to deal with windy and turbulent conditions on river and lake. Connor provides a lively account of this three-week trip, based, most likely, on letters that are no longer extant or possibly on interviews of which there is no record, since closely paraphrasing sources without citation is Connor's signature manner.[26] Lampman's strenuous and sometimes reckless activities during this trip appear to have been the first of such exertions to aggravate the heart condition that began to trouble him that winter, the original cause of which was a bout of rheumatic fever he suffered as a child.

The other trip, really a side trip, took place in late August of 1898. At this time Lampman was on an extended leave from work and friends had paid for him to travel east to Montreal, Quebec, Digby, and Boston, to benefit his health. In Montreal, another friend, the poet William Henry Drummond, arranged for him to stay at a lodge belonging to the St Maurice Club on Lake Wayagamack, 120 kilometres north of Three Rivers.[27] Here, where he could "breathe the great air of the wilderness free of labour or care," as he wrote to Scott, he was happy. The lake, he said, was "a good deal like Achigan, but about three times as large and much more beautiful." He spent his days fishing and exploring "in a little birch bark canoe which is about as taxing to navigate as if I were mounted on a feather." At the same time, he was coming to terms with the seriousness of his condition. "I am hardly any good," he wrote. "I am gradually reconciling myself to the fact that I am an invalid and shall remain so as long as I live, which I imagine can hardly be long – not many years."[28] It would, in fact, be less than half a year. This was to be his last sojourn in the wilderness.

The wilderness sonnets – four from the earlier trip and only one from the last – are notable for their simplicity. They are, with one partial exception, narrative-descriptive in their method, omitting references to the spirit inhabiting nature or to the observer's dream in nature, but emphasizing the details of weather and topography and highlighting the aboriginal place names that resonate with a northern ring: Temagami, Temiscamingue, Wayagamack. It seems to be enough for Lampman to evoke the wilderness setting and to place himself and his companions within it. The significance – the joy of being in the alternative world, at the opposite end of the experiential spectrum from the city – remains implicit. At the same time, the "dark" side of the wilderness is not lacking, but as we have come to expect, that is part of its beauty and charm. While these poems read like simple, rhyming journal entries, they were mostly completed well after the fact, when the experiences they are based on had become part of Lampman's "store" of memories. In part they have a documentary value, providing early poetic records of contact with the northern wilderness and its inhabitants. At the same time, they are carefully wrought productions, and their simplicity is part of their design, capturing the rawness of the experiences recorded.

Because only one of these sonnets was published in Lampman's life – "Temagami" in the March 1898 issue of *Blackwood's Magazine* – it is not known if they were intended to make up a discrete grouping. Manuscript copies of the ones from the 1896 canoe trip, however, are included with letters exchanged between Lampman and Scott in 1897–98,[29] so it is likely that Lampman saw at least these four as a gathering of some sort. I will treat the Temagami sonnets together as a record of an actual experience, and the single Wayagamack sonnet as a sort of summing-up.

Structurally, two of the Temagami sonnets ("Night in the Wilderness" and "In the Wilds") are of the Shakespearian type, while the other two ("Temagami" and "On Lake Temiscamingue") are hybrids, but closer to Shakespearian than was usual for Lampman, with two cross-rhymed quatrains followed by, in the former poem, a rhyming couplet and then a third cross-rhymed quatrain, and in the latter, six lines rhyming *eefggf* – altogether a good illustration of Lampman's point that he had "no very profound respect for rules and regulations" in his sonnet writing. ("Wayagamack," by contrast, is a Petrarchan sonnet.) In each case, however, Lampman employs the two-part structure of the Petrarchan form to good purpose. By using the "turn" to signal either a change in perspective or a time shift, he creates temporal and spatial relationships that add a new layer of meaning to the poems. The travellers' involvement with their surroundings and the emotional impact of the scenes and events described are conveyed largely through this structural device. The drawing of explicit morals is thus rendered superfluous. Although such a traditional form as the sonnet, even if modified, may seem an unlikely vehicle for imparting the spirit of the wilderness in nineteenth-century backwoods Canada, this template proves remarkably well adapted to the successful conveyance of that theme.

In "Temagami," the scene is set "Far in the grim Northwest beyond the lines / That turn the rivers eastward to the sea." The speaker is back in the south, removed now from the poem's setting, but with vivid memories of the distant lake, situated in terms of the large-scale geographical image of the watershed. The remoteness of the lake is emphasized, but so is its regal beauty, for it is "Set with a thousand islands, / crowned with pines." It is magnificent. Next, in the second quatrain, the hunters and trappers who frequent this environment are introduced. The place is "Wild" – already the second occurrence of this word – "with the trampling of the giant moose, / And the weird magic of old Indian tales." Enter the travellers, first mentioned in the couplet that Lampman has placed ahead of the final quatrain, as the poem shifts from purely descriptive to narrative and from present tense to past: "All day with steady paddles toward the west / Our heavy-laden long canoe we pressed." Their arms are busy with the physical work of paddling, but their eyes are alert to the dramatic surroundings. They observe "the thunder-travelled sky / Purpled with storm" and watch, in the closing lines, "the broken sunset die / In crimson on the silent wilderness." As that last phrase implicitly announces, in terms of both the real journey into the backwoods and the symbolic journey into the alternate world of unsullied nature, the seat of spiritual restoration, the sojourners have arrived. Words such as "grim," "dark," "trackless," "storm," "broken," and "die" may suggest to some readers "an ominous cross-current of suggestion," but the evident enthusiasm of the travellers, who have worked hard to reach their destination, suggests rather that this harsh and forbidding, yet beautiful, locale is entirely to their liking.

By following a purely descriptive segment (the first two quatrains) with an action-focused completion (couplet and third quatrain), Lampman is using essentially the same technique he employs in the sonnets "Solitude" and "A January Morning," where the effect of the intrusion is not to spoil the speaker's pleasure in observation but rather to enhance it by providing a new point of focus and to set off the first part by contrast. In this case, though, it is the speaker and his companions who are the intruders. The rugged ideal of the wilderness scene has been evoked, as in a painting, and then into that picture joyously sail the visitors – observed (by the reader-viewer) from behind as they advance into the frame and followed as they proceed westward into the distance, silhouettes diminishing in size against the fading light. Another difference from the earlier sonnets is the shift from present (general) to past tense (specific). It is as if to say, with the fervour of announcing a completed pilgrimage and holding up an artistic representation of Mecca, "here it is, and we remember – we were there."

The titles of the other three sonnets from the Temagami trip all emphasize the presence of the speaker and his companions "in" or (in the case of water) "on" their new environment: "In the Wilds," "Night in the Wilderness," and "On Lake Temiscamingue," corresponding to the "in" and "among" of Lampman's earlier nature poems. Instead of a farmer's field or a time of year, however, it is the northern wilds that the titles emphasize – not, as hypothetically it might have been, "Among the Trees" or "In July," but "On Lake Temiscamingue." That is the chief wonder the travellers experience – amazement at the in-ness and on-ness, linking the region to themselves. The first two poems, diary-like, record activities, while the third, inspired by a scene encountered on the home journey, is more purely descriptive.

"In the Wilds" imparts the intensity of pleasure the travellers derive from their engagement with their surroundings by means of a series of six end-stopped lines at the beginning, each one an encapsulated experience, with terminal semicolons emphasizing their separateness: "We run with rushing streams that toss and spume; / We speed or dream upon the open meres." The attitude of the group toward the rigours of the wilderness experience is captured in the line "The rain we take, we take the beating sun," where the chiasmus, balancing the antithetical rain and sun, shows their enthusiasm for all conditions. At line seven, catching his breath, the speaker slows the pace by running the statement over two lines, aptly with the focus on the end of day when, lying on the "rough earth," the exhausted travellers "slumber even in the storm's despite." Having listed their activities, the poem then shifts in the third quatrain to a consideration of effects: "The savage vigour of the forest creeps / Into our veins, and laughs upon our lips." The men are renewed, feeling within themselves a vitality associated with the primitive past as the "warm blood kindles from forgotten deeps."

With reference to laughter, Ernest Voorhis, one of the brothers-in-law who took part in this trip, has left the following account of Lampman's behaviour "in the wilds": "There was never a time when he could not see the humour in every happening. Often as we paddled in silence by the hour, resting his paddle, he would suddenly break into that hearty laugh of his at the recollection of some humorous incident and start the echoes bounding from shore to shore and rousing the solitary loon."[30] This report captures the delight Lampman took in the wilderness. He felt invigorated, alive, happy, and these are the feelings that the "effects" section of this sonnet enthusiastically records. By implication, the corrupt and stultifying environment of the city has been supplanted by the beauty and, in a sense, honesty of the lake setting, where the severe conditions are, to allude once again to the magical forest of Arden, not false flatterers, but "counsellors / That feelingly persuade me what I am."[31]

In contrast to the multiple situations referred to in "In the Wilds," "Night in the Wilderness" presents just one: the travellers gathered around the camp fire tended by the "good fire-ranger" – the historical David Maclaren – who "cooks his bouillon with a hunter's pride." With the fire as the central image, its "fount of sailing sparks" illuminating the nearby trees, a feeling of comfort and warmth prevails. (On the actual canoe trip, a long day of portaging, paddling, and running rapids preceded the welcome respite of the ranger's hospitality, his tent, according to Connor, "large and capacious enough to hold them all.")[32] At this juncture, the new sentence beginning at the fourth foot of line eight, serving as the imported Petrarchan "turn," signals the shift from evening to night. As the campers "sink at last to sleep," the perspective zooms out and pans the forest:

> On every side,
> A grim mysterious presence, vast and old,
> The forest stretches leagues on leagues away,
> With lonely rivers running dark and cold.

Lakes, bays, and the "stars above the pines" are evoked until, at the end of line thirteen, we encounter a full stop, the second of four in the last three lines of the poem. There is silence. One of the campers, it seems, is not yet asleep, but listening in the dark: "The wind scarce moves." Full stop. "An owl hoots from the hill." The simple language and the stops and starts capture with precision the immediacy of the experience: the silence, the speaker's attentiveness, and the breathing of the forest outside the tent. We appreciate simultaneously the vastness of the wilderness that dwarfs the human presence and, paradoxically, the speaker's expanded consciousness as he takes it all in. By means of simple statements and his skilful handling of form, Lampman conveys a keen sense of both the landscape and the human encounter with it.

"On Lake Temiscamingue," the last of the poems from the Temagami trip, depicts a scene encountered on the return journey. Lampman and one companion – the others had already departed – have arrived back at the lake they had traversed on their way in. Written in the manner of his purely descriptive pieces, devoid of event and lacking reference to any thematic idea, this sonnet, too, conveys meaning – in this case, of a valedictory nature – by means of a Petrarchan-style "turn."

The opening lines, sketching the scene, read like the verbal equivalent of the familiar tree images – Tom Thomson's *The Jack Pine*, for example – characteristic of the Canadian landscape painters of the first half of the twentieth century:[33]

> A single dreamy elm, that stands between
>   The sombre forest and the wan-lit lake,
> Halves with its slim gray stem and pendent green
>   The shadowed point.

The perceiving eye then looks past the tree to where "Bold brows of pine-topped granite bend away," further described as "fading off in grand / Soft folds of looming purple," before returning to the point of land. The granite is hard, but the tree-covered cliffs look soft in the dying light. Shifting the focus at line nine, the speaker states, "Two rivers meet beyond it" – that is, beyond the point – and "wild and clear, / Their deepening thunder breaks upon the ear." The present tense makes it seem as though the confluence of these rivers can be seen and heard in the present, but that seems doubtful. For one thing, the sound would break upon the ear only if one were approaching it; otherwise it would remain steady. As well, the passage goes on to describe contrasting features of the two rivers upstream beyond the confluence, presumably not visible from this side of the point. It would appear that the speaker is referring to a recent rather than current experience. He knows the sound

– the "race of tumbled rocks" and the "roar of foam" – because he has heard it, and now, in memory, he hears it again. Thus, without overt mention, the sonnet captures the experience of reaching the end of a journey and, implicitly, the emotions associated with that experience – sadness combined with gratitude.

In "Wayagamack," the one work that derives from his visit to the St Maurice Club lodge on Lake Wayagamack, completed on 30 August 1898, Lampman adopts the apostrophizing style of "The Lake in the Forest," written one year before. This piece lacks the immediacy of the earlier wilderness sonnets, but it provides a retrospective commentary on those works. The word "beauty" does not occur in the Temagami sonnets; in "Wayagamack" it (or its adjectival derivative) occurs three times. As the speaker looks out over the pristine landscape, his response is simply: "Beautiful are thy hills, Wayagamack." Raymond Knister once disparaged this line as an example of "weak-kneed banality" calculated to please a certain quality of old-fashioned reader with its outmoded rhetoric.[34] Kathy Mezei, by contrast, quotes the line and the four that follow it to illustrate a refreshing "starkness" of expression in Lampman's wilderness sonnets, with "the ornate frills" and "hackneyed echoes from the English pastoral tradition" now "happily absent."[35] Concerning the one line disdained by Knister, I would argue that the simplicity of the pronouncement, combined with a metric reversal in the first foot (trochaic instead of iambic) to suggest a burst of emotion, successfully conveys the intended lyric joy. What is clear is that the concept of beauty is central. It comes up again where the "twilight solitude" is "beautiful," and once more in a reference to the "austere beauty" of the wilderness, whose remoteness and roughness render it, Lampman imagines, secure from the encroachments of civilization.

It is in this context we see the relevance of this sonnet to the earlier ones. Where the language of the Temagami sonnets remains descriptive or narrative rather than interpretative, the emphasis on beauty in "Wayagamack," similar to them in every other respect, confirms what is no surprise – that the beauty of nature is the implicit theme in those works as well. The forest may be grim, the waters black and cold, the twilight eerily silent, and the storms severe, but the beauty of nature is all-pervasive. The wilderness poems simply extend this philosophy and make the inclusive irony stronger by depicting a version of nature where the extremes are more extreme.

Winter and Death: Two Sonnets

In the summer and fall of 1898, though his health was compromised, Lampman could not have anticipated that his annual attack of "the grippe" (influenza) that winter would become fatal. It is noticeable, however, that in his nature-focused sonnets of these final months, a strong sense of endings and departures is present. In "To the Ottawa," the river, lovingly evoked ("Dear dark-brown waters"), is traced from its wilderness origins past various rapids and other markers to where the "beryl waters" of its "comrade," the "mightier stream," wait to embrace it and carry it on "In that great bridal journey to the sea." In "Sunset," alternately titled "The Passing of the Sun,"[36] the objects tinged with the fading light at sunset – "trees and towers" – are likened to a host who goes to the doorway and, "With yearning and with smiles," takes leave of "the parting guest." And a note of finality is poignantly sounded in "Last Child,"[37] where the speaker observes his six-month-old son's seer-like contemplation of a sunbeam on a wall. As the title phrase makes clear, there will be no more children. We are left with the impression that the "ripest age" of human life, whose wisdom the child seems to possess, may not be in store for the one who chose this title for the poem. More emphatically, a sense of impending death is noticeable in two winter sonnets wherein the attention of the speaker, walking alone at night, is irresistibly drawn from the earth to the star-filled sky, depicted in such a way as to suggest the timeless realm to which all time must succumb.

"The Winter Stars," a Petrarchan sonnet, begins in typical fashion by identifying aspects of landscape and weather: the silence, the "keen wind," and certain ridges in the distance that "glimmer faintly bright," the oxymoron capturing to a nicety the surprising luminescence of the rock reflecting the nocturnal light. At this point an odd juxtaposition is introduced. The ridges resemble "hills on some dead planet hard and gray." As if prompted by this celestial imagery, the speaker looks skyward and encounters the everlastingness of space: "Divinely from the icy sky look down / The deathless stars that sparkle overhead." On one level comforting, the god-like presence of the undying stars, contrasting the hills on the imagined "dead planet," is also eternity's reminder of the transience of all things mortal.

These lines bring us only to the end of line six. Entirely dominating the sestet and reaching back into the octave, as it were, is a sustained meditation on the night sky. The speaker's glance never returns to earth. He identifies stars and constellations by name, notes the mythic significance of those names, observes the resemblance of the northern lights to "mystic dancers in the Arctic air," and closes by emphasizing the grand scale of the celestial scene: "The Dragon strews his bale-fires, and within / His trailing and prodigious loop involves / The lonely Pole Star and the Lesser Bear." On one level this cataloguing can be viewed as nothing more than an eloquent version of the casual noting of familiar objects in the skyscape, as people like to do on starry nights. In the light of the life-death imagery of the opening lines, however, the sky-watching takes on another level of significance. The cold, the wind, the "iron-bound silence" of the winter setting all suggest death, and the speaker's observations of the universe are the surface record of his contemplation of eternity in relation to his own small life.

Just as "April," the first poem in Lampman's first book, apart from the title piece "Among the Millet," stands symbolically as the work that marks the beginning of his career, "Winter Uplands," symbolically and in actuality, marks the end.[38] Bookended by these two poems lie the many depictions of nature that constitute Lampman's exploration of this favoured theme – at once a linear record of a life largely devoted to capturing the multiplicity of natural-world phenomena and a representation, as in *Lyrics of Earth*, of the everlasting annual cycle. And although the one bookend is fresh and forward-looking, on spring's doorstep, and the other, set in a winter's dying dusk, retrospective and redolent of finality, both affirm the joyousness of an encounter with beauty in nature.

Like "The Winter Stars," "Winter Uplands" places the speaker in a cold winter landscape at night, but in this case he is more open and receptive to the range of imagery before him. Having lingered on the snowy landscape, his attention is drawn to the sky, but then returns to earth as he retires from the scene to snowshoe his way home. If "The Winter Stars" is a meditation on eternity, "Winter Uplands" is a final celebration of what it means to be alive, and aware, in the here and now.

Syntactically, this Shakespearian sonnet is unusual in that it consists entirely of descriptive phrases, sometimes expanded with qualifying clauses, without the finality of a single full statement. In numerous poems, Lampman presents only narrative or descriptive information, with thematic content implicit. Here he takes that approach one step further, omitting sentences. Images, conveying perception, are the central feature of his nature poems and, in this last effort, the only feature.

The opening lines, following the pattern established in earlier poems of natural-world observation, such as "Solitude," locate the speaker already present in the scene of significance, receptive and alert:

The frost that stings like fire upon my cheek,
The loneliness of this forsaken ground,
The long white drift upon whose powdered peak
I sit in the great silence as one bound.

The placement of the only statement in this passage ("I sit") in a subordinate clause modifying "drift" has the effect of keeping our attention on the focus of the speaker's attention, even while we see peripherally the seated figure as part of the scene. The cumulative effect of the catalogue of images is to make us shiver – and relax. We are presented with the kind of chilling, sombre landscape that Lampman loves. Its "forsaken ground," as in the sonnet "In November," where "Fast drives the snow, and no man comes this way," is not disturbing. It is engaging. It is conducive to silent meditation.

As the speaker sits perched on his throne of snow, mesmerized by the landscape, he continues to note features of the scene, and as he does, the pace slows. In the first quatrain, three images are presented in rapid succession, with lines one, two, and three all beginning with a definite article to indicate a new point of focus. No strong pause occurs until the semicolon at the end of the quatrain. In contrast, quatrain two consists of only two images, each of which occupies two lines ending with semicolons. The retarding effect allows for an unhurried appreciation of the scene. The speaker's eye travels across the "rippled sheet" of windblown snow extending "for miles" in the distance and then, further still, to the horizon where the city towers "roofed in blue" are softened, becoming a "tender line upon the western red." From here the perspective shifts naturally upwards to an image of greater distance yet, the darkening sky with its "stars that singly, then in flocks appear." Ironically these stars do not strike the speaker as remote or diminishing, but rather,

"So wonderful, so many and so near." They seem almost welcoming. But then, benignly on cue comes the "golden moon to light me home," and the poem closes with a description that concisely conveys Lampman's attitude to nature and its extremes: "The crunching snowshoes and the stinging air, / And silence, frost and beauty everywhere." It is entirely fitting that Lampman's last poetic utterance, with reference to a cold, snowy landscape, is the simple phrase "beauty everywhere."

It is difficult not to view this sonnet in the context of Lampman's life story and for non-literary reasons to interpret the uplands trek as a last visit to a sacred shrine. Even without such associations, however, it is possible to make those connections, for there are allusions in the poem, both personal and literary, that suggest a retracing of old steps. As in "The Lake in the Forest," the speaker is looking back, infusing an intense experience in the present with memories of the past.

The echoes of language and image from Lampman's own poems are numerous. The word "uplands," for example, recalls the "naked uplands" of the sonnet "In November" and the place in "Winter-Store" where the speaker anticipates he will "dream by upland fences." In the Ottawa region within walking distance of the city, there cannot have been many candidates for this destination, so it is likely that these poems refer to the same locale. In one case, the resemblance is unmistakable. In "Winter Hues Recalled," written eleven years before, the speaker remembers snowshoeing across the open country south of the city where, having at sunset "reached / The loftiest level of the snow-piled fields," he found a place to sit and rest:

> Ere yet I turned
> With long stride homeward, being heated
> With the loose swinging motion, weary too,
> Nor uninclined to rest, a buried fence,
> Whose topmost log just shouldered from the snow,
> Made me a seat, and thence with heated cheeks,
> Grazed by the northwind's edge of stinging ice,
> I looked far out upon the snow-bound waste,
> The lifting hills and intersecting forests,
> The scarce marked courses of the buried streams,
> And as I looked lost memory of the frost,

> Transfixed with wonder, overborne with joy.
> I saw them in their silence and their beauty.

This spot corresponds exactly to the location atop the "powdered peak" of a snowdrift where the speaker in "Winter Uplands" pauses to rest, to the extent that the more concise expression of the sonnet makes comparison possible. In "Winter Uplands" the fence is not mentioned – but something must create the drift; the log is not mentioned – but snow alone would make an insubstantial seat. In both poems we have snowshoeing; the frost stings and the speaker's cheeks are heated; the speaker is entranced by the scene before him; and characterizing that scene are similar qualities, with the "silence" and "beauty" (and "frost") of "Winter Uplands" highlighted as well in "Winter Hues Recalled." As the title of the earlier poem indicates, moreover, its focus is on the colours of the scene, mostly associated with the sunset, and in "Winter Uplands" no fewer than six colours are mentioned, progressing roughly from bleak and stark to regal: white, blue, red, silver, violet, and gold. Finally, the moon appears toward the end of both poems – in "Winter Hues Recalled," just "an arc of rose"; in "Winter Uplands," a phase substantial enough to provide light for the return journey – as the speaker's thoughts in each case turn to home. Whether consciously for the last time or not, Lampman is clearly revisiting familiar territory in "Winter Uplands," both geographically and poetically.

The literary echoes in "Winter Uplands" suggest another kind of looking back, as if, around the time when this poem was written, Lampman had been rereading or recalling works by writers he admired that were now fresh in his mind. In the opening line of his sonnet "The Winter Fields," Charles G.D. Roberts makes reference to "frost that bites like steel," an image partly mirrored in Lampman's "frost that stings like fire" in the first line of "Winter Uplands."[39] While Lampman's image is perhaps superior, since fire stings more naturally than steel bites, still, it seems likely that Lampman's phrase is an adaptation of Roberts's. Thoroughly acquainted with Roberts's poems, Lampman at this time would have been familiar with his *Songs of the Common Day*, published in 1893, in which "The Winter Fields" appears. A second stylistic echo occurs toward the end of "Winter Uplands." Not the words but the phrasing in Lampman's "So wonderful, so many and so near" recalls

Matthew Arnold's "So various, so beautiful, so new," from "Dover Beach."[40] Finally, it is revealing that, in a rejected version of the closing couplet, Lampman had written, "The truth of beauty haunts us everywhere," alluding to Keats's famous equation of beauty and truth in "Ode on a Grecian Urn," but as Scott has observed, he changed it for the better in the final version of the poem.[41] What such echoes suggest is that, in addition to revisiting his own earlier writing, Lampman was reflecting back over the poetry that in various ways informed his own, and building into the very fabric of his poem, however subtly and however unconsciously, the traces of that process.

A point of circumstantial irony is that, following Lampman's death on 10 February 1899, his sonnet "The Winter Stars" appeared in the March issue of *Scribner's Magazine*. This is the poem in which the stars remain the focus until the end, with no return home recorded.

The seasons continuously turn, and even though each person's participation in the everlasting cycle is limited by the time-bound nature of all mortality, the participation itself makes possible the experience of involvement in the eternal presence of all nature, achieved through conscious meditation on, or simply exposure to, the objects of perception to be found in nature. Lampman's nature-focused poems both depict and celebrate that experience, and from the perspective of people living in the twenty-first century, with assaults on the natural environment rampant and the effects of largely human-induced climate change increasingly and alarmingly evident, those poems serve as an injunction to preserve an ecosystem – "nature" – on which both the body and the spirit may depend for their survival.

PROGRESS

Through Lapse and Strife

CHAPTER 8

Ideas of Progress

"Archibald Lampman's greatest gift to us," wrote Duncan Campbell Scott in 1943, "is his interpretation of nature in its varied aspects, from the gentleness of spring flowers to the wildness of winter storms." But this was not his only gift: "He had other powers, for he was greatly interested in men and affairs; he has said some memorable things about life and has made plain what was his ideal for the good life. It is no disparagement to say that he was first of all the poet of nature and there is no derogation of that finest of his powers to say that, at the end of his days, he was dealing with life's larger problems and even with heroic action."[1] Four years later, in a letter to Ralph Gustafson, Scott reiterated his point and sought to correct what he regarded as a common misperception. Lampman, he wrote, "was interested in both life and nature and there was no 'confusion' or 'contradiction' in this."[2] Gustafson had argued that Lampman "felt it his poetic duty" to deal with the social sphere in his writing even though his real inclination was toward natural-world description. The resulting push and pull led to a "confusion of purpose and personality" and to "contradiction" in poems such as "At the Ferry," where the speaker, following "some nine stanzas of distinctive power" in which he had closely observed "the Canadian scene," shifts his focus at the end: "I look far out and dream of life." Gustafson found this ending "unconscionable."[3]

Given the number of poems Lampman wrote on the subject, the variety of strategies they embody, and the strong feelings they express, there can be little doubt that Lampman was deeply interested in social issues – the conditions under which people lived and the directions that society might take to ameliorate the deprivations and inequities he saw as characterizing social relations in his time. His social-political outlook had a place in his nature poetry to the extent that exposure to nature had a curative effect that all human beings could benefit from, clearing their perspective and freeing them from materialistic and acquisitive tendencies in a manner consistent with Romanticism and also in harmony with ecologically minded thinkers of our own time. It did not, however, satisfy Lampman to confine his exploration of social issues to this facet of his philosophy of nature. His feelings and convictions were strong and he wished to foreground them in his poetry. The results were by turns angry poetic critiques of greed and corruption, realistic depictions of human suffering in the contemporary world, and prophetic works designed to show by contrast what kind of future, good or ill, might result from the alteration of current trends or their continued pursuit, all written with a view to forwarding the cause of social betterment.

Lampman's social-political poems reflect a journey that took him variously down paths of commitment, struggle and doubt, and reaffirmation. This journey was largely a solo affair; none of his poetic contemporaries incorporated social criticism or protest into their poems to anything like the same extent. But it should not therefore be assumed that Lampman wrote these poems in an ideological vacuum. The late nineteenth century was a period rife with the questioning of religious, philosophical, and social norms, and in conservative Canada the issues of the day were reported and discussed in the popular press to an extent that might surprise the average lay reader today. For this reason, I provide in the present chapter, first, an introduction to those aspects of Lampman's cultural milieu that relate to his social-political poems, and second, an examination of the prose writings wherein he himself engaged with the issues and ideas that in part defined his era. Just as the local climate and terrain were determining factors in the shaping of Lampman's aesthetic in relation to nature poetry, the intellectual climate in which his thoughts developed informed his writing in the social-political sphere.

The Ideological Context for Lampman's Progressivism

Central to Lampman's thinking on social issues was the nineteenth-century concept of progress toward a more enlightened social order in the future, derived in part from the publication of *On the Origin of Species* by Charles Darwin (1809–1882) in 1859, the book that introduced "descent with modification," soon termed "evolution," to a thunderstruck world.[4] The great debate over science and religion, still raging today in some quarters, had begun. I say "in part" because theories of progress that challenged biblical authority were already extant. For example, the French positivist philosopher and founder of the scientific study of human society, or "sociology," Auguste Comte (1798–1857), had earlier sought to replace traditional religion with a "religion of humanity," based on his belief in an ever-advancing human race.[5] And in England, the socialist and reform-minded manufacturer Robert Owen (1771–1858) articulated with great conviction his belief in social progress, as in his 1841 declaration that the social and political conditions of the day, together with advances in science, all "indicate with unerring certainty that a great change is coming over the nations of the earth; and that the wise, the good, the happy existence of man approaches with gigantic strides; in fact, that the millennium is not far distant."[6]

Darwin's role from this standpoint was to provide a scientific basis for a new evolutionary and, for the most part, progressive theory of human development. Darwin himself did not emphasize progress, but stressed rather the adaptation of species to prevailing conditions. His famous incendiary claim that "man is descended from a hairy, tailed quadruped, probably arboreal in its habits,"[7] however, suggests progress, if we may assume that complex social organization, sophisticated language, and artistic, technological, and intellectual attainment qualify as advancements. Certainly the concepts of evolution and progress became closely linked during this period, and the debates over evolution that raged throughout the Western world were focused largely on whether an evolutionary progressivist view could be reconciled with religion.

In Canada, as Carl Berger has observed, "most naturalists in the last four decades of the [nineteenth] century maintained a puzzling reticence on the idea of evolution. After the flurry of reviews of the 1860s, they seldom wrote general appraisals of the theory and kept to themselves whatever spiritual anguish this new view of life may have caused them."[8] (Berger's "naturalists" can be generalized to "scientists" since, in the same context, he mentions Sir William Dawson, a geologist.) The "flurry of reviews," to be sure, as A.B. McKillop has demonstrated, constituted long and carefully considered rebuttals of the Darwinists on the part of scientists such as Dawson and Daniel Wilson, both of whom, as McKillop points out, were "as much men of religion as they were of science."[9] But following the first decade of the Darwinian era, dated from 1859, those members of the scientific community who had given conscientious attention to evolution – with the exception of Dawson, who continued to put forward scientific arguments in defence of a Bible-based theology in many publications through the remainder of the century – did seem to retire from the field.

Where the scientists left off, prominent thinkers such as philosopher John Watson (1847–1939), psychologist and Whitman acolyte Richard Maurice Bucke (1837–1902), and preeminent man of letters Goldwin Smith (1823–1910) stepped in, publishing books and articles that kept the issues raised by the new science in the public eye. For the most part they accepted evolution and either enthusiastically or reluctantly sought to find an accommodation with, or substitute for, traditional religious belief. As Smith, in the reluctant camp, unhappily declared, "the Evolutionary theory is pregnant with momentous truth."[10] Common to the responses of these disparate writers was an adherence to the idea of human progress, founded on the new science, within a loosely theological framework. Their theories involved the advancement of humanity through a series of evolutionary stages toward an ideal state of being: for Watson, one in which distinctions between self and other would become all but extinct and the Christian virtue of selflessness a way of life; for Bucke, a condition of "cosmic consciousness," characterized by a sense of oneness with the universe on the part of the elevated individual; and for Smith, less systematically, a more enlightened condition of being, both intellectual and moral, corresponding to the ideal that reason revealed as the proper goal of all human aspiration.[11]

During his long tenure as resident "Bystander" (his journalistic pseudonym) in Canada, Smith inaugurated and supported a number of periodicals that served to raise the level of public awareness of the issues of the day, among them the *Canadian Monthly and National Review* (1872–78), *Rose Belford's Canadian Monthly* (1878–82), and the *Week* (1883–96). The stated goals of the last-mentioned, whose time line corresponded almost exactly to that of Lampman's writing career, were "to reflect and summarize the intellectual, social and political movements of the day," "to keep ... readers well abreast of the intellectual progress of the age," to be politically "thoroughly independent" and "untrammelled by party connections," and "to further ... the free and healthy development of the nation."[12] In addition to covering scientific, political, and philosophical issues, the *Week* published poetry. Lampman was very familiar with this magazine, praising its publisher (Smith) for setting a high critical standard and for supplying "its pages with so much really excellent matter."[13] His own first publications appeared in those pages, accepted by Charles G.D. Roberts, who served briefly as its editor, followed later by some of his best-known works of social-political protest, including "The Modern Politician" and "To a Millionaire," as well as "Sebastian," a poem in which he portrays the title character, a mill hand, as a visionary worker preparing for his part in an imminent social transformation.[14]

A frequent contributor to all three periodicals and to numerous others both national and international was William Dawson LeSueur (1840–1917), characterized by Smith as "*far* away the best writer in our nation's periodicals on all serious subjects."[15] Lampman's friend J.E. Collins was similarly impressed. In his social-political history *Canada under the Administration of Lord Lorne* (1884), Collins wrote, "Mr. Le Sueur has the 'scientific style'; and his special characteristics are a sober but uncompromising logic, and a facility for apt illustration, all expressed in pure incisive English."[16] These high estimates of LeSueur from his own time are supported in ours by McKillop, who has described the essayist as "arguably Canada's foremost man of letters in the last quarter of the nineteenth century."[17] LeSueur, like Smith, believed in rational inquiry over all else as a means of ascertaining the truth of things. Unlike Smith, he embraced the scientific discoveries of the age with enthusiasm, incorporating the theory of evolution into a progressivist philosophy derived partly from the positivism of Comte, with its belief in humanity and a future age of egalitarian enlightenment, and partly from an idealism that posited reason as the means to the working-out of a divine plan over time. Comte coined the term "altruism" to denote the kind of behaviour that would come to replace egoism.[18] With his Christian perspective, Watson would, and did, take issue with Comte's substitution of humanity for deity. He nevertheless agreed entirely that time and effort would move humanity toward an age of altruistic harmony. LeSueur's genius was to unite these perspectives in what McKillop has described as a blending of Comte and St Paul in "an implicit union of evolutionary naturalism and philosophical idealism."[19]

While such writers as Watson, Bucke, and Smith were in the outer circles of Lampman's world, LeSueur had a much more personal connection. When Lampman arrived in Ottawa in 1883, LeSueur, who was born in the city of Quebec, was well established in the civil service – he worked in the Post Office department into which Lampman had just been hired – and in the cultural life of the city. In 1869 he had been a founding member of the Ottawa Literary and Scientific Society, and the annual reports of that society to the Royal Society of Canada, with which it was affiliated, indicate his active participation.[20] He gave frequent talks, participated in a program of evening classes sponsored by the society, and served nine times as its president, as well as occupying other posts in the intervening years.[21] The Ottawa Literary and Scientific Society lasted until the middle of the First World War, which was also when LeSueur died. It appears he was indeed the animating force behind the organization.

The nineteenth century was an age of societies, and LeSueur was also involved with other groups, including the Ottawa Field Naturalists' Club, founded in 1879, and the Progressive Society of Ottawa. In an account of the inception of the latter group included in his *Unitarians in Canada*, Phillip Hewett provides insight into its ideology. In February of 1877, a group of Canadian Unitarians attempted, not for the first time, to establish a congregation in Ottawa. As soon became apparent, the field of potential members was divided, for "among those who turned out in response to the Unitarian announcements, there were not only liberal Christians, but a substantial number of people who could be described as freethinkers, rationalists or humanists." These people, though allies in being "liberal of spirit," "in another sense ... were competitors for the same constituency to which Unitarianism might have been expected to appeal." Mentioned as one member of the freethinker group was LeSueur. In the end the Unitarians gave up – for the present – but the freethinkers, "now that they had been made aware of each other's existence," decided to form an organization, and in May of that year they inaugurated the Progressive Society of Ottawa, "whose members," according to Hewett, pledged "to pursue truth in the spirit of charity, with a view to its application as far as possible to their own lives, and to its triumph in the world." This society lasted until 1894, after which the Unitarians returned, with a more successful outcome. Both the association of the freethinkers with the Unitarians, and their divergence, presumably on the basis of wanting to distance themselves from the Unitarians' Christian stance, reveal the Progressive Society of Ottawa as a radical presence in that conservative and church-going city.[22]

In addition to publishing articles on science and religion, philosophy, and intellectual history, LeSueur was involved over many years with the movement spearheaded by Sandford Fleming to reform the parliamentary system and eliminate "partyism" from Canadian politics.[23] As well, he took an anti-war position during the First World War, serving as vice-president of the Peace and Arbitration Society, an organization that sought to bring "an honourable end" to the war as quickly as possible. As biographer Clifford G. Holland comments, "LeSueur's stand on the war ... was not popular in some quarters and he was subjected to severe criticism, even though he published no actual articles opposing the war."[24] A final irony, however, is that the greatest controversy of LeSueur's life revolved around a successful legal challenge mounted by the family and associates of William Lyon Mackenzie King to prevent the publication of LeSueur's biography of King's grandfather and namesake, William Lyon Mackenzie, whose liberal legacy LeSueur had challenged.[25]

It did not take long, after his arrival in Ottawa in early 1883, for Lampman to become involved with the various organizations LeSueur was associated with. In March of 1885 he delivered a lecture, "The Modern School of Poetry in England," at a meeting of the Ottawa Literary and Scientific Society, the first of numerous lectures and poetry readings that he gave to this group over the years.[26] It seems highly likely that he also used the society's headquarters as a place to meet friends and discuss the issues of the day. The society's annual reports to the Royal Society of Canada indicate an active reading room containing over 2,600 books and "all the leading newspapers and magazines" of the day and notable for "its popularity as a meeting-place for members." Through this reading room, the society intended doing "all in its power to keep the members informed of current events, and in touch with modern thought."[27] The kinds of gatherings that took place there can be imagined in the light of Connor's account, with reference to the Ottawa of the 1880s and 1890s, of a community of people "typical of their century in intellectual curiosity but superior perhaps to most Canadians, in their serious and persistent interest in the social and political problems." Included in their number were LeSueur; the Reverend Albert Walkley, who in 1900 became the first Unitarian minister in Ottawa; A.C. Campbell, with whom Lampman "would argue vigorously but never be quite converted by him to Henry George's views of single tax"; J.H. Brown, radical socialist and author of *Poems Lyrical and Dramatic*, reviewed by Lampman in the Toronto *Globe*; James Macoun, whose "flaming socialism" Connor supposes had an influence on Lampman; and the poets Wilfred Campbell and Duncan Campbell Scott.[28]

That Lampman developed friendships with LeSueur and others of this group is made clear by numerous references in letters, as where Lampman reports to his wife, "I had Mr. Lesueur in to see me night before last [sic], and John Brown last night," and where Scott relates to an ailing Lampman during the latter's trip to the east coast in 1898, "I see Lesueur occasionally and I know he would like to hear from you."[29] In a later essay, Scott recalls that LeSueur had "much close and friendly intercourse with Lampman" and took a "special interest in Lampman and befriended him whenever possible."[30] The three people who coordinated the effort to publish Lampman's *Poems* in 1900 with a view to generating support for his family, and who identified themselves as concerned friends in a circular they sent out to solicit subscriptions for the book, were Scott, S.E. Dawson, and LeSueur.[31] On or near the fourteenth anniversary of Lampman's death, a "Lampman evening" was held at a public hall in Ottawa, attended by a full house, according to Scott, despite "no public invitation," and among those who gave talks were LeSueur, Brown, and Scott.[32] On 23 September 1917 LeSueur died, and at his funeral, presided over by the Unitarian minister Albert Lazenby, a poem by Lampman – the last sonnet of the three-sonnet sequence "The Largest Life" – was read, having been provided for the occasion by Scott, who commented in a letter to Lazenby, "I thought you could not use for quotation a more appropriate poem than the one I enclose; it was written by a friend of Dr. Le Sueur's, Archibald Lampman, and I think it expresses very clearly Dr. Le Sueur's faith."[33]

Despite Lampman's stated view of how "utterly destitute of all light and charm" the cultural climate of Canada was in his time, leaving the writer with no support beyond "himself and nature,"[34] it would appear that Ottawa of the 1880s and 1890s offered him some degree of intellectual stimulation. And it was within, and subject to the influence of, this social environment that his social-political outlook took shape and developed, just as it was within, and subject to the influence of, its geographical setting that his outlook on nature evolved. Both his poetry and prose, to the extent that they engage with the issues of human destiny and social justice, reflect this influence. It is of course the poems that are of prime importance, particularly as Lampman may fairly be adjudged the first accomplished poet in Canada to articulate a radical social vision. The prose provides insight into the theoretical foundation on which he built those poems. As an essayist, he is confident and optimistic, sometimes strident, in his pronouncements; as a poet, he is concerned, as always, with the personal dimension of experience, and his treatment is at once more visceral, more strategic, and more complex.

Prose Writings on Progress and Social Issues

Lampman first sets out his progressivist views in the course of challenging what he sees as the amorality of the Pre-Raphaelite poets, mainly Rossetti and Swinburne, in his lecture "The Modern School of Poetry in England."[35] To counter the destructive elevation of passion over reason on the part of these writers, he offers the following as a guiding principle of criticism, which according to Scott can be taken as a statement of "Lampman's creed":[36]

> Life is not a dreary thing. Human beings are not mere hopeless play things in the hands of chance, utter[ly] governed by a multitude of passions, that must mar and twist them, befoul them or beautify them as they will. Human nature may be represented by the ancient Pan – half human and half beast – but the human is the

mightier part, and the whole is ever striving to be divine. The main current of the human spirit through many changes, and many falls is setting eternally toward a condition of order and divine beauty and peace.[37]

In opposition to a philosophy that would see human beings as forever subject to their baser instincts in a directionless world in which no inherent values give meaning to behaviour – by implication, a world of violence and lust, war and domination – Lampman sides with the idealism of progressivist thought, which is, he asserts, in tune with the "main current of the human spirit." The members of the "modern school," he suggests, "have been led almost to glorify and treat as things divine some of the very passions, which it has been the aim of social progress to soften and command." While he cannot resist praising the artistry of the Pre-Raphaelites – their "*glowing* delight in nature" and their innovations in word choice and metrics, "the sweetest mysteries of sound" – he predicts future obscurity for them on the grounds that their ideas run counter to the forward movement of human society. In suggesting that progress may be impeded by "many changes, and many falls," however, Lampman allows for the possibility that the path of social progress will not be smooth or straight.[38]

Pronouncements of this sort recur in Lampman's literary criticism. In one lecture he dismisses Byron as having a "disturbing influence" inconsistent with the "divine progress" of human nature, and in another praises Keats for his expressions of beauty that "cannot disturb" but rather are "in harmony with the indestructible impulse of the general soul of humanity toward love and knowledge and peace."[39] The phrase "indestructible impulse" would seem to suggest that progress was as inevitable as gravity. As certain of his poems indicate, however, Lampman was not always so sure of this. For him – and perhaps for the age – the issue of progress was, exactly like religion, one of faith. There was no doubt that society should advance toward a condition of greater harmony, but whether it would do so was a different question, for it depended on human agency. Lampman wrote poems expressing both views. The difficulty did not have to do with what was right, but only, and distressingly, whether human beings could be counted on to do what was right.

The *Globe* column "At the Mermaid Inn" provided Lampman with an outlet for many of his ideas and opinions on contemporary issues. Passing references in several of his contributions indicate that progressivism had by 1892–93, when the column ran, become well established in his mental makeup. In one article, he speaks of the emancipation of women in the context of progressive social change already under way: "Of the many inspiring phenomena that make this teeming age wonderful and noteworthy, the most hopeful and the most significant is the change which is so rapidly taking place in the social position of women."[40] In another piece on the same subject, he responds sympathetically to an article, "Are We Really So Bad?" taking issue with two female commentators who had written negatively about the changes in women's behaviour inspired by feminism:

> I cannot understand the objection that many women have to the growth of wider tastes, more robust activities, and freer manners among their own sex. It is absolutely necessary that this change should take place if the race is to reach its noblest and fullest development, and if, as in our time, the new state of things leads to some extravagances and unseemliness, that is simply the effect of a natural reaction from the condition of stunted growth and "intolerable ennui" which were the boast of the past.[41]

It is true that Lampman idealizes the new woman in a way that later feminism might wish to critique – the women of the age of "our children's children" will be "superhumanly beautiful, superhumanly wise" – but among the range of opinions that were prevalent in his day, his views were decidedly of the progressive sort, which is how he presents them.

On a subject dear to his heart, that of work and leisure, Lampman observed that attitudes were changing in favour of shorter working hours, and this, too, he interpreted in the context of progress. Objecting to the prevalent view "that the mass of mankind were only made to be 'worked,' to be kept at the mill from dawn till sunset," he suggests that this philosophy is not held in southern countries and that "even among us the opinion is growing, and growing fast, that it is not absolutely essential that a man should have to work laboriously for six, eight, ten, or even fourteen hours out of the twenty-four."[42] In these comments, not only is a progressivist perspective noticeable, but also a proletarian one, as it is again where he notes the disparity according to which "a certain portion of the people are compelled by an irresistible force to carry out ... production" while "a large other portion sits by in comparative idleness and enjoys the spectacle." These conditions, however, were about to change. "The new idea is that every man shall work, that the work done shall be no more than necessary, and that in consequence the whole may be divided up into very moderate apportionments for each citizen." The socialist thinking here is reinforced by Lampman's statement that "the time will come, no matter how many generations from now, when every man on earth will be obliged to do his share of the world's work, but no more than his share, and that share will probably keep him employed for three or four hours a day, with frequent holidays."[43]

Even where social advancement is not the main subject, references to the idea of progress abound in Lampman's prose. In one instance, writing from Boston of the cultural heritage of the city, he relates in passing that "it may be that when the social movement, which the increasing strain of the present condition of things is bringing daily nearer, really begins, it will proceed from Boston, just as the anti-slavery movement did forty years ago." In another, on "the servant question," he asserts that unequal relations between human beings are no longer tenable and comments, "Democracy advances rapidly, and not only liberty, but fraternity and equality also are becoming more and more the sine qua non of a contented human race."[44]

Lampman perceived in society a need for change and also saw signs that change was under way. At the same time, his casual pronouncements remain vague as to the specific terms of his beliefs, standing more as public declarations of a progressive outlook. In two key prose pieces, however, he sets out in more detail his understanding of, in the first case, the ideological context within which the next stage of social advancement will occur, and in the second, the direction in which he would like to see it go, the first being philosophical and the second political.

In the "Mermaid Inn" for 8 April 1893, Lampman writes a short essay – actually a long single paragraph – that, according to Scott, "conveys a faith that he held most firmly and which in truth actuated his thinking and influenced his outlook on human affairs."[45] Carl Ballstadt has suggested that this piece reflects "one of the major studies of the evolution of a new intellectual, creative conception or consciousness by another Canadian, Dr. Richard Maurice Bucke, in his *Cosmic Consciousness: A Study in the Evolution of the Human Mind* (1901)."[46] (Lampman did not live long enough to have seen the publication of this book, but Bucke's study *Man's Moral Nature*, in which he sets out the theory behind *Cosmic Consciousness*, appeared in 1879.) In his "Mermaid Inn" essay, Lampman outlines two views of the human condition, one bleak and hopeless and the other – his own – forward-looking and optimistic. His strategy, following the logic of certain of his own sonnets, such as "Earth – the Stoic," is to present in the "octave" as discouraging a view as possible and then in the "sestet" to turn the tables with the result that, seen from another angle, the seemingly hopeless dilemma is miraculously resolved.

To introduce the negative view, Lampman loosely quotes "one of those terrible sayings" that may be attributed to either the disillusioned egoist or the disillusioned philosopher – "that life is one long disease, and this world nothing but a gigantic hospital, and [German poet and essayist Heinrich] Heine added that the great doctor is death." The egoist will have reached this conclusion by finding at the end of self-indulgence only "emptiness and spiritual annihilation," and the philosopher by examining "the desperate obliquity of human institutions and the hopeless inaptitude of human character," implicating both society and the individual. To illustrate the desperate state of the human condition, Lampman invites the reader to consider the unhappy parade of humanity in evidence at any busy street corner – "the multitude of faces unceasing in their variety, but all marked with the struggle and care of the crooked propensities of life," some tired or sick, some "hardened, withered or distorted with the countless maladies of the soul, greed, ambition, lust, drunkenness and many another," and scraping the bottom of the barrel, "some even that will fright you with a nameless suggestion of vileness and loathsome degradation" – presumably a reference to thieves, prostitutes, pimps, and the like. With this spectacle in mind, Lampman suggests, the reader will be ready to agree with the nihilistic statement with which he began.

Having set out the problem, Lampman executes his "turn" with a simple "But, patience!" The solution, he claims, is already evident, although only in embryonic form. Again appealing to the reader's own experience for confirmation, he asks rhetorically, "may we not perceive the dawning of a new hope? Have we not already noted the beginning and spreading of a new conception of the higher life – a conception which has not yet reached the masses of mankind, but we certainly hope may do so eventually, though not in our day?" The implication is that the old conceptions of the higher life – a phrase that meant for Lampman and his contemporaries the life of moral and spiritual exertion – have become outmoded, leaving humanity spiritually destitute and unable to find a remedy for the ills already enumerated. Loss of faith, then, is at the root of the problem, and therefore the new conception of the higher life has a new ideological foundation – science. As Lampman explains, "This conception is the child of science, reinforced by the poetry that is inherent in the facts of the universe and all existence. Thus reinforced, the conception is a religious one." (The title of Lampman's most famous poem, interestingly, is identical to the main title of John Tyndall's popular manual *Heat: A Mode of Motion*, first published in 1863 – perhaps a deliberate importation of a scientific term to reflect "the poetry that is inherent in the facts of the universe.") It is religious in a new way, however. It does not, like the "ancient creeds," "trust for its effects to any system of post-mortem rewards and punishments." Rather, its power rests on a broadening of consciousness with respect to the workings of life and the universe:

> It comes to those whom the new knowledge has made acquainted with the vast facts and secrets of life, arming them with a breadth and majesty of vision which withers away from the soul the greeds and lusts and meannesses of the old, narrow and ignorant humanity. The small ambitions and petty passions of this world seem infinitesimal indeed to him who once enters into the new conception and lives, as it were, in the very presence of eternity.

To have insight into the nature of mortal existence and the workings of the universe, Lampman implies, is to be raised to a new level of being, not only intellectually, but also morally, since the enlightened person understands selfhood in the context of the larger perspective, and spiritually, since, in a kind of scientific natural theology, the divine is revealed in the truths of the physical world. In terms of how the new outlook relates to progress, Lampman concludes by saying that although "this new spiritual force" has thus far affected only a few, "its growth is sure," and ultimately, "with the steady extension and dissemination of culture, from mass to mass, it may in the end work its way into the mental character and spiritual habit of all mankind," at which point "the world will become less and less a hospital, and the old cankerous maladies gradually decline and disappear."

Notwithstanding its rhetorical hyperbole, this essay is animated by strong conviction, complementing rather than contradicting Lampman's philosophy of nature. Discoursing on beauty in nature in a passage quoted earlier, Lampman asserts, "The happiest man is he who has cultivated to the utmost the sense of beauty." For this person, "every moment comes ... laden with some unique enjoyment, every hour is crowded with a multitude of fleeting but exquisite impressions. If health and a reasonable destiny attend him he cannot be otherwise than happy; pessimism for him is impossible."[47] The same point is made about those people "whom the new knowledge has made acquainted with the vast facts and secrets of life, arming them with a breadth and majesty of vision which withers away from the soul the greeds and lusts and meannesses of the old, narrow and ignorant humanity." For them, too, pessimism is impossible.

In addition to echoing his own statements about beauty in nature, Lampman's ideas about the "new conception of the higher life" closely resemble those of LeSueur, who in discussing "the spirit of intellectual liberty" in opposition to doctrinal belief, which he styles as skepticism, characterizes the modern truth-seeker as the true optimist: "He whose thought has been emancipated may find himself compelled to deny, or at least to question, many things commonly accepted, but the general tone of his mind is not negative, but positive. In a certain sense he feels as though he could believe all things, for he is prepared to welcome truth from any quarter, and the universe seems to him full of truth, while error dwindles away to the most insignificant dimensions."[48] It is LeSueur's view that the gradual displacement of "error" by "truth" will lead to a future societal harmony. As he says, "faith in reason and faith in progress are sentiments so closely allied that they are seldom seen apart." Citing an observation by the French philosopher Edgar Quinet, he adds, "what the mightiest church the world ever saw failed to accomplish – the unification of humanity – science, which is nothing but embodied reason, is every day hastening to a consummation."[49] By adopting ideas like these, Lampman extended his optimistic view of the effects of natural-world contemplation to a progressivist philosophy based on the revelations of science, expressed in such diverse poems as "Alcyone," in which an awareness of the immense distances between ourselves and the stars, while diminishing one's sense of self-importance, expands one's consciousness to encompass the vast reaches of space, and "The Largest Life," which asserts, "There is a beauty at the goal of life, / A beauty growing since the world began."

The second prose piece, focusing more on the social-political directions Lampman believed would constitute progress, is his untitled essay on socialism, written circa 1895.[50] It has sometimes been suggested that Lampman was merely a "mild" or "pale" socialist, and only for a brief period in the mid-1890s.[51] There is, however, considerable evidence to indicate a firm and lasting commitment to socialist politics on Lampman's part. The anti-capitalist stance evident in the 1887 poem "Freedom" would suggest an early beginning. Numerous references in "At the Mermaid Inn," such as where he outlines, and shows sympathy and support for, the socialist policies of contemporary New Zealand, reveal continued engagement in 1892–93.[52] The statement "He describes himself as a socialist" included in the entry on Lampman in the 1898 handbook *The Canadian Men and Women of the Time* would appear to extend the time frame further.[53] And the information given in an obituary notice – the one Milton Acorn "read … aloud in a voice flowing with intimations of his own passing"[54] – suggests that Lampman continued to promote socialism until the end of his life. The anonymous writer of this notice, having said that Lampman "was formerly a member of the Fabian Society of Ottawa, and was one of the leading Socialists of the city," reports: "One of the last views Mr. Lampman expressed with reference to Canadian nationality and the purpose of a national life was that 'Canada has an opportunity of giving the world an object lesson in the adoption of socialism as a form of government, which would not only make us a nation, but give us a unique place in the world's history.'"[55] It is also the case that Lampman included in *Alcyone*, the proofs of which he had just completed correcting when he died, poems that reflected his socialist outlook, notably "The Land of Pallas." As Connor observes, "the ideal end of socialism was always in his mind."[56] Although Scott seemed to change his mind about the nature and extent of Lampman's socialism, writing in 1925 that for a short period Lampman "belonged to a group of friends who were playing lightly with socialistic ideas,"[57] the account he gives in his 1900 memoir, when his memories were the freshest and before his own political attitudes had shifted, is perhaps the most accurate. "In the wider politics," Scott relates, "he was on the side of socialism and reasonable propaganda to that end, and announced his belief and argued it with courage whenever necessary."[58] In his 1947 letter to Gustafson, Scott declares that Lampman "was a confirmed socialist of the Fabian type, the only coherent association anywhere in the English-speaking world."[59]

The Fabian Society, having formed in London in 1884, no doubt had a powerful influence on Lampman and his socialist friends, who evidently had inaugurated their own chapter in Ottawa in the early 1890s. In 1889, marking the one hundredth anniversary of the French Revolution, the society published *Fabian Essays*, with contributions by seven members, including George Bernard Shaw and Sidney Webb, articulating their belief in social progress, their conceptualization of progress as the gradual displacement of capitalist disparity and exploitation by a new social order of equality and a proper standard of living for all, and their dedication to educating and advocating for their cause. The book was a runaway success, with numerous editions selling out in short order, so it seems altogether likely that copies made their way to the reading room of the Ottawa Literary and Scientific Society.[60] D.M.R. Bentley has suggested that "The Land of Pallas" was influenced by *Fabian Essays*,[61] and certainly Lampman's pronouncements in his essay on socialism and elsewhere seem inspired at least in part by the Fabians' radical, if gradualist, ideology of societal transformation. It is the case, however, that the obituary writer's statement that Lampman was "formerly" a member of the Ottawa Fabian group sits somewhat uncomfortably with Scott's 1947 avowal that his friend was a "confirmed" Fabian. It may be that the Fabians' principle of gradualism and peaceful evolutionary rather than revolutionary change – not clear in their early years but well established by 1889[62] – became less important to Lampman than the necessity for change, by whatever means.

In some ways the most outspoken of his social-political pronouncements, Lampman's essay on socialism nevertheless reflects ideas he expressed elsewhere in his writing, supporting and extending those ideas. The essay – or perhaps it was intended as a speech – begins with a rousing declaration:

> The cause of Socialism is the cause of love and hope and humanity: the cause of competition is the cause of anarchy, pessimism and disbelief in a possible manhood for human nature just emerging from its barbarous infancy. The human soul is the highest thing of which we have any knowledge. If this soul is incapable of ever adapting itself to conditions of equality, community and brotherhood, then had we better never have been born, for reason, the capacity for faith, and the love of beauty were given to us in vain.[63]

The reference here to "hope" in opposition to "pessimism" echoes the statement in his "new conception" essay that "a new hope" will displace "the greeds and lusts and meannesses of the old, narrow and ignorant humanity," as well as his earlier declaration about the state of mind of the person who is appreciative of beauty in nature, for whom "pessimism ... is impossible." The larger context for "hope" is that of progress, and Lampman makes clear that he conceives of socialism as being consistent with the evolutionary development of the "human soul." But he also emphasizes that progress could be thwarted. With its vehemence and emotional appeal, his essay seems largely motivated by the desire to promote the cause of socialism in the face of opposition or indifference in large sectors of humanity. Finally, Lampman's claim that human beings, if they cannot adapt themselves to a society of socialist values, would be better off never to have existed, is a modified version of the bleak outlook attributed to the despairing egoist and philosopher in the "new conception" essay, to which the new conception itself is the antidote. In that essay, the nihilistic view prompted by perceptions of human misery and degradation would be justified if it were not for the saving grace of the new outlook; in the present essay, that same nihilism would again be justified if the new understanding failed to inspire actual change. Lampman is arguing, in effect, that at this stage of evolution it is the responsibility of human beings to create a more equitable, socialist society. The further entrenchment of capitalism would constitute a subversion of destiny, a failure to develop.

Lampman goes on to challenge the argument that the unequal treatment of human beings under the present system is the unavoidable result of the workings of economics. He refers with scorn (and mocking capitals) to "the Law of Supply and Demand." The idea that human beings should, on the basis of such a rationale, suffer unemployment or inadequate employment and in many cases be reduced to "conditions of unspeakable horror and degradation" fills him with outrage. Human beings, he reminds the reader or listener, are "the noblest product of the forces of life." To justify the perpetuation of their suffering with an argument of economic necessity is a travesty of false reasoning. "What a desperate piece of mockery this is to the man with a human heart watching the misery of the world," he states, "yet the economist speaks to us without a smile." The so-called "law," he insists, is nothing more than a chimera, like the mysterious force that, in dreams, holds our hands back as we reach for something; it is the "baseless nightmare of the human race."[64]

At the root of the problem, Lampman argues, is the "wrong and unhuman principle" by which one person can, through private ownership, "take possession of the common earth" and subjugate others to a kind of slavery through the power of wealth. Lampman's indignation, again, is patent where he describes how the individual "who has land and money" – he first wrote "capitalist" – "takes possession of the strength and intelligence of men who have none." He allows that the relationship between capitalist and worker "may not sound so very bad in the ears of those who possess land and money and are bred to this system," then tellingly adds, "but look at the result." It is the human cost that irrevocably tips the scales, the "frightful inequality" between "accumulating pride and luxury" on the one hand and "accumulating vice and misery" on the other.[65] As in his "new conception" essay, Lampman is troubled by "vice," a character flaw, but as he makes clear in the present essay, the "brutalizing vices" to which people succumb are "begotten of" the "misery and despair" of deprivation.[66]

There are, Lampman asserts, just "two alternatives" for society, "the competitive plan and the collective." Since the one has been tried and not worked – "it has led to the inequality, the injustice, the misery that you see" – it is time to try the other, based on justice and "a generous estimate of the capabilities of the human soul." At this point he returns to the high rhetoric of all or nothing: "If this should fail then we shall have to agree with the pessimists and acknowledge that it is all a mistake; that life is a failure and not worth living." If progress cannot be made, then a nihilistic response seems most appropriate.[67]

With respect to how the transformation to socialism might be achieved, Lampman takes the view of the Fabians, predicting that the change "will work itself out gradually and intelligently from possibility to possibility." At the same time, he observes with equanimity that there are other means closer to revolution than to evolution. His forecast that there will be "probably no violence of any great account in connection with Socialism" is not calculated to reassure an audience more concerned with social stability than social transformation. In considering the possibility that without "gradual ameliorative changes" there could indeed be social upheaval, Lampman writes with cool composure.[68] It is when he addresses the subject of people's suffering and the desperate need for change that his tone heats up. For society's disparities, he declares, there is "no cure ... under the compet[it]ive system, none whatever." Since this is the case, "[t]he evil can only increase; and unless the humane social theory prevails, it will increase to the exploding point, when the conditions of life can no longer be borne."[69] Lampman takes the stance of an advocate who sees that, one way or another, the change must come.

The displacement of capitalist by socialist values, Lampman believed, would be consistent with the evolutionary progress of humankind, since capitalism was retrograde, amounting to institutionalized inequity, and socialism, founded on humane principles of public ownership, collective rights, and equal opportunity for all, was in tune with the ideals that constituted the projected end point of the evolutionary trajectory that science had illuminated. Highly disturbing, however, was the possibility that what science and nature sanctioned, humanity would fail to realize. Lampman's poetry on this subject ranges across the field of possibilities, sometimes expressing "faith" in humanity's forward movement toward an ideal end of "order and divine beauty and peace," but often revealing deep misgivings about human potential and expressing in various ways, hortatory and prophetic, the need for societal change. Neither does he exclude himself from the host of those who are subject to conflicting thoughts and feelings about these issues, and in certain poems he explores his own doubts as well as his personal struggle to follow the isolating path of commitment. Lampman's essays on "a new conception of the higher life" and on socialism give confident expression to his convictions about science and religion, progress, and social rectification; his poetry explores a complex personal engagement with those same issues.

CHAPTER 9

Poems of Progress

It is sometimes argued that Lampman's retreat to nature and his progressivist outlook constitute what L.R. Early has called "one of the deepest rifts in his imagination," compromising the integrity of his work overall.[1] This view would appear to rest on two assumptions: first, that natural-world primitivism cannot be squared with evolutionary idealism, and second, that a progressivist must take the view that everything will always improve regardless of what people may do to advance or impede the process. These assumptions, I suggest, are not a good fit for the progressivism we encounter in Lampman. Nevertheless, in turning now to his social-political poems, it is just as well to consider the relationship between the themes of nature and progress.

On the face of it, a conflict may appear in the sense that the retreat to nature is a move "backwards" to an Arcadia-like golden age of harmony, while the poems of progress are concerned with advancement toward what LeSueur described as "that golden age of the future to which all the noblest minds of the present generation instinctively look forward, and the hope of which grows stronger in the breast of humanity with each succeeding year."[2] Certainly Lampman would sometimes see in nature the residual traces of an imaginary idyllic past, as in "Favorites of Pan," where he interprets the springtime voices of the frogs mythically as a surviving remnant of Pan's music. However, to see this as anti-progressive would be to take the poet's mythologizing too literally. Milton in *Paradise Lost* references classical mythology repeatedly and with deep respect, but the poem's theology is never in question. It must be remembered, moreover, that Lampman's visions of Arcadia are only one aspect of his complex interpretation of nature and, further, that the natural world he loved was frequently not idyllic in aspect. What is true is that Lampman sometimes saw great lapses in progress and sometimes despaired of humanity's willingness or ability to effect progressive change. The poems that express a complete confidence in progress thus may be seen as contradicting those that entertain doubts, but the contradictions are those of shifting degrees of certitude or faith within the same belief system.

The larger question to consider is whether the two ideals of natural-world harmony (associated with the past) and social harmony (envisioned in the future) can be seen as complementary. In Lampman's view, they could. This is why he could describe human nature as "working forward slowly surely and ever infinitely nearer to what is pure and noble and beautiful" and, in the same essay, praise Wordsworth for his "calm and joyous devotion to wild nature in her freshness and strength and eternal youth."[3] Put simply, contact with beauty in nature clears one's head, lifts one out of the petty realm of worldly concerns, and restores one's sense of purpose. It predisposes one to believe in the possibility of creating a better world in the social sphere. And the reflection (or creation) of beauty in art is itself consistent with humanity's advancement in the sense that beauty "ennobles the heart."[4]

"Man's Future"

Lampman gives at once his most serene declaration of faith in progress and his clearest indication of how both nature and humanity may be understood in relation to progress in "Man's Future," a kind of reverse sonnet of rhyming couplets in which the sestet comes first. Completed on 1 May 1898, this poem dates from the period of general tranquility that followed the storm and stress of the mid-1890s. It seems fitting that, even though the belief it conveys is essentially that which Lampman articulated in prose more than a decade earlier in lectures for the Ottawa

Literary and Scientific Society, it was only now that he could give that belief such placid expression in a poem, since poetry and not prose is where the struggles of Lampman's imagination are recorded.

The logic of the poem is simple. Moved by the beauty of a nearby elm tree "towering at its perfect ease," the speaker asks himself if any human being could "match its clean perfection." The answer is no since, unlike humanity, "that noble and harmonious tree / Fulfills its law of being utterly." Rather than exhort people to action or lament their failures, however, he contents himself, in the closing octave, with a far-off vision of human perfection:

> What nature meant the elm for from of yore
> Even now it is, and time can do no more.
> But man is still unfinished: many an age
> Must bear him slowly onward stage by stage
> In long adjustment, – mind and flesh and soul
> Finally balanced to a rhythmic whole,
> Installed at last in his appointed place,
> Divine in beauty and undreamed of grace.

Although humankind, with its intellectual, physical, and spiritual (and moral) dimensions, will require further growth, the speaker is confident that the "long adjustment" will be made. The word "must" is not a directive. But as the words "many an age," "long," and "finally" imply, the process will be lengthy. Whatever disillusionment Lampman has experienced with respect to the human potential for achieving betterment is here channelled into an acceptance of the large time frame required to bring about the necessary changes. He takes comfort in the idea that a glorious destiny awaits the species, even if not the individual alive today. Redemptive concepts can take many forms – immortality of the soul, immortality of the body brought back to life, a return to life in a different form, a merging of the self with the energy of the universe. Here Lampman adopts the positivist belief in a future human society that has reached the promised land of a joyous maturity as his agent of redemption. That the speaker is untroubled by the remoteness of the event reinforces the idea that faith in "man's future" does indeed have the power to assuage the spiritual yearnings of those who live here in the unfinished past of human history.

"The City" and "The Better Day"

By contrast, angry impatience is the mood of two earlier poems: "The City," a pessimistic lyric that questions whether the current trend of society's relentless preoccupation with commerce and frivolous diversions can ever be altered; and "The Better Day," a terse piece of rhetoric that strongly implies a negative answer. First published in the *Week* in 1892 and included in *Alcyone* in 1899, these poems apparently had a lasting significance for Lampman, valued, perhaps, as warnings and incitements.[5] I doubt Lampman could have written them in the last few years of his life; that he still wished to publish them, however, indicates an ongoing belief in the importance of the issues they raise.

Framed by almost identical stanzas in which the speaker, apostrophizing the city itself, rhetorically asks, "Shall never an hour bring pity, / Nor end be found for care," "The City" imparts a feeling of desperation. It is the relentlessness of the city's pursuits that is most troubling – an unstoppable momentum. In its purely physical aspect, the city is beautiful, with its towering buildings "high in heaven" and its rivers winding at their base. "Thou art fair as the hills at morning," the speaker declares, offering high praise; "And the sunshine loveth thee." The cityscape looks glorious in the early light. The "soul" of the city, however, is "no longer free," for the "curses of gold" have enslaved its inhabitants. "One madness" has infected them; "One battle blind and shrill" preoccupies them. Capitalism has entirely taken over, dominating all aspects of life. Perhaps this would not be so bad, as Lampman observes in his essay on socialism, if it were not for the human cost. As it is, crowds rush by in a trance, so intent on their business that they "neither laugh nor weep," and the noise of industry and transport disturbs the peace of the urban setting continuously: "Through doors that darken never / I hear the engines beat."

The repeated "I see" and "I hear" in this poem have exactly the opposite effect of the same phrases in poems like "Among the Timothy," where they signify the sensory absorption of curative natural-world imagery. Here the senses admit the horrors of the non-stop clatter and shriek of industry into one's consciousness. And of no comfort are the entertainment night spots, where "the guest-hall boometh and shrilleth, / With the dance's mocking sound." For the workers in its thrall, this is a world of hopeless servitude, one in which "toil hath fear for neighbour" and life has become "one long labour, / Till death or freedom come." The reference to "freedom" is the only positive note in the poem. It hints that a social transformation could alleviate the suffering, but the ending reinforces the impression of a dehumanizing system deeply entrenched. The angry outburst "Canst thou not rest," repeated in the closing stanza from stanza one, evokes an image of society, both oppressors and oppressed, incapable of pausing in the interest of social betterment.

A less complicated poem, omitting topical references as well as any use of the first person singular, but effective in its brevity and directness, is "The Better Day." The speaker begins by listing in quick succession a host of sins to which humanity is susceptible, all of which, functioning as "choking sands" that "Perplex the stream of life" or as "cankers of the loftier will," impede progress. The imagery of suffocation and disease suggests a corruption of the norm. A healthy humanity would pursue its path to betterment, but in its blighted condition seems incapable of such action.

The fear that humanity will fail to realize its potential for good and will succumb to corruption inspires a lament that comprises the final three stanzas of this five-stanza poem – looking forward, but mourning in advance the loss of the enlightened future that never will be:

> Oh, shall there be no space, no time,
>   No century of weal in store,
> No freedom in a nobler clime,
>   Where men shall strive no more?

The question invites a positive refutation of its dismal outlook, but the negative phrasing – the word "no" occurs five times in four lines – casts doubt on that possibility, assuming a reluctance or disinclination on the part of those who could negate the negation. The next stanza envisions what will be lost, asking, is this what the future does not hold – a place "Where self shall be the unseen part, / And human kindness all?" The gloomy alternative to "the better day" is described in a final question – will "we" simply "cease to rave" and disappear, having found love only in our dreams and "peace but in the grave?"[6] Oblivion is the only "better day" that the melancholy speaker sees humanity as capable of achieving. As Richard Arnold puts it, "the ironic conclusion is that there is *no* better day coming."[7] That is the clear implication of this poem, but it is not Lampman's last word on the subject.

With its focus on sins – "Pride and hot envy and cold greed" – and on the conflict between, essentially, good and evil, "The Better Day" has an evangelical ring. The salvation that seems in doubt is not supernatural; rather, it is the apotheosis of a society evolved beyond its present state. Since, for Lampman, humanity was in the process of working out its own redemption – or of failing to do so – the religious and the secular are blended in his thinking. Lampman was not concerned, as many thinkers in the near future would be, that life had no meaning; life had meaning; the horror for him was that humanity might permanently disassociate itself from that meaning, in effect destroying what by nature was to be its "better day." The strategic purpose behind poems of such negativity, then, can be seen as one of provocation – to spark awareness and by that means inspire a will to change the direction in which society was headed.

Offsetting the negative view of present-day society in both "The City" and "The Better Day" is a faintly sounded note of nostalgia in the former poem. The soul of the city is "no longer free," implying a time when it was free. Listening to the "clash and clang" of the cymbals in the music hall, the speaker laments that "the days are gone like a vision / When the people wrought and sang." The purpose of the poem, however, is not to turn the tables on progressivism by depicting a bleak future and a rosy past. For Lampman, progress was the rule, consistent with an ordered and in some way divinely informed universe; but he recognized that progress was not a smooth road to the future, even when he was not considering the more dire possibility of ultimate failure on the part of humanity to achieve its destiny. He believed, moreover, that certain societies in the past were enviable in living a simpler life, more in tune with nature. Thus a primitivism is part of his intellectual make-up, as it would almost have to be in a poet so responsive to the pristine beauty of nature in wilderness settings. The challenge was for humanity to preserve or regain the innocence of its youth and to carry that quality into the more complex arena of present-day society and on into the future.

That Lampman could be nostalgic for the past and at the same time adhere to a progressivist view of human development is nicely illustrated in the narrative poem "Phokaia," about a sea-going people who lived in the Ionian city of Foça in present-day Turkey. A nostalgia for the simple virtues of the Hellenistic past is evident from the start:

> I will tell you a tale of an ancient city of men,
> > Of men that were men in truth:
> The world grows wide now; 'twas smaller and goodlier then,
> > And the busy shores of the little islanded sea
> > > Were filled with beautiful folk,
> A people of children and sages, untouched by the yoke,
> > Eager, far-venturing, fearless and free,
> > > In the pride and glory of youth.

The narrator goes on to give an account of how the Phokaians, forced from their city home by the aggressive Persians and denied succour by the people of Chios, resolve to resettle on the island of Kyrnos, at which point the following lines of commentary appear:

> For stormy times and ruined plans
> Make keener the determined will,
> And Fate with all its gloomy bans
> Is but the spirit's vassal still:
> And that deep force, that made aspire
> Man from dull matter and the beast,
> Burns sleeplessly a spreading fire
> By every thrust and wind increased.

In this passage, more in the spirit of Tennyson than Homer, we recognize the concept of evolutionary progress, suggesting that, although advancement may be difficult, and the loss of a simpler past regrettable, the two positions do not cancel each other out. To use the analogy implicit in "Phokaia," nostalgia for the past need not be at odds with a belief in progress any more than the fond recollection of childhood is at odds with the idea that only in maturity can one experience the richest and profoundest joys of life.

"The Clearer Self" and "To the Prophetic Soul"

Two poems in which the progressivist outlook of "Man's Future" is reiterated, but with the focus on an individual's relationship to the process, are "The Clearer Self" and "To the Prophetic Soul." Written in January 1894 and September 1893 respectively, these poems anticipate "The Largest Life," completed in January 1897, which is Lampman's fullest treatment of the theme of evolutionary progress and the individual person's role within it. Lampman included "The Clearer Self" and "To the Prophetic Soul" side by side in *Alcyone*, followed by "The Land of Pallas." The three poems map out the psychic journey of the speaker from lack of clarity in relation to purpose through uncertainty to an envisioning, in fantasy-like terms, of the goal of social-political struggle.

"The Clearer Self" conveys the same confidence about progressive change as is expressed in "Man's Future," but complicating the issue is a nagging question. Mired in the past, so to speak, the speaker wishes to know what the future holds in store for humanity if only human beings will work toward its attainment. Armed with that knowledge, he will possess a more complete sense of identity; he will have purpose and direction. He seeks, in other words, a vision of the ideal so he can then contribute to the process of making it real. The implication is that if he cannot participate, then he has no "higher life." He is like the citizens of the modern world in the sonnet "To Chaucer" who, in contrast to the people of Chaucer's day with their enviable firmness of belief, are victims of their own improved understanding: "Too well we see / The drop of life lost in eternity." His desire to play a role in the process stems from a need for meaningful engagement with life in relation to ultimate things. "The Clearer Self" was one of two poems by Lampman selected for inclusion in *The Oxford Book of English Mystical Verse*, published in 1917, the other being "Peccavi, Domine," a prayer-like expression of self-abnegation and remorse.[8] The editors recognized the spiritual yearning that "The Clearer Self" embodied.

The contrast between the vast time frame of humanity's evolution and the relative brevity of the speaker's own transient existence, introduced in stanza one, establishes the tension in the poem:

> Before me grew the human soul,
>   And after I am dead and gone,
> Through grades of effort and control
>   The marvellous work shall still go on.

The tone is confident, the message affirmative, but the speaker's consciousness of self and personal mortality – altogether missing in "Man's Future" – raises the question of the individual's place in the larger picture. In a general way, the speaker knows what his role should be:

> Each mortal in his little span
>   Hath only lived, if he have shown
> What greatness there can be in man
>   Above the measured and the known.

To participate meaningfully in life, each person must in some way bear witness to the human potential for reaching a more advanced state of being and seek the means by which the human spirit "Feels upward to some height at last / Of unimagined grace and power." Cast as everyman, the speaker is not up to the task. He understands there is an evolutionary process at work, but his understanding is abstract and unsatisfactory. He needs to know more. The problem is that, as of yet, "the sacred fire be dull" – humanity has only a dim sense of its own destiny – and "In folds of thwarting matter furled," that is, obscured by contrary ideas or beliefs. Here we have an instance of how it is altogether possible for non-progressive ideologies to interfere with progress, however much progress is in tune with what science has revealed about the evolution of human life from a "monstrous past" to whatever glorious state of being awaits (potentially) in the future.

Troubled by the faintness of the fire and especially by the prevalence of the "thwarting matter" – we can infer the entrenched capitalism depicted in "The City" – the speaker beseeches the "Master Spirit of the world" to enlighten him "Ere death is nigh, while life is full" so he can involve himself in the "higher life," contributing to the progress of humanity, and not feel lost like a drop in the ocean of eternity:

Grant me to know, to seek, to find,
  In some small measure though it be,
Emerging from the waste and blind,
  The clearer self, the grander me.

The "clearer self" is at once the human soul advancing to its more elevated state of being, of which the speaker is potentially a part, and, seen the other way around, the part of himself that is consistent with and contributes to the advance. The speaker longs to know what links him to the undying larger "self" of humanity within which he may find his own redemption. Armed with this knowledge, he will be better able to combat the forces of "thwarting matter" and thus to play his part in bringing about the redemption of all.

"The Clearer Self" is Lampman's version of a prayer wherein the petitioner seeks from the deity a strengthening of faith by means of some message or sign. Typically the conclusion such a person comes to is that faith can and must find its own way. Lampman's poems advocating socialist principles and exposing the failings of capitalism indicate that he had worked out at least to some degree what progress meant, even if, as in "The Clearer Self," he sometimes had questions about what the ideal future would look like and how best one could contribute to its achievement. At the same time he was not immune to the allure of worldly distractions – not money, but frivolous or morally reprehensible pursuits that, by his own standards, were at odds with his devotion to the ideal of human betterment and, in general, with a code of upright behaviour. In "To the Prophetic Soul," in keeping with his practice of examining not just ideas but the human responses to them, he incorporates his own internal struggle. Thus the struggle itself constitutes part of the record of his engagement with the idea of progress and involvement in the "higher life."

The seven-stanza poem opens with a four-stanza, single-sentence question about the mysterious and perplexing beings that the speaker sees before him:

> What are these bustlers at the gate
>   Of now or yesterday,
> These playthings in the hand of Fate,
>   That pass and point no way …?

The repetition of "these" – the pattern continues in the next two stanzas – suggests the immediacy of a direct encounter, but the language remains obscure. Scott has rightly described "To the Prophetic Soul" as "that enigmatic poem."[9] Certain facts, however, can be discerned. The bustlers are focused on the present or the recent past and are directionless, subject to forces outside their own volition. The phrase "playthings in the hands of fate" echoes the passage from Lampman's essay "The Modern School of Poetry in England" where, in support of his contention that "[l]ife is not a dreary thing," he insists that "[h]uman beings are not mere hopeless play things in the hands of chance, utter[ly] governed by a multitude of passions, that must mar and twist them, befoul them or beautify them as they will." This declaration of what people are not contrasts sharply with the characterization of the "bustlers" in "To the Prophetic Soul," who are indeed "mere hopeless play things." (The word "fate" in "To the Prophetic Soul" suggests not preordination but simply a lack of self-determination on the part of the subject – that is, "chance.") In his essay Lampman defines human nature as being, like Pan, "half human and half beast – but the human is the mightier part, and the whole is ever striving to be divine."[10] The bustlers – never assigned a name that would identify them as human – evidently lean more toward the bestial. Allowing themselves to be buffeted about randomly, following whatever direction their appetites lead them, they have relinquished their higher nature. They are "clinging bubbles" that coalesce into "Vain foam that gathers and expires / Upon the world's dark stream"; they are "gropers betwixt right and wrong," as likely to be moral in their behaviour as not; they are possessed of "mock fires" that contrast the "sacred fire" of human destiny in "The Clearer Self." As these phrases all attest, the speaker's scorn is palpable – and yet he is intrigued.

Addressing the "Soul" – his own – of the title, the speaker now completes the question to which his various cryptic descriptions were preliminary, asking, "What are they, then, O Soul,"

> That thou shouldst covet overmuch
>   A tenderer range of heart,
> And yet at every dreamed-of touch
>   So tremulously start?

For all the ephemeral and purposeless behaviour of the "playthings," the speaker finds them attractive and admits to desiring, and at the same time fearing, more intimate contact with them.[11] Although there is an erotic component to the language, the attraction may not be sexual so much as one of, more generally, human contact, but in the context of meaningless, unfocused "play." As the remaining stanzas make clear, the speaker – or his "Soul" – is lonely. (The use of "Soul" suggests the inner or essential self: it may be that the speaker engages with the bustlers superficially, but on a deeper level remains aloof.) The busy thoroughfare represents the lure of some kind of companionship, making it hard to turn away.

The speaker strenuously resists the tug that pulls him toward the bustlers, but as he gives his reasons, his claim that his "Soul" is possessed of a "hatred ever new / Of the world's base control" is too strong. The word "hatred" is cold in the wake of his expressed desire for affection. It betrays his emotional pain. At the same time, the speaker has an accurate sense of self. He knows that, with his "vision of the large and true," he cannot join in with the "clinging bubbles whose mock fires / For ever dance and gleam," no matter that their sparkle catches his eye. With bitter recognition he affirms that his "Soul" has been formed "in a rarer clay"; the bustlers "are not of thy kind." In the end, as he delivers his final adjuration to his "Soul," his resolve is triumphant, but his sense of lonely isolation remains:

> Be strong, therefore; resume thy load,
>   And forward stone by stone
> Go singing, though the glorious road
>   Thou travellest alone.

The dark night of the soul has passed. What the speaker's inner self, Christ-like, must do is difficult, but right, and the rewards, perhaps, greater than those of the bustlers, which have no lasting value, but vanish into oblivion.

Several parallels between this poem and one of those making up John Keble's *The Christian Year* suggest that here again Lampman found inspiration in the poetry of this well-known Anglican cleric. In Keble's poem for the Eighteenth Sunday after Trinity,[12] the "we" of the poem – members of the Christian community or, possibly, a wayward clergy – are susceptible to widespread "iniquity." With salvation within reach, they become distracted by the lures of the material realm: "Back to the world we faithless turned." Because these people have been exposed to the teachings of the church, however, it is not, or should not be, an option for them, as it is for the unenlightened "heathen," "To worship every monstrous shape" to which they may feel drawn:

> Vain thought, that shall not be at all!
>   Refuse we or obey,
> Our ears have heard the Almighty's call,
>   We cannot be as they.

Whether or not these people respond to God's call, they cannot pretend ignorance; they are doomed to knowing the difference between false gods and true. This entire stanza is closely echoed in the penultimate stanza of "To the Prophetic Soul," in terms of content and form:

> Nay, for they are not of thy kind,
>   But in a rarer clay
> God dowered thee with an alien mind;
>   Thou canst not be as they.

As well, Keble's "Vain thought" is partly matched by Lampman's "Vain foam," both initial phrases in their lines, and Lampman's expression of antipathy to "the world's base control" picks up "world" from Keble's "Back to the world we faithless turned." Finally, the odd plurals in "To the Prophetic Soul" – "bustlers," "clinging bubbles," "gropers" – can be traced to the initial phrase of Keble's lines, "Weak tremblers on the edge of woe / Yet shrinking from true bliss," descriptive of the non-committal quality of the subjects in his poem, caught between damnation and salvation (Lampman's bustlers are situated "betwixt right and wrong"). The echoes, which may well derive from memories of boyhood, when Lampman would have been exposed to the literary tastes of his Anglican minister father, point to a religiosity in Lampman's thinking and a concern with the struggle of "faith" versus "doubt" that are pervasive in his writing, extending even to his progressivist social philosophy, reinforcing the idea that commitment to the cause of human advancement was to him an issue of eschatological dimensions.

In some respects, "To the Prophetic Soul" is a flawed production. The abstract language is overly obscure, the speaker and his "Soul" are hard to distinguish, and the expression is sometimes cluttered, as where the speaker's "Soul" is said to possess a "quickness of the soul." At the same time, and perhaps justifying the obscurity, the poem has a surreal, hallucinatory quality, as if the speaker's conflict were being visualized through the blurry lens of a troubling dream. Its great strength, however, is its honesty. Playing his own strategic trick on himself, Lampman has the speaker build a case against the bustlers, only to reveal his fascination. The reader is surprised by the guileless confession of interest, and then taken aback by the evidence of resentment woven into the positive ending, where the speaker reaffirms his faith and determination to follow his lonely path. (Keble's wayward Christians can at least share each other's company.) The poem is strongly critical of others, but it is also self-critical in the sense of showing the human frailty of the speaker, whose ultimate decision, all things considered, we approve of, but whose self-denial we cannot help but regret.

"The Largest Life"

A poem in which a similar conflict is resolved less ambiguously is the well-known "The Largest Life," a sequence of three Shakespearian sonnets that explores the theme of human needs and desires in relation to a person's commitment to the great but impersonal cause of human betterment. The first sonnet depicts the speaker's isolation and loneliness, as in "To the Prophetic Soul," although with sadness more than bitterness. The second extols the virtues – and benefits – of selflessness, and the third describes humanity's progress toward its glorious destiny with a serenity that recalls "Man's Future," but incorporates as well the idea that in one's involvement in the process lies one's own salvation. It was not until near the end of his life that Lampman combined the three sonnets into one work. The first sonnet was written in August of 1894, not long after "The Clearer Self" and "To the Prophetic Soul" were completed; the second and third, in December 1896 and January 1897 respectively, when he had resolved his personal conflicts and achieved some degree of inner peace. It is as much a part of Lampman's purpose to show the process as to express the optimistic outlook at the end. Both his own evolution and humanity's are of interest to the poet.

After its first publication in the *Atlantic Monthly* in March of 1899 (apparently having been submitted by Lampman in the usual way, and likewise accepted, since no mention is made of his death the previous month), "The Largest Life" passed through a period of considerable popularity, often anthologized, and then went out of favour. In the wake of two world wars, the fall of communism in the USSR, and the widespread though not quite universal triumph of capitalism, its assurances of advancement toward a new age of egalitarian harmony seemed to fall flat. The poem stands, however, as an eloquent statement of belief in the ultimate achievement of a more humane society, despite setbacks, and of personal fulfillment derived from altruistic devotion to the common good.

The setting of the first sonnet, called in manuscript "The Soul's Solitude,"[13] is a bedroom. Outside the window is a neighbourhood, no doubt Lampman's own, as opposed to the fields or woods, where one might experience a different kind of "solitude." The predominant feeling is one of alienation from one's fellow human beings despite their close proximity. The echoes of Matthew Arnold's "Dover Beach" in the opening lines[14] suggest that Arnold's dismal vision of a world divided and bereft of spiritual meaning is part of the consciousness informing the present poem:

The moon is rising through the glistening trees;
And momently a great and sombre breeze,

With a vast voice returning fitfully,
Comes like a deep-toned grief.

The rushing of wind through the branches of trees eerily visible in the moonlight takes on for the speaker, who lies awake on his bed, a larger significance associated with human suffering. As earlier in the closing stanzas of "Winter-Store," the speaker's awareness of the unknown life stories of other people and of his own isolation from those people has overwhelmed his consciousness. And as in "To the Prophetic Soul," where the river of life is "dark," here "the dark march of human destiny" is one that seems to disallow any knowledge on the part of individuals of their fellow marchers.

Unique to the opening sonnet of "The Largest Life," however, is a broadening of the perspective to include others, with "I" and "they" experiencing the same dilemma:

What am I, then, and what are they that pass
Yonder, and love and laugh, and mourn and weep?
What shall they know of me, or I, alas!
Of them? Little.

The more inclusive stance is developed further as, switching from "I" to "we," the speaker acknowledges that the feeling of existential loneliness is common to all: "At times, as if from sleep, / We waken to this yearning passionate mood, / And tremble at our spiritual solitude." This broadening gesture is significant, for never in the remainder of the sequence does the focus return to the first person singular. It is as if the remedy for the spiritual malaise were already there in 1894, but it was not until the end of 1896, with the writing of sonnet two, that Lampman was able to give it full expression.

Responding directly to the *crie de coeur* in sonnet one, the speaker in sonnet two asserts that the antidote to "spiritual solitude" lies in people's recognition of their common humanity: "Nay, never once to feel we are alone, / While the great human heart around us lies." Made up of a single, complex sentence, this sonnet goes on to present a series of examples of selfless behaviour expressed in noun phrases, following the pattern established with "to feel" in line one, but without the negation – for example, "To make the smile on other lips our own" – all leading to a final affirmation of the true source of happiness in the closing couplet – grammatically necessary, but almost superfluous, since the evident relief and assured attitude of the first twelve lines convey the message. The recommended altruism has proved to be its own reward. "Divinest self-forgetfulness," the speaker relates, "at first / A task, and then a tonic, then a need," is hard to enact, but then quickly becomes the driving force in one's nature. To live according to this code, the couplet affirms, "is to see the beauty that God meant, / Wrapped round with life, ineffably content." As in "In November," where, observing the beauty of the harsh winter landscape, the speaker feels warmed by its effects on his consciousness – "Wrapped round with thought" – the speaker here, gazing upon a different kind of beauty, feels similarly protected. Vying for advantage in the public or private arena, Lampman seemed to feel, was intolerable. Preferable were the fields or the philosophy that would remove one from the bitter realms of competition and selfish desire.

To present-day sensibilities, the advocacy of selfless behaviour in "The Largest Life" may seem extreme to the point of absurdity, as where the speaker recommends, albeit figuratively, that the best policy is "only for another's wound to bleed." One suspects an irony, only to find there is none. It is nothing more than Christian morality that is being promoted, however, and a strong current of thought among the progressivists of Lampman's day (and later) was that, while Christian dogma and literal interpretations of the Bible must be abandoned, Christian morality was part of the evolutionary design of progress, carrying with it the notion that *self*-motivated behaviour – competing, fighting, and killing for personal and familial advantage – was being over time displaced by selfless behaviour, based on one's identification with others and with the universe as a whole. In Canada, the philosopher John Watson was only the most prominent of many thinkers who took this view.

The link between the ethic of altruism and a vision of, in Watson's phrase, "a higher nature within nature"[15] is precisely what we find in the climactic sonnet of "The Largest Life." This sonnet is the piece that was read at LeSueur's funeral and said by Scott to express "very clearly Dr. Le Sueur's faith."[16] The concept underlying Lampman's poem is that human destiny is an ever-brightening manifestation of divine design, with selfish motivations on the part of humanity gradually being displaced by those of community and love, pictured as "beauty":

> There is a beauty at the goal of life,
> A beauty growing since the world began,
> Through every age and race, through lapse and strife
> Till the great human soul complete her span.

Just as beauty is the quality in nature that Lampman finds redemptive in its effect on the sympathetic observer, so progress toward a glorious future for humankind, also redemptive, is understood in similar terms.

Notwithstanding the assured, stately tones of those opening lines, it is noticeable that Lampman is careful to include the qualification "through lapse and strife," echoing his phrase "through many changes, and many falls" in his prose statement from years before. In the second quatrain he elaborates on this theme, employing an oceanic metaphor to express the paradox of regress within progress:

> Beneath the waves of storm that lash and burn,
> The currents of blind passion that appall,
> To listen and keep watch till we discern
> The tide of sovereign truth that guides it all.

Whereas Arnold in "Dover Beach" sees the tide of the "Sea of Faith" in permanent ebb, exposing "the vast edges drear / And naked shingles of the world" to the godless new order,[17] Lampman evokes a large tidal movement containing within its waters those instances of human behaviour that go against, but do not ultimately impede, progress.

As poems such as "The Better Day" attest, Lampman did not always find it easy to discern the tide of truth through the waves and currents of adverse trends. Indeed he wrote bitterly about the extent to which unenlightened, corrupt, and retrograde behaviour seemed to dominate in human institutions. Two further instances of Lampman's anxieties occasioned by "lapse and strife" occur in unpublished works, the first a fragment from a rough notebook and the second a poem intended for inclusion in "The Land of Pallas, and Other Poems," the original compilation of *Alcyone*, but omitted from the final cut.[18] In the fragment – apparently the sestet of a sonnet that has not come to light – the far-off, better future, though not despaired of, is overshadowed by present conditions:

> All this we know & say the times are ill
> Aye, ill, and shall be worse! for we behold
> Only the van of evils; the old way
> Is sick to death & past the healer's skill,
> And ere the new be risen, slow decay
> And cankerous ruin must consume the old.[19]

Almost the inverse of the third sonnet of "The Largest Life," here the "evils" are foregrounded and the coming new age reduced to a brief mention. The speaker is grieved to live in a time so far from the goal, on the verge of greater catastrophe rather than of the apotheosis that eventually will follow.

A similarly gloomy attitude infects "Non Nobis Futura" ("not the future for us"), a poem whose ostensible purpose is to celebrate the anticipated glories of the new age to come, despite the non-participation of the current generation. The poem is narrated from the point of view of those in the present engaged in a Comtean worship of the future, as suggested by the antiphonal quality of stanza one:

> The great world rolls on its old bright way –
>   Great is the world! –
> The last age droops, but the coming day
>   Is a flag unfurled.

The same feeling is evident in stanza five, where a three-stanza closing apostrophe to the future begins like a prayer:

> O things of the marvelous age to come –
>   O fair and sweet! –
> When the wise were chequered with doubt, half dumb
>   We fell at your feet.

In a complicated adjustment of tenses, the future is spoken of in this passage first as future and then as present as the real present is shifted into the past. The speaker cannot, however, by an act of will catapult his own generation into the future, and a note of sadness compromises the otherwise clarion optimism of the poem. "The might of some lordlier tongue shall sing," he declares, "When we are dead." And in contrast to the stirring opening, the closing stanza brings the focus back from the glorious future to the dismal present:

> And yet we could never be free and whole,
>   As the lords of your day,
> But often in bond to a flagging soul,
>   We sank by the way.

The "flagging soul" of the present stands, or rather falls, in bathetic contrast to the image of the future as "a flag unfurled" in stanza one.

In "The Largest Life," by contrast, Lampman does not permit such thoughts to put him off his course. Despite the impediments to progress, acknowledged but denied their power, the poem ends with an eloquent declaration of purpose and affirmation of faith:

> So to address our spirits to the height,
> And so attune them to the valiant whole,
> That the great light be clearer for our light,
> And the great soul be stronger for our soul:
> To have done this is to have lived, though fame
> Remember us with no familiar name.

Following on the quatrain in which the contrary influences are mentioned, this passage conquers them by moving past them. The ideal of a generous-hearted devotion of the one to the all, expressed in simple language, with repetitions of wording lending a chant-like quality to the passage, is unclouded by the doubts that are so overwhelming in "The Better Day." As a declaration of selfless devotion to a cause, overriding any concerns about the ability of contrary forces to prevent the realization of the envisioned goal, no matter how distant, this passage stands as a model of its rhetorical type – and a moving testimony of the serenity of mind that Lampman had reached toward the end of his life.

Two Prophetic Visions

So far in this discussion of Lampman's social-political poems the focus has been on those that deal more or less directly with the idea of progress, reflecting his belief that the discoveries of science had given rise to "a new conception of the higher life" that promised to fill the moral and spiritual vacuum created by the reassessment of theology prompted by Darwinism. Salvation achieved through humanity's evolutionary advance toward a future of peace and harmony, rather than through a "system of post-mortem rewards and punishments," was the new ideal. The future society would be characterized by a selfless code of behaviour that would replace the materialism and greed of the present day, of which capitalism was the institutional manifestation.

This belief constitutes the philosophical foundation of all Lampman's poems that deal with social issues. In many of these poems, however, the belief is less the focus of concern than the social issues themselves. Among the social poems that are not primarily disquisitions on progress are to be found Lampman's strongest indictments of free-enterprise capitalism and industrialization, and of their promulgators. These poems I have clustered into three distinct categories. The first consists of two contrasting prophetic visions representing the alternative futures for humankind that would result from choices made by contemporary society, "The Land of Pallas" and "The City of the End of Things." The second is a group of shorter critiques and exposés of corruption and greed in which sympathy for the poor and disadvantaged is matched by a carefully controlled but not mitigated anger directed at the exploiters. The last category, explored in chapter 10, comprises two works – Lampman's long narrative poem *The Story of an Affinity* and the lesser-known "Sebastian" – involving the anticipated roles of the main characters in shaping the world of the future. Although the idea of progress may be seen as the philosophical basis of these poems, the concern is more with proselytizing than with philosophizing. Progress might be the law; social rectification is the goal.

In "The Land of Pallas" and "The City of the End of Things," Lampman projects two future states of being for human society, corresponding, within his world view, to heaven and hell – the ideal become real through human effort over time in the one case and the horrific inverse of that outcome in the other. The heavenly projection sees the soul of humanity expanded to its full potential in maturity; its infernal counterpart envisages the soul's destruction.[20] That Lampman saw the two poems as companion pieces is suggested by the fact that they were to appear together as the first two poems in "The Land of Pallas, and Other Poems" and by Lampman's employment of old-style alternative titles, later excised, that appear with the main titles in the proof sheets of *Alcyone* as follows: "The Land of Pallas, or, The Country of the Ought-to-Be" and "The City of the End of Things, or, The Issue of the Things that Are."[21] In *Alcyone* "The City of the End of Things" is left near the beginning, but "The Land of Pallas" is shifted to the middle of the book, where it follows "To the Prophetic Soul," as if to suggest the directive at the end of that poem, "Go singing, though the glorious road / Thou travellest alone," were now being followed by the visionary narrator of the longer piece.

Neither poem is meant to be seen as realistic. As Lampman said of "The City of the End of Things," it is "intended to represent – in an exaggerated way of course – what we are coming to, if the present ... developments of machinery continues [sic] under the present social and economic conditions."[22] The pair are rather complementary utopian and dystopian visions based, like most works belonging to these genres, on evidence derived from the present but stretched to extremes and spiced with hyperbole. The aim of such works is always to comment on the current state of society and to reveal "in an exaggerated way of course" how conditions could be infinitely better if known methods were applied to make them so, or drastically worse if nothing were done to curtail existing trends.

Although progressivism in "The Land of Pallas" takes a back seat to the simple idea that it is, or "ought to be," possible for humanity to move beyond the disparities and injustices inherent in capitalism and to establish a more enlightened way of living, the "happy land" of the poem is clearly an idealization of the future that Lampman saw as people's rightful destiny, if only they could steer their way to that place.

This future, as numerous commentators have pointed out, is largely based on the utopian society depicted by William Morris in *News from Nowhere*. Early has called Lampman's poem "a versified reduction" of *News* and, as such, an example of "derivative work," while Munro Beattie has dismissed it as "little more than a mixture of Morris and water."[23] The idea of basing a narrative poem on a prose model – of producing a "versified reduction" – is of course sound in itself and has many precedents, from Chaucer's renderings of Boccaccio onward. The question is whether or not the poem is convincing as a utopian projection and successful at exposing through contrast the unsatisfactory social conditions in the present. Like Morris, Lampman employs a dream-vision frame in order to render the ideal society believable – anything can happen in a dream – and to create a strange-seeming alternative against which to measure real life in the contemporary world. Many readers will find the utopian land too placid and lifeless. Scott himself, explaining his decision to omit the poem from *Lyrics of Earth: Sonnets and Ballads*, comments that "the dream-pastoral society which he imaginatively substituted for the present is as passionless as a wall painting by [nineteenth-century French painter Pierre] Puvis de Chavannes." Lampman's utopia "may be momentarily attractive as a contrast to our perilous existence," Scott adds, "but cannot serve the ambitious heart as a goal or the eager mind as a logical resting place."[24] This criticism could be applied with equal justice to many literary utopias, beginning with Eden and not excluding *News from Nowhere*. Scott's point regarding contrast, though, is telling. Certainly the contrast that emerges at the end of "The Land of Pallas," when the speaker returns to the real world after a lengthy stay in the placid alternative realm, does indeed engender something of a shock. Society's failings in the present come more sharply into focus in the light of the utopian ideal, and a better future, even if not precisely the one imagined, seems worth striving for.

Lampman's utopia embodies the values he extols in his other progressivist writings. It is a land, first of all, where "beauty dwelt supreme," the same, we can assume, as the "beauty at the goal of life" evoked in "The Largest Life." In this alternative realm, then, the quality that Lampman found perennially in nature would finally have its human equivalent, and humankind, no longer semi-evolved, as in "Man's Future," would have reached the perfection in human terms that the elm tree had manifestly attained. As the narrator, who has visited the ideal land, now recalls,

> But all the children of that peaceful land, like brothers,
>   Lofty of spirit, wise, and ever set to learn
> The chart of neighbouring souls, the bent and need of others,
>   Thought only of good deeds, sweet speech, and just return.

The selflessness of these people corresponds to the ideal of altruism set out in the second sonnet of "The Largest Life," where it is stated that to live for others "is to see the beauty that God meant," and in "The Better Day," where the future of which the less-optimistic speaker is doubtful is described as one in which "self shall be the unseen part, / And human kindness all." Finally, to take note of a more specific correlation, the image in the opening stanza of a society "where strife and care were dead, / And life went flowing ... like a placid river" recalls that of the society in which meanspiritedness and cruelty "keep this restless world at strife" and "like choking sands, / Perplex the stream of life" in "The Better Day," only now life is cured of its malaise. The "century of weal" has arrived.

The narrator of the poem recalls imagining that he journeyed through a happy land where he witnessed a thriving, harmonious society operating on socialist principles: labour equally shared, public ownership of resources, and a widespread belief in the common good. The main focus is on the rural scenes, where workers till the land "with joy" and without compulsion. Also mentioned, though, are the "great fair cities" in which the greed and disparity characterizing the cities depicted in "Freedom" and "The City" are singularly absent. In place of the struggle for the "power of gold" has arisen a "golden calm." Neither is it only in their way of life that the citizens of this land are different from the people of the narrator's own time. Both the men and women are "fairer / Than even the mightiest of our meaner race," and the women, "strong, and subtly wise," stand "equal with the men." A sex-based division of labour, however, remains in place, as the women, described as "calm counsellors," do not work in the fields but rather bring baskets of food to the men, whom they "[bless] ... with their lofty beauty and blithe speech." The men, for their part, are "like gentle children, great of limb, yet rarer / For wisdom and high thought, like kings for majesty." These men and women are not immortal, but live "long lives in proud content unbroken," for, as the narrator succinctly recalls, "no man was rich, none poor, but all were well." They engage in a "priestless worship" of Pallas Athena, representing wisdom. Lampman's analysis of Christianity, as conveyed in a letter to Thomson, was that "[a]s long as there is sorrow on earth, the pathetic figure of Christ will stand."[25] With sorrow, born of suffering, left behind in the "age of fear," Christianity can now, in the happy land, take its place with "many a vanished creed." Instead of seeking the solace of a personal salvation in the Christian sense, the citizens of the land endeavour to advance their society further, and so "to kindlier ends and vaster / Moved on together." Though already living an ideal life, "a life made more divine," they continue to reach for greater heights of ideality.

Part of what makes Lampman's "verse reduction" of *News from Nowhere* distinct from its source is the poetry itself, and indeed the formal elements of "The Land of Pallas" are particularly well chosen to convey its thematic concerns. The four-line stanzas, with feminine and masculine endings alternating throughout and rhyming *abab*, reinforce the idea of social interconnectedness and wittily imply the harmonious relations between the sexes.[26] The hexameters are open and expansive, in keeping with the narrator's enthusiasm for what he is recalling and wanting to report. In addition, they are marked by irregular pauses and variations of stress, along with understated rhymes, that together reduce the effect of monotony that hexameters can create:

> And when the great day's toil was over, and the shadows
>   Grew with the flocking stars, the sound of festival
> Rose in each city square, and all the country meadows,
>   Palace, and paven court, and every rustic hall.

Not all stanzas offer as much variation as does this one, with its partial rhymes and its metrical reversals in the initial feet of the last three lines, along with skilfully deployed enjambment and caesural rests, but in general Lampman's handling of the verse form gives the poem an easy, natural expression suitable to the depiction of the unruffled lives of its subjects.

In the end, the narrator records that, as in a dream – a dream within a dream – he lost his way and found himself in a land of "baser men" whose activities "Were urged by fear, and hunger, and the curse of greed." In other words, he was back in the present. Coming after his, and our, full immersion in the harmony of the ideal land, extended over thirty-one stanzas, the familiar scenes – the gross inequities, the defeated looks of "bowed men" and the sorrows of "piteous women" – are disconcerting. The sharp contrast has the effect of making one wonder if there could not after all be a better way. The narrator further relates that, motivated by feelings of "deep solicitude and wondering pity," he embarked on a mission to convert the masses to the new way of thinking, but in vain: the powerful "Rebuked [him] as an anarch" while "they that served them," bearing their suffering with "bitter patience," dismissed him as mad. The obvious irony of this reaction is calculated to inculcate the idea that a shift in values is urgently needed to help society move forward.

For the conclusion of the poem, Lampman considered alternative stanzas, much discussed as the "pessimistic" and "optimistic" endings. In the one, the narrator frantically tries to find his way back to "that land of blessing," but cannot; in the other, despite rejection, he continues to promote his cause, knowing that "somehow" the changes must take place to bring about a future of harmonious living in this world.[27] The contrast seems to be one of despair versus hope. The pessimistic ending, however, does not rule progress out, and the optimistic ending can be read as vain, wishful thinking. It may well be that Lampman's reason for preferring the latter was simply that artistically it made more sense. The narrator has been exposed to the benefits of an altruistic way of life. It would seem inconsistent for him now to abandon his fellow sufferers, however much they might scorn his efforts. Still, the narrator's desperate efforts in the pessimistic ending to find his way back to the happy land are revealing of how much Lampman loathed the capitalist system and longed to escape its influence.

"The Land of Pallas" succeeds in outlining a positive vision of what human life could be if human beings would only make it happen. The implicit suggestion is that the goal of a classless society of enlightened individuals or, short of that, improvements in that direction would be worth striving for. If advancement toward the socialist ideal was in tune with Lampman's progressivist view of how human society should and could be evolving, however, it was not the direction in which he saw it actually moving in his own time, as poems such as "Non Nobis Futura" make clear. This direction is what he sets out to describe in "The City of the End of Things" – a nightmarish vision of what the future will look like if present trends continue.

Written in the summer of 1892 and first published in the *Atlantic Monthly* for March 1894, "The City of the End of Things" proved to be one of Lampman's most successful and popular poems, although it has had its detractors.[28] Of the five Lampman selections included in Stedman's 1895 *A Victorian Anthology*, it was the exception in being the one poem not taken from Lampman's only published book at that time, *Among the Millet* (1888). Since its publication in *Alcyone* (1899) and *Poems* (1900), it has been frequently anthologized. Its repeated appearance alongside "Heat" and other nature poems has prompted some commentators to perceive a schism in Lampman's writing between nature (symbolically the idyllic past) and the city (symbolically the horrific future). William Toye, for example, states that "[t]he antithesis of the values he found in nature is given rein in his nightmarish vision of a lifeless, mechanistic city" in "The City of the End of Things,"[29] implying a logical equivalency between nature on the one hand and one projection of the future on the other, as if the nightmarish vision *were* (in Lampman's view) the future and the escape to nature a way of hiding one's head in the sand. As Lampman's contemplated alternate titles to the poems under consideration indicate, the real antithesis is rather between soul-fulfilling and soul-destroying visions of the future, both of which are possible. The one future would result from humanity's success in transforming society into what "ought to be," and the other from its failure to do so. As in conventional religion, there are prescribed behaviours, consistent with "truth," but people are free to disregard them at their peril.

In *Poems*, "The City of the End of Things" is divided into three sections: a brief introduction to establish the setting, a description of the prevailing conditions and inhabitants, and an account of the history and destiny of the city. It should be noted, however, that in the texts Lampman approved, two further breaks appear, the first after line twenty-eight, separating conditions from inhabitants, and the second after line sixty-four, dividing past and future. My discussion will follow this five-part division.[30]

The imagery of the brief opening section establishes the setting in mythic terms. The city is located in "the leafless tracts / And valleys huge of Tartarus," an abyss of eternal punishment that lies in the lowest region of the classical Greek underworld. The references to the geography of Hades are important in capturing the dark, death-ridden, apocalyptic setting of the poem, but Lampman is careful not to overdo the parallels to classical mythology. This would only distract readers from his main purpose, which is to evoke a symbolic image of where humanity is heading "under the present social and economic conditions." And as we soon discover, if this is hell, it is a specific kind of hell, for what the "iron towers" and "thousand furnace doors" evoke is nothing more nor less than a massive factory, a fitting image of the world remade in the interests of capitalist greed. No sunlight penetrates its walls; nothing grows; and the familiar divisions of time have been collapsed into one perpetual round of production, an extension of the shift work that keeps the factories in the real world going around the clock. The connection of this dystopia to the present world is reinforced by the parallel between its shift-work imagery and that of "The City," set in the present, where "Through days and nights that follow / The hidden mill-wheel strains." In "The City of the End of Things," "The beat, the thunder and the hiss / Cease not, and change not, night nor day."

This environment is antithetical to what it means to be human. The continuous noise of machines creates, in a choice phrase, a "gigantic harmony" of "inhuman music," in a place where "no man is, / And only fire and night hold sway" and the very air is poisonous. Anyone "of our mortal race" stumbling on the city would either be struck dead or, "caught by the terrific spell," meet with an equally horrific fate: "Each thread of memory snapt and cut, / His soul would shrivel and its shell / Go rattling like an empty nut." The death-like, soulless existence of this person, with every connection to the natural and the human now lost, contrasts the state of being of the inhabitants of the Land of Pallas, who have attained "a life made more divine." Lampman's clear message is that humanity's ultimate fate, amounting to its salvation or damnation, rests in the hands of people today, who must choose their future.

The effect of the city's toxic atmosphere on the hapless human wanderer raises a question as to who or what the city's inhabitants – "figures that / Obey a hideous routine" – are:

They are not flesh, they are not bone,
They see not with the human eye,
And from their iron lips is blown
A dreadful and monotonous cry.

It is sometimes assumed that these are automatons in a world in which people have entirely ceased to exist. E.K. Brown, for example, proposes that "[m]an will not be able to sustain life in [the city's] mephitic atmosphere: he will be superseded by machines."[31] But why would robots cry? And why would it be necessary to insist on their inhuman qualities? The much more frightening prospect is that these figures, who, as Bentley has observed, "with their 'clanking hands' and 'iron lips,' have come to resemble the machines that they serve,"[32] are the degraded creatures that human beings have become. By this interpretation, what Lampman is depicting "in an exaggerated way of course" is the effect of industrialization on workers and, by extension, the effect of capitalism on humanity.

Commentators have noticed a plethora of influences on "The City of the End of Things," most notably James Thomson's "The City of Dreadful Night," Poe's "The City in the Sea," and Books 8 and 9 of Wordsworth's *The Excursion*.[33] John Sutherland, tracing echoes of Poe in "The City of the End of Things," not altogether convincingly, as Bentley has shown,[34] is highly critical of Lampman's imitative methods, whereas Bentley sees Lampman's "discerningly eclectic" selection of source material in a positive light.[35] Either way, the emphasis falls on the threads that tie Lampman's poem to precedents, making it seem, for better or worse, a prophesy based on borrowings from the past. Less appreciated is the forward-reaching quality of Lampman's vision. The imagery of the poem anticipates Fritz Lang's classic silent film *Metropolis* (1927), featuring a subterranean mass of robot-like worker-slaves whose labour supports the city above them, and Charlie Chaplin's *Modern Times* (1936), in which we see the protagonist leaving a factory still twitching and jittering after hours of repetitive bolt twisting, and in another scene becoming caught up, literally, in the cogwheels of a huge machine. He, too, has become machine-like – that is, dehumanized – as a result of being exploited by capitalists in an industrial setting. Lang's imagery of industrial enslavement and Chaplin's exaggerated depiction of the effects of mechanization on the individual worker come close to illustrating Lampman's method in "The City of the End of Things," written decades before these ground-breaking films were made.

The last two parts of the poem (following Lampman's original divisions) outline the history and destiny of the city. Unlike the narrator of "The Land of Pallas," the speaker here, fully informed by his dreams, has an omniscient perspective. In the forgotten past, which we understand to be the present or the near future, when the blessings of sunlight and human joy were still in evidence, "multitudes of men" built the city "in their pride" and then "withered age by age and died," the victims of their own creation. The implication of this biblical language involving the fabricating and worshipping of a false god, vaguely reminiscent of the story of the golden calf (Exodus 32), is that humanity has contravened the dictates of its own better nature in creating a system that is soul-destroying. The "beauty at the goal of life" anticipated in the third sonnet of "The Largest Life" has thus became a lost potential, the law of supply and demand that Lampman derides in his essay on socialism having supplanted the law of progress.

Employing obscure symbolism but powerful imagery, Lampman concludes the poem with an account of the last survivors of the human race and finally the apocalyptic "end of things." Three figures "like carved idols" remain for a time, facing each other, implying the insular quality of capitalism. These seem like magnates: industrialists in an infernal parody of the holy trinity. They are "the masters of [the city's] power," so when they ultimately die, as the speaker knows they will, the factory wheels will grind to a halt and, presumably, the worker-slaves who had existed only to do their bidding will likewise perish. Meanwhile a grotesque and ominous fourth figure, perhaps based on the classical Erebus, the personification of the utter darkness of the underworld, is introduced. This creature, described as a mindless, soulless "bulk that never moves," sits at the city gate, gazing with "dreadful eyes" at "the lightless north, / Beyond the reach of memories," destined to remain in its place forever as the living monument of our lost civilization. No other signs of life will survive. When the factory noises cease and the fires die out, the city will become a silent mausoleum, with trees, grass, rain, and wind all absent. Not the stillness and silence of the sonnet "Solitude," infused with the breathings of nature, but "A stillness absolute as death" and "The silence of eternal night" will prevail.[36] Since these events are spoken of in the future tense, it follows that we are situated at the almost-end of things, with the city-factory in full production, looking back on the time (the present era) when humankind could have prevented its own demise and forward to a state of oblivion. Symbolically the poem reveals the anti-human (and anti-nature) directions of capitalist society. Something like the subjugation described in the first parts of the poem and, following that, something like the destruction of all things we value will be the result of failing to change "the present social and economic conditions" under which the dehumanizing effects of industrial labour are felt.

As prophetic dream visions, "The Land of Pallas" and "The City of the End of Things" both focus on the far future, but each reflects an engagement with the present age of conflict and strife that, if changed, could lead to the peace and harmony of the former poem, but if not changed seems bound for the disaster spelled out in the latter. The comic outcome would be in tune with the law of progress, but the socioeconomic conditions in Lampman's day were, in his judgment, tending more toward the tragic. Humanity was in danger of losing its humanity. It was this kind of concern that fed his anger at the oppressor as well as his compassion for the oppressed in a small group of shorter poems with a social-political focus.

Short Exposés and Poems of Social Protest

When Lampman shifts his focus from country to city and from trees and fields to human beings, he also typically changes the form and style of his poems, producing prophetic visions, philosophical meditations, and introspective lyrics. On occasion, however, he will employ exactly the same method as in his descriptive nature poems that concentrate on the outward appearances of things, with one difference. In place of the feeling

Poems of Progress

of content that emanates from the observations of beauty in nature, he will express a troubled sympathy for the inhabitants of the urban arena. The sonnets "The Railway Station" and "Reality" are of this type.

In "The Railway Station," a jarring mood is established by the reference to the contravention of the natural cycles of day and night as in the poems that feature shift work, in this case caused by the glaring lights and noise of the station: "The darkness brings no quiet here, the light / No waking." We observe people's rushed farewells – "the clasp, the flight" – before "the hoarse wheels turn" and the train departs. As in "The City," the speaker's repeated "I see" echoes the same words from any number of Lampman's nature poems, but the urban scene produces a contrary impression, one of wonderment at the unknown: "What threads of life, what hidden histories, / What sweet or passionate dreams and dark distresses, / What unknown thoughts, what various agonies!" Reiterating an idea expressed in "The Largest Life," the speaker laments the obscurity within which people live their private lives and experience their hopes and disappointments, each isolated from the others despite physical proximity. In this case, though, the image is more precise. The bustle of activity at the train station evokes a scene still recognizable today, often encountered in airports, of strangers brought together by a common purpose yet remaining separate and obscure to one another. Contemporary life is alienating.

A more beleaguered sample of humanity is presented in "Reality,"[37] in which a pair of bag ladies and a blind beggar compete for the speaker's attention with a screaming child and a howling dog, all part of a noon-hour scene "upon the heated flags" (paving-stones) of a busy intersection. The scene is one of noise, ugliness, and misery. Although horror more than pity is sparked by this snapshot of city life, the urban nemesis of Lampman's "Heat," there is an evident desire to record accurately the terrible consequences of current social conditions.

"Reality" was one of two sonnets published by Lampman in "At the Mermaid Inn," part of a satirical fiction wherein the narrator purports to be outraged by the inappropriateness of the topics chosen for treatment in sonnets by his "friend the sonneteer." In response to the first of these, a delightful study of the experience named in its title, "Falling Asleep," "Lampman" (the narrator) asks, "could you not have arranged to cast your impression in some more suitable form a little less ridiculously inapplicable to the smallness and homeliness of your subject?" to which the "friend" replies, "No, I couldn't." Things get worse. Upon hearing the sonneteer recite "Reality," the narrator is beside himself, declaring, "Certainly you have outdone yourself this time" and "You have violated every law of moral dignity and literary decency." Curiously, in the course of arguing that the Confederation poets opted for a conservative formalism in their compositional practice, Bentley takes these comments at face value. "Clearly evident in these humorous remarks," he states, "is a serious moral-aesthetic whose roots lie in the classical theory of decorum: the sonnet is more 'suitable' (Lampman's word) to some themes and subjects than to others – a rule of propriety that the fictitious 'sonneteer' chooses to flout in order to offend the poet's sense of seemliness and decency."[38] By this interpretation, Lampman wrote the poems featured in his satire specifically to illustrate a wrongheaded approach to the employment of the sonnet form. But as F.W. Watt has pointed out, Lampman "allowed ['Reality'] to stand in his manuscript book without any special apologies,"[39] indicating that he regarded the poem not simply as the vehicle of a satire but as a genuine poetic utterance, a point that is reinforced by the fact that Lampman wrote the sonnet in August of 1889, almost three years before incorporating it into his "Mermaid Inn" satire. "Reality" – the title drawing attention to its stark realism – strikes a note that Lampman did not sound frequently, but at the same time its descriptive technique is typical. As Scott, who seemed not to know what to make of the poem, has observed, "The artistry is there and the keen observation, but no hope."[40] It is the inverse of Lampman's nature studies, offering an implicit critique of society, just as those poems offer an implicit celebration of natural-world beauty.

A different sort of poem, one that makes clear in its closing phrases the source of much human suffering, but which develops its theme by way of analogy, is "A Night of Storm." This Petrarchan sonnet, written in November 1887, may be seen as a transitional work paving the way for those poems that point to a need for social rectification. A winter storm has "sewn" the streets with "restless drift" – the wind keeps changing the shapes of the snowdrifts – and the city's inhabitants have retreated indoors. In the dark, the windows of the houses "dim and many / Gleam red across the storm." Only "the fierce wind's sweep and moan" disturb the silence. Then, with the sestet, comes the parallel, continuing the apostrophe to the city that is employed throughout: "Darkling and strange art thou thus vexed and chidden; / More dark and strange thy veilèd agony." The Arnoldian (or perhaps Keblian)[41] poeticism "Darkling" is momentarily distracting, but the overriding metaphor has heartfelt impact as we consider the "stormier woes" and the effects of "time's heavier sleet" on the citizens in their dwellings – "Rude fates, hard hearts, and prisoning poverty." The red light emanating from the windows, contrasting the grey of the storm and the white of the snow, now takes on a poignant suggestiveness, symbolizing the suffering of the mortals within, caused partly by misfortune ("fates") and emotional cruelty ("hard hearts"), but largely the result of the socioeconomic conditions ("prisoning poverty") that help to create these problems. As John Bell, who chose "A Night of Storm" to represent Lampman in his 1992 anthology *Ottawa: A Literary Portrait*, relates, "In this sonnet, Lampman paints a bleak canvas of a city beset by relentless natural and social forces. Clearly evident are his distaste for the modern city and his socialist views on class oppression."[42] This is a poem in which he combines his descriptive powers and his social conscience to good effect.

Lampman's empathy for those beset by "Rude fates, hard hearts, and prisoning poverty," together with his anger at the system that either causes or intensifies their suffering, may be seen as fuelling such purposeful attacks on capitalist greed as "To a Millionaire" and "Epitaph on a Rich Man."

The world of "To a Millionaire" is one of "gloom and splendour"; it is, in other words, the familiar world in which magnificent buildings and other signs of opulence exist side by side with deprivation and misery. The millionaire of the title is possessed of "that old distorted dream / That makes the sound of life an evil cry" – what Lampman calls in a "Mermaid Inn" piece on a similar subject "a purely brute instinct," in contrast to the motivations of those who seek knowledge, produce art, or engage in "political or social reform" or works of charity.[43] For all his backwardness, however, the millionaire triumphs, winning respect into the bargain:

> Good men perform just deeds, and brave men die,
> And win not honour such as gold can give,
> While the vain multitudes plod on, and live,
> And serve the curse that pins them down.

Society's standards are wrong, virtue is undervalued, and the masses of people of the working class are reduced to conditions of servitude. With these points established, the octave of this Petrarchan sonnet comes (almost) to an end. What remains to be said?

As in Lampman's essay on socialism, the problem is not merely injustice, which might seem an abstract concern or "not sound so very bad in the ears of those who possess land and money and are bred to the system," but it is also, and mainly, the human cost. "But I," says the speaker, addressing the millionaire but wishing, no doubt, to be overheard by those who suffer and who should nurture a desire for change,

> Think only of the unnumbered broken hearts,
> The hunger and the mortal strife for bread,
> Old age and youth alike mistaught, misfed,
> By want and rags and homelessness made vile,
> The griefs and hates, and all the meaner parts
> That balance thy one grim misgotten pile.

The catalogue of negative effects that stem from capitalist greed is the speaker's best argument, and the top-heavy quality of the sestet, with its long list of ills so out of proportion to the millionaire's single benefit, which they "balance," formally underlines the point. The fact that the final line appears on its own in one of Lampman's notebooks in the proximity of poems written earlier than "To a Millionaire," completed in October 1891, suggests that the idea of constructing a tower of words on the base of this simple adjective clause was indeed the original conception for this poem.[44]

Although he does not cite the proverb "It is easier for a camel to go through the eye of a needle, than for a rich man to enter into the kingdom of God" (Matthew 19:24; Mark 10:25; Luke 18:25), Lampman does argue in his essay on socialism that those who devote their lives to the accumulation of riches, if they believe in an afterlife, must realize that they are contributing to the "degradation" of their own souls.[45] In "Epitaph on a Rich Man," one such man is now dead. In the text Lampman has supposedly prepared for the subject's tombstone, however, he does not focus, good or ill, on the afterlife, but instead makes reference to what he regards as the true concern of spiritual endeavour – social progress. To have contributed to that goal, as stated in "The Largest Life," would be "to have lived, though fame / Remember us with no familiar name." By this standard, the rich man has not lived – has not done anything worthwhile with his life. His influence on the masses of humankind has been negative. Accordingly, he is dismissed as a "glittering fellow," one who has "reaped plentifully / From the black soil of human misery" and now has been buried "With splendour that the people's want makes grim." His riches have won for him the honours that, in "To a Millionaire," fall to the wealthy more than to the virtuous, but his legacy will be of a different sort, for as the speaker predicts in the closing lines, the day will come when "he shall not be called to mind / Save as the curse and pestilence of his kind."

This deliberately provocative language is an example of what Scott called Lampman's "force" of expression.[46] It was very likely because of this "force" that Lorne Pierce, editor-in-chief of Ryerson Press, listed this poem and two others with politically charged content among those he wished to see omitted from the posthumous *At the Long Sault*. As Scott commented to E.K. Brown, Pierce was "probably nervous about 'Liberty,' 'The Usurer,' and 'The Epitaph.'" As joint compilers of *At the Long Sault*, Scott and Brown prevailed in having all the poems that Pierce had questioned included in the book.[47]

Besides rich industrialists, there was one other group that Lampman liked to vent his spleen upon, namely, the politicians of the day, whose activities he could observe at first hand as an Ottawa resident and employee of a government department. Something of his attitude can be gleaned from the half-serious rants with which he entertained Thomson on various occasions over the course of their eight-year correspondence. In one letter, angry with the sitting government for imposing longer hours and more adverse working conditions within the civil service, he wishes he had "some knowledge in political history" and "practice in writing about politics" so he could "have a hand in smashing them"; in another, nothing more than the appearance of members of Parliament "prowling about" – "What are they after? Vipers, blood-suckers!" – prompts a panegyric on Guy Fawkes, whose attempt to blow up the British parliament in 1605 made him worthy of sainthood.[48] Typical of Lampman's diatribes is the following from 10 February 1893:

> No sooner has the weather moderated than we have that other worse disaster the assembly of the great national dunghill or Dominion cess-pool, everything connected with which gives me sensations of unutterably [sic] loathing and horror. At present I am engaged in endeavouring, through the few friends I have in the House to save a friend of mine here who has been most unjustly and arbitrarily dismissed by the <u>Hon</u>. John Haggart, a person whose existence makes me regret that the old theological fable of Hell-fire is not true.[49]

Conservative member of Parliament John Graham Haggard, at that time minister of Railways and Canals, had been postmaster general, 1888–92, making him Lampman's top boss. By occupation he was, according to Parliament of Canada records, a "mill owner." Given these facts, it may well be that Lampman's indignation at the firing of his friend was reinforced by a more personal as well as philosophical antipathy.[50]

In "The Modern Politician," the amoral, opportunistic world of modern political practice is contrasted with the genuine heroics of the past. The speaker of this Petrarchan sonnet is incredulous that a human being could stoop so low as to manipulate truth for political gain: "What manner of soul is this to whom high truth / Is but the plaything of a feverish hour, / A dangling ladder to the ghost of power!" The politician's machinations are, in the speaker's eyes, a pathetic echo of "the grandeurs of the world's iron youth / When kings were mighty, being made by swords." Instead of swords, the politician uses "specious words" to deceive voters and further his own ambition. His is the "transit age, the age of brass," and his type are clowns instead of kings. The "transit age" may be necessary to progress, but lamentably so, with opportunism and empty rhetoric standing in for the rigours of power secured by strength.

To the politician-clowns of the present day, the speaker continues in the sestet, all values and beliefs – "faith, kinship, truth" – become merely "the counters at a desperate play," like pieces in a board game that one moves or trades off to further one's advantage. Careless of "what the end may be," they are happy as long as "they glitter, each his little day, / The little mimic of a vanished king." The repeated "little" is of course a disparagement, emphasizing how poorly the new breed of power-seekers measures up against the old, and the evident aim of this poem overall is to heap scorn on its subject with as much vehemence as can be neatly accommodated within the decorous confines of a sonnet. As Louis K. MacKendrick has suggested, "The Modern Politician" is "an astringent and bitter piece of invective," its language "metaphorically rich, colloquial and strong, and brutally affective."[51]

Lampman's criticisms of politicians may be seen as a reflection of a more widespread discontent. A decades-long struggle against "partyism" in Canadian politics, born in the early days of the Canada First movement in the 1870s, was in full force in the 1890s. The participants in this struggle objected to what Carl Berger terms the "pointless partisanship" they saw as characterizing the system of two parties opposing each other for the sake of opposing, and showing more interest in power than truth.[52] "The Modern Politician" was written in December 1890 and was first published in the *Week* in November 1894.[53] In 1892 Sir Sandford Fleming, the Scottish-born Canadian engineer famous for inventing the global system of standard time and for promoting the construction of the Canadian transcontinental railway, published *An Appeal to the Canadian Institute on the Rectification of Parliament*, arguing for the abolition of the party system in Canada. As Fleming makes clear in a postscript included with *An Appeal*, he saw parliamentary reform in the context of social progress: "We recognize that we are in an age of evolution: the arts and sciences are expanding civilization in every sphere of activity, and it appears inconsistent with the law of progress that the domain of government should remain non-progressive." He adds, "The evidence before us leads to the conviction that to enter on the path of progress, popular government must stand on a broader and sounder basis than that of party."[54] The author of "The Modern Politician" could only agree wholeheartedly with this assessment. As A.B. McKillop has observed, "The Modern Politician" epitomized the widespread disenchantment with politics and politicians associated with the movement to reform Parliament. Having quoted Lampman's poem in full, he comments, "To each of these lines, which mirror the disappointments and unease of an age, could be added a half-dozen sermons, speeches, and articles which echoed the poet's sentiments."[55]

Among the supporters of parliamentary reform in Canada were intellectuals of many stripes. As Berger relates, "The distaste for the chicanery of politicians and the undignified and pointless wars between parties united such various figures as the continental unionist Goldwin Smith and the loyalist Colonel Denison, the French-Canadian nationalist Henri Bourassa and the imperialist Stephen Leacock, the engineer Sandford Fleming and the controversialist William Le Sueur."[56] Lampman's friend LeSueur was, indeed, a tireless advocate of the cause. Included in an appendix to Fleming's *Appeal* is LeSueur's essay "Partizan Government," in which he too writes of the "amazing hollowness" of the party system.[57] In an earlier essay, he provides what could be taken as the logical foundation of Lampman's more impassioned castigation of "the modern politician." While the "immoralities of a grosser kind" – scandals and the like – are familiar to everyone, he suggests,

> what is not so thoroughly understood is the intellectual and moral confusion, the desolating scepticism, both as to men's motives and as to the validity of all logical processes, produced by the permanent spectacle of two bodies of men professing to speak the truth upon public questions, and yet, with monotonous regularity contradicting one another on every point. Is it any wonder that, under such a system, true and false, honest and dishonest, should come to be regarded as words empty of meaning; since what is false to one party is true to the other, while the patriots and heroes of the one are the intriguers and corruptionists of the other? It is only necessary to talk to half a dozen average voters in succession to find how little they feel the force of any appeal to conscience or reason in connection with politics, and how very feebly, if at all, they identify the interests of the country with their own.[58]

When LeSueur encountered Lampman's politician-clowns "Blinding the multitude with specious words" and cynically referencing ideals only to

Poems of Progress 257

manipulate opinion and help them reach "the ghost of power," he must have recognized regretfully, but with appreciation, the type he had described so long before.

Also a staunch supporter of the anti-party movement was another friend, journalist and author J.E. Collins (1855–1892), esteemed by Lampman for his appreciation of literature, especially poetry, and for his early and vital encouragement of "two or three – perhaps more – young writers, whose names are now well known in the Dominion."[59] Lampman would be thinking here of Roberts, possibly Bliss Carman, and himself. Collins may or may not have been the "somebody" who in 1881 or 1882 (the date is uncertain)[60] famously lent Lampman a copy of Roberts's recently published *Orion, and Other Poems*, which put Lampman into "a state of the wildest excitement" at the thought "that such work could be done by a Canadian, by a young man, one of ourselves" and "was like a voice from some new paradise of art calling to us to be up and doing." Certainly "it was through Collins that [the] correspondence [between Lampman and Roberts] first began in the early 1880s."[61] John Coldwell Adams has noted Collins's role as mentor to both Roberts and Lampman,[62] and Bentley has gone further, characterizing Collins, an ardent advocate of Canadian independence and a strong new literature worthy of the Canada he envisioned, as the driving force behind the assortment of writers later known as, in Bentley's phrasing, "the Confederation group of Canadian poets."[63] In the preface to his *Canada under the Administration of Lord Lorne*, Collins showed no hesitation in declaring his position vis-a-vis parliamentary reform:

> Our system of government – and this is a sad admission for a Canadian who has no interest in either side to make – has now become the most painful spectacle known to us. The fetters which bind our parties grow stronger; and from day to day the partizan teaches himself to look less beyond the circle that bounds him. It is in deference to the needs of such a hard-and-fast combination that men stoop to actions which, if done in private life, would bring upon them the reproach and scorn of every upright man.

Collins goes on to advocate the creation of "a Third Party ... led by a body of strong, honest, patriotic men," one that would sit "between the two factions" and be "potent enough to thwart any evil projected by the stronger" and to mitigate partisanship so effectively that the old style of politicking would soon disappear.[64] While Collins disassociates himself from any ideology or political stance, and in this regard differs from Lampman, who "was on the side of socialism and reasonable propaganda to that end," nevertheless his critique of the two-party system and his vilification of the politicians who kept it going would have found a receptive ear in the young Lampman, and more so as the years went by.

Lampman's attitude toward the politicians of his day, made clear in "The Modern Politician," is nowhere expressed so succinctly than in an epigram that E.K. Brown retrieved from among Lampman's papers:

> From the seer with his snow-white crown
> > Through every sort and condition
> Of bipeds, all the way down
> > To the pimp and the politician.[65]

The quasi-scientific language gives the quatrain a blackly humorous appearance of objectivity: the speaker is simply analyzing types, just as the botanists of Lampman's day would categorize and name the various fungi they observed. At the top of the vertical scale is wisdom, for Lampman the highest of qualities, as indicated by his decision to name his utopian country of the future after Pallas Athena, goddess of wisdom. At the bottom are the lowliest examples of their kind, with the politician fitted securely into place by the anticipated rhyme and the alliteration that links the two nouns at the end. This is a methodically arranged expression of contempt, lacking, admittedly, any stated rationale for its negativity – "The poem seems to hang in the air without any support," commented Scott[66] – but rhetorically effective in its calculated strategy of association.

A more complex and self-disclosing work, but equally outspoken, is the sonnet "The True Life," written in 1894 but published for the first time in 1943 in *At the Long Sault*. The title is Scott's; Lampman called the poem simply "Life."[67] Partly a study of the individual's struggle for authenticity in a world that demands conformity, the poem is also an indictment of an establishment that impedes progress by mouthing platitudes that reinforce the status quo and pressure others to go along with the falsehoods.[68] In an early draft, Lampman's target was the church, or rather its conservative congregation, those people whom, along with industrialists and politicians, he saw as bolstering a retrograde and destructive social order.[69] Over time, however, Lampman changed some of the phrases to broaden the scope and possibly to avoid offending the very churchgoers the poem might have implicated. Even so, when he sent a copy of the revised version to his sister Isabelle and her husband, her reply was, "Thank you for sending us your poem – I am not as much impressed by it as I am usually by your work."[70] In an earlier letter, this same sister confessed that "[o]f late I have come to agree with others that when you are simply expressing your perceptions of Nature you are best." Such responses, though discouraging, did not prevent Lampman from including "Life" in an early manuscript version of the collection that was to become *Alcyone*.[71] As it happened, he removed all sonnets from that collection in hopes of including them in a separate volume of sonnets, and after that plan fell through, he reinstated in the final compilation of *Alcyone* twelve nature sonnets. Since it did not qualify as a nature sonnet, "Life" was not among them.

In Lampman's manuscript copy book for this time period, "Life" comes after "The Clearer Self," on the same page as the final stanza of that poem, which runs over from the previous page.[72] The effect is that Lampman's expressed wish to know "The clearer self, the grander me" is followed immediately by an outcry of frustration at how difficult it is to have that wish fulfilled:

This life is a depressing compromise
Between the soul and what it wills to do
And what your careful neighbours plan for you,
Often the thing most odious in your eyes,
A makeshift truce, whereby the soul denies
The birthright of a being bright and new[,]
Puts on a mask and crushes down the true,
And lolls behind a fence of courteous lies.[73]

The word "careful" – not Lampman's first choice – is heavily loaded in the context of these lines. The neighbours lack boldness; their conservatism makes them timid of change, and through their influence, "you" are also curtailed. They are filled (-*ful*) with worry or anxiety (*care*), in the sense that humanity in "A Prayer" is beset by "glooms and cares" and city dwellers in "Freedom" are trapped in the "furnace of care." The neighbours are not joyful. Mainly, however, they are solicitous of others, full of concern, caring, the heavy irony of this significance being made clear in the line that follows. This complex use of a term not normally pejorative, forcing us by its context to ascertain its intended significance, demonstrates the skill with which Lampman could hone what comes across as a spontaneous outburst.

Originally, the "careful neighbours" were "pious brethren," a pointedly sarcastic reference to fellow worshippers. Lampman's attitude to churchgoing was never very positive. "Sunday," he complains in a letter to Thomson, "is a day that drives me almost to madness. The prim black clothes, the artificial dress of the women, the slow trooping to church, the bells, the silence, the dreariness, the occasional knots of sallow & unhealthy zealots whom one may meet at a street corner whining over some awful point in theology – all that gradually presses me down till by Sunday night I am in despair, and would fain issue forth with pot & brush and colour the town crimson."[74] The staid and conventional behaviour of the attendees, in whose company he seems obligated to remain, fills him with a desire to break free, as from prison or a straightjacket, and give vent to a bottled-up passion. It is not to paint the town red, however, that the speaker yearns in "The True Life," but rather just to call nonsense nonsense, to speak of what really matters, and to engage in activities that would support a more satisfying, less hypocritical existence.

As in "The Modern Politician," it is the falseness of people's behaviour that is their most offensive trait – the speaker's own, because he wishes to break free but feels compelled to conform, but mostly that of the neighbours who seem actively involved in thwarting his desires. Whereas living authentically, untrammelled by tradition and restriction, could lead to beneficial change and expansion of the human soul, conformity to false ideals is soul-destroying. Thus in the sestet, apostrophizing a now expanded version of "neighbours," the speaker declares his truth:

> O, world of little men, how sweet a thing
> The true life is, what strength and joy it hath,
> What grandeur and what beauty it might bring,
> Could we but sweep forever from our path
> Your cant rules and detested casuistries,
> Your clap-trap, and your damned hypocrisies.

The word "true," in its simplest sense, means genuine, contrasting the falseness against which the speaker rails. At the same time, "the true life" is a phrase that suggests a religious life or a life devoted to high moral and spiritual purpose, in contrast to the false semblance of this. It is used in this way by John Watson, who states, "the religious interests of man can be preserved only by a theology which affirms that all forms of being are manifestations of a single spiritual principle in identification with which the true life of man consists," or again, "the highest life of man can only be realized through the consciousness that he has no true life which can be severed from life in God."[75] Lampman's "Could we but," echoing identical phrases in the sonnets "Sight" and "An Old Lesson from the Fields," laments the failure of society to free itself of the high-sounding but false and stultifying ideologies of the "little men" and to embrace "the true life," similar to people's failure in "Sight" to distinguish "True ends from false, and lofty things from low," an ability that would liberate them, for "Then should the wonder of this world draw near / And life's innumerable harmonies." Indeed the critiques of humanity in these two poems are remarkably similar, highlighting a consistency between the nature-loving Lampman of *Among the Millet* and the radical Lampman of *Alcyone*. Despite the similarities, however, and with all due respect to Lampman's sister, who likely would have had no qualms about praising "Sight," the disarming directness and verbal "force" of "The True Life," expressive of raw emotion, make it the stronger poem.

This "force" is particularly noticeable in the closing lines. The critique of conventional religion in the earlier draft of the poem, evident in the excised phrase "pious brethren," was also conveyed in Lampman's original use of "church talk," replaced by "clap-trap." The choice of "clap-trap" was inspired. It reinforces the anger and frustration that the poem overall expresses. "Church talk" is scornful, but "clap-trap" is entirely dismissive. The ending is also made stronger and more emphatic than it might otherwise have been by Lampman's use of a rhyming couplet in what is otherwise a Petrarchan sonnet. The climactic "damned hypocrisies," with its single plosive occurring in the last stressed syllable, to be spat out with disdain, sounds all the more final for the close proximity of the rhyme. It is interesting to note that, as late as 1942, Scott was of a mind to soften the ending by changing "damned" to "rank," but in the end agreed with Brown that the poem should stand "Damned and all."[76]

In the social poems under examination, Lampman's position, explicit or implicit, is that a shift in society toward socialism is what *should* happen, and he is variously optimistic and pessimistic about whether such a shift *will* happen. As to the means by which the process will, or should, take place, for the most part he seems to adopt the Fabian position, anticipating incremental changes "from possibility to possibility," despite inevitable lapses. Another scenario, however, was that the downtrodden majority, unwilling to abide relentless oppression, would rise up in revolt against the established order and bring about change by force. In his essay on socialism, Lampman cites as historical precedent the French Revolution. Despite the horrors of the Reign of Terror and the murders and atrocities carried out by the citizenry during the September Massacres, he argues, the ideal of freedom from "feudal chains" was present throughout, "hanging over the heads of the rough multitude," and as a result, Europe still owes "the debt of political liberty" to the Revolution, for through it "civilization was advanced another stage."[77] (The logic here is similar to that of Lampman's defence of "some extravagances and unseemliness" on the part of the newly liberated women of his time, which should be accepted as "a natural reaction from the condition of stunted growth and 'intolerable ennui' which were the boast of the past.")[78]

A poem in which the possibility of revolution is sympathetically addressed, and in which the French Revolution is once again referenced, although without the same equanimity with respect to the new regime, is "Liberty," written in January 1898. Like "Epitaph on a Rich Man" and "The True Life," this poem was culled from Lampman's notebooks by Brown and first published in *At the Long Sault* in 1943.

The title "Liberty" alludes to the phrase "liberty, equality, fraternity," the motto of the French Republic that was coined during the French Revolution. It was "Just a hundred years ago," the speaker relates, that "the shout of freedom" resonated throughout the world, and people everywhere believed that the cry would act as a sword to conquer "Hate, injustice, tyranny," replacing those evils with "Plenty, brotherhood, and peace." But even though "the tyrant kings are gone" and a new order has come into being, the anticipated change has not occurred: "the justice comes not." Worse yet, a new oppression is perpetrated under a revolutionary banner:

> Still the ancient curse survives
> Making wreck of human lives;
> Pride and slavery and shame
> Prosper in the people's name.

True liberty has not taken hold, for the "master" is still in control and the "toiler" still does his bidding, and while "Golden ladies" lounge on cushions as in the past, "the stricken trull goes by / With her wild and haunted face."

As always, it is the subjugation of the labouring classes to the will of the monied classes – the majority suffering for the benefit of the minority – that Lampman finds objectionable. In the next stanza, the sixth of seven, the speaker asks rhetorically,

> Was it for this – for this? we cry
> That you made the peoples free,
> That your vessels plough the sea,
> And your buildings climb the sky ...?

The pronouns are confusing, but the idea seems to be that, following the French Revolution, the revolutionary movements of the world ("you") made their societies "free" of monarchic tyranny, but people today ("we") find that conditions remain effectively the same. The pronoun "this" refers to the retrograde idea "that one should hold / All that kings possessed of old" while "the other" has "service for his lot." It is true that, with those vessels and buildings, there is evidence of prosperity, but the age-old disparities remain. In short: was aristocratic tyranny overthrown just so we could have capitalism?

The rhetorical question of stanza six marks the point at which Lampman might have been expected to leave off, as in "The Better Day," which concludes with a series of such questions. This time the ending is more explicit. Was it for this, the same oppression under a new name, that the great changes initiated by the French Revolution were brought about?

> This! my Masters, Nay!
> For there comes at last the day
> When the meanest and most poor
> Having scanned the ages' flow[,]
> Probed his hurt, and guessed the cure
> Shall rise up and answer – No!

A new revolutionary consciousness will take hold among the oppressed, with whom the speaker himself identifies, referring to the oppressors as "my Masters." Poor but intelligent, the suffering masses will come to see that evolution ("the ages' flow") points to progress, and since exploitation is not progressive, they will "rise up" to bring about change.

In a short poem that has never before been published, Lampman envisions a march of demonstrators who are engaged in just such an action:

> Do you hear the cry of the people?
>   There is thunder in their tone;
> They march with a banner uplifted[.]
>   Do you see what is written thereon?
>
> "What need that the one should flourish
>   And the ten should sink and fall;
> There's enough in the old earth's granaries,
>   There's enough in her looms for all."

In the decades ahead, of course, workers would organize, in some places mounting revolutions and in others demanding and receiving significant gains in such areas as working conditions, hours, and salary. Lampman's forecast in "Liberty" of a working-class movement that would effect a social transformation was to some degree prescient.

Although "Liberty" has an unfinished quality about it and is marred by occasional awkwardness and ambiguity, it is a powerful expression of the idea that oppression masquerading as freedom is a travesty of justice, one that the oppressed will not abide. Its seven-syllable trochaic line, with substitutions here and there of a five-syllable line, is suitably taut, harnessing the anger, while its uneven stanza lengths and haphazard end rhymes give the poem a free-form, content-driven feel.

Whether its strategy is to threaten the powers that be so that they will relent and introduce reforms or to embolden the masses themselves, "Liberty" is a poem that resonates from nineteenth-century Canada with a decidedly angry, radical voice, not only offering a harsh critique of the inequities of capitalism but also advocating – the tone seems to go beyond forecasting – revolutionary change. Irving Layton found it impressive. The poems "Epitaph on a Rich Man" and "Liberty," he relates in his 1944 review of *At the Long Sault*, came to him "like two mortar blasts," revealing "an unexpected social awareness in Lampman." "Liberty," he suggests, "without its somewhat antiquated rhetoric about Kings and Tyrants, might have been written by some aspiring poet in the *New Masses* or the *Canadian Tribune*" – Marxist publications from the American and Canadian radical left, respectively.[79] The word "aspiring" may seem to dampen the praise, but Layton's point is that "Liberty," apart from some of its language, sounds modern and radical, ahead of its time.

Lampman's prophetic visions and poems of social protest strike many notes. They range from hopeful to despairing and from angry to placidly serene. Common to all, however, is a belief in progress and a conviction that the power structure responsible for social inequity and exploitation must be challenged – the former philosophical, the latter political. Not surprisingly, given Lampman's pathfinding role in this realm of poetic expression, the poems are unequal in quality, but at their best they exhibit a power and eloquence that make of political persuasion, memorable art.

CHAPTER 10

Heroic Visionaries of Future Progress

Two social-political poems that do not employ the rousing language of "Liberty" and "The Modern Politician" but that nevertheless reflect Lampman's radical social conscience are the narrative-descriptive "Sebastian" and what Lampman called his "small novel in blank verse," *The Story of an Affinity*.[1] These are both character-focused works featuring descriptive realism in an overtly Canadian setting within which socially aware main characters are seen to be readying themselves for significant, though unspecified, involvement in the struggle for societal transformation. If ever the future ideal envisioned by Lampman's progressivist philosophy is to be realized, these poems suggest, the social movement sparking the change is likely to be led by such characters as these intelligent, sensitive, heroic members of the working classes – farmers and labourers.

The main focus of *The Story of an Affinity* is its love theme, of interest for its autobiographical aspects. The descriptions of the female lead, Margaret, slim and tall and with "calm grey eyes," precisely match those of Katherine Waddell in Lampman's love poems relating to her, and the working-out of the relationship between Margaret and her male counterpart can be read as a vicarious fulfillment of the frustrated love between Lampman and Waddell.[2] The growth of love and the maturing of the two main characters as they prepare for their roles at the vanguard of a new social order, however, are themes not simply parallel but integral to each other, since love is what fosters the marriage-bound couple's determination and commitment. In "Sebastian," by contrast, the focus is entirely on the development of the main character's social-political outlook; the love theme is entirely lacking.

"Sebastian"

First drafted in May 1889 and revised in 1892, "Sebastian" was published in the *Week* on 17 May 1895.[3] Slated for inclusion in *Alcyone*, it was omitted from the final version of that collection.[4] Lampman changed the name of the title character several times over the course of revising the poem. At one point it was Paolo, perhaps suggesting Saint Paul; later Amico, meaning friend; and finally Sebastian, with Greek roots signifying "revered" or "venerable."[5] The character seems, by turns, a visionary, a friend to the people, and a man with potential to become a beloved leader; in the poem, all these associations apply.

As noted by Howard O'Hagan in his 1901 *Canadian Essays*, Lampman gave a reading of "Sebastian" "at a meeting of the Royal Society of Canada" – possibly the "literary and musical evening" held on 19 November 1897 that included "A. Lampman, reading."[6] This reading would indicate that the poem was a work of importance in the eyes of its author. It has remained obscure in the critical literature largely because it did not appear in *Poems*, despite Scott's claim that "almost everything that [Lampman] had written was included."[7] Since then, it has been republished only once, in a gathering of "fugitive poems" in the academic journal *Canadian Poetry: Studies, Documents, Reviews*.[8] O'Hagan may be implying a criticism of Scott when, wishing to give "some insight into the spirit and character of Lampman's workmanship," he quotes forty-eight lines from the poem as his only example of Lampman's writing.[9] Presumably O'Hagan had heard the reading he mentions and was favourably impressed.

It is difficult to know why Scott would omit "Sebastian" from *Poems*. It represents Lampman at the height of his descriptive powers and broadens the palette of his social-political poems, featuring a mill worker in the heroic mould of visionary labourer whose cause is progressive social change.

It does these things, moreover, within a recognizably local setting that features contemporary logging and mill work, evoked with documentary accuracy. Both character and setting bespeak a desire on Lampman's part to imbue his immediate surroundings with a mythopoeic significance.

A poem of 127 lines, "Sebastian" is divided into seven sections, the first three largely descriptive of the main character, the workplace, and the work itself, and the last four depicting Sebastian's behaviour as he readies himself mentally for the role he is to play. The cinematic opening lines focus closely on the main character's appearance in order to establish his heroic stature and suitability for that role:

> Tall and loose-limbed, leading upon his pole,
> Rapt yet alert, a giant in a dream:
> Drooped shoulders, head thrust slightly forward, hair
> Curled duskly over wide and wave-like brows,
> Long hands with lean and supple fingers, cheeks
> High-boned, tanned red as leather.

The camera then zooms in on his "watchful eyes," which from "far within" are "Fed by a tranquil and perpetual fire." The passage concludes, "So leans Sebastian with unharassed gaze / That marks the hour, but seems to watch beyond." Sebastian's calm, confident demeanour is central to his character. He is not impulsive. His judgments will be sound and his actions well considered. He is in touch with the here and now, and at the same time focused on the larger picture (of the history and destiny of humankind, as it turns out) – both realist and dreamer.

The focus then shifts to local surroundings, seen through the mill hand's eyes: the "heavy river" that "o'er its fall of rocks / Roars down in foam and spouted spray and pounds / Its bed with solid thunders"; the "river shepherds" or log drivers who "with their spiked poles / Herd [the logs] in flocks, and drive them like blind sheep / Unto the slaughterer's hand"; and the mill's interior "cool with the scent of pines" where "the crash and clamour shake the floors" and "All day"

> The pitiless saws creep up the dripping logs
> With champ and sullen roar, or round and shrill,

> A glittering fury of invisible teeth,
> Yell through the clacking boards.

The descriptive language reveals the poem's protagonist as both close observer of nature and interpreter alert to the plight of the victims of oppression, whose tragic lot he reads in the cutting of the timber. To be able to provide this level of detail, it is clear that Lampman had stepped inside a functioning mill and stood within its "Dim and low-roofed" confines to make his firsthand observations. He had, moreover, observed its operation at night as well as in the daytime. Thus he can describe the "fierce light" emanating from its walls:

> Through every hole and crack, through all the doors,
> A stream upon the solid dark, it lights
> The black smooth races and the glimmering booms,
> And turns the river's spouted spray to silver.

Inside, the glare illuminates, along with the saw blades and the logs, "the wild crowd of men" working night shift, and these rough workers, too, he must have observed. His goal in this poem, at least in part, is to provide accurate reportage.

Within the mill environment, Sebastian is pictured as both thoughtful observer and supremely capable worker. In the former role, he glances outside through "the great square door" of the mill and his "quiet eyes" take in the river rapids and in the distance "The pale blue cloud line of the summer hills." He is like the speaker of Lampman's "At the Ferry":

> Beyond the tumult of the mills,
>   And all the city's sound and strife,
> Beyond the waste, beyond the hills,
>   I look far out and dream of life.

This stanza brings "At the Ferry" to a close, but in "Sebastian" we are given further insight into the content of the dream. As he looks past "the heat and roar," Sebastian "Skirts the cool borders of an ampler world,

/ Decking the hours with visions." He is thinking about social progress. At the same time, as worker, he is alert to the task at hand:

> Up the shaken slides
> With splash and thunder come the groaning logs.
> Sebastian grasps his cant-dog with light strength,
> Drives into their dripping sides its iron fangs,
> And one by one as with a giant's ease
> Turns them and sets them toward the crashing saws.

These lines vividly capture the workplace in terms of task and equipment, exhibiting at the same time the formidable skill of the protagonist.

Altogether the descriptions in the first part of the poem provide a detailed record of mill work in the heyday of the sawn wood industry in the Ottawa region, which according to a governmental record was at its height between 1882 and 1902.[10] The poem does not specify a precise setting, but one can be inferred. An undated manuscript poem depicting river and mill and employing similar language includes the following apostrophe to the Ottawa River: "And so thou comest ever journeying home / To where the narrow Chaudiere breaks in foam / The torrent of thy water."[11] This poem cannot be classified as an early draft of "Sebastian," since the main character and central focus of the latter are entirely lacking, but with its descriptive passages echoed and in some cases repeated verbatim in "Sebastian," it qualifies as a precursor. It is therefore safe to identify the mill in "Sebastian" with the one in the manuscript poem, situated at the base of the once-magnificent Chaudière Falls, just west of Parliament Hill, where the great lumber mills in the Ottawa of Lampman's day were clustered.[12]

As for the temporal setting, a phrase from "Sebastian" is instructive. As the main character looks out on the river's rapids, his gaze reaches beyond the "piered and buttressed bridge." This is clearly the suspension bridge over the Chaudière, featuring four piers or towers supporting cables, built in 1843 and replaced by a different kind of bridge in 1889.[13] To prepare for the replacement, the suspension bridge was demolished the previous year.[14] Unfortunately the manuscript poem is not dated, although it is written out on Post Office stationery inscribed July 1885.[15] The vignette of mill work captured in "Sebastian," then, would appear to reflect the scene as it was between 1885 and 1888 – most likely the latter half of this period since the tautness and immediacy of some of the descriptive language is characteristic of the poetic maturity that Lampman had attained by 1887.

Lampman's depiction of sawmill activity in "Sebastian" may be compared with a description of the Chaudière mills made by "a tourist" during the height of the lumber trade. In his 1927 *Ottawa Past and Present*, A.H.D. Ross quotes the visitor as follows:

> Great chains and hooks descend and drag the logs up a trough-like incline into the dens where the myriad teeth of the terrible saws await them. After they are "slabbed off" to the proper thickness they pass under heavy rollers to the "gates." In each gate thirty or forty saws dart up and down in a gigantic dance, and against their lance-like teeth the logs are steadily and irresistibly driven until the steel bites its way from end to end. Beyond each gate endless chain-conveyors carry forward the planks and boards to be "edged." Behind each saw there shoots a curving yellow spray of sawdust, and the timber divides as swiftly as though it were the impalpable fabric of a dream. Next the boards are squared off at the ends by circular saws revolving so fast that they appear to be stationary. As each touches the innocent-looking humming disk there rises a soaring shriek which may quaver through the whole gamut, the chaos of strange and strident noises being simply indescribable, and the whole scene of ceaseless activity a most novel and impressive one. By day the whole scene is enacted in the yellow gloom of a low-roofed timber structure housing the powerful and complicated machinery of the mill, and by night the continuous rending and biting of the saws is carried on beneath the white glare of countless electric lights.[16]

This record matches Lampman's in several particulars, including the size and efficiency of the operation, the level and quality of noise, the round-the-clock activity, and the details of chain and saw, together with the dramatic impressiveness of "the whole scene." Noticeably absent, though, are the workers. A reader might conclude from the description here that the entire operation was automated. For Lampman the "river shepherds" and the "wild crowd of men" in the mill are a vital component. Indeed, the main purpose of his adaptation of his original manuscript was evidently to introduce the larger human story – that of social change emanating from the working class – while rendering the mill symbolic of the dehumanizing forces of industrialization that the poem's hero sees beyond in his vision of "an ampler world."

In the remainder of the poem, the focus is on Sebastian's growth toward a state of readiness for what seems his predestined role in bringing about social change. We see the mill hand after hours (he "only works by day") leaning over the windowsill of "the small upper chamber where he sleeps." He looks out across the night "with that ample front / And those calm, capable, untroubled eyes," his own qualities reflecting those of the better world he imagines. Two questions are juxtaposed: "What thought is in yon city's moving heart?" and "What thoughts are in Sebastian's soul?" Superficially, the city's inhabitants may not be thinking very deeply. The voices he hears "from the rooms below" – "Threats, curses, drunken songs" – suggest no questing after truth. These people are indulging in the "poor makeshifts" and "common lures" of life, "Wine, lust, or play," to which Sebastian pays no heed. At some deeper level, however, all humanity yearns for the happier state of being that evolutionary progressivism points to as its destiny, and Sebastian's thoughts seem the embodiment of that yearning:

> The future! What shall the great future bring?
> He dreams not yet; but this, unconsciously,
> Sown with the very seed of life, he knows,
> That all his being like yon city's heart,
> Brain, flesh, and spirit, by encumbered paths,
> To some large purpose moves serenely on.

We recognize this vision of the future from Lampman's poems of progress, such as "Man's Future," where "mind and flesh and soul" will be balanced in "a rhythmic whole" when humankind at long last attains its "appointed place" in the society of the future. Sebastian, like the speaker in "The Clearer Self," is not sure what the new world and the new humanity will be like, but in contrast to that pleading individual, he is on the verge of knowing. In his room, we are told, he has books:

> And there Sebastian sits, and with grave brow,
> Keeps vigil stouter than a knight of old,
> Questing through lands beset with doubt and toil
> His modern Sangreal.

In the mythopoesis of Lampman's poem, Sebastian is the type of the emerging hero who will find the path and then lead the way to humanity's predestined future. The books he reads, admittedly, reflect "doubt and toil," and people's paths are "encumbered," but Sebastian, serene and sure, is the opposite of those pessimists (Lampman himself sometimes among their number) who despair of positive change:

>   not for him
> Is doubt; might hath begotten might; the hours
> Move onward, widening to eternity.
> Sebastian sees them, and his eager gaze
> Grows firmer and more trustful day by day,
> More spacious and more solemn.

While resembling Lampman himself in his "dreaming" of the future, Sebastian has the confidence, determination, and patience that his creator lacked but saw as necessary in one who could lead the way to social transformation.

The closing segment of the poem shows Sebastian on the threshold of readiness for a call to action. His self-education has empowered him. Still, he continues to study, and "each point of knowledge gained" brings him ever closer to his goal:

> It is a key to open stanchioned doors
> And lift the lids of coffers yet unsearched,
> A golden gleam on many a dark recess,
> A sword laid by that may be some day drawn.

The symbolic key, light, and sword will together enable him, and, with him, other progressives, to remake society. Whatever the method of transformation turns out to be, it is his learning that is his strength. Through his studies – following, we might say, Lampman's "new conception of the higher life," the effect of which is to arm participants "with a breadth and majesty of vision which withers away from the soul the greeds and lusts and meannesses of the old, narrow and ignorant humanity" – he has been building up "the conquering fabric of his brain."[17] And since progress is aligned with truth, his knowledge of the laws of the universe and the history and destiny of humankind will enable him to urge society in a forward direction. The readiness is all: "When he is ready, horsed, and fully armed, / The occasion shall not pass unmarked. His hour / Will bid him with an unmistakable touch." This conclusion leaves us on the threshold of change.[18] Knight-like, Sebastian is confident, steadfast, and devoted to an ideal. Yet our modern Galahad is a mere labourer, albeit a learned one. In this character, Lampman has blended the scientific preoccupations of his age with a proletarian consciousness to situate an enlightened mill hand at the forefront of imminent progressive social change. Sebastian embodies the future.

"The Story of an Affinity"

Around the time he was revising his original draft of "Sebastian" in advance of its publication in the *Week*, Lampman put much conscientious effort into the writing of a long narrative poem with which the earlier work had much in common. *The Story of an Affinity* is a kind of poetic Bildungsroman about the development of the main character, Richard Stahlberg, from a strong but naive farmer's son to a sensitive and erudite young man (aged twenty-nine) ready to play his part in some great enterprise, motivated throughout by his devotion to the wise and virtuous Margaret Hawthorne, whose character development is also part of the story.[19] It appears, however, that Lampman made no attempt to publish it. A tracing of the evolution of the poem from inception through enthusiastic progress reports in letters to Thomson and others to its sudden disappearance from Lampman's correspondence is revealing of the sometimes unhappy commingling of the creative and personal realms.

As Kathy Mezei notes in her discussion of Lampman's conscious desire to evoke a "sense of place" and "transform history into myth" in his poetry, the genesis of *The Story of an Affinity* can be traced to a letter Lampman wrote in the summer of 1884 to his college friend J.A. Ritchie, where he mentions his plan to write "a strictly Canadian poem, local in its incident and spirit, but cosmopolitan in form and manner" set "in the Niagara district, among the old farmsteads there."[20] However, serious planning did not begin until October 1892, when Lampman wrote Thomson, "I am trying to work myself up to commence something long; and I should not be surprised if I succeed."[21] He then put all his energy into the project, informing Thomson in November that an essay he had been writing on Keats had "gone to the wall" because he was so busy with the poem, and apologizing to J.E. Wetherell a few days later for not having yet read a book Wetherell had sent him, explaining, "I have been very hard at work on a certain piece of writing."[22] Some fifteen months later, on 2 February 1894, he wrote Thomson that he was "almost finished," adding, "I verily believe it will be a good thing, and will bring me credit." By 28 February he could report to his sister Isabelle, "I have finished and am working over a long piece which has occupied me for more than a year. It is called 'The Story of an Affinity', is a sort of novelette in blank verse, and contains about 2000 lines." He comments, "I believe that it is a good thing and will do more to make me a name than any other thing or things I have written," but concedes, "I think this to-day: perhaps to-morrow I shall be damning it!"[23] The last surviving reference to the poem in Lampman's correspondence is his promise on 25 April 1894 to send his manuscript "in a little while" to Thomson for evaluation. "If it does not gain the suffrages of the wise," he states, "I shall take it that I must stop doing that kind of work."[24] At this point all discussion of the poem (in the extant correspondence) ceases, and there is no evidence to show that Lampman ever sent it to a publisher. What happened?

One could speculate that, upon hearing Thomson's criticisms, Lampman changed his mind about the artistic merits of the poem, or one could adopt Bentley's explanation that Lampman wrote the poem with a view to having it published in the United States, only to find that in the American periodicals and publishing houses of the day there was no niche for the long poem.[25] To at least one perceptive reader, however, the reason for the sudden disappearance was of a more personal nature. As Lampman's confidant, Thomson must have recognized that the life parallels – Margaret's resemblance to Katherine Waddell and the similarity between Richard's love for Margaret and Lampman's for Waddell

– were all too obvious. And he would have seen that the poem's negative characterization of marriages lacking "affinity" reflected badly on Lampman's own marriage. For these reasons, he advised his friend against publishing the work while still a married man; and Lampman, whose love for Maud, his wife, is often lost sight of in considerations of his marital difficulties, agreed.[26] Although Lampman may never have damned his cherished tale in verse, he did consign it to Limbo, where it languished for six years until Scott included it, with several lengthy excisions, in the posthumous *Poems*. In Bentley's edition of the poem, used in the present discussion, the original text is fully restored.

The Story of an Affinity – loosely based, as Wanda Campbell has shown, on a story by Goethe, part of a larger work whose title, *Elective Affinities*, signals an association with Lampman's poem[27] – is mainly concerned with the relationship between the two main characters, but in treating the themes of love and marriage, Lampman also explores issues of self-discovery, self-fulfillment, and meaningful engagement in life. For him, personal happiness was contingent on one's success in finding and following one's own inclinations and not getting caught up in what is referred to in "The True Life" as the "depressing compromise" that can exist "Between the soul and what it wills to do / And what your careful neighbours plan for you, / Often the thing most odious in your eyes." The title of another sonnet developing this theme, "Salvation," indicates the importance Lampman placed on nurturing rather than stifling one's particular gift. Following one's inclinations, however, had also to do with emotional needs, and the conflict sparked on occasion by the contrary pulls of passion (sexual desire) and morality (doing right by others) was for Lampman deeply troubling. In his poems on progress and moral purpose, he sometimes found it necessary to have the speaker resist "the world's base control" mentioned in "To the Prophetic Soul" (re-spun as "the passions' dark control" in "Peace") in order to proceed "alone" down the "glorious road" of selfless devotion to the cause of social progress. Omitted from this solution is all possibility of romantic or conjugal love, or even shared affection.

In *The Story of an Affinity*, passion, personal fulfillment, and work devoted to the advancement of humanity – corresponding to the Freudian trinity of id, ego, and superego – are reconciled and harmonized by love. Prior to his transformative meeting with Margaret, Richard is a brooding and unhappy young man at the mercy of strong but unfocused passions, his mind a cauldron of formless potential. His love for Margaret gives direction to his passions. At the same time, Margaret awakens him to his own ambition – he wants to develop his mind – and then inspires him to pursue his goal of acquiring an education, which will make him a more eligible husband for Margaret. Because it flourishes within love, passion now feeds rather than stifles Richard's energy for meaningful engagement with the world; and since contributing to the progress of humanity is for him and Margaret, as for Lampman, the most important work one can do, the poem has the ultimately happy lovers embarking on a life's journey of active involvement in the cause of social betterment, empowered by their love. Much difficult terrain must be crossed, however, before this journey can begin.

As is consistent with Lampman's 1884 plan, the country portions of *The Story of an Affinity* (the first and last of its three parts) take place in what is clearly the Niagara fruit belt, where a hundred years earlier some of Lampman's own United Empire Loyalist forebears had settled and farmed.[28] In Part 1, the two main characters, having been playmates as children, become estranged in their adolescence, as do their counterparts in *Elective Affinities*. During this period, Margaret travels to "the great city" where she attends school and learns "other thoughts and ways" while Richard develops into a physically powerful man but one who, despite having shown "flashes of a strange intelligence" as a boy, remains mentally and emotionally immature. He is afflicted by a "strange infirmity" whereby his ability to act in a constructive manner is subverted by the passions to which he finds himself subject. On one occasion, significantly just before he becomes reacquainted with Margaret, he exhibits the effects of his affliction. Profoundly moved by the beauty of the wind roaring in the trees above his head and sweeping across nearby fields of wheat "in swift pale glimmering waves," he feels the need for "some tremendous word / Or violent deed," and lacking recourse to the former, he seizes "in both his hands / The trunk of a young birch-tree" and, bracing himself, rips the tree from the ground and flings it into the nearby field. "The deed," we are told, "relieved him." This auto-erotic violence, described by Early as "a perverse expression of sexual energy," shows the deep frustration of the young man who, though capable by nature (as we discover) of great achievement, remains at this point helpless to act creatively, in thrall to his undirected passion.[29]

It is at this crucial juncture that Richard, at age nineteen, stumbles on Margaret, newly returned from the city, asleep on a "rustic bench" with a book lying open at her feet.[30] In proper romantic fashion, he is struck "As if a blow / Had met him in the forehead from some hand / Invisible" by the appearance of this beautiful young woman. Fully mature, educated, and refined, she is everything he (now) desires, both as an object of love and as a model for his own self-improvement. The sight of her inspires a kind of personal revelation, linked in an extravagant parallel to a biblical precedent:

> A vision, rare and beautiful to him
> As any by [the] Saint in Patmos seen,
> Had slid beneath the cloud-bands of his soul,
> And flooding all with one enchanted gleam
> Had driven them far asunder.

As with all mystical visions, Richard has, in a moment, experienced enlightenment. "With ever-deepening pierce," we are told, "he saw the world / And his own life, and comprehended all." He feels empowered; transformed. A few minutes before, he had approached the spot where Margaret was resting "With plodding gait and wasteful eyes, wherein / That mindless grief and impotent hunger burned." Now, "At one stroke / Life rose beneath him like a magic tower." The mix of religious and sexual imagery in this part of the poem underlines the close connection between spiritual and sexual fulfillment, both made possible by love.

Richard soon finds, however, that his awakening also has its fearful side, for he now recognizes "his own ignorance" and the gulf of knowledge that divides him from Margaret. The book she has been reading, he observes, contains "curious words and unknown type" – the Hellenist Lampman, we can speculate, has her studying Greek[31] – and he feels intimidated. How could she, the playmate of his childhood, have become so learned? Margaret assures him that "If you will to learn, / You may," and Richard's life-changing response to this is endearingly spontaneous:

"I am resolved", he said[,] "to live my life anew
And follow manfully where your steps have gone,
Margaret; and this book shall be my guide –
The thing I prize beyond all else on earth –
If you will let me keep it for my own."

She gives him the book, now imbued with talismanic significance, and assures him that "some day in a future year" they will "read it through together." For Richard, a bond has thus been established, even though for Margaret, it appears, no such tie exists, notwithstanding that the seed of love has been planted in her heart.

It is notable that Richard's illumination occurs at noon on a hot day in "the blazing heart of June" – the same time of day and close to the same time of year as when the speakers of "Among the Timothy" and "Heat" experience profound transformations of consciousness.[32] The situational and linguistic details reinforce the connection. The description of Margaret's arrival at the rustic bench "ere the burning sun / Had robbed the shadowy dock-leaves of their pearls," not with scythe, to be sure, but "Swinging her wide-brimmed hat," echoes the account of the mower entering the scene in "Among the Timothy":

Long hours ago, while yet the morn was blithe,
  Nor sharp athirst had drunk the beaded dew,
A mower came, and swung his gleaming scythe
  Around this stump.

In both cases, the arrival sets the stage for the mystical experience that is to follow, and as the scene in *The Story of an Affinity* unfolds, several additional references reinforce the parallel. Margaret's father, we are told, delights in his daughter's "sun-like presence," and it is in her presence "at the stroke of noonday" that Richard feels the clouds oppressing his soul disperse. Then, instead of fading, the noon expands, taking even fuller possession of the scene. In the aftermath of his encounter with Margaret and following the midday meal he shares with her family, Richard feels the need to wander the fields by himself before returning home. In this scene, during which we find him at one point "wading among timothy," he is exposed to the sun at full strength: "Now perfect noon with not a single cloud, / A measureless kingdom of content, shone down / On the still meadows and heat-drowsèd fields." It is under the influence of this (for Lampman) most intensely charged of all temporal settings that Richard, having felt confused about what his spiritual awakening might mean and dismayed by thoughts of his "unworthiness," can focus productively on his situation. The parallel with "Heat" is quite precise. Just as, in the earlier poem, the speaker's "thoughts grow keen and clear" under the intense rays of the midday sun, Richard's "quieted will" now shapes "the tumult of his thoughts / Into an ordered counsel, bringing forth / A single stream of purpose large and clear." Uniting the themes of personal regeneration in nature and salvation through love, the parallels reveal Lampman expanding his mythopoeic design to encompass human relations and, with them, his social-political concerns – for the "purpose large and clear" is gradually revealed in the poem to be one of dedication to the greater good of humankind. Richard, whose name carries the meaning of "powerful leader," will soon be joining Sebastian, figuratively speaking, in the movement to further the cause of social betterment.

Part 2 recounts Richard's ten-year educational sojourn in the city – presumably Toronto in the late 1870s and early 1880s when Lampman was a student there at Trinity College – providing in the process intriguing glimpses of its physical space and inhabitants.[33] We see, for example, the industrial blight of the urban landscape as the train pulls into the yards of what is likely the second of three incarnations of Union Station, which opened on 1 July 1873,[34] and are introduced to a wide range of character types, from affluent society ladies (sympathetically portrayed) to one Charlotte Ambray, a performer of charitable acts in "the tenements of the poor," with whom Richard enters into a mutually rewarding friendship. Richard's introduction to the society ladies is facilitated by another new friend, an unnamed poet, who, described as "somewhat tall, / With thin clear cheeks, bright eyes and lofty brow," may well be the second appearance of Duncan Campbell Scott in Lampman's semi-autobiographical poetry, the first being Euktemon in "An Athenian Reverie," discussed in chapter 1.[35] When the two friends talk, "The poet, as each thought / Flashed by before them, capped it with some strain / Or proverb from the famous lords of rhyme" – quite believable of Scott, whose writing in "At the Mermaid Inn" and elsewhere is interspersed with poetic quotations. Whereas in real life Lampman was Scott's poetic mentor, in the poem the roles are reversed. Thus Lampman, if this conjecture is correct, can be seen as honouring his friend by making him the teacher of the second, after Sebastian, of his own fictional alter egos, Richard.

It is in this middle section of the poem that the parallels with "Sebastian" are most evident. Having made his way to an area of town where "the little cottages / Of artisans" replace the opulent homes of the city's "broad and stately thoroughfares," Richard meets a "workman and his wife," who take him in as a boarder. Ensconced now in his "attic chamber," recalling Sebastian's "small upper chamber," he immediately begins his studies, first with a private tutor and then at school in the company of children, a "humble giant at their petty tasks." These two young men, each alone with his books and struggling to acquire the knowledge he will need to contribute to societal transformation, seem cut from the same cloth. But there is one key difference between them. Whereas the mill hand Sebastian is already familiar with the urban proletariat, whose inarticulate aspirations he divines, Richard knows only the life of the farm. Consequently, as part of his education, he cultivates friendships with various "workmen," who respond to his wide-eyed curiosity by filling him with "endless learning" about "the ways of trade" and even about their equipment – "The wonders of their mightiest and subtlest arts, / And all the mysteries of machinery." In an early, untitled draft of "The City of the End of Things," Lampman wrote "The City of Machinery" in place of the title phrase in line eight.[36] In light of this positive reference to machinery in *The Story of an Affinity*, however, it appears that Lampman was no Luddite. Industrialization *per se* was not the problem; capitalism was the problem.

With his social conscience enriched by human contact and with his mind made more incisive by the study of science, history, and classical literature, among other subjects, Richard develops a critique of society that is recognizably a reflection of Lampman's own:

He saw how fair and beautiful a thing
The movement of the busy world might be,
Were men but just and gentle, yet how hard,

> How full of doubt and pitiless life is,
> Seeing that ceaseless warfare is but man's rule
> And all his laws and customs but thin lies
> To veil the pride and hatred of his heart.

Bolstering this social philosophy, presented here in general terms, are Richard's more specific observations of various categories of corrupt society – the "rich and proud" attending church but remaining deaf to the message of "love and brotherhood" preached from the pulpit; "the strong" growing fat and thriving "upon the general need" and hiding "cruel and remorseless hands / Behind a mist of custom and the law"; and Lampman's favourite target, the "public leaders"

> Gulling men openly with fulsome lies,
> And on the trustful ignorance of the just
> And the blind greed and hatred of the base
> Building the edifice of their own power.

Lampman's poems of social criticism, such as "To a Millionaire" and "The Modern Politician," are works that Richard could at this point appreciate, if not compose.

The apparent negativity of Richard's critique might make it seem as though he were becoming more of a nihilist than a social reformer. But the very quality in Richard that sharpens his perceptions, distinguishing him from those who either close their eyes to human suffering or "seeing, do not care," also keeps him immune to the kind of cynicism to which those perceptions might lead in another. Possessed of a childlike innocence, he is able to resist the disillusionment that his clear-sightedness might otherwise engender:

> Yet also because his soul was fresh and stout
> And of a natural birth, he lost not faith,
> Nor grew distempered, as the weaker may,
> Amid this forceful fraudulent air of life.

Echoing such phrases as "Yet they quail not" ("Sapphics") and "And yet to me" ("Heat"), the wording here ("Yet also") indicates an unexpected response to prevailing conditions in the form of Richard's persistent faith in the possibility of change for the better. Richard's stance matches that of Sebastian, of whom we are told that "not for him / Is doubt," but rather, "his eager gaze / Grows firmer and more trustful day by day." In the world of *The Story of an Affinity*, moreover, evidence of impending change within society is not lacking, for Richard has already met "many that in heart and head" are "of the better world and the securer path," men and women he recognizes as "the pioneers / Of man's advancement and the larger life." For both protagonists, belief in progress toward a future of greater social harmony and justice becomes ever stronger as their reading, combined with experience, convinces them this is the direction in which society must (should and will) proceed.

To the extent that *The Story of an Affinity* is, as suggested earlier, a poetic Bildungsroman tracing Richard's growth to maturity, the work at this point is all but complete, requiring only that Margaret, like Penelope, welcome her Odysseus home, and that the reunited couple be married.[37] Lampman chose, however, to extend the poem by a third approximately equal part. He had two main reasons for this. One was to develop Margaret's different and archetypically female story during the ten years of Richard's absence, since it is the character makeup of two, not one, ideal types of the future, the Adam- and Eve-like prototypes of a new social dispensation, that the poem sets out to delineate.[38] The second reason was that the theme of "affinity" had to be explored, and to this end Lampman followed Goethe in complicating the plot by introducing a credible rival for Margaret's hand.

Over the ten years that Richard has been heroically engaged in "triumphant toil," circumstances have created a "different destiny" for Margaret. We know from Part 1 that she had earlier suffered a reversal in the form of disappointed hopes. Having shown great aptitude for learning, she had built for herself "A dream of onward and heroic toil, / Of growth and mind-enlargement for herself, / And generous labour for the common good." Her father, however, who originally had helped to foster this outlook, sending her away to school so she might have a "larger future than the farm could give," subsequently changed his mind and "resolved / To have her henceforth near him." Margaret, it seems, had made herself too helpful and too cheerful a presence for him to be without. As a result, she had reconstituted "in another lowlier shape / The ruined fabric of her hope." She would carry out her housekeeping duties, read in her spare time, and try to be a loving and sympathetic companion to those around her, this being her "old dream smiling in a lowlier guise." But as we now discover, Margaret cannot obliterate her original dream as easily as she thought. For a time she is moody and unpredictable, expressing her frustration through "wayward and unusual deeds, and storms / Of secret weeping," but even after she fights her spirit down and feels her "bondage" inexorably increase with the death of her mother, she never quite lets go. As friend and adviser to the people in her farm community and unofficial teacher and storyteller to the local children, she creates for herself a "sturdy happiness," but remains haunted by a "sense of lost desire" and stifled potential. She cannot suppress an "adventurous yearning for the freer sway."

Enter John Vantassel, a local lawyer and political campaigner who has come to the farm to secure votes for an unidentified candidate during a "fierce-fought electoral campaign" – possibly the federal election of 1878, the year Lampman turned seventeen, when the Liberals of Alexander Mackenzie were defeated after one term in office by the resurgent Conservatives under John A. Macdonald. There is no clear sense in which the two suitors represent the two political parties of the time, but the electoral battle in the background parallels the contention between the rivals in the main action of the poem. Vantassel (who is referred to primarily by his last name) admires Margaret's intelligence and charm, and she finds him a welcome distraction, interesting and congenial. The friendship persists and develops over years, Vantassel having "divined" that "His suit must be a long and difficult one," until finally Margaret realizes she must confront the prospect of marriage. She does not feel in any way obligated to Richard, who as far as she can tell has disappeared from her life, but sees with trepidation that by marrying Vantassel she would deny herself forever the fulfillment of her girlhood dream of entering into the life of the world beyond the farm and becoming involved in the struggle for human betterment.

A second issue is that of sexual fulfillment. Fundamental to the poem is the idea that those who share an "affinity" must not deny their desire for each other. Margaret rationalizes to herself, however, that she feels for Vantassel "such friendship as not love / Could have made truer, albeit passion-free." In a surrender to circumstances, trapped in the home of her father and with Vantassel offering her – given her sense of propriety and obligation – the only way out, she decides after lengthy soul-searching that she will accept Vantassel:

> Rebellion seemed a vain and hopeless thing.
> Her life with John Vantassel would be still
> The same long round of plain activities,
> Performed upon a little larger field.

Taking solace in the "little larger field" that life with Vantassel, who lives in a nearby town, would provide, Margaret gives her assent, not to Vantassel, but to herself, sealing her inward promise "with sacred vows." Thus the field has been prepared for the "election" battle between Richard, soon to present himself as her destined life companion, and Vantassel, whom she has decided (unbeknownst to him) to marry.

Margaret's life during the period of Richard's absence has been one of repression and constraint. Family obligations have curtailed her intellectual development and all but squelched her deep-seated ambition to learn and, in some way commensurate with her abilities, contribute to "the common good." She is, moreover, honourable to a fault. Thus when Richard returns, now fully matured, she is confronted with a dilemma. Seeing in him not "the pale student lured at last / Back to old scenes and former friends" but "the strong lover," she yearns to join with him in a life of mutual love, for she realizes beyond all doubt that here is "her spirit's answering type." In addition, she perceives that Richard has returned "Like a bright herald from the outer world," reawakening thoughts of "the old dreamed of path," while marriage to Vantassel, she realizes, would mean "certain failure of one half her life." Yet she has knowingly permitted Vantassel to court her and, more than that, has given in her heart her "solemn troth" to marry him. Her struggle is between desire and conscience, and such is Margaret's "queenly honour" that conscience must prevail. To Richard's desperate argument that the only bond that matters is the one in their hearts, she can only reply, "I must be true." When pressed by Vantassel for an answer, however, unable to be false the other way, she rejects him as well. Feeling hopeless and possibly suicidal, for she has left behind a letter cryptically described as the "final sad memorial of her strife," she wanders out into the midnight fields. Such is the predicament of the woman who is loved by three, but for her own happiness finds all doors closed.

While Lampman has sympathetically portrayed Margaret's limiting circumstances, however, it is not to his purpose to create a tragic outcome but rather to show the power of "affinity." Richard may be wrong to insist that Margaret break her vow, but it is still the argument of the poem that a way must be found to unite the lovers who belong together. Accordingly Lampman constructs a nocturnal confrontation between the two rivals, initiated by Vantassel, who wants to strike out at the man who has undermined his hopes, but who finishes by relinquishing his claim on Margaret. On one level it is an epic battle, for Richard must ward off the other's "wild attack" and, when Vantassel will not hear him speak, exert his giant's strength by lifting his opponent into the air and pinning him "like a feather to the earth." But more important is the convincing power of the story that Richard recounts of his longstanding involvement with Margaret and of "his labour and his love" for her. Even if Vantassel were to succeed with Margaret, he points out, they would experience "the fate of all unmated things, / The incurable curse of blight and emptiness," whereas there is a "bond between [himself and Margaret], sacred and inherent" that unites the two. Realizing that Margaret does not and never will love him, Vantassel concedes the victory, announcing that he will "release her from all debt" to him. The way is now clear for the two soulmates to marry and for the poem to reach its comedic conclusion. It is, however, an emotionally exhausted Margaret who encounters Richard in the closing scene. They meet again at the "rustic bench" of Part 1, now under a full moon – the counterpart to the noontide sun of the earlier scene – and with a look, but no words, Margaret accepts him. Having struggled on both sides, they have found at last the "portals of the perfect fields of life" and can see, in the closing line, the "endless road before them, clear and free." This road recalls "the glorious road" of labour devoted to the cause of social betterment down which the speaker resolves to proceed in "To the Prophetic Soul." Not "alone" like that unhappy individual, however, but supported by the love they share, with passion now united with purpose, the protagonists of Lampman's magnum opus have a much better chance of succeeding because joy, not bitterness, is the emotional component of their resolve.

Richard and Margaret are meant to be seen as ideals. Their "story" is simple, but driven by passions, as in opera. Both must outface external as well as internal obstacles. There are no flat-out villains, but Margaret's father emerges as an interesting character, his generosity turning to selfishness as he clings to Margaret and virtually imprisons her, as the title character of Verdi's *Rigoletto* does his daughter Gilda, with tragic results. Fundamental to Lampman's poem, though, is its happy ending, as well as its optimistic social conscience. Both hero and heroine rise from their humble origins as children of the farm to become paragons of their sex, Margaret grown to "perfect womanhood" and Richard the model of manhood with his great strength and stature complemented by sensitivity and intellectual attainment, and both devoted to the cause of social reform. As such, they are at once the activists who will play a part in transforming society and the precursors of the humanity of the future. Their union, a triumph over adversity, prefigures the harmony that, after a struggle, will displace competition and greed when the work begun by the pioneers of progress, whom they will join, has succeeded in ushering in a new era of social enlightenment. As we know, Lampman's confidence in humanity's ability to achieve progressive change would wax and wane as he oscillated between "faith" that society would "somehow" find its way and "doubt" that it ever would. In *The Story of an Affinity*, he maintains an optimism about the ability of such dedicated and capable individuals as Margaret and Richard to bring about the necessary changes. To do so is possible, he seems to say, making this poem, the most ambitious of all his writings, a statement of "faith" rather than of "doubt."

Conclusion

Implicit in all Lampman's nature poems, and explicit in some, is a critique of the social and political institutions of his day, often imaged as a crowded and noisy urban centre from which the speaker must escape. We see this in the early poem "Freedom," where a group of friends abandon a city rife with greed and contention in favour of the purity of the hills. Lampman's nature poems are not all about escape; they are about a love of nature; but nature provides for Lampman a place of refuge from the flawed institutions and behaviour of city life. Another way of dealing with the ill effects of capitalism is to change society. For Lampman, the conceptual foundation of such change was that of evolutionary progressivism, an ideology that flowered in the nineteenth century but survived far beyond it, the word itself, tied to the idea of social advance, being prominent in the minds of Canadians from the time of the Progressive Society of Ottawa in the 1890s to that of the Committee of Progressive Electors in the city of Vancouver in the 1990s, a municipal party now somewhat overshadowed by the relatively new Vision Vancouver party, whose goal as I write is to bring "bold, progressive leadership back to City Hall."[39]

In this progressive ideology, Lampman read the promise of a new age of social harmony, but in the world around him he saw a disheartening reluctance or lack of initiative on the part of humanity to bring this new age into existence. We encounter, then, the need, the hope, and the fear, all of which figure prominently in his ongoing exploration of this theme. The result is a rich and complex body of work, comprising poems that chronicle a personal struggle with the issue of commitment to a cause, exemplified by "To the Prophetic Soul"; eloquent declarations of belief in a future society profoundly transformed, such as "The Largest Life"; prophetic works that challenge the reader to examine the possible directions society might take, represented by "The City of the End of Things" and "The Land of Pallas"; two heroic narratives envisioning worker agency in effecting social change; and perhaps most significant of all, biting critiques of contemporary society in which strong feelings are melded with a radical perspective to give us the first credible instance in Canada of social-political poetry that succeeds on both fronts – advocacy and art.

One of Lampman's most noticeable personal traits was stubbornness. Scott draws our attention to this when he speaks of preferring over all others the portrait of his friend included as the frontispiece of *Lyrics of Earth: Sonnets and Ballads*, in part because it shows "a sort of stern, almost obstinate set of the mouth," one that was "quite characteristic."[40] It is to this quality as much as to any other that we owe his distinctive voice. Because he will not see it *their* way – "And yet to me" – we are invited to see it his way, and the result, at its best, is poetry that makes us think harder about the issues raised and look again, with greater appreciation, at the poetry itself.

APPENDIX A

Index of Poems in The Poems of Archibald Lampman (including At the Long Sault)

Presented here is a combined index of *The Poems of Archibald Lampman* (1900) and *At the Long Sault, and Other New Poems* (1943), published in facsimile under one cover as *The Poems of Archibald Lampman (including At the Long Sault)* (1974). The page numbers of poems from *At the Long Sault*, which has separate pagination, are prefixed by the abbreviation ALS. Auxiliary components, such as introductions, are omitted.

Abu Midjan ... 54
Across the Pea-Fields ... 262
After Mist ... 287
After Rain ... 144
After the Shower ... 264
After Snow ... 318
Alcyone ... 177
Ambition ... 295
Among the Millet ... 3
Among the Orchards ... 210
Among the Timothy ... 13
Amor Vitae ... 250
April ... 4
April in the Hills ... 127

April Night ... 185
April Voices ... 257
Aspiration ... 113
At Dusk ... 269
At the Ferry ... 150
At the Long Sault ... ALS, 1
Athenian Reverie, An ... 90
Autumn Landscape, An ... 157
Autumn Maples ... 120
Autumn Waste, The ... 228
Avarice ... 285
Baki ... 340
Ballade of Summer's Sleep ... 23
Ballade of Waiting, A ... 45

Beauty ... 258
Before the Robin ... 289
Before Sleep ... 46
Better Day, The ... 226
Between the Rapids ... 36
Bird and the Hour, The ... 143
Bird Voices ... 321
By an Autumn Stream ... 160
By the Sea ... 272
Child's Music Lesson, The ... 88
Chione ... 187
Choice, The ... ALS, 17
City, The ... 118
City, The ... 215
City of the End of Things, The ... 179
Clearer Self, The ... 199
Cloud-Break ... 145
Cloud and Sun ... ALS, 25
Comfort ... 106
Comfort of the Fields ... 148
Coming of Winter, The ... 62
Crete ... ALS, 30
Cup of Life, The ... 280
David and Abigail ... 357
Dawn on the Lievre, A ... 290
Dead Cities ... 269
Death ... 288
Death of Tennyson, The ... 275
Deeds ... 112
Despondency ... 107
Distance ... 143
Dog, The ... 121
Drought ... 317
Earth – The Stoic ... 283
Easter Eve ... 63

Emperor's True-Love, The ... ALS, 11
Epitaph on a Rich Man ... ALS, 19
Estrangement ... ALS, 22
Euphrone ... 261
Even Beyond Music ... ALS, 27
Evening ... 198
Fair Speech ... ALS, 36
Falling Asleep ... 278
Fate ... ALS, 24
Favorites of Pan ... 131
Forecast, A ... 116
Forest Moods ... 129
Forest Path in Winter, A ... 286
Freedom ... 17
Frogs, The ... 7
Frost Elves, The ... ALS, 5
Gentleness ... 108
Godspeed to the Snow ... 126
Goldenrod ... 292
Good Speech ... 226
Growth of Love, The ... ALS, 37
Heat ... 12
Hepaticas ... 321
Impression, An ... 10
In Absence ... 264
In Beechwood Cemetery ... 288
In the City ... 259
In March ... 179
In May ... 137
In November ... 158
In November (sonnet) ... 117
In October ... 21
In the Pine Groves ... 267
In the Wilds ... 294

APPENDIX A

Indian Summer ... 225
Ingvi and Alf ... 348
Inter Vias ... 183
Invocation, An ... 255
Islet and the Palm, The ... 194
January Morning, A ... 286
June ... 140
King Oswald's Feast ... 325
King's Sabbath, The ... 51
Knowledge ... 110
Lake in the Forest, The ... 313
Lament of the Winds ... 22
Land of Pallas, The ... 201
Largest Life, The ... 300
Liberty ... ALS, 28
Life and Nature ... 138
Little Handmaiden, The ... 52
Loneliness ... ALS, 26
Loons, The ... 119
Love ... 282
Love-Doubt ... 104
Love-Wonder ... 106
Man and Nature ... ALS, 13
Man's Future ... ALS, 34
March ... 119
March Day, A ... 289
March of Winter, The ... 280
Martyrs, The ... 115
May ... 261
Meadow, The ... 134
Midnight ... 34
Midnight Landscape, A ... 270
Midsummer Night ... 118
Minstrel, The ... 305
Modern Politician, The ... 277
Monk, The ... 75

Moon-Path, The ... 146
Morning on the Lievre ... 19
Morning Summons, A ... 255
Music ... 109
Music ... 260
Mystery of a Year, The ... 242
Nesting Time ... 256
New Year's Eve ... 39
New Year's Eve ... ALS, 15
Niagara Landscape, A ... 272
Night ... 263
Night of Storm, A ... 115
Night in the Wilderness ... 294
October Sunset, An ... 6
Ode to the Hills, An ... 221
Old House, The ... 321
Old Lesson from the Fields, An ... 111
On the Companionship with Nature ... 258
On the Death of Tennyson ... ALS, 33
On Lake Temiscamingue ... 293
One Day ... 41
Organist, The ... 71
Ottawa ... ALS, 20
Outlook ... 107
Passing of Autumn, The ... 312
Passing of the Spirit, The ... 266
Passing of Spring, The ... 296
Passion ... 44
Passion ... 279
Paternity ... 310
Peace ... 310
Peccavi, Domine ... 219
Perfect Love ... 105

Persistence ... ALS, 23
Personality ... 185
Phokaia ... 328
Piano, The ... 260
Pilot, The ... 273
Poets, The ... 113
Poet's Possession, The ... 157
Poet's Song, The ... 210
Portrait in Six Sonnets, A ... ALS, 43
Power of Music, The ... ALS, 32
Praise and Prayer ... ALS, 39
Prayer, A ... 109
Railway Station, The ... 116
Re-assurance, A ... 156
Refuge ... 184
Return of the Year, The ... 129
Ruin of the Year, The ... 279
Salvation ... 263
Sapphics ... 217
September ... 154
Sight ... 110
Sirius ... 268
Sleep ... 42
Snow ... 162
Snowbirds ... 162
Solitude ... 120
Song ... 40
Song, A ... 48
Song of Pan, The ... 193
Song Sparrow, The ... 182
Song of the Stream-Drops ... 35
Sorrow ... 281
Sostratus ... 327
Spanish Taunt, A ... 344
Spirit of the House, The ... 257
Spring on the River ... 10

Stoic and Hedonist ... 284
Storm ... 30
Storm Voices ... 276
Story of an Affinity, The ... 409
Strife and Freedom ... 312
Summer Evening, A ... 298
Sun Cup, The ... 173
Sunset ... 164
Sunset at Les Eboulements ... 273
Sweetness of Life, The ... 125
Temagami ... 292
Thamyris ... 274
Three Flower Petals ... 43
Three Pilgrims, The ... 59
Thunderstorm, A ... 214
To Chaucer ... 271
To the Cricket ... 193
To Death ... 282
To a Flower ... 309
To a Millionaire ... 276
To My Daughter ... 186
To the Ottawa ... 297
To the Ottawa River ... 297
To the Prophetic Soul ... 200
To an Ultra Protestant ... 285
To the Warbling Vireo ... 265
True Life, The ... ALS, 35
Truth, The ... 114
Unrest ... 40
Uplifting ... 290
Usurer, The ... ALS, 18
Vain Fight, The ... 283
Vase of Ibn Mokbil, The ... 336
Violinist, The ... 345
Virtue ... 277
Vision of April, A ... ALS, 8

APPENDIX A

Vision of Twilight, A ... 195
Vivia Perpetua ... 229
Voices of Earth ... 218
War ... 243
Wayagamack ... 298
Weaver, The ... 57
We Too Shall Sleep ... 228
What Do Poets Want with
    Gold? ... 50
White Pansies ... 227
Why Do Ye Call the Poet
    Lonely? ... 11
Wind's Word, The ... 320
Winter ... 24
Winter-Break ... 252
Winter Dawn, A ... 291
Winter Evening ... 243
Winter Hues Recalled ... 27
Winter Solitude ... *ALS*, 21
Winter Stars, The ... 295
Winter-Store ... 165
Winter-Thought ... 112
Winter Uplands ... 299
With the Night ... 139
Woodcutter's Hut, The ... 247
Xenophanes ... 266
Yarrow ... 308

APPENDIX B

Table of Contents of "Afoot with the Year" and Lyrics of Earth

The list of the contents of "Afoot with the Year," never published, is from the manuscript book "Miscellaneous Poems," held by the Library of Parliament, Ottawa. The inclusion of "An Ode to the Hills" and "A Midwinter Phantasy" in "Afoot with the Year," along with the positioning of "An Ode to the Hills" at the beginning and of "The Sweetness of Life" later in that list, would indicate that "Afoot with the Year" is the early version of Lyrics of Earth under discussion between Lampman and Thomson in 1895. See chapter 6, part I, for a tracing of the genesis of Lyrics of Earth. The titles "Successors of Pan" and "Favorites of Pan" refer to the same poem, as do "The Possession" and "The Poet's Possession." "A Midwinter Phantasy" appears in At the Long Sault as "The Frost Elves."

AFOOT WITH THE YEAR	LYRICS OF EARTH
An Ode to the Hills	The Sweetness of Life
April in the Hills	God-speed to the Snow
A Godspeed to the Snow	April in the Hills
Forest Moods	Forest Moods
Return of the Year	The Return of the Year
The Meadow	Favorites of Pan
Successors of Pan	The Meadow

AFOOT WITH THE YEAR

In May
The Sun Cup
Life & Nature
With the Night
Refuge
June
The Bird & the Hour
After Rain
The Sweetness of Life
Cloud break
The Moon path
Comfort of the Fields
At the Ferry
September
Re-assurance
The Possession
An Autumn Landscape
In November
By an Autumn Stream
Snow birds
Snow
Sunset
Winter store
A Midwinter Phantasy
After Snow
A Snowshoer's Halt

LYRICS OF EARTH

In May
Life and Nature
With the Night
June
Distance
The Bird and the Hour
After Rain
Cloud-Break
The Moon-Path
Comfort of the Fields
At the Ferry
September
A Re-assurance
The Poet's Possession
An Autumn Landscape
In November
By an Autumn Stream
Snowbirds
Snow
Sunset
Winter-Store
The Sun Cup

Notes

Information on Locating Poems and on Abbreviations Used in Notes

See Appendix A for an index to *The Poems of Archibald Lampman (including At the Long Sault)*, provided because neither the original publications nor this combined facsimile reprint includes an index. All references to Lampman's poems, unless otherwise noted, are to this edition, and individual poems can be located therein by using this index. The following abbreviations are employed in the notes:

AER *Addresses, Essays, and Reviews*, by Scott
ALS Facsimile reprint of *At the Long Sault* in *The Poems of Archibald Lampman (including At the Long Sault)*
AMI *At the Mermaid Inn: Wilfred Campbell, Archibald Lampman, Duncan Campbell Scott in The Globe 1892–93*, by Campbell, Lampman, and Scott
ER *Essays and Reviews*, by Lampman
LAC Library and Archives Canada
LE:SB *Lyrics of Earth: Sonnets and Ballads*, by Lampman
LE:WT *Lyrics of Earth: A Working Text*, by Lampman
L-TC *An Annotated Edition of the Correspondence between Archibald Lampman and Edward William Thomson (1890–1898)*, by Lampman and Thomson

"Mermaid Inn" Any essay from the column "At the Mermaid Inn," originally published in the Toronto *Globe* and reprinted in AMI, individually identified by date

Poems Facsimile reprint of *The Poems of Archibald Lampman* in *The Poems of Archibald Lampman (including At the Long Sault)*

PTRSC *Proceedings and Transactions of the Royal Society of Canada*

SFU Simon Fraser University

"SFU Letters" "The Letters of Archibald Lampman in the Simon Fraser University Library," edited by Sommers

SFU manuscript book The single bound manuscript book held by Simon Fraser University

U of T manuscript book The single bound manuscript book held by the Thomas Fisher Rare Book Library, University of Toronto

INTRODUCTION

1 Howells, "Editor's Study," 823; Thomson, "Among the Millet," 97; "Canadian Poet," 52.
2 Connor, *Archibald Lampman*, 11.
3 Brown, "Archibald Lampman," 15.
4 Gnarowski, introduction to *Selected Poetry*, by Lampman, 24.
5 Ware, "Archibald Lampman (1861–99)," in *Northern Romanticism*, 123–4.
6 Daniells, "Lampman and Roberts," 406.
7 Collin, in "Archibald Lampman," 142, quotes the phrase "a small, pure stream," which he applies to Lampman's poetry, from an anonymous "Mermaid Inn" contribution, 26 November 1892, in AMI, 197, where it is employed in another context. A.J.M. Smith, in *Book of Canadian Poetry*, 176, assuming Lampman to be the author of the original "Mermaid Inn" contribution, quotes the phrase again, believing that Lampman had hit upon an image that was applicable to himself. The "small clear flame" statement is from Daniells, "Lampman and Roberts," 408. Nesbitt, in "Gift of Love," 142, quotes Daniells's phrase, with emphasis on the pun: "Archibald Lampman is rightly remembered for the few nature poems illuminated by his personal 'small clear flame.'"
8 Manguel, *City of Words*, 139.
9 Lampman, letters to John A. Ritchie, quoted in Connor, *Archibald Lampman*, 66, 67, 78. The first two letters are from early 1883, not long after Lampman moved to Ottawa following a short-lived stint as a school teacher in Orangeville, Ontario, and the last is from the summer of 1884. Connor does not precisely date his excerpts, and today the whereabouts of the letters are unknown.

10 Connor, *Archibald Lampman*, 196.
11 Scott, "Who's Who in Canadian Literature: Archibald Lampman," in *AER*, 2:372.
12 Bentley, *Confederation Group*, 147–57.
13 On Poe, see Sutherland, "Edgar Allan Poe in Canada," 169–78, challenged by Bentley in "Thread of Memory," 87–9. On Emerson, see Davies, "Lampman and Religion," 113–22; Richard Arnold, "'The Clearer Self,'" 35–48, and "'Thoughts Grow Keen and Clear,'" 170–2; and Klinck, "'The Frogs,'" 30–5.
14 Early, *Archibald Lampman*, 151.
15 Ibid., 27.
16 Ibid., 29–30.
17 Ibid., 85. Like Early, Nesbitt, in "Lampmania," 47–8, sees Lampman's participation in, and then abandonment of, a Romantic aesthetic as central to his achievement: Lampman "defined – indeed accomplished – the break between colonial romanticism and a variety of close-focussed poetic imagism which articulated whatever would be understood as the essence of Canadian poetry for at least a generation." Nesbitt's point is consistent with a continued focus on nature; Early, on the other hand, notes a thematic shift in the direction of "the more human contexts of his dreams: the city, and erotic love."
18 Early, *Archibald Lampman*, 150.
19 Ibid., 150, 152.
20 Bentley, "Romantic Lampman," 89.
21 See, for example, Ware's "D.C. Scott's 'The Height of Land' and the Greater Romantic Lyric" and his "Generic Approach to Confederation Romanticism."
22 McLeod, "Canadian Post-Romanticism," 2.
23 Ibid., 11–12.
24 The title of Bentley's 2004 study, *The Confederation Group of Canadian Poets, 1880–1897*, indicates his preferred name for the poets of Lampman's generation. For his explanation, see *Confederation Group*, 4.
25 Bentley, *Confederation Group*, 18.
26 Smith, *Book of Canadian Poetry*, 175. Compton, in "Poet-Impressionist," 33, does not quote Smith's statement that Lampman's "descriptive method ... is that of impressionism," but does quote the sentence that immediately follows it, indicating her familiarity with the passage.
27 Early, *Archibald Lampman*, 76, cited by Compton in "Poet-Impressionist," 35.
28 Compton, "Poet-Impressionist," 35–6.
29 Ibid., 47.
30 Ibid., 46.
31 Ibid., 33.

32 Ibid., 44, 53.
33 Ibid., 40–2, 46–7, 49.
34 Ibid., 38–9.
35 Smith, *Book of Canadian Poetry*, 175–6; Compton, "Poet-Impressionist," 33.
36 Daniells, "Lampman and Roberts," 414, 410; Compton, "Poet-Impressionist," 40.
37 Compton, "Poet-Impressionist," 48.
38 Ibid., 39; Early, *Archibald Lampman*, 51–2.
39 Davies, "Lampman and Religion," 114.
40 Ibid., 104, 107, 116–17.
41 Ibid., 122.
42 Klinck, "'The Frogs,'" 30–1.
43 Early, *Archibald Lampman*, 63–6; Ower, "Story of an Affinity," 285–9.
44 Arnold, "'The Clearer Self,'" 45.
45 Ibid., 48.
46 McMullen, *Lampman Symposium*, xiii.
47 Bentley, review of *Lampman Symposium*, 89.
48 McMullen, *Lampman Symposium*, xiii.
49 See Mathews and Steele, eds., *Struggle for Canadian Universities*.
50 Mathews, "Lampman's Achievement," 122.
51 Bentley, review of *Lampman Symposium*, 90.
52 Steele, "Lampman's Achievement," 126–7.
53 On the first point, see Bentley, *Gay/Grey Moose*, 135–7, 191–2, 195–200. On the second point, see *Gay/Grey Moose*, 15–42. The chapter in *Gay/Grey Moose* to which the first references apply, entitled "The Poem in Its Niche: Lampman's 'The City of the End of Things' and Its Origins," is reprinted in *Northern Romanticism*, ed. Ware, 447–67.
54 McLeod, "Canadian Post-Romanticism," 23–5.
55 Arnold, "'Thoughts Grow Keen and Clear,'" 170, 175.
56 Early, *Archibald Lampman*, 33.
57 Doyle, "Politics of Nature," 21–3. In this article as well as in his *Progressive Heritage*, Doyle credits Marxist writer and editor Margaret Fairley with being among the first to recognize the consonance between Lampman's nature poems and socialist poems. As he writes in *Progressive Heritage*, 29, by selecting poems of both types for inclusion in her New Frontiers Pamphlet anthology *The Stone, the Axe, the Sword and Other Canadian Poems* (1955), designed to illustrate the historical basis of a progressive culture in Canada, Fairley "demonstrated the unity of Lampman's love of nature and his desire for a better society."
58 Watt, "Literature of Protest," 478, 483. For a brief history of the Socialist Party of Canada, see Gambone, *Impossibilists*, 1–4; the dates of the party journal, the *Western Clarion*, are given in a list of journal articles, 24.

59 Early, in *Archibald Lampman*, 41, comments that "Lampman's hunger for transcendence was so powerful that it seized on at least four different strategies. Occasionally, it compelled something akin to a conventional piety, but more often it focused on natural beauty, or utopian conjectures, or romantic love."
60 Murray, *Tom Thomson*, 64–5. See also Grace, *Inventing Tom Thomson*, 70–1.
61 Blom, "Archibald Lampman."
62 Hill, "Tom Thomson, Painter," 112.
63 One sign of incipient radicalism in Canada during Lampman's lifetime was the increasing power and influence of labour unions. As Carole Gerson, in her introduction to "Marie Joussaye's 'Labor's Greeting,'" 88, states, "In Canada as in other industrialized countries, the last two decades of the nineteenth century saw the growing militancy of the labour movement." Joussaye's poem, first published in 1901, dichotomizing "Labor" and "Greed" and declaiming sympathy for "strikers," provides some evidence of this development.
64 On the positive side, see Watt, "Literature of Protest," 478, and Doyle, "Politics of Nature," 23–8; and on the negative, Beattie, "Archibald Lampman," 78–80, and Gustafson, "Life and Nature," 5–6.
65 Anonymous response to Brown's introduction to *At the Long Sault*, quoted in Brown to Scott, 2 December 1943, in *Poet and Critic*, 85.
66 Doyle, *Progressive Heritage*, 197.
67 Brown, in *On Canadian Poetry*, 97, describes Lampman at his best as the creator of "great nature poetry," and Deahl, in his introduction to Acorn's *I Shout Love*, 9, states that "[t]o some readers Acorn is Canada's finest nature poet, a poet alive to the beauty and pattern of the non-human world."
68 Acorn, "Knowing I Live in a Dark Age," in *Dig Up My Heart*, 81.
69 Gudgeon, *Out of This World*, 222–3.
70 Wayne, "Shouting Love," 15–17.
71 Acorn, preliminary material, in *I've Tasted My Blood*, [v].
72 Wayne, "Shouting Love," 17.
73 Acorn, "Tirade by Way of Introduction," in *Jackpine Sonnets*, 21.
74 Acorn and Deahl, dedication, in *A Stand of Jackpine*, [v].

CHAPTER ONE

1 Lampman, "To Chaucer." See Appendix A for an index to *Poems* and ALS.
2 Lampman, "Sapphics." Lampman's phrase is perhaps a play on Keats's "forgetfulness divine," from the sonnet "To Sleep," in *Poems of Keats*, 510.
3 Pacey, note on "Tantramar Revisited," in *Collected Poems of Sir Charles G.D. Roberts*, 406.

4 Lampman to Thomson, 25 April 1894, in *L-TC*, 119.
5 Keats, "To Autumn," in *Poems of Keats*, 653. I have chosen this title as the best readily available critical edition of Keats' work. Jack Stillinger, in his "all-purpose reading edition," *Complete Poems* (Cambridge, MA: Belknap Press, 1982), 413, calls it "the most fully annotated of the critical editions." More recent publications tend to be reprints of earlier editions or selected editions.
6 The close similarity (despite opposite intent) between the characterizations of the same month in the opening lines of "The Waste Land" and in the first two stanzas of "April" raises the question of whether Eliot could have been influenced by Lampman's poem. In both cases April is described with a superlative adjective ("sweetest" and "cruellest") and is depicted as, in Eliot's phrasing, "mixing / Memory and desire." The line "A tangle of Desire and Memory," from Lampman's "Ambition," has been described by Beattie, in "Archibald Lampman," 79, as "a curious prestatement of the emotional emphasis of *The Waste Land*." Did the young Eliot at some point come across a copy of *Among the Millet*, published in 1888, the year he was born, or of *Poems*, published and widely distributed twelve years later, and re-issued in 1901, 1905, and 1915? As part of a well-educated family that spent its summers in Massachusetts, where Lampman was known in literary circles, and with a mother who was herself interested in poetry, it is conceivable that he did.
7 Early, "Chronology," 77. The composition dates of Lampman's poems referred to in this study are from this chronology, unless otherwise noted.
8 In "Chronology," 80, Early gives the composition date as "c. 1885–88." A letter from Lampman to Maud Emma Playter (later his wife), 21 September 1885, in "SFU Letters," 19, suggests the fall of 1885. "I have completed a long poem, a story in verse, and am at work polishing it up," Lampman reports, specifying that in this poem, in contrast to an earlier one, "there are no rhymes." The theme of marriage is present both in the letter and the poem (in the former, Lampman is ardent and keen; in the latter, the narrator has his doubts). Although Lampman does not mention the title of the poem he is referring to, the description fits, and the lack of another obvious candidate makes it fairly certain that he is referring to "An Athenian Reverie."
9 Lampman, "The Harvest of Time," Lampman Papers, LAC, vol. 2, 831.
10 Fuller, *Gnomologia*, 188; Stevenson, *Home Book of Quotations*, 1293.
11 For a list of Warnock's numerous articles and links to the articles themselves, see "Mary Warnock."
12 Warnock, *Memory*, 75–7.

13 Ibid., 141–2.
14 Scruton, "Continental Philosophy," 224–5.
15 Wordsworth, "Lines Composed a Few Miles above Tintern Abbey," in *William Wordsworth: The Poems* (referred to subsequently as *Poems*), 1:359.
16 Keats, "Ode on a Grecian Urn," in *Poems of Keats*, 537; Lampman, "Athenian Reverie," 94.
17 The parallels between the narrator's mixed feelings about marriage in "An Athenian Reverie" and Lampman's own thoughts on this subject during his lengthy courtship of Maud Player reveal Lampman's penchant for incorporating his life experiences into the fiction of his poems. In his 21 September 1885 letter to Maud, in "SFU Letters," 20, Lampman gives no hint of having doubts about marriage, saying only, "I work [on the poem] till I am tired and then sit back and dream – of you, and the future." But in another letter, dated 21 January 1887, in "SFU Letters," 42–3, he teasingly tells Maud that if she were to find "another young man," he would "cut the Service, put a knap sack on my back and start for Europe – travel all over the world and give myself up body, soul and spirit to Art, literature and Bohemia." The week before, in a letter dated 11 January 1887, in "SFU Letters," 33, he had likened himself to Mr Ingram, a character in the novel *A Princess of Thule* by William Black, which he had just been reading. "That's me," he tells Maud, "the same careless, inelegant, unsocial kind of body exactly. The other principal character would have suited you better – Mr. Lavender – [h]e was very social – dreadfully so." It appears that the doubts couched in Lampman's facetious comments sparked in Maud some doubts of her own. In a letter dated 25 January 1887, in "SFU Letters," 48, Lampman writes, "You shouldn't dream of marrying another man, my Maud; that will never do. Whenever I dream of marriage I am always faithfully married to you." Maud had apparently had a dream in which she married another man.

Lampman and Maud were married on 3 September 1887; he was 25 and she was 20. A frequently occurring error in writings on Lampman is that Maud at this time was only 18. Whitridge, in her introduction to *Lampman's Kate*, 13, declares, "the moment [Maud] was eighteen she married him," and Adams, in *Confederation Voices*, writes, "Once Maud turned eighteen, her father withdrew his opposition, despite his lingering reservations, and the young couple were married." As Early points out in *Archibald Lampman*, 154n18, Maud was in fact born on 3 January 1867, as indicated by a notice in the *Daily Globe* of Toronto for 5 January 1867, and confirmed (since the notice does not name the baby) by a letter from Lampman to Maud, dated 3 January 1887, in "SFU Letters," 27–8, in which he acknowledges her twentieth birthday.

Sommers, in "SFU Letters," 27n1, traces the error through Connor, *Archibald Lampman*, 89, to Voorhis, "Ancestry," 119, where Maud's dates are incorrectly given as 1869–1910.
18 Warnock, *Memory*, 140.
19 This parallel was first noticed by E.W. Thomson in "Among the Millet," his 1889 review of Lampman's first published volume, 95–6.
20 This passage is inscribed on the memorial cairn erected in 1930 in Lampman's honour in his home town, Morpeth, Ontario. See Scott, Stringer, and others, *Addresses Delivered*, 1.
21 Arnold, "Resignation" and "To a Republican Friend, Continued," in *Matthew Arnold*, 43 and 52, respectively.
22 Arnold, "To a Republican Friend, 1848," in *Matthew Arnold*, 51–2.
23 Milton, "When I consider how my light is spent," in *Complete Poetry*, 157–8.
24 Seen in terms of its autobiographical implications, "An Athenian Reverie" provides a fascinating portrait of both Scott and Lampman himself. Euktemon (there is even a similarity between this name and "Duncan") is nothing like the narrator. He is a brooding individual, "gloomy and austere," whereas the narrator is talkative and always ready with a smile. Unlikely companions, they discover a liking for each other and embark on a long walk – "our first together" – that somehow is not hard to transpose from the road to Corinth to the Experimental Farm in Ottawa. The narrator concludes the poem with words that bespeak a close attachment fully consistent with the fictional construct and yet revealing of a personal regard:
   There is no hand that I would gladlier grasp,
   Either on earth or in the nether gloom,
   When the gray keel shall grind the Stygian strand,
   Than stern Euktemon's.
Scott, we know, worked tirelessly all his long life to build and secure Lampman's reputation, and the image of Lampman extending his hand to welcome his old friend to the afterlife is charmingly affecting. Here on earth, however, as perhaps would not have surprised the marriage-shy young narrator, the Lampman-Scott friendship suffered some strain during their married years, for as Sandra Gwyn reports in her gossipy but insightful study *The Private Capital*, 447, their wives, "to put it bluntly, did not get on."
25 Lampman, "Happiness," in *ER*, 196. In his account of the publication history of this essay, in *ER*, 360, Bentley mentions three reprints that omit the original ending: the essay in pamphlet form (Toronto: Ryerson, 1925) and the versions published in *Archibald Lampman's Letters to Edward William Thomson*, ed. Bourinot, 48–52, and *Archibald Lampman: Selected Prose*, ed. Davies, 105–10. A fourth reprint with

the same omission appeared in the journal *Canadian Poetry* 30 (1967): 40–3.

CHAPTER TWO

1. Davies, "Forms of Nature," 79.
2. Brown, in *On Canadian Poetry*, 89, comments, "Everything in the manner of ['Winter Hues Recalled'] is imitative of 'The Prelude,' slavishly imitative, if you will; what is significant is that taking so much from Wordsworth, as he does, the young poet applies it so surely and so sharply to scenes and situations in his own immediate world."
3. Lampman, early draft of "Winter-Store," undated but proximate to poems written in the summer and fall of 1887, in Lampman Papers, LAC, vol. 6, 2712–14; "Vision," in "Mermaid Inn," 19 November 1892, in *AMI*, 191–2.
4. Arnold, "'Thoughts Grow Keen and Clear,'" 170–2.
5. *Lyrics of Earth* is dated 1895, but a publisher's colophon note indicates that the actual printing of 500 copies was done in March 1896. By 8 April 1896 Lampman still had not received word that the book was out. In a letter to his wife on that date, in "SFU Letters," 111, he declares with facetious, yet unattractive, violence, "My book is not out yet and I am getting mad. I shall go down to Boston one of these days with a seven shooter and open a lot of little holes through somebody."
6. Lampman to Thomson, 25 March 1895, in *L-TC*, 137.
7. Lampman, first dated manuscript of "Winter-Store," in Lampman Papers, LAC, vol. 3, 1441–9; second dated manuscript, in U of T manuscript book, 57–65. The U of T manuscript book is the one known as Lampman's "gift of love" to Katherine Waddell, the woman with whom he was emotionally involved in the mid-1890s. See letters exchanged between Scott and Brown in *Poet and Critic*, 133–7. See also Nesbitt, "Gift of Love," 142–3; Whitridge, introduction to *Lampman's Kate*, by Lampman, 18–19; Early, "Lampman's Love Poetry," 117–18; and Campbell, "Love in the Langevin Block," single-page newspaper feature.
8. Early, *Archibald Lampman*, 84–5. See also Arnold, "'The Clearer Self,'" 45 and 48, where Arnold makes a similar point but identifies "Emersonian Transcendentalism" as the belief system being abandoned.
9. Ibid., 81.
10. Lampman, "Winter-Store," in U of T manuscript book, 57–65.
11. Greig, "Check List," pt. 2, 25.
12. Lampman to Herbert Copeland of Copeland and Day, publishers of *Lyrics of Earth*, 30 September 1895, in Greig, "Check List," pt. 2, 16.

The notion that "The Sun Cup" serves well as a "coda" in *Lyrics of Earth* originates with Bentley in his "Same Unnamed Delight," 33–4.
13 It should be noted that, according to a holograph list of the contents of an earlier compilation of the collection that was to become *Lyrics of Earth*, entitled "Afoot with the Year," "Winter-Store" was to be the fourth-to-last poem, followed by three additional winter poems, a position that would militate against the idea that this poem was designed to draw our attention back to the beginning of the volume. On the other hand, Lampman's ultimate placement of the poem at the end of the book (discounting for the moment the complications created by the poem's new ending) suggests he may well have wished it to perform this function. See Appendix B. For a discussion of the genesis of *Lyrics of Earth*, see chapter 6.
14 Lampman, undated partial draft of "Winter-Store," Lampman Papers, LAC, vol. 6, 2714–12 (pages are numbered backwards). This notebook includes poems written circa 1887. The draft of "Winter-Store" follows "Heat," written in the summer of 1887. The date 26 November 1889 appears at the end of a more complete draft of "Winter-Store," in Lampman Papers, LAC, vol. 3, 1449.
15 Warnock, *Memory*, 77.

CHAPTER THREE

1 Connor, *Archibald Lampman*, 64; Scott, "Archibald Lampman" (1943), in AER, 2:478–9; Early, *Archibald Lampman*, 4–5; Adams, "Archibald Lampman (1861–1899)," *Confederation Voices*.
2 Scott, memoir, in *Poems*, xxiii.
3 When the subject of a possible position at Cornell University first comes up in Lampman's correspondence with Thomson, in a letter dated 16 September 1891, Lampman is keen – "I hope it may indeed be!" – but mostly for the sake of his wife, who is "immensely [pleas]ed with the Professorial castle in the [air]." A few weeks later, Lampman is not so sure, describing himself on 4 October 1891 as "overcome with doubt and fear." In the same letter, he says he must write to Moses Coit Tyler, the Cornell professor who was making the arrangements, to indicate how unqualified he is, having devoted his time in recent years to "scribbling" instead of to academic study. On 20 November 1891, he assures Thomson that he did not write the letter to Tyler, but one can sense his relief at the lack of news about the job. Since "the matter will not come to anything anyway," he sighs, "there will probably be no need for me to write it." The quotations are from *L-TC*, 17, 20, 25.
4 Scott, memoir, in *Poems*, xvii.
5 Lampman, "Mermaid Inn," 4 February 1893, in AMI, 255.

6 Marshall, *Harsh and Lovely Land*. Charles G.D. Roberts's phrase "this rough, sweet land," from his "An Ode for the Canadian Confederacy," in *Collected Poems*, 90, captures the same idea.
7 Keats, "Ode on a Grecian Urn," in *Poems of Keats*, 537.
8 Scott, introduction to LE:SB, 39.
9 Emerson, in chapter 3 of *Nature*, entitled "Beauty," in *Collected Works*, vol. 1, 17, presents a similar idea, developed, however, in an ideological direction consistent with his transcendental philosophy, to which Lampman's "Beauty" makes no reference: "Beauty, in its largest and profoundest sense, is one expression for the universe. God is the all-fair. Truth, and goodness, and beauty, are but different faces of the same All." Lampman contents himself with the simple conjoining of beauty, truth, and goodness, complicated only by the paradoxical unity-within-trinity whereby beauty is, at once, one of three named and the name of three in one.
10 Lampman, "Mermaid Inn," 18 June 1892, in AMI, 94.
11 The terms "loafer" and "spear of grass," together with the overall celebration of resting at ease and observing nature, constitute a sympathetic referencing of the opening section of Whitman's "Song of Myself," in *Leaves of Grass*, 26, which Lampman may have read in the immediate wake of Whitman's death. Two months earlier, in "Mermaid Inn," 23 April 1892, in AMI, 60–1, he had written feelingly of "the venerable old Scald just dead in Camden," distancing himself from Whitman's "loud-mouthed" defenders, but taking pleasure in castigating the genteel critics in the anti-Whitman camp, one of whom "professes to be unable to find out what Whitman's message to humanity is." Lampman apparently had no such difficulty.
12 Lampman, "Poetic Interpretation," in ER, 126.
13 Emerson, *Nature*, in *Collected Works*, vol. 1, 14, 17. See also note 9 above.
14 Ibid., 17.
15 Bentley, editorial note, in ER, 305–6.
16 Ibid., 306.
17 Bentley, for example, in "Watchful Dreams," 17–18, argues that in "Freedom" the speaker's credibility must be questioned since it is only by distancing himself at the end of the poem from the dark realities of nature that he can claim to have achieved "freedom," which, however, when properly understood, is "not freedom at all, but an exclusive, misanthropic, and entrapping state of childish dependence on 'mother earth.'" According to this reading, the "negative" imagery infuses the poem with an irony that subverts its otherwise superficial and self-deluding celebration.
18 Brown, *On Canadian Poetry*, 95.
19 Swinburne, "The Triumph of Time," in *Selected Poetry and Prose*, 107.

20 See Bentley, *Confederation Group*, 177–87, for a discussion of Lampman's "therapeutic conception of nature" in the context of "the American mind-cure movement" and notions of nature as "mental restorative" in the writings of, among others, Wordsworth, particularly as understood by American landscape architect and proponent of "natural scenery" as "therapeutic agent" Frederick Law Olmsted and Scottish critic John Campbell Shairp. If it seems uncertain that Lampman was directly influenced by the mind-cure movement, Bentley's evidence nevertheless reveals the currency of the idea, during Lampman's life and indeed throughout the nineteenth century, that modern life required respite from materialistic preoccupations and what we now call workaholism.
21 Gnarowski, note on "Among the Timothy," in *Selected Poetry*, by Lampman, 107. In the text of the poem, Gnarowski restores Lampman's "reaper," suggesting that in referring to a scythe "Lampman had named the wrong agricultural tool," instead of agreeing with Scott that Lampman had named the wrong agricultural worker. Ware, in *Northern Romanticism*, 127, 284, follows Gnarowski.
22 Arnold, "The Scholar-Gipsy," in *Matthew Arnold*, 208.
23 Early, *Archibald Lampman*, 70; Mezei, "Lampman Among the Timothy," 62.
24 In *Matthew Arnold*, 546, the editors note the influence of Keats's "Ode to a Nightingale" stanza on Arnold's "The Scholar-Gipsy" stanza. In addition, they state that "Keats's influence diffusely pervades the poem" and cite "specific echoes" of "Ode to Autumn" and "Ode to a Nightingale."
25 Mezei, "Lampman Among the Timothy," 63.
26 Shakespeare, Sonnet 29, in *Norton Shakespeare*, 1956.
27 See, for example, Barry, "Prominent Canadians – XXXV," 13, and Coblentz, "Archibald Lampman," 346–7.
28 Davies, "Forms of Nature," 89.
29 Bentley, "Watchful Dreams," pt. 2, 19. See also Bentley, *Confederation Group*, 185.
30 Trehearne, "Style and Mind," 75, 83.
31 Ibid., 75.
32 Ibid., 83.
33 Ibid., 67–8, 75–6, 78–9.
34 Ibid., 70–3. The references to "reciprocity" and "blind" appear on 72.
35 Ibid., 68.
36 Ibid., 90.
37 Ibid., 86–7.
38 Donne, Holy Sonnet 10 (14 in other editions), in *John Donne's Poetry*, 140.

39 Lampman to Thomson, 2 February 1894, 6 November 1893, 25 April 1894, in *L-TC*, 103, 97, 119.
40 Doyle, "Archibald Lampman and Hamlin Garland," 38.
41 Lampman to Garland, 4 April 1889, quoted in Doyle, "Archibald Lampman and Hamlin Garland," 39.
42 Lampman to Thomson, 22 November 1893, in *L-TC*, 101.
43 Doyle, "Archibald Lampman and Hamlin Garland," 40.
44 Lampman to Garland, 25 April 1889, quoted in Doyle, "Archibald Lampman and Hamlin Garland," 40. Doyle, following Lynn, in *L-TC*, 26n1, and followed by Trehearne, in "Style and Mind," 68, writes "to my plan." Lampman's phrase in the original letter, in the Hamlin Garland Collection, for better or worse, is "in my plan."
45 "Archibald Lampman," obituary notice in the *Globe*, 11 February 1899, 24.
46 In *Archibald Lampman*, 63, Early argues that "[i]n 'The Frogs,' Lampman makes Keats not so much his model as his resource," with echoes forming "a meaningful pattern of allusion," and in "Story of an Affinity," 285, Ower provides a similar analysis in relation to Tennyson.
47 Perkins, "John Keats," in *English Romantic Writers*, ed. Perkins, 1117–18.
48 Ower, "Story of an Affinity," 285.
49 Keats, "Ode on a Grecian Urn," in *Poems of Keats*, 535.
50 Wittgenstein, *Tractatus Logico-Philosophicus*, 87, quoted in LePan, "Responsibility and Revolt," 220.
51 Stringer, "Glance at Lampman," 23.
52 A tricky issue of spelling arises in relation to the word "rapt" in "The Frogs," where it occurs three times. Lampman spells it "wrapt" in *Among the Millet*, and in *Poems* Scott changes it to "rapt." In *Selected Poetry*, 42–4, Gnarowski restores the original spelling on the assumption that "Lampman intended to mean enveloped" (108), and Ware, in *Northern Romanticism*, 135–7, follows Gnarowski (see Ware's note in *Northern Romanticism*, 284). There are instances in other poems where Lampman uses "wrapped" in the sense of enveloped. In "Winter-Thought" the buttercups are "thought-wrapped" and in the sonnet "In November" the speaker is "Wrapped round with thought" (both unchanged in *Poems*). In "The Organist," on the other hand, where the meaning of entranced or enraptured seems intended, the spelling in *Among the Millet* is the same as in these cases ("wrapped"), and Scott once again changes it to "rapt" in *Poems*. In "The Frogs," it seems most likely that Lampman's "wrapt," like his "wrapped" in "The Organist," means "rapt." For one thing, even though "Wrapt with your voices" could mean enveloped, the phrases "wrapt ears" and "wrapt delight" seem clearly wrong, whereas "rapt" fits the idea that the listeners,

subject to "enchanted reveries," are entranced by the frogs' music. According to the *Oxford English Dictionary*, "wrapped" can be defined as "Absorbed or engrossed *in* thought, contemplation, etc.," a meaning "[p]erhaps partly suggested by RAPT." Historical examples include "wrapt in wonder" (James Beattie, 1771), "wrapt in prayer" (George Eliot, 1859), and "wrapped in delight" (Baring-Gould, 1894). If this – despite the absence in "The Frogs" of the "in" construction – is the intended meaning, as I believe it is, then for readers today the "wrapt" spelling must be confusing. Assuming, then, that the meaning is "absorbed" rather than "enveloped," and given that the standard spelling in that sense is "rapt," Scott's emendations appear sound.
53 Keats, "Ode to a Nightingale," in *Poems of Keats*, 532.
54 Early, *Archibald Lampman*, 66.

CHAPTER FOUR

1 Scott, introduction to LE:SB, 46.
2 Scott, introduction to LE:SB, 46–7; Roberts to Lampman, 10 November 1889, in *Collected Letters*, by Roberts, 111; "Canadian Poet," 53; [Machar], "Some Recent Canadian Poems," 4; Stedman, *Victorian Anthology*, 659–60.
3 Scott, introduction to LE:SB, 47.
4 The parallels with "Tantramar Revisited" and "Tintern Abbey" are noted by Mezei in "Lampman Among the Timothy," 65, where, at odds with Daniells and Early, she praises "Between the Rapids" for its evocation of the Canadian past, "creating a sense of tradition and locality."
5 Scott, introduction to LE:SB, 46; Clough, "Les Vaches," in *Poems of Clough*, 207–8.
6 Bentley, *Confederation Group*, 86.
7 Arnold, "A Dream," in *Matthew Arnold*, 65–6. Daniells, in "Lampman and Roberts," 405–6, although he does not name "A Dream," quotes lines from "Between the Rapids" as an illustration of Lampman's propensity to produce "re-creations of the poetic world of Arnold." Early, in "Archibald Lampman (1881–1899)," 138, comments, "It is startling ... to discover that the frequently praised 'Between the Rapids' (1886) is, quite evidently, an approximate copy of Matthew Arnold's 'A Dream,'" and in *Archibald Lampman*, 113, he dismisses the poem as a "tissue of Arnoldian cadences and forced nostalgia." Bentley, in *Confederation Group*, 86, points out that Lampman's "Heaven gleams and then is gone" echoes "the light / Gleams and is gone" from Arnold's "Dover Beach."
8 Arnold's opening question, "Was it a dream?" (see previous note),

echoes the closing lines of Keats's "Ode to a Nightingale, "Was it a vision, or a waking dream? / Fled is that music ... Do I wake or sleep?" in *Poems of Keats*, 532. Likewise, Arnold's description of the ghost-like female forms that emerge onto the balcony of the cottage in "A Dream" – "Clad were they both in white" – recalls Milton's image of the ghost of his dead wife who, appearing before him in a dream, "Came vested all in white," in his Sonnet 23, in *Complete Poetry*, 163. All literature feeds on itself, however, and conventions take hold. Thus one detects in Milton's "Methought I saw my late espousèd saint / Brought to me like Alcestis from the grave" (alluding to Euripides's *Alcestis*) an echo of the opening line of the first of Walter Raleigh's commendatory verses attached to Spenser's *The Faerie Qveene*, titled "A Vision vpon this conceipt of the *Faery Queene*," 721, which reads, "Me thought I saw the graue, where *Laura* lay," alluding to Petrarch's idealized beloved. Through imitation and allusion, the connections multiply.

9 In *Among the Millet*, 21, Lampman has the title as "Morning on the Lièvres." In *Poems*, Scott changes it to "Morning on the Lievre." In *Selected Poetry*, Gnarowski restores the original spelling, noting, 107, that the Rivière du Lièvre, as it is now officially known, was once called the Rivière aux Lièvres. In representing this title, I have respected Scott's editorial decision to omit the *s*, but restored the accent. Ware, in *Northern Romanticism*, 131, 284n, follows Gnarowski.

10 Wordsworth, "I wandered lonely as a cloud," in *Poems*, 1:619.

11 Richard Hovey, in his "Down the Songo," in *Songs from Vagabondia*, coauthored by Bliss Carman, 18, echoes Lampman's "Sky above and sky below" in his phrase "Above us sky, beneath us sky." And as Veronica Strong-Boag and Carole Gerson point out in *Paddling Her Own Canoe*, 152, Pauline Johnson's poem "Shadow River" "can be compared to Lampman's 'Morning on the Lièvre,' as Johnson suspends the canoeing speaker 'midway 'twixt earth and heaven,' in a moment of idealized understanding." Charlotte Gray, in *Flint and Feather*, 128, makes a similar observation. The similarity of phrasing can be seen in Johnson's description of the speaker as floating "upon the sapphire floor, a dream / Of clouds of snow, / Above, below." According to Strong-Boag and Gerson in *Collected Poems and Selected Prose*, by Johnson, "Shadow River" was first published in *Saturday Night* on 20 July 1889. Lampman's poem was written in 1886 and published in *Among the Millet* in 1888.

12 Beattie, "Archibald Lampman," 85. The idea that intimations of the "ominous" and "sinister" may be found in Lampman's portrayal of nature occurs as well in Richard Arnold, "'The Clearer Self,'" 38; in *Encyclopedia Canadiana*, 160, where George L. Parker points authori-

tatively to Lampman's "ambivalence towards the natural world"; and in the entry on Lampman in *Oxford Companion to Canadian Literature*, 618, where Zailig Pollock asserts that "[i]n many of Lampman's finest poems ('April', 'Heat', 'In November', 'Winter [U]plands') the celebration of nature is touched by unease, even fear." Northrop Frye, in his famous "Conclusion to a *Literary History of Canada*," in *Bush Garden*, 225, speaks of being impressed by "a tone of deep terror in regard to nature" in Canadian literature, adding that "[n]ature is consistently sinister and menacing in Canadian poetry" (142). This perspective has on occasion been visited upon Lampman. For example, McLeod, in "Canadian Post-Romanticism," 11–12, quotes Frye and goes on to argue that Lampman and his contemporaries felt the terror and expressed it in an effort to undercut their ostensibly positive celebrations of nature, as discussed in my introduction. And to cite a recent example, art historian Ross King, in *Defiant Spirits*, 42–4, credits Lampman and Wilfred Campbell with presenting "harrowing portraits of spectral woods and frigid winds" in a land characterized by "loneliness and isolation – the lack of any other human presence" in poems that prefigure the paintings of the Group of Seven. King's chapter title "Eerie Wilderness" is a phrase from Lampman's poem "Storm."

13 Arnold, "'The Clearer Self,'" 38.
14 Bairstow, *Morning on the Lièvre*.
15 Lampman, "Happiness," in ER, 194.
16 Muddiman, "Archibald Lampman," 68.
17 Lampman to Thomson, 30 October 1895, in L-TC, 159.
18 Lampman to Carman, 23 February 1891, in "Letters to Carman," by Campbell, Lampman, and Scott, 57.
19 In *Lampman's Sonnets*, Whitridge includes 177 poems, but some, such as "To Chicago," 118, and "Cloud and Sun," 144, bear only a vague resemblance to the sonnet form.
20 Roberts, "The Sower" and "The Potato Harvest," in *Collected Poems*, 82, 91.
21 "The Sower," first published in July 1884, appeared in Roberts's *In Divers Tones* in 1886, the year of Lampman's canoe trip with Scott. "The Potato Harvest," written no later than 7 April 1886, the date inscribed on a holograph manuscript of the poem, is included in the same book. (The subject matter of the latter poem suggests it was written in the fall of the previous year – 1885.) See Pacey's notes in Roberts's *Collected Poems*, 410–11, 421–2.
22 Lampman, "Two Canadian Poets," in ER, 102, 107; Lampman, "Mermaid Inn," 21 January 1893, in AMI, 240.
23 Lampman, "Two Canadian Poets," in ER, 94–107. Lampman's two "Mermaid Inn" contributions dealing entirely with Roberts are those for 19 November 1892, in AMI, 193–4, and for 21 January 1893, in

AMI, 239–41. His third contribution mentioning Roberts, on sonnets, is for 17 September 1892, in *AMI*, 152–3.
24 Although Scott, in his introduction to *LE:SB*, 46–7, traces "A Dawn on the Lièvre" to the 1886 canoe trip, there may have been a lag between inspiration and composition. Supporting Early's estimate of "c. Nov 1889," in "Chronology," 80, is the fact that the poem does not appear in *Among the Millet*, published in 1888.
25 Lampman, "Two Canadian Poets," in *ER*, 94–5.
26 Crawford, "The Dark Stag," in *Collected Poems*, 78–80.
27 Crawford, "The Dark Stag," *Toronto Evening Telegram*, 28 November 1883, 4.
28 Thomson to Lampman, 3 June 1893, in *L-TC*, 83.
29 Lampman, "Mermaid Inn," 26 March 1892, in *AMI*, 43.

CHAPTER FIVE

1 Lampman, "Happiness," in *ER*, 196.
2 Lampman, "Mermaid Inn," 28 January 1893, in *AMI*, 248.
3 Lampman, "Mermaid Inn," 2 April 1892, in *AMI*, 44–5.
4 Shakespeare, Sonnet 116, in *Norton Shakespeare*, 1985.
5 Scott, "Mermaid Inn," 18 February 1893, in *AMI*, 260.
6 Lampman Papers, LAC, vol. 6, 2717–15 (pages are numbered backwards). The instances in which the sequencing of passages in Lampman's notebook draft differs from the published version of "Heat" are as follows: the last four lines of stanza four appear after stanza one; the second half of stanza two appears for the first time in a revised version of that stanza that follows stanza five; stanza six appears after stanza three; and stanza four, incorporating as its last four lines those that were written immediately after stanza one, appears at the end.
7 Shakespeare, Sonnet 65, in *Norton Shakespeare*, 1968.
8 Pacey, in "Reading of Lampman's 'Heat,'" 182, suggests the "not this or that" passage is "an obvious reference to the pairs of opposites of which we have seen the poem to be composed." Gnarowski, in his introduction to *Archibald Lampman*, xxvi, demurs: "Yet, methodical and convincing though [Pacey's reading] is, one is left wondering if the 'problem' of the last stanza of 'Heat' is really solved or satisfactorily explained." Davies, in "Forms of Nature," 95, interprets the first two lines to mean "that life is not an occasion for the extremes of optimism or pessimism, that it is a mixture of joy and sorrow, triumph and tragedy." McLeod, in "Canadian Post-Romanticism," 31–2, proposes that these lines indicate that the speaker "cannot always distinguish [one thing from another] sharply, though nature is sweetest and he is most himself when he can. 'This' and 'that,' therefore, also have the implication of 'subjective' and 'objective.'" Early, in *Archibald Lamp-*

man, 68, states, "I take 'this or that' to refer to the two kinds of consciousness mentioned at the opening of the preceding stanza: 'dreams,' or the approach to visionary insight, and their 'intervals' of sensory alertness to outward things." And Bentley has evolved his reading over time: in "Watchful Dreams," pt. 1, 191–2, he suggests that the closing stanza indicates that the speaker, who has been "struggling to clarify his thoughts and perceptions" and to "regain rational coherence and perceptual clarity in 'the pale depth of the noon,'" has finally "won his struggle, albeit conditionally and with difficulty"; in *Gay/Grey Moose*, 102, he sees that stanza as expressing "a privileged moment of intense, rational insight" and as emphasizing "spiritual significance over objective fact, the recording mind over the objects seen"; and in *Confederation Group*, 153–4, he speaks of a "mental equipoise that begins fully to emerge in the final stanza of the poem."

9 Lampman Papers, LAC, vol. 6, 2716.
10 Davies, in "Forms of Nature," 96, notes that "[t]he hour, the noon, has become a 'furnace,'" and explains, "The furnace is the instrument for the melting, fusing, and transmutation of ore, the basic poetic material, into pure gold, complete poetic expression."
11 Newman, *Apologia Pro Vita Sua*, 42.
12 Martin, *John Keble*, 17, 52–4; Griffin, *John Keble*, 27, 71–4.
13 Ibid., 110–13.
14 Ibid., 110, 169–70. See Shaw, "*In Memoriam* and *The Christian Year*," for a detailed examination of the parallels as well as contrasts in the composition, content, style, and impact of the two poems.
15 Martin, *John Keble*, 111.
16 Griffin, *John Keble*, 29. The year the college opened is given in "About Keble," on the Keble College website.
17 Headon, "George Whitaker," 918; cited in Bentley, *Confederation Group*, 205.
18 Reed, *History of the University of Trinity College*, 88–9; cited in Bentley, *Confederation Group*, 205n. The chairs "in memory of two great Oxford teachers" were established at the request of an anonymous Oxford graduate, who, in response to a fund-raising appeal for Trinity College carried out in England in 1885, had donated £5,000. Keble and Pusey had both made donations in response to a similar appeal in 1864. See Reed, 88–9, 71.
19 Lampman Papers, LAC, vol. 3, 144; U of T manuscript book, 17.
20 Quoted by Nesbitt in "Matthew Arnold in Canada," 53–4.
21 Lampman to Thomson, 2 November 1897, in *L-TC*, 193.
22 Karen Evans, librarian with the Anglican Church of Canada, in an e-mail to me dated 13 August 2007, writes, "It would be fair to say that most parts of the nineteenth century Anglican Church in Canada would have considered themselves as more on the 'Protestant' or 'Low

Church' side of the church," whereas "[t]he diocese of Toronto tended to be 'High.'" In *Confederation Voices*, Adams notes that Lampman Senior had once reprimanded "a young parishioner ... for associating with a Roman Catholic." This man, Reginald Drayton, later described the elder Lampman as "very narrow and small in his religious views." One could of course be anti-Catholic and still supportive of Anglo-Catholicism, and High Church leanings could explain what Adams refers to as the mystery of Lampman's father's early retirement in 1875 at the age of 53. Beyond the supposition that Lampman Senior approved of his son's enrolment in Trinity College, however, I have found no evidence to support the conjecture that he had High Church sympathies.

23 Griffin, *John Keble*, 76. See also Martin, *John Keble*, 110.
24 Martin, *John Keble*, 127.
25 Connor, *Archibald Lampman*, 35.
26 Keble, poem for the First Sunday after the Epiphany, in *Christian Year*, 33–5.
27 Keble, poem for the Twenty-Third Sunday after Trinity, in *Christian Year*, 173–5.
28 Handel, in *Messiah*, pt. 1, passages 6 and 7, sets only part of this text, as follows: "For he is like a refiner's fire. And He shall purify the sons of Levi, that they may offer unto the Lord an offering in righteousness."
29 Early, in *Archibald Lampman*, 67, states incisively that "[t]he poem's central paradox is that the atmosphere of intense heat evoked is felt as liberating rather than as oppressive."
30 Pacey, "Reading of Lampman's 'Heat,'" 178–84. Finding its "descriptive accuracy, perfection of tone and unwavering concreteness" not enough "to explain the spell which the poem weaves," Pacey explores the idea that "Heat" is "constructed on the principle of balanced opposites" and suggests that the imagery of "cyclical movement" gives rise to an epiphany wherein the various opposites are reconciled in a "vision of a unified world." Pacey's reading is endorsed either fully or in modified form by Daniells, in "Lampman and Roberts," 412; Davies, in "Forms of Nature," 93; Bentley, in "Watchful Dreams," pt. 1, 190–1; and McLeod, in "Canadian Post-Romanticism," 31.
31 Lampman, "Mermaid Inn," 3 December 1892, in *AMI*, 204.
32 Early, in *Archibald Lampman*, 68, observes, "'Heat' is a splendid example of Lampman's [R]omantic re-vision of his Christian heritage."
33 Keble, poem for the Twentieth Sunday after Trinity, in *Christian Year*, 167–9.
34 Carman's unconscious plagiarism was first pointed out by Joseph Edgar Chamberlin in his column "The Listener," *Boston Evening Transcript*, 28 January 1893, quoted in full in *L-TC*, 64n10. Carman's

acknowledgment of his "amazing theft" appears in a letter to Lampman, 26 February 1894, in "SFU Letters," 181–2.
35 For a complete account of the controversy sparked by Miller's article, with all contributions to the periodical press reproduced, see Hurst, *War among the Poets*.
36 [Campbell], "Poetry and Piracy," 30.
37 Miller, "After the Bard[s'] Battle," 86.
38 Carman, "War among the Poets," 91.
39 Tennyson, *The Princess*, in *Poems of Tennyson*, 1:223 (3.106); Aeschylus, passage from *Prometheus Bound*, quoted in English by Blathwayt, in *Through Life*, 59. The phrase "innumerable Rabble," appearing in George Chapman's translation of a Homeric epigram, given prominence as the final line of translated verse in *Chapman's Homeric Hymns*, 185, may have led to Miller's confusion over the source of the phrase "innumerable ripple."
40 Milton, *Paradise Lost*, in *Complete Poetry*, 365 (3.147).
41 Spenser, *Faerie Qveene*, 275 (2.12.35.6).
42 Davies, "Forms of Nature," 95.
43 Scott, "Archibald Lampman [1924]," in *AER*, 334.
44 Early, in "Poems of October," 35, detects in the description of wind-blown leaves in the first three lines of stanza four of "In October" an allusion to Shelley's "Ode to the West Wind" and, through this allusion, a consolatory hint of spring's return.
45 Early, "Chronology," 78, 86n5. In his note, Early explains that the first two stanzas of "In October" were written in October of 1883 and the remaining two in October of 1884.
46 Brown, *On Canadian Poetry*, 97.
47 "Canadian Poet," 52.
48 Isaiah 40:4.
49 Connor, *Archibald Lampman*, 102.
50 [Machar], "Some Recent Canadian Poems," 3, 5.
51 Expanding on his designation of "The Dog" as "a mongrel about a mongrel," Bentley, in "New Dimension," 14, calls the poem "an irregular sonnet describing a beast whose 'queer feet [are] / planted irregularly' and who chases a ball up to, but not beyond, a broken fence." In the somewhat modified version of the same essay included in *Gay/Grey Moose*, 24, the phrase "an irregular sonnet" becomes "a largely regular Petrarchan sonnet," which takes something of the force from "a mongrel about a mongrel," but this phrase is preserved. In *Confederation Group*, 125–6, Lampman's cur appears again, this time in the context of a broader discussion of form and style in the poetic practice of Lampman and his contemporaries. (See my discussion of "Reality" in chapter 9.) Having drawn the conclusion that Lampman "regarded the [sonnet] form as appropriate only for serious and elevat-

ing materials," Bentley assesses "The Dog" as anomalous, concluding, "it is an exercise in incongruity that aims to extract humour by treating a comically ugly subject in a serious form." Precisely the same analysis appears in the revised version of chap. 3 of *Confederation Group* that serves as the introduction to *English Canadian Poetics*, ed. Hogg, 52–3. It should be noted that the reference to "pigs" rhyming with "legs" in both of these last-mentioned sources must be the result of a typographical error, the correct word being "pegs."
52 Lampman, "Why Do Ye Call the Poet Lonely?" in *Poems*, 11.

CHAPTER SIX

1 Bentley, introduction to LE:WT, 9–10, 15. In my 1989 article "Life 'Only Sweet,'" pt. 1, 12–19, I presented my findings on this issue, at odds with Bentley's view on the one crucial point, but Bentley apparently remains unconvinced, for although he has never to my knowledge refuted my arguments, he has on numerous occasions reiterated his original position. In his 1996 introduction to ER, xxiii, having noted that both *Among the Millet* and *Alcyone* reflect Lampman's preference for "variety" of style and subject matter in a collection of poems, Bentley states that "*Lyrics of Earth* might have been similar if Lampman and Thomson, who helped to give it its final shape as a somewhat monotonous a [sic] cycle of nature lyrics ... had not recognized the difficulty of interesting a publisher in a collection of 'miscellaneous poems.'" Five years later, in "On the Confederation Poets' Companionship with Nature: Lampman," 7, he asserts that *Lyrics of Earth* was "[a]rranged with E.W. Thomson's help around the cycle of the seasons." This point is repeated in the revised version of the same essay that partly makes up chap. 4 of *Confederation Group* (2004), 138, and in chap. 3 of that book, 154, he writes, "Thanks to Edward William Thomson's 'better idea of constructing a book' for the American market, *Lyrics of Earth* took shape in the summer of 1895 as a sequence of lyrics of varying lengths organized around the seasonal cycle" – words that are repeated verbatim in the 2009 remounting of this essay as the introduction to *English Canadian Poetics*, ed. Hogg, 61–2.
2 Adams, *Confederation Voices*.
3 Lampman to Thomson, 28 October 1891, in L-TC, 23.
4 Early, "Chronology," 81.
5 Lampman to Thomson, 20 October 1892, in L-TC, 52.
6 Lampman to Thomson, 10 February 1893, in L-TC, 59.
7 Lampman to Scudder, 11 December 1893, in Greig, pt. 2, 14.
8 Lampman to Thomson, 18 April 1893, in L-TC, 76; 5 July 1893, in L-TC, 88; 6 May 1895 and 30 May 1895, in L-TC, 138, 143.
9 Lampman to Thomson, 30 May 1895, in L-TC, 143.

10 Bentley, introduction to *LE:WT*, 9–10. Connor, in *Archibald Lampman*, 172, also assumes that Lampman's reference to the three non-nature poems relates to *Lyrics of Earth*. Connor notes that Lampman "wished to retain" the poems, but makes no comment about the fact that they do not appear in *Lyrics of Earth*.
11 Bentley, introduction to *LE:WT*, 15.
12 Lampman to Thomson, 20 May 1895, in *L-TC*, 141–2.
13 Lampman, "Miscellaneous Poems," [191–6]. The lists of poems included in this volume are mentioned in Whitridge, "Annotated Checklist," 26.
14 Bentley, introduction to *LE:WT*, 9.
15 Lampman to Thomson, 6 June 1895, in *L-TC*, 144.
16 Lampman to Scudder, 30 September 1895, in Greig, pt. 2, 16.
17 "Forest Moods," "The Bird and the Hour," and "An Ode to the Hills," according to Early's "Chronology," 82, were written on 24 May 1893, 6 June 1893, and 11 August 1893, respectively.
18 Lampman to Thomson, 5 July 1893, in *L-TC*, 88.
19 Carman to Lampman, 26 February 1894, in "SFU Letters," 182.
20 Lampman, "Miscellaneous Poems," [191–3].
21 The three poems alluded to are "The City of the End of Things," "War," and "The Land of Pallas" – all included in *Alcyone*.
22 Bentley, introduction, *LE:WT*, 17.
23 Griffin, *John Keble*, 68, 75.
24 Canadian parallels of this inclusive vision of nature may be found in non-literary artistic expression – for example, in Tom Thomson's portrayal of beauty throughout the year in his northern images, as discussed in the introduction to this book, and in Harry Somers's musical composition *North Country: Four Movements for String Orchestra* (1948), a work that interprets each of the four seasons. Regarding the latter, Grace and Haag, 110–11, take issue with an analysis by musicologist David Parsons. Where Parsons – "[i]n language that is reminiscent of Northrop Frye's and Margaret Atwood's interpretations of the Canadian landscape" – hears "an overwhelming, threatening landscape conveyed by the music," they counter that the music "need not be read in negative terms." Following musical analysis, they conclude, "Rather than representing a negative or hostile landscape, *North Country* could be said to capture the variety, drama, energy, beauty, and expectation that Somers finds in the North."
25 Lampman, "The Lesson of the Trees," in *The Owl* 7 (1894): 243.
26 Lampman, "The Lesson of the Trees," in "Twenty-Five Fugitive Poems," 60.
27 Lampman, "Two Canadian Poets," in *ER*, 93.
28 Tennyson, "The Oak," in *Demeter*, 171–2, and in *Poems of Tennyson*, 3:219.

29 Fry, *Ode Less Travelled*, 91.
30 Early, *Archibald Lampman*, 78.
31 Tennyson, *Maud*, in *Poems of Tennyson*, 2:565 (1.912–13).
32 Tennyson, "The Voice and the Peak," in *Poems of Tennyson*, 3:3–4.
33 Lampman, "Mermaid Inn," 10 December 1892, in AMI, 206–7.
34 Thomson to Scott, 4 April 1923, in *Some Letters*, by Scott, Lampman, and others, 15.
35 Another instance of this phenomenon of wanting to hold on to a fading experience and then finding compensation in its successor occurs in Lampman's "An October Sunset." This poem is from *Among the Millet*, not *Lyrics of Earth*, and the image is diurnal, not seasonal, but the idea is the same and nowhere more simply and yet evocatively expressed. The "slim cloudflakes" at sunset are imagined as leaning in the direction of the vanishing "king," the sun, wishing to kiss his hand, and "Paying no reverence to the slender queen," the moon, set beautifully in the eastern sky, nor to the "small stars that one by one unfold." The courtier-like, sun-worshipping cloudflakes pay no reverence, but the speaker does, the unstated action being that he has turned regretfully from the fading western light, to be surprised and delighted by the alternative splendour of a different kind of beauty, what Lampman calls "the darker dawn" in another short lyric on a similar theme, "With the Night."
36 The quoted passages are from "In May" and "In November."
37 Lampman Papers, LAC, vol. 2, 959.
38 Keith, "Archibald Lampman," 21–2.
39 Both Lampman's fear that his writing could be prolix and his preference for simplicity of expression are evident in his 8 February 1892 response to a letter from Bliss Carman praising his "Comfort of the Fields," in Greig, pt. 1, 13. "I feel your approval to be something very pleasant [and] very valuable," Lampman writes, "and the fact that my poem has given you satisfaction enables me to regard it with greater favour than I had before done. Your attributions to its quality of simplicity pleases [sic] me better than anything else, for I had cut, and changed and re-written the verse many times in order [to] reduce the formal and some what cataloguing effect that they seemed to me to have, and I was afraid they still produced an impression of that kind." Greig suggests that the poem under discussion is "Sunset" because, in another letter included in the Douglas Library collection that he is analyzing, dated 11 November 1891, Lampman indicates that he is sending Carman that poem for possible publication in *The Independent*. But in a letter not included in the Douglas Library collection, dated 25 January 1892, in "SFU Letters," 178, Carman offers a critique of "Comfort of the Fields," which he had likely seen in *Scribner's Magazine* 11 (1892): 255–6, and it is clearly this letter to which

Lampman is referring in his response two weeks later. In a letter to Thomson dated 28 October 1891, in *L-TC*, 22, Lampman mentions that he had recently sold "Comfort of the Fields" to *Scribner's*. He describes the poem as consisting of "six or seven heavy stanzas" and comments, "I do not know what they took it for, they have refused & sent me back many a better piece of work."

40 Lampman to Thomson, 6 November 1893, in *L-TC*, 97.
41 Lampman, "The Hermit Thrush," with "The Cup," by Scott, Christmas greeting card, 1894.
42 A contrary view has been advanced by Davies in "Forms of Nature," 90–1, suggesting that in "Snow" we are presented with "the exact opposite of the process described in 'Heat,'" one in which the speaker's thoughts are "accompanied by a sense of threatening force and menace." This is part of Davies's "quarternary" approach to Lampman's poems, within which winter is archetypically negative: "It is the withdrawal of the life-force, the absence of the sun, a world without light or heat, a body bereft of the quickening warmth, and a mind without illumination. It is petrification." According to this analysis, the beauty of the landscape, the stillness, the calm are not meant to be soothing; the very silence of the falling snow has "a sinister meaning."
43 Loreena McKennitt has twice recorded her version of "Snow": one version appears on *To Drive the Cold Winter Away* (1987) and the other on *A Winter Garden* (1995). The five tracks of the latter recording, together with eight others, are included on *A Midwinter Night's Dream* (2008).
44 Lampman, "Poetic Interpretation," in *ER*, 126–7.
45 Lampman, "Love-Wonder," in *Poems*, 106.
46 Ralph Gustafson, "Among the Millet," 153.
47 The story that Katherine Waddell commissioned the memorial plaque in St Margaret's Church is one that Whitridge tells in her introduction to *Lampman's Kate*, by Lampman, 22–3. Whitridge does not say where the rumour originated. Scott, in a letter to Pelham Edgar, 4 February 1905 (in *More Letters*, by Scott, Lampman, and others, 26), writes, "I have noticed your efforts in the A.L. memorial fund. We are doing something the same here, but ours is to be a plain brass, a very handsome one however." In a brief bibliography by R.H. Hathaway, tacked onto Scott's "Who's Who in Canadian Literature: Archibald Lampman" (1926), in *AER*, 374, it is stated that the tablet was "erected by Lampman's friends." It may well be that Whitridge based her sourcing of the tablet on supposition. The story has often been repeated, however. Sandra Campbell, for example, in "Love in the Langevin Block," A14, writes, "[Waddell] in fact anonymously commissioned the plaque at St. Margaret's Church after the poet's early death."

48 Lampman to Copeland and Day, 30 September 1895, in Greig, pt. 2, 16.
49 Bentley, "Same Unnamed Delight," 33–4. Despite finding "The Sun Cup" a "pleasing coda" to *Lyrics of Earth*, Bentley apparently took Lampman's statement that the poem "would do just as well at the end" to be sanctioning an unsatisfactory expedient and restored it to its original position in his "working text" edition of the book. See Bentley, introduction to *LE:WT*, 11–12.
50 According to Early, in "Chronology," 77, 83, the earliest poem in *Lyrics of Earth*, "Godspeed to the Snow," was written in April of 1883, and the latest, "Distance," c. 1894.

CHAPTER SEVEN

1 Knister, in "Poetry of Archibald Lampman," 114, sees "Sapphics" as embodying "an oft-repeated conception of the relation of nature and human destiny, as far as could be wished from jingling banality." Logan, in "Literary Group," 559, praises the poem for its "faultless technic, for spiritual vision of nature and for the beautiful application of noble ideas to life," calling it "an indubitable contribution to poetic art, and peculiarly Canadian." Lampman himself, less effusively, says of the poem in a letter to Thomson, 21 October 1895, in *L-TC*, 156, "I rather like it," adding, "I flatter myself that these [stanzas] are real Sapphics, and the proof of it is that the movement is musical." Daniells, in "Lampman and Roberts," 412, agrees, stating that Lampman "was rightly pleased with his 'Sapphics,' a real test of skill surmounted without apparent effort." And Early, in "Poems of October," 59, identifying the poem as "Lampman's final autumnal elegy," calls it "one of his finest achievements in the form."
2 Lampman to Thomson, 21 October 1895, in *L-TC*, 156.
3 Logan, in "Literary Group," 559–60, and Early, in "Poems of October," 57, make the same divisions.
4 Unwin, "Poetry of Archibald Lampman," 92.
5 [Willison], in "The Attack on Bliss Carman," an unsigned contribution to the debate over plagiarism in the Toronto *Globe* (discussed in chapter 5), 46, writes, "As to the line taken from Mr. Lampman without acknowledgment, surprise is only felt that he should have done so. The lyricist has no need to borrow from the didactic poet." Scott, in his memoir, in *Poems*, xxiv, recalls that "[i]t amused him when he was called a didactic poet" since the poems that might be called didactic were "written from fulness of conviction and experience and prompted only by the joy of production."
6 Logan, "Literary Group," 560–2.

7 Similar diction is evident, for example, in Bliss Carman's Lyric 3 from his *Sappho: One Hundred Lyrics*, 5, where the speaker asks, "Whom shall we life-loving mortals / Serve and be happy?" and again, "Lo now, your garlanded altars, / Are they not goodly with flowers?" This lyric is reprinted in Ware, *Northern Romanticism*, 190.

8 Early, in "Poems of October," 59, notes the stoic philosophy present in "Sapphics," but sees the poem – "dynamic" rather than "static and dubiously triumphal" – as shifting its stance in the last two stanzas, allowing the speaker "to move beyond the posture of heroic stoicism and embrace the contingencies of experience." I would argue that there is no intent in the poem to repudiate the hard-won main claim in what amounts to a (movingly emotional) coda. Rather, the closing stanzas are offered as a bittersweet extension of the main position. It is true that sometimes Lampman strove to distance himself from stoicism, as where, in a passage quoted by Early, 59, he describes the object of his frustrated love, Katherine Waddell, as "too human for the stoic's part," but "Sapphics," in my reading, does not "develop" in that direction. The shift at the end, where the music becomes softer, is one of tone, not theme.

9 Early, in "Chronology," 85, gives the date "Sep 1897?" for "The Lake in the Forest," presumably based on the criteria he employs, as explained on 77, for undated poems: their place in Lampman's manuscripts or "other circumstantial evidence."

10 Milton, *Paradise Lost*, in *Complete Poetry*, 360 (3.8–9).

11 Shelley, "Ozymandias," in *Poems*, 310–11.

12 Dudek, "Significance of Lampman," 193.

13 In his sonnet "Voices of Earth," Lampman once again links natural-world imagery – in this case auditory – to a spiritually imbued prehistory. Elemental sounds "are the voices of earth's secret soul, / Uttering the mystery from which she came." Canadian composer Ruth Watson Henderson uses Lampman's poem as the centrepiece of her prize-winning choral composition *Voices of Earth*, in which excerpts from six Lampman poems – "The Sun Cup," "The Moon-Path," "The Wind's Word," "Winter-Store," "May," and "Voices of Earth" – are paired with extracts from St Francis's "Canticle of the Sun," emphasizing the connection between nature and the divine. For a detailed analysis of the linking of the texts in this work, see Ryan J. Herbert, "Conductor's Study," 12–20.

14 John 1:1: "In the beginning was the word."

15 The image of "Channels ... turned to stone" recalls that of "water like a stone" in Christina Rossetti's poem "A Christmas Carol," in *Complete Poems*, 216–17, well known today by the title "In the Bleak Midwinter," with musical settings by, among others, Gustav Holst and Harold Edwin Darke.

16 In a letter to Thomson dated 6 June 1895, in L-TC, 144, Lampman speaks of having "a special liking" for "An Ode to the Hills." On a manuscript copy of the poem in Lampman Papers, Simon Fraser University, MsC-7.1.5.12, someone has written, "[sent to Isabel Voorhis]," and in a letter to Isabelle Voorhis, 29 November 1893, in "SFU Letters," 147, Lampman says he is enclosing a poem "which is the first piece in my new volume" and asks for her opinion. The "new volume" would have been "Afoot with the Year," of which the opening poem was "An Ode to the Hills" (see Appendix B). In "Report of Section Two," PTRSC, 2nd series, vol. 3 (1897), lxxiv, it is mentioned that Lampman read "An Ode to the Hills" and "Ingvi and Alf" to a meeting of that section. This report was delivered in June 1897. In a letter to Maud Playter Lampman dated 22 June 1897, in "SFU Letters," 118, Lampman writes, "Tomorrow I read my poems" – hence the date of 23 June 1897.
17 Longfellow, *The Song of Hiawatha*, in *Poems and Other Writings*, 144. The quoted terms appear in Part I of the poem, "The Peace-Pipe," lines 3–4 and 12.
18 Crawford, *Malcolm's Katie*, in *Collected Poems*, 202 (2.138), 215 (4.38).
19 Early, *Archibald Lampman*, 138–9.
20 Lampman, "A Fantasy," in "Twenty-Five Fugitive Poems," 56.
21 In *Poems*, 316, a period occurs, apparently by error, at the end of the second-to-last line, which is here omitted.
22 Lampman to Thomson, 17 February 1898, in L-TC, 199.
23 Adams, *Confederation Voices*.
24 Lampman associates "An Invitation to the Woods" with the Lake Achigan canoe trip in a letter to Thomson, 1 October 1897, in L-TC, 191–2; and Bourinot, in *Archibald Lampman's Letters to Edward William Thomson*, 40, links "The Lake in the Forest" to the same trip, as noted by Early, in *Archibald Lampman*, 138.
25 Lampman, "An Invitation to the Woods," in "Twenty-Five Fugitive Poems," 67. As Early explains, 70, this text is based on the version of the poem published in *Youth's Companion*, 23 June 1898, 304; no manuscript copy has come to light. Lampman's comment on the poem appears in Lampman to Thomson, 1 October 1897, in L-TC, 191–2. The term "hound" in the first line quoted may refer to the "hare and hound" races that avid canoeists and others engage in, where one group, the hares, starts first and the hounds race to catch up.
26 Connor, *Archibald Lampman*, 177–87.
27 Ibid., 191–2.
28 Lampman to Scott, 6 August 1898 and 21 August 1898, in *Some Letters*, by Scott, Lampman, and others, 3–5.
29 Lampman Papers, LAC, vol. 1, 515–27.

30 Voorhis, "Ancestry," 104.
31 Shakespeare, *As You Like It*, in *Norton Shakespeare*, 1637 (2.1.10–11).
32 Connor, *Archibald Lampman*, 178.
33 Early, in *Archibald Lampman*, 51–2, notes that "On Lake Temiscamingue," and in particular the single tree, anticipates the work of the Group of Seven painters as well as the landscape poems of F.R. Scott and A.J.M. Smith; and Toye, in his highly readable *On Canadian Literature*, 133, makes exactly the same point, which he may be repeating from Early, but, consistent with his method throughout this book, he provides no documentation.
34 Knister, "Poetry of Archibald Lampman," 104–5.
35 Mezei, "Lampman Among the Timothy," 61.
36 Lampman, "The Sunset" or "The Passing of the Sun," in *Lampman's Sonnets*, 172. This sonnet is not included in *Poems*. In Lampman Papers, LAC, vol. 5, 2403, Lampman gives the title as "Sunset."
37 Lampman, "Last Child," in *Lampman's Sonnets*, 174. This sonnet is not included in *Poems*.
38 Burpee, in "Archibald Lampman," 64, makes a similar observation: "It is not, perhaps, altogether without significance that while [the verses of "April"], some of his earliest, are devoted to Nature's spring-time, his last word was given to midwinter." In a manuscript notebook, Lampman Papers, LAC, vol. 5, 2415, "Winter Uplands" is dated 29 January 1899. On the previous page appears a sonnet addressing a woman who is clearly Katherine Waddell, beginning "You talk of age," also dated 29 January 1899. A more finished copy of "Winter Uplands" incorporating the changes Lampman made to the notebook version appears in a copy book, Lampman Papers, LAC, vol. 2, 1045, dated 30 January 1899. This is the latest composition date to appear in Lampman's manuscripts.
39 Roberts, "The Winter Fields," in *Collected Poems*, 128.
40 Arnold, "Dover Beach," in *Matthew Arnold*, 136.
41 Lampman Papers, LAC, vol. 5, 2415. Scott discusses Lampman's emendation of the closing line of "Winter Uplands" in his introduction to *LE:SB*, 39.

CHAPTER EIGHT

1 Scott, "Archibald Lampman," in *AER*, 2:475.
2 Scott, "Copy of Letter," 156. Scott's letter, as reproduced in *The Fiddlehead* in 1959 and in *Archibald Lampman*, ed. Gnarowski, in 1970, is dated 17 July 1945, but as Lynn points out in *L-TC*, xxvii, the correct date is 17 July 1947.
3 Gustafson, "Among the Millet," 148–50.

4 Darwin, *Origin of Species*, 123, 340, 456. Darwin does not use the word "evolution" in *Origin*, but in his closing sentence, with reference to the origins of life on earth, he declares that "from so simple a beginning endless forms most beautiful and most wonderful have been, and are being, evolved."
5 Alexander, *Short History*, 546–51; Walsh, *History of Philosophy*, 414–16.
6 Owen, quoted in Breach, *Documents*, 164–5.
7 Darwin, *Descent of Man*, 603.
8 Berger, *Science, God, and Nature*, 69.
9 McKillop, *Disciplined Intelligence*, 101. McKillop provides a detailed summation of the reviews of *On The Origin of Species* by Dawson and Wilson, both of whom objected to the "unwarranted speculation" they found in Darwin. See 99–110.
10 [Goldwin Smith], "Bystander," column in the *Week*, 2 October 1884, 692. As Regius Professor of Modern History at Oxford University in the 1850s, Smith propounded views that were, as Malcolm Ross, in "Goldwin Smith," 40–1, has argued, fundamentally Christian. A strong advocate of free inquiry, however, Smith gave close consideration to the claims of the evolutionists and, finding the evidence incontrovertible, was forced to abandon, one by one, the precepts of his faith. As Ross observes, "A study of his religious opinions from the Oxford lectures of the fifties to letters written just before his death would reveal a slow but sure drift away from orthodoxy" (36). Smith was deeply troubled by the idea that the foundations of Christian salvation had been undermined by science, but his firmest commitment was to reason rather than faith. "If there is anything which ... our nature tells us," he wrote in the preface to *Guesses at the Riddle of Existence* in 1897, vi–vii, "it is that our salvation must lie in our uncompromising allegiance to the truth" – by which he meant the truth derived from "free and hopeful inquiry." Both his anxiety and his belief in free inquiry are encapsulated in the title of a book he published eleven years later, near the end of his life: *No Refuge But in Truth*.
11 See Watson, *Christianity and Idealism* and *Philosophical Basis of Religion*; Bucke, *Man's Moral Nature* and *Cosmic Consciousness*; Goldwin Smith, *Guesses at the Riddle of Existence* and *No Refuge But in Truth*. While some of these books were published late in Lampman's life or after his death, they reflect the thoughts of their authors made known in various writings throughout the last three decades of the nineteenth century.
12 [Goldwin Smith], "Prospectus of the Week," *The Week*, 13 December 1883, 30.
13 Lampman, "Mermaid Inn," 19 March 1892, in *AMI*, 38.
14 As Connor, in *Archibald Lampman*, 74–5, points out, Lampman's "A

Monition" (later titled "The Coming of Winter"), "Three Flower Petals," and "A Fantasy" were published in the *Week* on 6 December 1883, 17 January 1884, and 7 February 1884, on pages 6, 102, and 155, respectively. "The Modern Politician" and "To a Millionaire," two of ten sonnets collectively titled "A Sheaf of Sonnets," appeared in the same publication on 30 November 1894, page 10, as did "Sebastian" on 17 May 1895, page 585.

15 Goldwin Smith to George W. Curtis, editor of *Harper's Weekly*, 24 October 1876, quoted by McKillop in his introduction to *Critical Spirit*, by LeSueur, xvii.
16 Collins, *Canada under the Administration of Lord Lorne*, 350.
17 McKillop, *Contours*, 59.
18 Philips, "August Comte," 388.
19 McKillop, *Contours*, 59.
20 See "Report of the Ottawa Literary and Scientific Society," PTRSC, 1st series, vol. 3 (1884), xxi–xxii, and similar reports in subsequent years.
21 Holland, *William Dawson LeSueur*, 28–9.
22 Hewett, *Unitarians in Canada*, 108–15.
23 See McKillop, introduction to pt. 3, "On Morality and Politics," in *Critical Spirit*, by LeSueur, 160. See also LeSueur, "Party Politics," in *Critical Spirit*, 170, where LeSueur advocates the replacement of the endless "see-saw" of government and opposition switching sides with a system "more in accordance with reason, and more favourable to true progress."
24 Holland, *William Dawson LeSueur*, 39.
25 Ibid., 242–62. See also McKillop, introduction to "The Critic as Historian," pt. 4 of *Critical Spirit*, by LeSueur, 247–86; McKillop, introduction to *William Lyon Mackenzie*, by LeSueur, viii–xi; and LeSueur's 1915 preface, in *William Lyon Mackenzie*, xliii–xliv.
26 "Report of the Ottawa Literary and Scientific Society," PTRSC, 1st series, vol. 3 (1884), xxii.
27 "Report of the Ottawa Literary and Scientific Society," PTRSC, 1st series, vol 11 (1893), xx, and vol. 12 (1894), xxxiii–xxxiv.
28 Connor, *Archibald Lampman*, 84. Lampman's review of Brown's *Poems Lyrical and Dramatic* appears in "Mermaid Inn," 17 December 1892, in AMI, 210–12. The information on Albert Walkley is from Holland, *William Dawson LeSueur*, 113.
29 Lampman to Maud Lampman, 10 April 1896, in "SFU Letters," 112; Scott to Lampman, 16 September 1898, in *Some Letters*, by Scott, Lampman, and others, 8.
30 Scott, "Archibald Lampman [1924]," in AER, 2:328.
31 The circular sent out in 1899 to solicit subscriptions for *Poems* (1900), signed by Dawson, LeSueur, and Scott, is quoted in full by Whitridge in her biographical note included in *Poems* (1974), xxx–xxxiv. See

also the note, signed by the same people, at the end of *Poems* (verso of 473).
32 Scott to Pelham Edgar, 16 February 1913, in *More Letters*, 44. Scott does not give the specific date of the evening.
33 Scott, "Extracts from Letter," [6].
34 Lampman, "Mermaid Inn," 27 February 1892, in AMI, 24, and 27 August 1892, in AMI, 140.
35 See Bentley, "Editorial Notes," in ER, 245–51, for a discussion of the writings of some of Lampman's apparent sources, including Matthew Arnold and John Campbell Shairp.
36 Scott, "Archibald Lampman [Memorial]," in AER, 2:386.
37 Lampman, "Modern School of Poetry," in ER, 58–9.
38 Ibid., 68–9.
39 Lampman, "Poetry of Byron," in ER, 115, 124; "Character and Poetry of Keats," in ER, 142, 143. Lampman delivered the Byron lecture to the Ottawa Literary and Scientific Society in 1884, as mentioned in the report of that society to the Royal Society of Canada, in PTRSC, 1st series, vol. 4 (1886), xxvii. He read the Keats lecture in January 1893 in Kingston – see "SFU Letters," 96n5 – and again on 23 February 1893 to the Ottawa Literary and Scientific Society, as noted in its report, in PTRSC, 1st series, vol. 11 (1893), xx.
40 Lampman, "Mermaid Inn," 9 April 1892, in AMI, 47.
41 Lampman, "Mermaid Inn," 27 August 1892, in AMI, 138.
42 Lampman, "Mermaid Inn," 25 March 1893, in AMI, 281.
43 Ibid., 281–2.
44 Lampman, "Mermaid Inn," 13 May 1893, in AMI, 313, and 3 June 1893, in AMI, 320.
45 Lampman, "Mermaid Inn," 8 April 1893, in AMI, 290–1. Scott's comment appears in his introduction to LE:SB, 15.
46 Ballstadt, introduction to *Search*, xliii–xliv. Although Lampman did not live to see the publication of *Cosmic Consciousness*, he may well have been familiar with Bucke's 1878 study, *Man's Moral Nature*, which sets out the ideology behind the later book. As Ballstadt states, "It is probable that the Confederation poets were familiar with some of Bucke's writing" (xliv). Bucke experienced at age 36 what he described as a mystical awakening, and in *Man's Moral Nature* he "sought to embody the teaching of the illumination" (*Cosmic Consciousness*, 8). The result was an elaborate theory of human evolutionary progress characterized by the gradual displacement of hate and fear, the "negative functions" of the moral faculty, by love and faith, the "positive functions" (*Man's Moral Nature*, 49). By this process, according to Bucke in *Cosmic Consciousness*, "the race of man" will ultimately achieve a "higher life than any heretofore experienced or even conceived," dwelling in a world "as far removed from the world of to-day

as this is from the world as it was before the advent of self consciousness" (19, 4).
47 Lampman, "Mermaid Inn," 18 June 1892, in AMI, 94.
48 LeSueur, "Intellectual Life" (1875), in *Critical Spirit*, 32.
49 Ibid., 33–4.
50 Lampman, "[Socialism]," in ER, 186–90. In his notes to "[Socialism]," 351–2, Bentley explains that the estimated date of composition is based on proximity to other writings in the manuscript notebook where the essay appears.
51 MacDonald, in *Canadian Portraits*, 224, writes that Lampman "developed into a mild socialist of the intellectual type." With this kind of reference in mind, Nesbitt, in "The New Lampman," 103, makes reference to "what has come to be called rather condescendingly [Lampman's] pale or Fabian socialism." Three years later, in his entry on Lampman in *Great Writers of the English Language: Poets*, 573, Nesbitt – now opting for condescension – notes that Lampman "associated with a minuscule group of pale socialists in Ottawa, and occasionally wrote poetry of social protest."
52 Lampman, "Mermaid Inn," 1 April 1893, in AMI, 285.
53 Morgan, *Canadian Men and Women*, 554.
54 Wayne, "Shouting Love," 17.
55 "Death of Mr. A. Lampman," 3.
56 Connor, *Archibald Lampman*, 84.
57 Scott, introduction to LE:SB, 41.
58 Scott, memoir, in *Poems*, xxii.
59 Scott, "Copy of Letter," in Gnarowski, 155. Brown, in a memoir included in *Selected Poems of Duncan Campbell Scott*, xxi, reports that Scott himself was active in "the Ottawa group of the Fabians" in the 1890s.
60 See Briggs's introduction to *Fabian Essays*, by Shaw, Webb, and others, 11–12, for an account of the publication history of the book.
61 Bentley, *Confederation Group*, 227.
62 See McBriar, *Fabian Socialism*, 9–19, for a discussion of the influence of both liberalism and Marxism on the early Fabians and of the society's initial openness – at least on the part of some members – to revolutionary social transformation.
63 Lampman, "[Socialism]," in ER, 186. Where Bentley, transcribing from Lampman's notebook, has written "inequallity [sic]," I have corrected the error and omitted the marker.
64 Ibid., 186–7.
65 Ibid., 187. Where Bentley, transcribing from Lampman's notebook, has again written "inequallity [sic]," I have corrected the error and omitted the marker. The excised "capitalism" is mentioned in the notes to "[Socialism]," in ER, 356.

66 Ibid., 186. Where Bentley, transcribing from Lampman's notebook, has written "dispair [sic]," I have corrected the error and omitted the marker.
67 Ibid., 187. Where Bentley, transcribing from Lampman's notebook, has for a third time written "inequallity [sic]," I have corrected the error and omitted the marker.
68 Ibid., 189–90.
69 Ibid., 187.

CHAPTER NINE

1 Early, *Archibald Lampman*, 33.
2 LeSueur, "Intellectual Life," 34.
3 Lampman, "Poetry of Byron," in *ER*, 124, 116.
4 Lampman, "Character and Poetry of Keats," in *ER*, 142.
5 Lampman, "The Better Day," *The Week*, 13 May 1892, 374; "The City," *The Week*, 1 July 1892, 486.
6 The pessimistic ending of "The Better Day" is echoed in Lampman's "War," a poem in which the history of military conflict in various locations throughout the world is catalogued in thirteen carefully wrought stanzas, with each of the first ten representing a particular conflict. The last three stanzas indicate that finally a more enlightened outlook is taking shape: humanity gazing "From behind the bolted visor" sees at last "the horror / And the guilt." The change is too slow, however, for the speaker perceives a new war – the second Boer War? – on the horizon and caustically predicts that only after "the strength of man is shattered" and "the powers of earth are scattered" will peace arise.
7 Arnold, "'The Clearer Self,'" 52.
8 Lampman, "The Clearer Self" and "Peccavi, Domine," in *Oxford Book of English Mystical Verse*, ed. Nicholson and Lee, 445–6, 446–8.
9 Scott, introduction, *LE:SB*, 42.
10 Lampman, "Modern School of Poetry in England," in *ER*, 58–9.
11 A similar dilemma, but stated with more philosophical reserve, may be found in "Personality," Lampman's highly successful experiment in free verse. The self-aware speaker notes his uneasiness in the presence of a stranger, though subject to an "ineradicable longing / For tender comradeship." In a closing extended simile, he ponders his fascination and his fear, comparing himself to "one that comes alone at night / To a strange stream" – darkly mysterious, yet superficially comforting and attractive, "silvered by the familiar moon."
12 Keble, poem for the Eighteenth Sunday after Trinity, in *Christian Year*, 162–5.
13 Lampman Papers, LAC, vol. 9, 69.
14 See Arnold, "Dover Beach," in *Matthew Arnold*, 135, lines 1–5.
15 Watson, *Christianity and Idealism*, 297.

16 Scott, "Extracts from Letter," [6].
17 Arnold, "Dover Beach," in *Matthew Arnold*, 136.
18 Lampman, "Non Nobis Futura," in SFU manuscript book, 15–16. This title may be adapted from Psalm 115, beginning "Non nobis Domine," translated in the King James Bible as "Not unto us, O Lord." The psalm has often been set to music and employed in devotional services. In 1934 the opening phrase was incorporated into a poem by Rudyard Kipling – "Non Nobis Domine!" – which in turn was set to music by Roger Quilter.
19 Lampman, fragment, Lampman Papers, LAC, vol. 3, 1550.
20 Herbert, in "There Was One Thing," 86, connects Lampman's two forecasts (the positive one represented by "A Vision of Twilight" rather than "The Land of Pallas") to similar projections in the writing of William Morris, but adds that Morris over time "relinquishes hope."
21 Lampman Papers, LAC, vol. 3, 1176, 1209.
22 Lampman to H.E. Scudder, in Greig, pt. 2, 13.
23 Early, "Archibald Lampman," 142; Beattie, "Archibald Lampman," 79.
24 Scott, introduction to *LE:SB*, 41.
25 Lampman to Thomson, 2 November 1897, in *L-TC*, 194.
26 Bentley, in "New Dimension," 13, observes that the lines in "The Land of Pallas" "are arranged in cross-rhymed quatrains whose rhymes are, perhaps – but only perhaps – fortuitously, both masculine and feminine."
27 The "pessimistic" ending of "The Land of Pallas" appears in U of T manuscript book, 111.
28 Early, in *Archibald Lampman*, 99, ranks "The City of the End of Things" as "one of Lampman's finest poems"; Gustafson, in "Life and Nature," 6, calls it "a pastiche, a grade B movie; unmoving and cliché."
29 Toye, *On Canadian Literature*, 132.
30 The five-part structure of "The City of the End of Things" appears in the *Atlantic Monthly* 73 (1894): 350–2, and in *Alcyone*, 5–8, but not in *Poems*. In *Selected Poetry*, 84–6, Gnarowski restores Lampman's divisions.
31 Brown, *On Canadian Poetry*, 94.
32 Bentley, *Gay/Grey Moose*, 197.
33 With respect to the literary influences on "The City of the End of Things," Whitridge, in her introduction to *Poems* (1974), xxiv, mentions James Thomson's "The City of Dreadful Night," Poe's "The City in the Sea," and as a "secondary influence" Coleridge's "The Ancient Mariner"; Collin, in "Archibald Lampman," 135–6, refers to Arnold as well as to Thomson; Brown, in *On Canadian Poetry*, 94, writes that

in this poem Lampman "projects a Butlerian nightmare of man as victim of mechanical civilization," referring to Samuel Butler, author of the satirical fiction *Erewhon*; Sutherland, in "Edgar Allan Poe in Canada," 169–78, traces numerous verbal echoes of Poe, especially from "The City in the Sea"; Herbert, in "There Was One Thing," 84, states that "Lampman's dystopian poem suggests and redesigns the psychological settings of several [of Morris's] *Earthly Paradise* tales and, in particular, of the 'Prologue,'" and notes parallels to Edward Bellamy's *Looking Backward*; and Bentley, in "Thread of Memory," 89–91, makes a convincing case for the influence of Wordsworth's *The Excursion*. In terms of the poem's inception, Bentley, in *Gay]Grey Moose*, 191–2, 199, contends that Lampman was inspired by the essay "Why Socialism Appeals to Artists," by British illustrator and William Morris associate Walter Crane, published in 1892 in the *Atlantic Monthly*, two years before Lampman's poem appeared in the same magazine. In following through with his self-assigned "Commission," Lampman employed the method of extracting from his various sources just those features that fitted his purposes, "part of a complex and purposeful process of importation and adaptation in which what Lampman chose to reject or ignore is as important as what he chose to appropriate and deploy."

34 Bentley, "Thread of Memory," 87–9.
35 Bentley, *Gay]Grey Moose*, 199–200.
36 Notwithstanding that Lampman's focus is on capitalism and exploitation, not environmental degradation caused by pollutants, it is hard not to detect in his prediction of what we might call "the end of nature" a vision of manmade ecological catastrophe of the sort anticipated by Bill McKibben and many other environmental scientists and activists in our own time. Lampman's "factory" emits poison, and no one can live within its precincts. The idea that human beings in the twenty-first century seem bent on disaster, or incapable of averting it, would not surprise him.
37 Lampman, "Reality," in "Mermaid Inn," 4 June 1892, in AMI, 88–9.
38 Bentley, *Confederation Group*, 125.
39 Watt, "Masks," 219; Lampman, "Reality," in U of T manuscript book, 16.
40 Scott, introduction to LE:SB, 30.
41 In his poem for the Sixth Sunday after the Epiphany, in *Christian Year*, 46, Keble begins, "There are, who darkling and alone, / Would wish the weary night were gone." Griffin, in *John Keble*, 69–70, suggests that "a careful reader might trace out the influence of this poem on two more celebrated poets, Matthew Arnold ('Dover Beach') and Emily Dickinson ('Success is Counted Sweetest')."

42 Bell, *Ottawa*, 57.
43 Lampman, "Mermaid Inn," 24 September 1892, in *AMI*, 157–8.
44 Lampman Papers, LAC, vol. 3, 1556.
45 Lampman, "Mermaid Inn," 24 September 1892, in *AMI*, 157.
46 Scott to Brown, 15 November 1942, in *Poet and Critic*, 1983.
47 Scott to Brown, 15 March 1943, in *Poet and Critic*, 58.
48 Lampman to Thomson, 15 December 1891 and 26 October 1894, in *L-TC*, 29, 127.
49 Lampman to Thomson, 10 February 1893, in *L-TC*, 58.
50 Parliament of Canada website, "Senators and Members," John Graham Haggard page.
51 MacKendrick, "Sweet Patience," 55–6.
52 Berger, *Sense of Power*, 69.
53 Lampman, "The Modern Politician," part of "A Sheaf of Sonnets," *The Week*, 30 November 1894, 10.
54 Fleming, *Appeal to the Canadian Institute*, 172–3.
55 McKillop, introduction to pt. 3, "On Morality and Politics," in *Critical Spirit*, 156.
56 Berger, *Sense of Power*, 200.
57 LeSueur, "Partizan Politics," in *Appeal*, by Fleming, 84–5.
58 LeSueur, "Old and New in Canada," in *Critical Spirit*, 187–8.
59 Lampman, "Mermaid Inn," 19 March 1892, in *AMI*, 40.
60 Adams, in "Roberts, Lampman, and Edmund Collins," 8, states, "it is quite possible that [Lampman] was referring to Collins," but Bentley, in *Confederation Group*, 33, points out that Lampman's recollection on 19 February 1891 that the event took place on a May evening "almost ten years ago" suggests May of 1881, whereas Collins did not arrive in Toronto, where Lampman was a student at Trinity College, until October of that year.
61 Adams, "Roberts, Lampman, and Edmund Collins," 8; Lampman, "Two Canadian Poets," in *ER*, 94.
62 In "Roberts, Lampman, and Edmund Collins," 11, Adams makes the point that Roberts "acknowledged Collins as his literary mentor," and in "Archibald Lampman," chap. 4 of *Confederation Voices*, he notes that Collins was also Lampman's mentor. In *Confederation Group*, 46–7, Bentley infers from Connor's references to various walks and visits shared by the two that in 1882–83 Collins was "Lampman's almost constant mentor."
63 Bentley, *Confederation Group*, 16–17, 24–36.
64 Collins, preface to *Canada under Lord Lorne*, ix–xi.
65 Lampman, "From the seer with his snow-white crown," in "Twenty-Five Fugitive Poems," 63. Brown, in *On Canadian Poetry*, 93, comments, "Nowhere in his published verse is his contempt for the politician so fierce as in this epigram."

66 Scott to Brown, 8 February 1943, in *Poet and Critic*, 54.
67 Lampman, "Life," in SFU manuscript book, 52; Scott to Brown, 15 November 1942, in *Poet and Critic*, 38.
68 For an insightful analysis of "The True Life" as a comment on Lampman's struggle for individual authenticity, see Watt, "Masks," 217–18.
69 Lampman, "Life," in SFU manuscript book, 52.
70 On a holograph, single-page copy of "Life," in Lampman Papers, SFU, item 7.1.5.11, someone has written "sent to Isabel Voorhis," that is, Isabelle Lampman Voorhis, Lampman's sister. Isabelle's comment about "your poem" – not named, but presumably the poem in question – appears in a letter to Lampman dated 7 July 1895, in "SFU Letters," 161. In this version of the poem, the original phrase "pious brethren" has been changed to "pious neighbours" (later changed again to "careful neighbours"), and the original phrase "church talk" has become "cant rules." The original phrases appear in a rough notebook copy of the poem, in Lampman Papers, LAC, vol. 2, 980.
71 "Life," in manuscript book "Alcyone," 84.
72 Lampman, "The Clearer Self" and "Life," in SFU manuscript book, 51–2.
73 The comma added at the end of line six in square brackets, missing in ALS, is consistent with Lampman's punctuation in manuscript versions of the poem.
74 Lampman to Thomson, 2 November 1897, in *L-TC*, 194–5. D.G. Jones, in his poetic suite entitled "Kate, these flowers ... (The Lampman Poems)," which presents Lampman in a series of monologues directed at Katherine Waddell, in *Under the Thunder*, 76, writes of kisses in a passage that alludes to this letter: "I who hate Sundays / dream how I will boldly / rush out and overnight paint / Ottawa crimson / I come / secretly to the fold, would find / election in your mouth." Jones's sensual treatment of the Lampman-Waddell relationship, used as a vehicle for a meditation on love and desire, is oddly convincing in its transmigration of the historically based subjects from their own world to his; or, perhaps more accurately, its transmission of a modern idiom back through time to 1890s Canada.
75 Watson, quoted in Irving, "Philosophical Literature," 457, and in Armour and Trott, *Faces of Reason*, 313.
76 See letters – Scott to Brown, 15 November 1942; Brown to Scott, 24 November 1942; Scott to Brown, 28 November 1942 – in *Poet and Critic*, 38, 40, 41.
77 Lampman, "[Socialism]," in ER, 189.
78 Lampman, "Mermaid Inn," 27 August 1892, in AMI, 138.
79 Layton, "Review of *At the Long Sault*," 14.

CHAPTER TEN

1 Lampman to Thomson, 25 April 1894, in *L-TC*, 120.
2 Lampman, *Story*, 10, 15. In his introduction to *Story*, xiii–xv, Bentley observes that the poem can be seen as "a vicarious autobiography," noting several parallels between Lampman and the protagonist Richard as well as differences that suggest a strategy of "wish-fulfillment" on Lampman's part, but apart from an oblique reference to "other parallels," he does not link Margaret with Katherine Waddell. In "Sizing up the Women," 55, having mentioned Margaret's grey eyes, Bentley observes that Lampman associates that image with wisdom, but does not mention that the sonnet in which the association is made, the first in the sequence "A Portrait in Six Sonnets," in *ALS*, 43, is about Waddell. These omissions perhaps indicate a deliberate resistance to gossipy speculation. Other commentators have noted the connection, including Djwa, in "Lampman's Fleeting Vision," 130; Nesbitt, in "Lampmania," 46; Early, in *Archibald Lampman*, 126–7; and Campbell, in "Educating Adam," 173. According to Djwa, 139, Lampman's sonnet sequence "implies that the higher vision is now [in the mid-to-late 1890s] to be associated with Katherine Waddell: 'Touched by her, / A World of finer vision I have found.'" The quotation is from sonnet IV of "A Portrait," in *ALS*, 45.
3 Lampman, "Sebastian," manuscript draft, Lampman Papers, LAC, vol. 3, 1395–9, dated July 1889; revised draft, vol. 4, 1999–2013, again dated July 1889 but proximate to poems with dates from the spring of 1892; published in *The Week*, 17 May 1895, 585.
4 Lampman, "Sebastian," in manuscript book "Alcyone," 114–19.
5 "Paolo" is from the 1892 draft and "Amico" from the "Alcyone" manuscript, where it is crossed out and replaced with "Sebastian." The name in the original 1889 version, as near as I can make out from Lampman's sketchy handwriting, is "Parnio." See notes 3 and 4 above.
6 O'Hagan, "Canadian Poets," 20; "Report of the Ottawa Literary and Scientific Society," *PTRSC*, 2nd series, vol. 4 (1898), liv.
7 Scott, introduction to *LE:SB*, 3.
8 Lampman, "Sebastian," in "Twenty-Five Fugitive Poems," 57–9. All quotations from the poem are from this edition.
9 O'Hagan, "Canadian Poets," 20–2.
10 Bond, *City on the Ottawa*, 97.
11 Lampman, untitled manuscript poem on mill work at the Chaudière Falls, on five loose leaves, Lampman Papers, SFU, item 7.1.5.16, lines 1–3.
12 In its natural state, the Chaudière impressed viewers with its power

and the beauty of its setting, later compromised by damming, bridging, and the construction and operation of the mills. See Eggleston, *Queen's Choice*, 98–9, and Ross, *Ottawa Past and Present*, 160–1.

13 *Early Days in the Ottawa Country*, 10. See also Davidson, "Bridges of the Chaudière Falls," featuring images of the various bridges across the Chaudière.

14 Tyrrell, in *History of Bridge Engineering*, 225, states, "The old Chaudiere highway suspension [bridge] over the Ottawa river at Ottawa, Canada, was removed in 1888." This sentence (somewhat garbled) is quoted in Bentley, "HypheNations," n16.

15 The Post Office stationery that the manuscript poem is written on has the printed dateline "Ottawa, ... 188 " (with a blank space for the last digit to be inserted) as well as a printer's note along the top margin that reads "33-5000-24-7-'85," which might be translated as "order number 33, 5000 copies, printed on 24 July 1885."

16 Ross, *Ottawa Past and Present*, 161–2.

17 In an apparent Freudian slip, Lampman first wrote "my brain" in his final version of the poem in the manuscript book "Alcyone," and then crossed out "my" and wrote "his." As the correlations between Lampman's values and those of his character attest, Lampman viewed Sebastian as a kind of alter ego – a more capable and robust version of himself in his role as prophetic visionary and social activist.

18 The emphasis on waiting and readiness has a parallel within the ideology of the Fabian socialists. The society named itself after the Roman general Fabius Maximus, whose military tactic of delay was reputed to have been highly successful. McBriar, in *Fabian Socialism*, 9, states that this choice of a model would appear to reflect the Fabians' "cardinal principle of gradualness." But standing as a corrective, McBriar goes on to say, is the explanatory note included in the group's first published pamphlet: "For the right moment you must wait, as Fabius did most patiently, when warring against Hannibal, though many censured his delays; but when the time comes you must strike hard, as Fabius did, or your waiting will be in vain, and fruitless." Lampman's Sebastian is ready for unspecified action, and by this association, the action could be of a militant nature.

19 Bentley, in his introduction to *Story*, xv, remarks that "if it were in fact a novel, [the] poem would indeed be classed as a *Bildungsroman*." Campbell, in "Educating Adam," 158–9, 166–8, explores this idea in relation to the influence of Goethe's *Elective Affinities* and Milton's *Paradise Lost* on Lampman's poem.

20 Mezei, "Lampman Among the Timothy," 58–9; Lampman to Ritchie, quoted in Connor, *Archibald Lampman*, 78. In his introduction to

Story, Bentley does not connect the poem with Lampman's letter from the summer of 1884, but in *Mimic Fires*, 308, and *Confederation Group*, 48, he does make the connection.
21 Lampman to Thomson, 12 October 1892, in L-TC, 50.
22 Lampman to Thomson, 9 November 1892, in L-TC, 55; Lampman to Wetherell, 14 November 1892, in Wetherell Papers.
23 Lampman to Thomson, 2 February 1894, in L-TC, 103; Lampman to Isabelle Voorhis, 3 March 1894, in "SFU Letters," 148. Lynn, in L-TC, 104n1, speculates mistakenly that Lampman's reference in his 2 February 1894 letter is to his verse drama "David and Abigail."
24 Lampman to Thomson, 25 April 1894, in L-TC, 120.
25 Bentley, *Gay/Grey Moose*, 136–7.
26 Florence Roy, in conversation with the author, 24 August 2009.
27 Campbell, in "Educating Adam," 159, notes that the story of "The Two Strange Children" in Goethe's *Elective Affinities* "parallels many of the basic plot elements" of Lampman's poem: "two children who grow up together and appear destined to marry are separated to undergo the process of education. Meanwhile, a new suitor arrives to whom the girl makes an unspoken commitment. After a series of complications, the old affinity reasserts itself and 'the two strange children' confirm their love." This is not quite accurate. The boy joins the army, the girl matures, the girl becomes openly engaged, and an early antipathy transforms into affinity. Nevertheless, the parallel is there, with emphasis on the power of affinity.
28 In an alternative opening, in Lampman Papers, LAC, vol. 5, 2228, and quoted by Bentley in his "Explanatory Notes" in *Story*, 75, Lampman conceived of a more localized setting than in the opening for which he eventually opted:
 Between the overlapping of two seas
 Ontario and Erie, lies a land
 Rich with wide fruits and sloped with berried vine
 The blossoming garden of this northern world.
All quotations from *Story* are from this Canadian Poetry Press edition. An online version of the same text appears on the press's website, where quotations can be easily traced.
29 Early, *Archibald Lampman*, 123. On the same page, Early suggests a parallel with Wordsworth's "Nutting," lines 43–5. Bentley, in a gloss on Part 1, lines 201–8, in *Story*, 77, notes a possible source in Milton's *Paradise Lost*, 2.542–6. James Reaney, in "Vision in Canada?" 945, simply reports, "All I could say when I first read this was 'Wow! – what next?'" adding, "a mural should be done of this for the provincial parliament building."
30 A fascinating re-spinning of this scene may be found in Jane Urquhart's novel *The Whirlpool*, in which a young poet named Patrick – based on

Lampman himself, but incorporating elements of Richard – is suddenly distracted from his bird-watching and transfixed by the sight of Fleda, the unconventional wife of a local military historian, sitting in the woods and reading Browning. Urquhart is highly selective in terms of the parallels she draws and does not hesitate to alter facts – as, for example, by making Fleda a married woman, unlike both the historical Katherine Waddell and the fictional Margaret – but the association is clear: Patrick is the son of a minister, his uncle has a farm in the Niagara region, he has been schooled in Latin (Lampman majored in classics), he loves nature, he is unhappily married and falls in love with another woman, and in 1889 he has recently published "a slim collection he had paid for himself" (69) – all suggestive of Lampman, although *Among the Millet* in reality was paid for with money from a bequest received by Maud, Lampman's wife. Intriguingly, Patrick has the desire "to capture [Fleda] somehow, to put her where she belonged in *his* story, back inside the fieldglasses where he could control the image" (126).

31 Campbell, in "Educating Adam," 163, similarly speculates that the text in Margaret's book is "possibly Greek."

32 Bentley, in his introduction to *Story*, xvii–xviii, notes that, as in Lampman's "lyrics of illumination, most notably 'Heat' and 'Among the Timothy,'" Richard's transformation takes place "when 'perfect noon with not a single cloud' suffuses 'the still meadows and ... fields' ... with heat and light."

33 In his 1884 letter to Ritchie, quoted in Connor, 78, Lampman contemplates a poem "maybe dated forty or fifty years back in rougher times." The descriptions of the city in *Story*, however, appear to represent the period of Lampman's own youth.

34 Boles, "Toronto's First Union Station."

35 Bentley, in *Mimic Fires*, 302, noting that Lampman's specific physical description of the unnamed poet "both encourages and frustrates identification," offers Keats, Lampman himself, Matthew Arnold, and Charles G.D. Roberts as candidates for the model. See also Bentley's introduction to *Story*, xiii–xiv, where Lampman's admiration for Roberts and "the probable influence of Roberts' 'The Pipes of Pan' on his own treatment of frogs in such poems as the 'Favorites of Pan'" are seen as lending support to the Roberts option.

36 Lampman, manuscript draft of "The City of the End of Things," LAC, vol. 4, 2030.

37 Early, in *Archibald Lampman*, 121, discusses Lampman's "fusion" of the Odysseus myth of journey and return and the story of Adam and Eve as recounted by Milton in *Paradise Lost*, the latter parallel being ironic in the sense that Lampman's ending suggests "homecoming rather than exile, a recovery rather than a loss of paradise." The point

about irony is well taken. It should be noted, however, that Richard and Margaret are not likely to remain on the farm. They will, like Adam and Eve, make a new beginning away from the "garden," but under the terms of a positive and voluntary exile, not banishment. Wanda Campbell, in "Educating Adam," 164–8, explores in detail Lampman's adaptation of the Adam and Eve story in *Paradise Lost*, noting parallels as well between Richard's education and that which Milton prescribes in his essay *Of Education*.

38 Early, in *Archibald Lampman*, 122, suggests that "[i]n 'The Story of an Affinity' Lampman affirms the potential glory of an essentially human dispensation, an ideal order largely unrealized in our familiar world of abused power and exploited ignorance, but achieved by Richard and Margaret on a personal level, through each other."

39 Vision Vancouver election brochure, 2008.

40 Scott, introduction, LE:SB, 22–3.

Bibliography

Listed here are all works cited in the text, including archives and both primary and secondary sources, together with a few additional sources consulted but not cited. See Appendix A for an index to *The Poems of Archibald Lampman (including At the Long Sault)*.

Acorn, Milton. *Dig Up My Heart: Selected Poems, 1952–83*. Toronto: McClelland and Stewart, 1983.
– *I Shout Love, and Other Poems*. Edited by James Deahl. Toronto: Aya, 1987.
– *I've Tasted My Blood: Poems, 1956–1968*. 1969. Reprint, Toronto: Steel Rail, 1978.
– *Jackpine Sonnets*. Toronto: Steel Rail, 1977.
Acorn, Milton, and James Deahl. *A Stand of Jackpine: Two Dozen Canadian Sonnets*. Toronto: Unfinished Monument, 1987.
Adams, John Coldwell. *Confederation Voices: Seven Canadian Poets*. London, ON: Canadian Poetry Press website. Notation in Preface: Toronto, 2007. Accessed 4 December 2012. http://www.uwo.ca/english/canadian-poetry/confederation/John%20Coldwell%20Adams/Confederation%20Voices/index.htm.
– "Roberts, Lampman, and Edmund Collins." In *The Sir Charles G.D. Roberts Symposium*, edited by Glenn Clever, 5–13. Ottawa: University of Ottawa Press, 1984.
Alexander, Archibald B.D. *A Short History of Philosophy*. Glasgow, UK: James MacLehose and Sons, 1908.
"Archibald Lampman." Obituary notice. *Toronto Globe*, 11 February 1899.

Armour, Leslie, and Elizabeth Trott. *The Faces of Reason: An Essay on Philosophy and Culture in English Canada, 1850–1950.* Waterloo, ON: Wilfrid Laurier University Press, 1981.
Arnold, Matthew. *Matthew Arnold.* Edited by Miriam Allott and Robert H. Super. Oxford, UK: Oxford University Press, 1986.
– *Poetry and Criticism of Matthew Arnold.* Edited by A. Dwight Culler. Boston: Houghton Mifflin, 1961.
Arnold, Richard. "'The Clearer Self': Lampman's Transcendental-Visionary Development." *Canadian Poetry: Studies, Documents, Reviews* 8 (1981): 33–55.
– "'Thoughts Grow Keen and Clear': A Look at Lampman's Revisions." *Studies in Canadian Literature* 10, no. 1 (1985): 170–8.
Bairstow, David, dir. *Morning on the Lièvre.* Montreal: National Film Board of Canada, 1961.
Ball, Eric. "Life 'Only Sweet': The Significance of the Sequence in *Lyrics of Earth.*" Pts. 1 and 2. *Canadian Poetry: Studies, Documents, Reviews* 25 (1989): 1–20; 26 (1990): 19–42.
Ballstadt, Carl, ed. *The Search for English-Canadian Literature.* Toronto: University of Toronto Press, 1975.
Barry, Lilly E.F. "Prominent Canadians – XXXV: Archibald Lampman" (1891). In Gnarowski, *Archibald Lampman*, 6–19.
Beattie, Munro. "Archibald Lampman." In Bissell, *Our Living Tradition,* 63–88.
Bell, John, ed. *Ottawa: A Literary Portrait.* Lawrencetown Beach, NS: Pottersfield Press, 1992.
Bentley, D.M.R. *The Confederation Group of Canadian Poets, 1880–1897.* Toronto: University of Toronto Press, 2004.
– *The Gay]Grey Moose: Essays on the Ecologies and Mythologies of Canadian Poetry, 1690–1990.* Ottawa: University of Ottawa Press, 1992.
– "HypheNations: Canadian and Canadian-American Bridges." In *Canadian Architexts: Essays on Literature and Architecture in Canada, 1759–2005.* London, ON: Canadian Poetry Press website. Accessed 18 August 2012. http://www.uwo.ca/english/canadianpoetry/architexts/index.htm.
– *Mimic Fires.* Kingston and Montreal: McGill-Queen's University Press, 1994.
– "A New Dimension: Notes on the Ecology of Canadian Poetry." *Canadian Poetry: Documents, Studies, Reviews* 7 (1980): 1–20.
– "On the Confederation Poets' Companionship with Nature: Lampman." Editorial preface. *Canadian Poetry: Studies, Documents, Reviews* 48 (2001): 5–12.
– Review of *The Lampman Symposium*, edited by McMullen. *Canadian Poetry: Studies, Documents, Reviews* 1 (1977): 89–91.

- "A Romantic Lampman." Review of *Archibald Lampman*, by Early. *Canadian Poetry: Studies, Documents, Reviews* 22 (1988): 89–94.
- "The Same Unnamed Delight: Lampman's Essay on Happiness and *Lyrics of Earth*." *Essays on Canadian Writing* 5 (1976): 25–35.
- "Sizing up the Women in *Malcolm's Katie* and *The Story of an Affinity*." *Studies in Canadian Literature* 14, no. 2 (1989): 48–62.
- "A Thread of Memory and the Fabric of Archibald Lampman's 'City of the End of Things.'" *World Literature in English* 21 (1982): 86–95.
- "Watchful Dreams and Sweet Unrest: An Essay on the Vision of Archibald Lampman." Pts. 1 and 2. *Studies in Canadian Literature* 6, no. 2 (1981): 188–210; 7, no. 1 (1982): 5–26.

Berger, Carl. *Science, God, and Nature in Victorian Canada*. Toronto: University of Toronto Press, 1983.
- *The Sense of Power: Studies in the Ideas of Canadian Imperialism, 1867–1914*. Toronto: University of Toronto Press, 1970.

Bissell, Claude T., ed. *Our Living Tradition: Seven Canadians*. Toronto: University of Toronto Press, 1957.

Blathwayt, Raymond. *Through Life and Round the World*. London, UK: George Allen and Unwin, 1917.

Blom, Brendan. "Archibald Lampman: Canada's Modest Master." Books section of *(Cult)ure Magazine*. 27 October 2010. Accessed 13 September 2012. http://culturemagazine.ca/books/archibald_lampman_canadas_modest_master_.html.

Boles, Derek. "Toronto's First Union Station." Heritage Toronto website. 16 June 2008. Re-posted at current address 6 January 2013. Accessed 16 January 2013. http://heritagetoronto.org/torontos-1st-union-station/.

Bond, Courtney C.J. *City on the Ottawa: A Detailed Historical Guide to Ottawa*. Ottawa: Minister of Public Works, 1961.

Breach, R.W., ed. *Documents and Descriptions in European History 1815–1939*. London, UK: Oxford University Press, 1964.

Brown, E.K. "Archibald Lampman, 1861–1899: What We Lost." *Saturday Night*, 8 February 1949.
- *On Canadian Poetry*. Rev. ed. 1944. Facsimile reprint, Ottawa: Tecumseh, 1977.
- "The Poetry of Our Golden Age." In Ware, *A Northern Romanticism*, 403–12. Originally published as "L'age d'or de notre poesie" in *Gants du Ciel* 11 (1946): 7–17.

Bucke, Richard Maurice. *Cosmic Consciousness: A Study in the Evolution of the Human Mind*. 1901. Reprint, Secaucus, NJ: Citadel, 1977.
- *Man's Moral Nature*. New York: G.P. Putnam's Sons, 1879.

Burpee, Lawrence J. "Archibald Lampman" (1909). In Gnarowski, *Archibald Lampman*, 62–7.

Butler, Joseph. *The Analogy of Religion [Natural and Revealed to the Constitution and Course of Nature]*. 1736. Reprint with an introduction by Ernest C. Mossner. New York: Frederick Ungar, 1961.

Campbell, Sandra. "Love in the Langevin Block." *Ottawa Citizen*, 3 October 1999.

Campbell, Wanda. "Educating Adam: Lampman's *The Story of an Affinity*." *Essays on Canadian Writing* 58 (1996): 158–75.

[Campbell, Wilfred]. "Poetry and Piracy" (16 June 1895). In Hurst, *War among the Poets*, 30–43.

Campbell, Wilfred, Archibald Lampman, and Duncan Campbell Scott. *At the Mermaid Inn: Wilfred Campbell, Archibald Lampman, Duncan Campbell Scott in* The Globe, *1892–93*. Edited by Barrie Davies. Toronto: University of Toronto Press, 1979.

– "Letters to Carman, 1890–92, from Campbell, Lampman, and Scott." Edited by Tracy Ware. *Canadian Poetry: Studies, Documents, Reviews* 27 (1990): 46–66.

"A Canadian Poet." Review of *Among the Millet, and Other Poems*, by Lampman. *Spectator* (London, UK), 12 January 1889, 52–3.

Carman, Bliss. *Sappho: One Hundred Lyrics*. 1903. Reprint, Toronto: Musson, n.d.

– "The War among the Poets" (13 July 1895). In Hurst, *War among the Poets*, 91–3.

Carman, Bliss, and Richard Hovey. *Songs from Vagabondia*. Boston: Copeland and Day, 1894.

Clough, Arthur Hugh. *The Poems of Arthur Hugh Clough*. Edited by F.L. Mulhauser. 2nd ed. Oxford, UK: Clarendon, 1974.

Coblentz, Stanton A. "Archibald Lampman: Canadian Poet of Nature." *Arizona Quarterly* 17 (1961): 344–51.

Collin, W.E. "Archibald Lampman" (1934). In Gnarowski, *Archibald Lampman*, 125–42.

Collins, J.E. *Canada under the Administration of Lord Lorne*. Toronto: Rose, 1884.

Compton, Anne. "The Poet-Impressionist: Some Landscapes by Archibald Lampman." *Canadian Poetry: Studies, Documents, Reviews* 34 (1994): 33–56.

Connor, Carl Y. *Archibald Lampman: Canadian Poet of Nature*. 1929. Facsimile reprint, Ottawa: Borealis, 1977.

Crawford, Isabella Valancy. *The Collected Poems of Isabella Valancy Crawford*. 1905. Toronto: University of Toronto Press, 1972.

Daniells, Roy. "Lampman and Roberts." In Klinck, *Literary History of Canada*, 1:405–21.

Darwin, Charles. *The Descent of Man, and Selection in Relation to Sex*. Rev. ed. 1874. Reprint, Detroit: Gale, 1974.

– *On the Origin of Species.* 1859. Facsimile edition with an introduction by Ernst Mayr. Cambridge, MA: Harvard University Press, 1966.
Davidson, Michael. "The Bridges of the Chaudière Falls." *Archaeological and Historical Landmarks of Ottawa.* 26 April 1998. Accessed 20 March 2012. http://aix1.uottawa.ca/~weinberg/ottawa.html.
Davies, Barrie. "The Forms of Nature: Some of the Philosophical and Aesthetic Bases of Lampman's Nature Poetry." In McMullen, *The Lampman Symposium,* 75–97.
– "Lampman and Religion." In Woodcock, *Colony and Confederation,* 103–23.
"Death of Mr. A. Lampman." Obituary notice. *Ottawa Evening Journal,* 10 February 1899.
Djwa, Sandra. "Lampman's Achievement." In McMullen, *The Lampman Symposium,* 111–14.
– "Lampman's Fleeting Vision." In Woodcock, *Colony and Confederation,* 124–41.
Donne, John. *John Donne's Poetry.* Edited by Donald R. Dickson. New York: Norton, 2007.
Doyle, James. "Archibald Lampman and Hamlin Garland." *Canadian Poetry: Studies, Documents, Reviews* 16 (1985): 38–46.
– "The Politics of Nature: Archibald Lampman's Socialism." *Canadian Poetry: Studies, Documents, Reviews* 45 (1999): 10–30.
– *Progressive Heritage: The Evolution of a Politically Radical Literary Tradition in Canada.* Waterloo, ON: Wilfrid Laurier University Press, 2002.
Dudek, Louis. "Significance of Lampman" (1957). In Gnarowski, *Archibald Lampman,* 185–201.
Early, L.R. *Archibald Lampman.* Boston: Twayne, 1986.
– "Archibald Lampman (1881–1899)." In *Canadian Writers and Their Works,* poetry series, vol. 2, edited by Robert Lecker, Jack David, and Ellen Quigley, 135–85. Downsview, ON: ECW Press, 1983.
– "A Chronology of Lampman's Poems." *Canadian Poetry: Studies, Documents, Reviews* 14 (1984): 75–87.
– "Lampman's Love Poetry." *Essays on Canadian Writing* 27 (1983–84): 116–49.
– "Poems of October: Lampman's Elegies." *Canadian Poetry: Studies, Documents, Reviews* 45 (1999): 31–65.
Early Days in the Ottawa Country: A Short History of Ottawa, Hull and the National Capital Region. Ottawa: Minister of Public Works, 1967.
Eggleston, Wilfrid. *The Queen's Choice.* Ottawa: Minister of Public Works, 1961.
Emerson, Ralph Waldo. *The Collected Works of Ralph Waldo Emerson,* vol. 1, edited by Robert E. Spiller and Alfred R. Ferguson. Cambridge, MA: Belknap Press, 1971.

Fairley, Margaret, ed. *The Stone, the Axe, the Sword, and Other Canadian Poems*. Toronto: New Frontiers, 1955.
Fleming, Sandford. *An Appeal to the Canadian Institute on the Rectification of Parliament*. Toronto: Copp, Clark, 1892.
Fry, Stephen. *The Ode Less Travelled: Unlocking the Poet Within*. London, UK: Hutchinson, 2005.
Frye, Northrop. *The Bush Garden: Essays on the Canadian Imagination*. Toronto: Anansi, 1971.
Fuller, Thomas, comp. *Gnomologia: Adagies and Proverbs, Wise Sentences and Witty Sayings, Ancient and Modern, Foreign and British*. London, UK: B. Barker, 1732.
Gambone, L[arry], ed. *The Impossibilists: Selections from the Press of the Socialist Party of Canada and the One Big Union, 1906–1938*. Montreal: Red Lion Press, 1995.
Garland, Hamlin. Papers. Department of Special Collections, University of Southern California.
Goethe, Johann Wolfgang von. *Elective Affinities*. Translated by David Constantine. Oxford, UK: Oxford University Press, 1994.
Gnarowski, Michael, ed. *Archibald Lampman*. With an introduction by Gnarowski. Toronto: Ryerson, 1970.
Grace, Sherrill. *Inventing Tom Thomson: From Biographical Fictions to Fictional Autobiographies and Reproductions*. Montreal and Kingston: McGill-Queen's University Press, 2004.
Grace, Sherrill, and Stefan Haag. "From Landscape to Soundscape: The Northern Arts of Canada." *Mosaic* 31, no. 2 (1998): 101–22.
Gray, Charlotte. *Flint and Feather: The Life and Times of E. Pauline Johnson, Tekahionwake*. Toronto: Harper Collins, 2002.
Greig, Peter E. "A Check List of Lampman Manuscript Material in the Douglas Library Archives." Pts. 1 and 2. *Douglas Library Notes* 15, no. 3 (1967): 8–16; 16, no. 1 (1968) 12–27.
Griffin, John R. *John Keble: Saint of Anglicanism*. Macon, GA: Mercer University Press, 1987.
Gudgeon, Chris. *Out of This World: The Natural History of Milton Acorn*. Vancouver: Arsenal Pulp, 1996.
Gustafson, Ralph. "Among the Millet" (1947). In Gnarowski, *Archibald Lampman*, 142–53.
– "Life and Nature: Some Re-Appraisals of Archibald Lampman." In McMullen, *The Lampman Symposium*, 1–8.
Guthrie, Norman Gregor [John Crichton]. *The Poetry of Archibald Lampman*. Toronto: Musson, 1927.
Gwyn, Sandra. *The Private Capital: Ambition and Love in the Age of Macdonald and Laurier*. Toronto: McClelland and Stewart, 1984.
Hartman, Geoffrey H. "Wordsworth, Inscriptions, and Romantic Nature Poetry." In *From Sensibility to Romanticism: Essays Presented to Freder-*

ick A. Pottle, edited by Frederick W. Hilles and Harold Bloom, 389–413. London, UK: Oxford University Press, 1965.

Headon, Christopher Fergus. "George Whitaker." *Dictionary of Canadian Biography*, 11: 916–18.

Henderson, Ruth Watson. *Voices of Earth*. Canadian Music Centre. Accessed 29 June 2012. http://www.musiccentre.ca/home.cfm.

Herbert, Karen. "'There Was One Thing He Could Not See': William Morris in the Writing of Archibald Lampman and Francis Sherman." *Canadian Poetry: Studies, Documents, Reviews* 37 (1995): 79–99.

Herbert, Ryan J. "A Conductor's Study of Ruth Watson Henderson's *Voices of Earth*." Ph.D. diss. Baton Rouge: Louisiana State University and Agricultural and Mechanical College, 2006.

Hewett, Phillip. *Unitarians in Canada*. Toronto: Fitzhenry and Whiteside, 1978.

Hill, Charles C. "Tom Thomson, Painter." In *Tom Thomson*, edited by Dennis Reid, 111–43. Exhibition catalogue. Toronto: Douglas and McIntyre, 2002.

Hogg, Robert, ed. *An English Canadian Poetics, vol. 1: The Confederation Poets*. With an introduction by D.M.R. Bentley. Vancouver: Talonbooks, 2009.

Holland, Clifford G. *William Dawson LeSueur (1840–1917): A Canadian Man of Letters*. San Francisco: Mellen, 1993.

Homer. *Chapman's Homeric Hymns, and Other Homerica*. Translated by George Chapman. Edited by Allardyce Nicoll. Princeton, NJ: Princeton University Press, 2008.

Howells, William Dean. "Editor's Study." *Harper's New Monthly Magazine* 78 (1889): 820–5.

Hurst, Alexandra J., ed. *The War among the Poets: Issues of Plagiarism and Patronage Among the Confederation Poets*. London, ON: Canadian Poetry Press, 1994.

Irving, John A. "Philosophical Literature to 1910." In Klinck, *Literary History of Canada*, 447–60.

Johnson, E. Pauline. *Collected Poems and Selected Prose*. Edited by Carole Gerson and Veronica Strong-Boag. Toronto: University of Toronto Press, 2002.

Jones, D.G. *Under the Thunder the Flowers Light Up the Earth*. Toronto: Coach House Press, 1977.

Joussaye, Marie. "Marie Joussaye's 'Labor's Greeting' (1901)." Edited by Carole Gerson. *Canadian Poetry: Studies, Documents, Reviews* 53 (2003): 87–95.

Keats, John. *The Poems of John Keats*. Edited by Miriam Allott. London, UK: Longman, 1970.

Keble. *The Christian Year: Thoughts in Verse for the Sundays and Holydays Throughout the Year*. 1827. London, UK: Longmans, Green, 1894.

Keble College. "About Keble." Accessed 7 October 2010. http://www.keble.ox.ac.uk/about.
Keith, W.J. "Archibald Lampman." In *Profiles in Canadian Literature*, edited by Jeffrey M. Heath, 1:17–24. Toronto: Dundurn Press, 1980.
King, Ross. *Defiant Spirits: The Modernist Revolution of the Group of Seven*. Vancouver: Douglas and McIntyre, 2010.
Klinck, Carl F. "'The Frogs': An Exercise in Reading Lampman." In McMullen, *The Lampman Symposium*, 29–37.
– ed. *Literary History of Canada: Canadian Literature in English*. 2nd ed. 3 vols. Toronto: University of Toronto Press, 1976.
Knister, Raymond. "The Poetry of Archibald Lampman" (1927). In Gnarowski, *Archibald Lampman*, 100–18.
Lampman, Archibald. "Alcyone." Manuscript book. Library of Parliament, Ottawa.
– *Alcyone*. Ottawa: James Ogilvy, 1899.
– *Among the Millet, and Other Poems*. Ottawa: J. Durie and Son, 1888.
– *Archibald Lampman: Selected Prose*. Edited by Barrie Davies. Ottawa: Tecumseh, 1975.
– *Archibald Lampman's Letters to Edward William Thomson (1890–1898)*. Edited by Arthur S. Bourinot. Ottawa: privately printed, 1956.
– *At the Long Sault, and Other New Poems*. Edited by Duncan Campbell Scott and E.K. Brown. Toronto: Ryerson, 1943.
– *Comfort of the Fields: The Best-Known Poems*. Edited by Raymond Souster. Sutton West, ON: Paget, 1979.
– *The Essays and Reviews of Archibald Lampman*. Edited by D.M.R. Bentley. London: Canadian Poetry Press, 1996.
– "The Hermit Thrush." With "The Cup," by Scott. Christmas greeting card, 1894. In *Canada, the Printed Record: A Bibliographic Register with Indexes to the Microfiche Series of the Canadian Institute for Historical Microreproductions*. Ottawa: Canadian Institute for Historical Microreproductions, 1985.
– Lampman Collection. Toronto: Thomas Fisher Rare Book Library, University of Toronto.
– *Lampman's Kate: Late Love Poems of Archibald Lampman, 1887–1897*. Edited by Margaret Coulby Whitridge. Ottawa: Borealis, 1975.
– *Lampman's Sonnets, 1884–1899*. Edited by Margaret Coulby Whitridge. Ottawa: Borealis, 1976.
– *Lyrics of Earth*. Boston: Copeland and Day, 1895.
– *Lyrics of Earth: Sonnets and Ballads*. Edited by Duncan Campbell Scott. Toronto: Musson, 1925.
– *Lyrics of Earth: A Working Text*. Edited by D.M.R. Bentley. Ottawa: Tecumseh, 1978.
– "Miscellaneous Poems." Manuscript book. Library of Parliament, Ottawa.

- Papers. Ottawa: Library and Archives Canada.
- Papers. Burnaby, BC: Simon Fraser University.
- *The Poems of Archibald Lampman*. Edited and including a memoir by Duncan Campbell Scott. Toronto: Morang, 1900.
- *The Poems of Archibald Lampman (including At the Long Sault)*. 1900 and 1943. Facsimile reprint with an introduction by Margaret Coulby Whitridge. Toronto: University of Toronto Press, 1974.
- *Selected Poetry of Archibald Lampman*. Edited by Michael Gnarowski. Ottawa: Tecumseh, 1990.
- *The Story of an Affinity*. Edited by D.M.R. Bentley. London, ON: Canadian Poetry Press, 1986.
- "Twenty-Five Fugitive Poems by Archibald Lampman." Edited by L.R. Early. *Canadian Poetry: Studies, Documents, Reviews* 12 (1983): 46–70.

Lampman, Archibald, and Edward William Thomson. *An Annotated Edition of the Correspondence between Archibald Lampman and Edward William Thomson (1890–1898)*. Edited by Helen Lynn. Ottawa: Tecumseh, 1980.

Layton, Irving. "Review of *At the Long Sault*" (1944). In *Engagements: The Prose of Irving Layton*, 14–15. Toronto: McClelland and Stewart, 1972.

LePan, Douglas. "Responsibility and Revolt." *Queen's Quarterly* 74 (1967): 201–21.

LeSueur, William Dawson. *A Critical Spirit: The Thought of William Dawson LeSueur*. Edited and with critical commentary by A.B. McKillop. Toronto: McClelland and Stewart, 1977.
- *William Lyon Mackenzie: A Reinterpretation*. Edited by A.B. McKillop and with a preface by the author. Toronto: Macmillan, 1979.

Logan, John. "The Literary Group of '61." *The Canadian Magazine* 37 (1911): 555–63.

Longfellow, Henry Wadsworth. *Poems and Other Writings*. Selection and notes by J.D. McClatchy. New York: Library of America, 2000.

MacDonald, Adrian. *Canadian Portraits*. Toronto: Ryerson, 1925.

[Machar, Agnes Maule]. "Some Recent Canadian Poems" (1889). In Gnarowski, *Archibald Lampman*, 1–5.

MacKendrick, Louis K. "Sweet Patience and Her Guest, Reality: The Sonnets of Archibald Lampman." In McMullen, *The Lampman Symposium*, 49–62.

Manguel, Alberto. *The City of Words*. CBC Massey Lecture. Toronto: Anansi, 2007.

Marshall, Tom. *Harsh and Lovely Land: The Major Canadian Poets and the Making of a Canadian Tradition*. Vancouver: University of British Columbia Press, 1979.

Martin, Brian W. *John Keble: Priest, Professor and Poet*. London, UK: Croom Helm, 1976.

Mathews, Robin. "Lampman's Achievement." In McMullen, *The Lampman Symposium*, 121–3.

Mathews, Robin, and James Steele, eds. *The Struggle for Canadian Universities: A Dossier*. Toronto: New Press, 1969.

McBriar, A.M. *Fabian Socialism and English Politics*. London, UK: Cambridge University Press, 1962.

McKennitt, Loreena. "Snow." On *To Drive the Cold Winter Away*, Quinlan Road Productions, 1987, CD 76310, track 5; *A Winter Garden: Five Songs for the Season*, Quinlan Road, 1995, CD 12290, track 4; *A Midwinter Night's Dream*, Quinlan Road, 2008, QRCD 112, track 8.

McKibben, Bill. *The End of Nature*. 2nd ed. New York: Anchor Books, 1999.

McKillip, A.B. *Contours of Canadian Thought*. Toronto: University of Toronto Press, 1987.

– *A Disciplined Intelligence: Critical Inquiry and Canadian Thought in the Victorian Era*. 1979. Reprint with a new introduction by the author. Montreal and Kingston: McGill-Queen's University Press, 2001.

McLeod, Les. "Canadian Post-Romanticism: The Context of Late Nineteenth-Century Canadian Poetry." *Canadian Poetry: Studies, Documents, Reviews* 14 (1984): 1–37.

McMullen, Lorraine, ed. *The Lampman Symposium*. Ottawa: University of Ottawa Press, 1976.

Mezei, Kathy. "Lampman Among the Timothy." *Canadian Poetry: Studies, Documents, Reviews* 5 (1979): 57–72.

Miller, Joseph Dana. "After the Bard[s'] Battle" (1 July 1895). In Hurst, *War among the Poets*, 83–6.

Milton, John. *The Complete Poetry and Essential Prose*. Edited by William Kerrigan, John Rumrich, and Stephen M. Fallon. New York: Modern Library, 2007.

Morgan, Henry James. *The Canadian Men and Women of the Time: A Handbook of Canadian Biography*. Toronto: William Briggs, 1898.

Morris, William. *News from Nowhere; or, an Epoch of Rest: Being Some Chapters from a Utopian Romance*. 1890. Edited by Krishan Kumar. New York: Cambridge University Press, 1995.

Muddiman, Bernard. "Archibald Lampman" (1915). In Gnarowski, *Archibald Lampman*, 68–80.

Murray, Joan. *Tom Thomson: Design for a Canadian Hero*. Toronto: Dundurn Press, 1998.

Nesbitt, Bruce. "Lampman." In *Great Writers of the English Language: Poets*, edited by James Vinson. London: Macmillan, 1979.

– "A Gift of Love: Lampman and Life." In Woodcock, *Colony and Confederation*, 142–7.

– "Lampmania: Alcyone and the Search for Merope." In *Editing Canadian Texts*, edited by Francess G. Halpenny, 33–48. Toronto: Hackert, 1975.

- "Matthew Arnold in Canada: A Dialogue Begun?" *Culture* 28 (1967), 53–4.
- "The New Lampman." In McMullen, *The Lampman Symposium*, 99–110.
Newman, John Henry. *Apologia Pro Vita Sua*. London, UK: Everyman, 1912.
Nicholson, D.H.S., and A.H.E. Lee, eds. *The Oxford Book of English Mystical Verse*. Oxford, UK: Clarendon, 1917.
O'Hagan, Howard. "Canadian Poets and Poetry." In *Canadian Essays Critical and Historical*, 11–53. Toronto: William Briggs, 1901.
Ower, John. "The Story of an Affinity: Lampman's 'The Frogs' and Tennyson's 'The Lotos-Eaters.'" *Canadian Literature* 115 (1987): 285–9.
Pacey, Desmond. "A Reading of Lampman's 'Heat'" (1953). In Gnarowski, *Archibald Lampman*, 178–84.
Parker, George L. "Literature, English Language." In *Encyclopedia Canadiana*, 152–73. Toronto: Grolier, 1975.
Parliament of Canada. "Senators and Members." Last updated 25 May 2011. Accessed 5 August 2011. http://www.parl.gc.ca/common/SenatorsMembers.asp.
Perkins, David, ed. *English Romantic Writers*. 2nd ed. New York: Harcourt, 1995.
Philips, R. Craig. "August Comte." In *World Philosophers and Their Works*, edited by John K. Roth, 1:386–9. 3 vols. Pasadena, CA: Salem Press, 2000.
Poe, Edgar Allan. *The Complete Poetry and Selected Criticism of Edgar Allan Poe*. Edited by Allen Tate. New York: New American Library, 1981.
Pollock, Zailig. "Lampman." *The Oxford Companion to Canadian Literature*, edited by Eugene Benson and William Toye. 2nd ed. Toronto: Oxford University Press, 1997.
Reaney, James. "Vision in Canada?" *University of Toronto Quarterly* 70 (2001): 937–46.
Reed, Thomas Arthur, ed. *A History of the University of Trinity College, Toronto, 1852–1952*. Toronto: University of Toronto Press, 1952.
Roberts, Charles G.D. *Collected Letters*. Edited by Laurel Boone. Fredericton, NB: Goose Lane, 1989.
- *The Collected Poems of Sir Charles G.D. Roberts*. Edited by Desmond Pacey. Wolfville, NS: Wombat, 1985.
Ross, A.H.D. *Ottawa Past and Present*. Toronto: Musson, 1927.
Ross, Malcolm. "Goldwin Smith." In Bissell, *Our Living Tradition*, 29–47.
Rossetti, Christina. *The Complete Poems of Christina Rossetti*, vol. 1, edited by R.W. Crump. Baton Rouge: Louisiana State University Press, 1979.
Royal Society of Canada. *Proceedings and Transactions of the Royal Society of Canada*. 1st series, vols. 1–12, 1883–94; 2nd series, vols. 1–12, 1895–1906; 3rd series, vols. 1–16, 1907–22. Montreal: Dawson Brothers,

1884–92; Ottawa: John Durie and Son, 1893–97; Ottawa: James Hope and Son, 1898–1913; Ottawa: Jas. Hope and Son, 1914–22.

Scott, Duncan Campbell. *Addresses, Essays, and Reviews*. Edited by Leslie Ritchie. 2 vols. London, ON: Canadian Poetry Press, 2000.

– "Copy of Letter by Duncan Campbell Scott to Ralph Gustafson" (1959). In Gnarowski, *Archibald Lampman*, 154–8.

– "Extracts from Letter from Mr. Duncan C. Scott to Mr. Lazenby." In *Extracts from Rev. Mr. Lazenby's Address at the Funeral of William Dawson Le Sueur*. Ottawa: n.p., 1917. Held by the Widener Library at the Harvard College Library.

– *More Letters of Duncan Campbell Scott*. Edited by Arthur S. Bourinot. Ottawa: privately printed, 1960.

Scott, Duncan Campbell, and E.K. Brown. *The Poet and the Critic: A Literary Correspondence between D.C. Scott and E.K. Brown*. Edited by Robert L. McDougall. Ottawa: Carleton University Press, 1983.

Scott, Duncan Campbell, Archibald Lampman, and others. *Some Letters of Duncan Campbell Scott, Archibald Lampman, and Others*. Edited by Arthur S. Bourinot. Ottawa: privately printed, 1959.

Scott, Duncan Campbell, Arthur Stringer, and others. *Addresses Delivered at the Dedication of the Archibald Lampman Memorial Cairn at Morpeth, Ontario*. London: Canadian Authors' Association, 1930.

Scruton, Roger. "Continental Philosophy from Fichte to Sartre." In *The Oxford Illustrated History of Western Philosophy*, edited by Anthony Kenny, 193–274. London, UK: Oxford University Press, 1994.

Shakespeare, William. *The Norton Shakespeare*. Edited by Stephen Greenblatt. 2nd ed. Based on the Oxford Edition. New York: Norton, 2008.

Shaw, George Bernard, Sidney Webb, and others. *Fabian Essays*. 1889. With an introduction by Asa Briggs. 6th ed. London, UK: George Allen and Unwin, 1962.

Shaw, Marion. "*In Memoriam* and *The Christian Year*." In *John Keble in Context*, edited by Kirstie Blair, 159–74. London, UK: Anthem Press, 2004.

Shelley, Percy Bysshe. *The Poems of Shelley*. Edited by Kelvin Everest and Geoffrey Matthews. 2 vols. Harlow, UK: Longman, 2000.

Sibley, Robert C. *Northern Spirits: John Watson, George Grant, and Charles Taylor – Appropriations of Hegelian Political Thought*. Montreal and Kingston: McGill-Queen's University Press, 2008.

Smith, A.J.M., ed. *The Book of Canadian Poetry*. 3rd ed. Toronto: Gage, 1957.

Smith, Goldwin. *Guesses at the Riddle of Existence, and Other Essays on Kindred Subjects*. New York: Macmillan, 1897.

– "The Immortality of the Soul." *Canadian Monthly and National Review* 9 (1876): 408–16.

– *Lectures on the Study of History*. Toronto: Adam, Stevenson, 1873.

– *No Refuge But in Truth*. 2nd ed. New York: G.P. Putnam's Sons, 1909.
Sommers, Carol Marie, ed. "The Letters of Archibald Lampman in the Simon Fraser University Library." M.A. thesis. Burnaby, BC: Simon Fraser University, 1979. Includes letters from Lampman to, and to Lampman from, various correspondents.
Spenser, Edmund. *The Faerie Qveene*. Edited by A.C. Hamilton. Harlow, UK: Longman, 2001.
Stedman, Edmund Clarence, ed. *A Victorian Anthology: 1837–1895*. Boston: Houghton Mifflin, 1895.
Steele, James. "Lampman's Achievement." In McMullen, *The Lampman Symposium*, 125–8.
Stevenson, Burton Egbert. *The Home Book of Quotations Classical and Modern*. 10th ed. New York: Dodd Mead, 1967.
Stringer, Arthur. "A Glance at Lampman" (1894). In Gnarowski, *Archibald Lampman*, 20–7.
Strong-Boag, Veronica, and Carole Gerson. *Paddling Her Own Canoe: The Times and Texts of E. Pauline Johnson (Tekahionwake)*. Toronto: University of Toronto Press, 2000.
Sutherland, John. "Edgar Allan Poe in Canada" (1951). In Gnarowski, *Archibald Lampman*, 159–78.
Swinburne, Algernon Charles. *Selected Poetry and Prose*. Edited by John D. Rosenberg. New York: Modern Library, 1968.
Tennyson, Alfred. *Demeter, and Other Poems*. London, UK: Macmillan, 1889.
– *The Poems of Tennyson*. Edited by Christopher Ricks. 2nd ed. 3 vols. Harlow, UK: Longman, 1987.
Thomson, Edward William. "Among the Millet" (10 August 1889). Review of *Among the Millet, and Other Poems*, by Lampman. With an introduction by Eric Ball. *Canadian Poetry: Studies, Documents, Reviews* 20 (1987): 90–9.
– *The Letters of Edward William Thomson to Archibald Lampman (1891–1897)*. Edited by Arthur S. Bourinot. Ottawa: privately printed, 1957.
Toye, William. *On Canadian Literature*. Toronto: Colombo, 2005.
Trehearne, Brian. "Style and Mind in Lampman's 'Among the Timothy.'" *Canadian Poetry: Studies, Documents, Reviews* 45 (1999): 66–98.
Tyrrell, Henry Grattan. *History of Bridge Engineering*. Chicago: privately printed, 1911.
Unwin, G.H. "The Poetry of Archibald Lampman" (1917). In Gnarowski, *Archibald Lampman*, 80–100.
Urquhart, Jane. *The Whirlpool*. Toronto: McClelland and Stewart, 1986.
Voorhis, Ernest. "The Ancestry of Archibald Lampman, Poet." *Proceedings and Transactions of the Royal Society of Canada*. Issued by the Royal Society of Canada. 3rd series, vol. 15. 103–21.
Walsh, Martin J. *A History of Philosophy*. London, UK: Geoffrey Chapman, 1985.

Ware, Tracy. "D.C. Scott's 'The Height of Land' and the Greater Romantic Lyric." *Canadian Literature* 111 (1986): 10–25.
– "A Generic Approach to Confederation Romanticism." Ph.D. diss. London, ON: University of Western Ontario, 1984.
– ed. *A Northern Romanticism: Poets of the Confederation*. Ottawa: Tecumseh, 2008.
Warnock, Mary. *Memory*. London, UK: Faber, 1987.
"Mary Warnock." Profile page. *Guardian* (London UK) online. Most recent essay 19 February 2012. Accessed 12 August 2012. http://www.guardian.co.uk/profile/marywarnock.
Watson, John. *Christianity and Idealism: The Christian Ideal of Life in Its Relations to the Greek and Jewish Ideals and to Modern Philosophy*. Rev. ed. New York: Macmillan, 1897.
– "Darwinism and Morality." *Canadian Monthly and National Review* 9 (1876): 319–26.
– "Science and Religion: A Reply to Prof Tyndall on 'Materialism and Its Opponents.'" *Canadian Monthly and National Review* 9 (1876): 384–97.
Watt, F.W. "Literature of Protest." In Klinck, *Literary History of Canada*, 1:473–89.
– "The Masks of Archibald Lampman" (1958). In Gnarowski, *Archibald Lampman*, 202–22.
Wayne, Joyce. "Shouting Love: Milton Acorn Remembered." *This Magazine*, December 1988, 12–18.
Wetherell, J.E. Wetherell Collection. Toronto: Thomas Fisher Rare Book Library, University of Toronto.
Whitman, Walt. *Leaves of Grass, and Other Writings*. Edited by Michael Moon. New York: Norton, 2002.
Whitridge, Margaret Coulby. "Annotated Checklist of Lampman Manuscripts and Materials in Known Repositories in Canada." PhD diss. Ottawa: University of Ottawa, 1970.
– "The Lampman Manuscripts: A Brief Guide." In McMullen, *The Lampman Symposium*, 131–6.
[Willison, John Stephen]. "The Attack on Bliss Carman" (19 June 1895). In Hurst, *War among the Poets*, 44–7.
Wittgenstein, Ludwig. *Tractatus Logico-Philosophicus*. Translated by D.F. Pears and B.F. McGuinness. London, UK: Routledge Classics, 2001.
Woodcock, George, ed. *Colony and Confederation: Early Canadian Poets and Their Background*. Vancouver: University of British Columbia Press, 1974.
Wordsworth, William. *William Wordsworth: The Poems*. Edited by John O. Hayden. 2 vols. Penguin, 1977. Reprint: New Haven, CT: Yale University Press, 1981.

Index

Works by Lampman are given in four separate listings headed by his name: poems, poetry collections, prose, and volumes planned but not published. "L" stands for Lampman throughout.

Acorn, Milton, 21–3, 212, 301n67
Adams, John Coldwell, 124, 180–1, 257, 303n17, 315n22, 332n60, 332n62
Aeschylus: *Prometheus Bound*, 115
Alcyone (L): changes to manuscript of, 130, 259; dedication of to L's father, 112; original compilation of, 126, 127; posthumous publication of, 47; as reflection of L's social-political views, 79, 212–13, 261
ambivalence to nature, L's supposed, 61, 90, 311–12n12
Among the Millet (L): contemporary reviews of, 3–4; perspective on nature in, 123; progressivism evident in, 79, 261

Anglicanism, 110–11, 231, 314–15n22. *See also* Keble, John
Arcadia, 147, 148, 218, 219
Arnold, Matthew: and "Among the Timothy," 71–2; and "Between the Rapids," 86–7, 310n7; influence on L, 6, 28; and "The Largest Life," 232, 235; and "A Night of Storm," 251; and "An Ode to the Hills," 172–3; and "Outlook," 37–8; and "Winter Uplands," 193–4; works by: "Dover Beach," 193–4, 232, 235, 251, 310n7, 331n41; "A Dream," 5, 86–7, 310n7, 310–11n8; "Resignation," 28, 37; "The Scholar-Gipsy," 71–2, 172–3; "Thyrsis," 172–3; "To a Republican Friend, 1848," 37; "To a Republican Friend, Continued," 37–8
Arnold, Richard, 12, 14, 305n8, 311n12; on "Vision," 46; on "The Better Day," 223
associationist psychology, 75
"At the Mermaid Inn" (*Globe*

column), 62, 207; L on beauty in nature, 62–3; L on Charles G.D. Roberts, 94, 312n23; L on dreamers and realists, 97–8; L on emancipation of women, work and leisure, slavery, servants, social disparity, shorter work day, 207–8; L on science and progress – "a new conception of the higher life," 208–11; L on socialist policies in New Zealand, 212; L on sonnet-writing "friend," 249–50; L on Tennyson, 142–3; L on wealth and social disparity, 251; L on Walt Whitman, 307n11
Atlantic Monthly, 232, 244, 331n33
Atwood, Margaret, 318n24

Bairstow, David, 90
Ball, Eric, 317n1
Ballstadt, Carl, 208–9, 327n46
Beattie, Munro, 90, 240, 302n6
beauty in nature, 16–17, 28, 190; effects of, 62–6; and "The Frogs," 81, 83; and "In October," 119; and "The Lesson of the Trees," 131, 133, 138; and *Lyrics of Earth*, 124, 131–2, 138–9, 143–4; and "The Old House," 131, 135–7, 138; and optimism, 62–3, 211, 214, 219; pervasiveness of, 60, 98, 103, 118, 318n24
Bell, John, 251
Bentley, D.M.R.: on mind-cure movement, 308n20; on "Among the Timothy," 74; on "Between the Rapids," 86, 310n7; on Canadian writing, 8–9, 14; on "The City of the End of Things," 246, 331n33; on "The Dog," 122, 316–17n51; on "Freedom," 307n17; on "Heat," 314n8, 315n30; on J.E. Collins as mentor of Confederation poets, 257, 332n60, 332n62; on John Campbell Shairp as influence on L, 64–5; on L on sonnet-writing "friend," 250; on "The Land of Pallas," 213, 330n26; on *Lyrics of Earth*, 124, 126–7, 130, 317n1; on *The Story of an Affinity*, 275, 334n2, 335n19, 336n29, 337n32, 337n35; on "The Sun Cup," 159, 306n12, 321n49
Berger, Carl, 199–200, 255, 256
Bergson, Henri, 33
biblical references: Exodus, 81, 247; Isaiah, 121; John, 322n14; Luke, 252; Mark, 252; Matthew, 252; Psalms, 141, 170, 330n18
Bildungsroman, 274, 283, 335n19
Black, William, 303n17
Blackwood's Magazine, 183
Blom, Brendan, 18
Boccaccio, 240
Boston Evening Transcript, 315n34
Bourassa, Henri, 256
Bourinot, Arthur S., 323n24
Brown, E.K.: on "The City of the End of Things," 246; on "From the seer with his snow-white crown," 332n65; on "In November" (sonnet), 120; on L's achievement, 4, 301n67; on "Liberty," 262; on "The Modern Politician," 258; on political poems in *At the Long Sault*, 20–1, 253; on "The True Life," 262; on "Winter Hues Recalled," 305n2; and "young communist," 21
Brown, J.H., 204, 326n28
Browning, Robert, 6, 337n30
Bucke, Richard Maurice, 200, 202, 209, 327n46

INDEX

Burpee, Lawrence J., 324n38
Burroughs, John, 6–7
Butler, Samuel, 330–1n33
Bystander. *See* Smith, Goldwin

Campbell, A.C., 204
Campbell, Alexander, 59
Campbell, Archibald, 59
Campbell, Sandra, 320n47
Campbell, Wanda, 276, 336n27, 337n31, 338n37
Campbell, Wilfred, 62, 114, 204, 312n12
Canada First movement, 255
Canadian Monthly and National Review, 201
Canadian Tribune (Toronto), 265
Canadianism, 3, 17–18, 60; and "Between the Rapids," 86, 310n4; and Charles G.D. Roberts, 94, 257; and "A Dawn on the Lièvre," 87, 93; E.K. Brown on L's, 4; and "Freedom," 69; John Logan on L's in "Sapphics," 164–5; and "Life and Nature," 158–9; and "Morning on the Lièvre," 87; and "On Lake Temiscamingue," 187; Robin Mathews on L's, 12–13; and "Sebastian," 266; and socialism, 22, 212–13; and "Solitude," 99; and *The Story of an Affinity*, 266, 275
capitalism, 16, 20, 21, 232, 238, 288; and "The City," 221; and "The City of the End of Things," 246, 247; and "The Clearer Self," 227; and "Freedom," 70; and "The Land of Pallas," 239; and "Liberty," 264, 265; and *The Story of an Affinity*, 281; and untitled essay on socialism, 214–17
Carman, Bliss: and "Comfort of the Fields," 319n39; and J.E.

Collins, 257; as literary adviser to Stone and Kimball, 129; and "Sapphics," 322n7; and "unconscious plagiarism" of L, 114–16, 315–16n34, 321n5; works by: "The Eavesdropper," 114, 115; Lyric 3 of *Sappho: One Hundred Lyrics*, 322n7
Catholicism, 109, 110–11, 315n22
Chamberlin, Joseph Edgar, 315n34
Chaplin, Charlie, 246–7
Chapman, George, 316n39
Christian Year, The. See Keble, John: works by
Christianity: and classicism, 62, 166; and "The Largest Life," 234; and nature philosophy, 113, 119; and "Sapphics," 166; and "To an Ultra Protestant," 110–11. *See also* Anglicanism; Catholicism; Protestantism
classicism, 6, 59, 62, 218–19; and "An Athenian Reverie," 31; and "Beauty," 61; and "The City of the End of Things," 245, 247; and "The Moon-Path," 160; and Pan poems, 146–7; and "Phokaia," 224–5; and "Sapphics," 163, 166; and *The Story of an Affinity*, 278
Clough, Arthur Hugh, 86
Collins, J.E., 201, 257–8, 332n60, 332n62
Committee of Progressive Electors (Vancouver), 288
Compton, Anne, 9–11
Comte, Auguste, 199, 201–2, 236
Confederation poets, 18, 250; the term, 8
Connell, J., 15
Connor, Carl Y.: on L's achievement, 4; on L's boyhood home, 111–12; on L's canoe trip to Temagami region, 181–2, 186; on

L's reading of Greek, 6; on L's socialism, 213; on social-political discussions in L's Ottawa, 204; on the unconventional in L's writing, 122
Copeland and Day, 48, 126
Cornell University, 59, 306n3
Coward, Noël, 108
Crane, Walter, 331n33
Crawford, Isabella Valancy: book by Milton Acorn dedicated to L and, 23; and "A Dawn on the Lièvre," 94–6; inclusion in *The Stone, the Axe, the Sword*, 21; and "The Lake in the Forest," 176; works by: "The Dark Stag," 94–6; *Malcolm's Katie*, 176
Crowell & Co., 127
(Cult)ure Magazine (Ottawa), 18

Daniells, Roy, 4–5, 10, 11; on "Between the Rapids," 310n7; on "Heat," 315n30; on "Sapphics," 321n1
Darke, Harold Edwin, 322n15
Darwin, Charles, 199, 238, 325n4
Davies, Barrie, 11; on "Among the Timothy," 74; on "Heat," 11, 116, 313n8, 314n10; on "Snow," 320n42; on "Winter-Store," 41
Dawson, S.E., 204
Dawson, William, 200, 325n9
Deahl, James, 23, 301n67
Denison, Colonel George Taylor, 256
Dickinson, Emily, 331n41
Djwa, Sandra, 334n2
Donne, John, 77, 106
Doyle, James, 14–15, 21, 78, 300n57
Drayton, Reginald, 315n22
Drummond, William Henry, 182
Dudek, Louis, 171

Early, L.R.: on "Between the Rapids," 310n7; on "The City of the End of Things," 330n28; on L's "fissured vision," 7, 14, 218; on "The Frogs," 83, 309n46; on "Heat," 313–14n8, 315n29, 315n32; on L and impressionism, 9; on "In October," 316n44–5; on "The Lake in the Forest," 178; on "On Lake Temiscamingue," 324n33; on "The Land of Pallas," 240; on L and mysticism, 301n59; on L and Romanticism, 7–8, 9, 12, 299n17; on "Sapphics," 321n1, 322n8; on *The Story of an Affinity*, 277, 336n29, 337n37, 338n38; on "The Sweetness of Life," 141; on "Winter-Store," 7–8, 48
Eliot, T.S., 5, 30, 302n6
Emerson, Ralph Waldo, 6–7, 46; *Nature*, 64, 307n9. *See also* transcendentalism
Euripides, 32, 311n8
Evans, Karen, 314–15n22

Fabian socialism, 213, 328n62; and L, 212, 213, 216, 262, 328n51; and "Sebastian," 335n18
Fabian Society of Ottawa, 212, 328n59
Fawkes, Guy, 254
Fleming, Sandford, 203, 255, 256
Francis of Assisi, St, 322n13
Fréchette, Louis, 111
French Revolution, 213; and "Liberty," 262–4
Fry, Stephen, 133
Frye, Northrop, 8, 312n12, 318n24
Fuller, Thomas, 32

INDEX

Garland, Hamlin, 10, 77–9
Gatineau Hills, 60, 85, 87
George, Henry, 204
Gerson, Carole, 301n63, 311n11
Globe (Toronto), 46, 62, 115, 204, 207; *Daily Globe*, 303n17
Gnarowski, Michael: on L's achievement, 4; and "Among the Timothy," 71, 308n21; and "The Frogs," 309n52; and "Heat," 313n8; and "Morning on the Lièvre," 311n9
Goethe, Johann Wolfgang von, 276, 277, 283, 336n27
Grace, Sherrill, 318n24
Greeks. *See* classicism
Griffin, John R., 111, 131, 331n41
Group of Seven, 11, 165, 312n12, 324n33
Group of the Sixties. *See* Confederation poets
Gudgeon, Chris, 21–2
Gustafson, Ralph: on "At the Ferry," 197; on "The City of the End of Things," 330n28; on L's social-political poems, 9, 197; on "Life and Nature," 158–9
Gwyn, Sandra, 304n24

Haag, Stefan, 318n24
Haggard, John Graham, 254
Handel, George Frederick, 112–13, 315n28
Harper's New Monthly Magazine, 39, 115
Heat: A Mode of Motion (Tyndall), 210
Heine, Heinrich, 209
Henderson, Ruth Watson, 322n13
Herbert, Karen, 330n20
Hewett, Phillip, 202–3
Hill, Charles C., 18–19
Holland, Clifford G., 203

Holst, Gustav, 322n15
Home Book of Quotations Classical and Modern (Stevenson), 32
Homer, 115, 224, 316n39
Houghton Mifflin, 126, 129
Hovey, Richard, 311n11
Howells, William Dean, 3, 77–8
Hurst, Alexandra J., 316n35

impressionism, 9–11, 20
inclusive irony, 17–18, 61, 65–6, 114, 122–3, 188, 318n24
influence, literary, 4–7, 310–11n8. *See also* individual critics and individual poets; Romanticism; Victorianism
Independent, The, 319n39
irony. *See* inclusive irony

Johnson, E. Pauline, 311n11
Jones, D.G., 333n74
Joussaye, Marie, 301n63

Keats, John: and "Among the Timothy," 72; and "April," 29–30; and "An Athenian Reverie," 34; benign expressions of beauty in, 206; and "A Dream" (Arnold), 5, 310–11n8; and "The Frogs," 79–80, 82–3; influence on L, 6, 29, 60; and "In October," 119; and "The Lake in the Forest," 175; L's lecture on, 275, 327n39; and "An Ode to the Hills," 172; and "Sapphics," 301n2; and "Winter Uplands," 194; works by: "Ode on a Grecian Urn," 34, 60, 79, 80, 83, 194; "Ode to a Nightingale," 72, 79, 82–3, 172–3, 175, 310–11n8; "To Autumn," 29–30; "To Sleep," 301n2
Keble, John, 109–12; association with Trinity College, 110,

314n18; and "Heat," 109, 112–14; influence on L, 6; and *Lyrics of Earth*, 130–1; and "Sapphics," 165–6; and "To the Prophetic Soul," 230–1; works by: *The Christian Year*, 6, 109, 110, 111–12, 130–1; Eighteenth Sunday after Trinity, 230–1; First Sunday after the Epiphany, 112; Sixth Sunday after the Epiphany, 331n41; Twentieth Sunday after Trinity, 113–14; Twenty-Third Sunday after Trinity, 112, 165–6
Keith, W.J., 148
King, Ross, 312n12
King, William Lyon Mackenzie, 203
Kipling, Rudyard, 330n18
Klinck, Carl F., 11–12
Knister, Raymond, 188, 321n1
Krieghoff, Cornelius, 103

Lampman, Archibald, poems: "Across the Pea-Fields," 103; "After Rain," 152–3, 154–6, 161; "After the Shower," 121; "Alcyone," 212; "Ambition," 30, 302n6; "Among the Orchards," 96; "Among the Timothy," 4, 66, 70–7, 78, 91, 106, 154, 164, 173, 221–2, 279–80; "Amor Vitae," 141; "April," 29–30, 118–19, 137, 190, 302n6; "April in the Hills," 144, 150–1, 161; "An Athenian Reverie," 31–2, 33–6, 38–40, 280, 302n8, 303n17, 304n24; "At the Ferry," 197, 269; "Avarice," 164; "Beauty," 61, 307n9; "The Better Day," 221, 222–3, 241; "Between the Rapids," 85, 86–7, 310n4, 310n7; "The Bird and the Hour," 146, 148–50; "By an Autumn Stream," 153–6, 164; "The Child's Music Lesson," 54–5; "Chione," 127; "The City," 221–2, 223–4, 227, 245; "The City of the End of Things," 239, 244–8, 281, 288; "The Clearer Self," 225–7, 228, 232, 259; "Cloud Break," 144–5, 146, 148; "Comfort of the Fields," 147, 148, 151, 319–20n39; "The Coming of Winter," 325–6n14; "A Dawn on the Lièvre," 85, 91, 92–6, 104; "The Dog," 120–2, 316–17n51; "Earth – the Stoic," 168–9, 170, 173; "Epitaph on a Rich Man," 20–1, 253, 265; "Falling Asleep," 249–50; "A Fantasy," 179; "Favorites of Pan," 146, 148, 218; "Forest Moods," 157–8; "Freedom," 66–70, 76, 212; "The Frogs," 79–83, 122, 140, 179, 309–10n52; "Godspeed to the Snow," 161; "The Harvest of Time," 32; "Heat," 40, 77–8, 104–9, 112–16, 122, 137, 279–80, 313n6; "The Hermit Thrush," *see* "The Bird and the Hour"; "Ingvi and Alf," 127, 323n16; "In May," 147; "In November," 147–8, 150, 151; "In November" (sonnet), 42, 116–18, 119–20, 148, 169, 192, 234; "In October," 118–20, 147; "Inter Vias," 135; "In the Wilds," 183, 185–6; "An Invitation to the Woods," 181, 323n24–5; "A January Morning," 98–9, 103–4, 109, 149, 179; "June," 143–4, 145–7, 160, 161; "The Lake in the Forest," 163, 170, 175–80, 181; "The Land of Pallas," 213, 225, 239–44, 245, 248, 288; "The Largest Life," 204, 212, 225, 231–5, 237–8, 240, 241, 247, 249, 253, 288; "Last Child,"

INDEX 359

189; "The Lesson of the Trees," 131–3, 138–9, 154; "Liberty," 20–1, 253, 262–5; "Life and Nature," 146, 157, 158–9; "Man's Future," 219–21, 226, 232, 240, 272; "May," 322n13; "The Meadow," 146; "The Modern Politician," 201, 254–7, 282, 326n14; "The Moon-Path," 147, 160, 322n13; "Morning on the Lièvre," 85, 87–91, 311n9; "Night in the Wilderness," 183, 185, 186–7; "A Night of Storm," 250–1; "Non Nobis Futura," 236–7, 330n18; "An October Sunset," 319n35; "An Ode to the Hills," 140, 170–5, 178; "The Old House," 48, 131–2, 134–9, 160, 161, 179; "An Old Lesson from the Fields," 61–2, 132, 261; "On Lake Temiscamingue," 183, 185, 187–8; "On the Companionship with Nature," 62; "Outlook," 29, 36–8; "Peace," 276; "Peccavi, Domine," 226; "Personality," 329n11; philosophical sonnets, 61–2, 66, 132, 261; "Phokaia," 224–5; "A Portrait in Six Sonnets," 334n2; "A Prayer," 62, 260; "The Railway Station," 249; "Reality," 249–50; "The Return of the Year," 146, 147; "Salvation," 276; "Sapphics," 109, 163–7, 168, 282, 301n2, 321n1, 322n8; "Sebastian," 201, 238, 266, 267–74, 281; "September," 144, 179; "A Sheaf of Sonnets," 326n14; "Sight," 62, 66, 132, 261; "Snow," 151, 320n42–3; "Solitude," 98–101, 103–4, 248; "Stoic and Hedonist," 167–8; *The Story of an Affinity*, 96, 266–7, 274–87; "The Sun Cup," 50, 144, 159–60, 321n49, 322n13; "Sunset," 189; "The Sweetness of Life," 128, 139–43, 160; "Temagami," 183–5; "Three Flower Petals," 31; "A Thunderstorm," 171; "To a Millionaire," 251–2; "To an Ultra Protestant," 110–11; "To Chaucer," 28, 225; "To the Ottawa," 96, 189; "To the Prophetic Soul," 109, 225, 227–31, 239, 276, 286, 288; "The True Life," 258–62, 276; "The Usurer," 20–1, 253; "Vision," 46, 47; "A Vision of April," 135; "Vivia Perpetua," 127; "Voices of Earth," 322n13; "War," 329n6; "Wayagamack," 182, 188; "Why Do Ye Call the Poet Lonely?" 122; wilderness sonnets, 48, 180–8; "The Wind's Word," 322n13; "Winter Hues Recalled," 43–5, 192–3; "The Winter Stars," 189–90; "Winter-Store," 41, 45–54, 144, 146, 179, 192, 322n13; "Winter-Thought," 42–3; "Winter Uplands," 41, 51, 137, 190–4; "With the Night," 319n35

Lampman, Archibald, poetry collections: *Alcyone*, see separate listing; *Among the Millet*, see separate listing; *At the Long Sault*, 20–1, 253, 265; *Lampman's Kate: Late Love Poems of Archibald Lampman, 1887–1897*, 303n17, 320n47; *Lampman's Sonnets, 1884–1899*, 312n19; *Lyrics of Earth*, see separate listing; *Lyrics of Earth: Sonnets and Ballads*, 85, 240, 288; *Lyrics of Earth: A Working Text*, 124, 321n49; "Miscellaneous Poems" (manuscript book), 127, 130, 294; U of T manuscript book, 305n7

Lampman, Archibald, prose: from "At the Mermaid Inn," *see* separate listing; "The Character and Poetry of Keats," 275, 327n39; "Happiness," 39–40, 91, 304–5n25; "The Modern School of Poetry in England," 7, 203, 205–6, 228; "Poetic Interpretation," 63, 155–7; "Poetry of Byron," 327n39; "Two Canadian Poets," 94; untitled essay on socialism, 212, 213, 214–16, 221, 247, 252, 262

Lampman, Archibald, volumes planned but not published: "Afoot with the Year," 127, 128–9, 294–5, 306n13, 323n16; "A Century of Sonnets," 127, 130; "A Gift of the Sun," 125; "The Land of Pallas, and Other Poems," 127, 129, 235–6, 239; "Pictures and Meditations," 125

Lampman, Archibald (father), 111–12, 114, 231, 315n22

Lampman, Archibald Otto (son), 181

Lampman, Arnold (son), 162

Lampman, Maud Emma Playter (wife), 3, 181, 276, 306n3, 337n30; and "An Athenian Reverie," 34–5, 302n8, 303–4n17

Lampman Symposium, 12–13

Lang, Fritz: *Metropolis*, 246–7

law of supply and demand, 215, 247

Layton, Irving, 265

Lazenby, Albert, 204

Leacock, Stephen, 256

LeSueur, William Dawson, 201–5, 211–12, 218, 326n23; and "The Largest Life," 204–5, 234; and "The Modern Politician," 256–7

"Listener, The." *See* Chamberlin, Joseph Edgar

Livesay, Dorothy, 22

Logan, John, 164–5, 321n1

Longfellow, Henry Wadsworth, 176

Lyrics of Earth (L): and "Afoot with the Year," 294–5, 306n13; and *The Christian Year* (Keble), 130–1; design of, 130–9; genesis of, 46, 123–30; and "The Lesson of the Trees," 131–2, 138–9; and "The Old House," 131–2, 135–6, 138–9; overriding theme of, 18, 60–1, 122, 140, 156–7, 160–1, 162; recurring images and motifs in, 143–51; and Tom Thomson, 19; and "Winter-Store," 50, 52, 53

MacDonald, Adrian, 328n51
Macdonald, John A., 284
Machar, Agnes Maule, 86, 122
MacKendrick, Louis K., 255
Mackenzie, Alexander, 284
Mackenzie, William Lyon, 203
Maclaren, David, 181, 186
MacMechan, Archibald, 8
Macoun, James, 204
Manguel, Alberto, 5
Manitou, 175–6
Marshall, Tom, 60
Marxism, 21, 265, 300n57, 328n62
Mathews, Robin, 12–13, 65
McArthur, Peter, 21
McBriar, A.M., 328n62, 335n18
McKennitt, Loreena, 151
McKibben, Bill, 331n36
McKillop, A.B., 200, 201, 202, 255–6, 325n9
McLachlan, Alexander, 21
McLeod, Les: on "Heat," 313n8;

on L and contemporaries as Post-Romantics, 14, 17, 312n12; and term Post-Romanticism, 8–9
McMullen, Lorraine, 12
memorial cairn in Morpeth, Ontario, 304n20
memorial plaque in St Margaret's Church, Ottawa, 159, 320n47
Messiah (Handel), 112–13, 315n28
Metropolis (Lang), 246–7
Mezei, Kathy: on "Between the Rapids," 310n4; on *The Story of an Affinity*, 274; on "Wayagamack," 188
Miller, Joseph Dana, 114, 115, 316n39
Milton, John: and "A Dream" (Arnold), 5, 87, 311n8; and "Heat," 115–16; influence on L, 6; and *Memory* (Warnock), 33, 54; and "An Ode to the Hills," 170, 171; and "Outlook," 37–8; and *The Story of an Affinity*, 336n29, 337–8n37; and "A Vision vpon this conceipt of the Faery Queene" (Raleigh), 5, 311n8; works by: *Paradise Lost*, 115–16, 170, 219, 336n29, 337n37; Sonnet 19 ("When I consider"), 37–8; Sonnet 23 ("Methought I saw"), 5, 311n8
mind-cure movement, 308n20
Modern Times (Chaplin), 246–7
Moore, Thomas, 86
Morning on the Lièvre (Bairstow), 90
Morpeth, Ontario, 3, 304n20
Morris, William: and "The City of the End of Things," 330n20; and "The Land of Pallas," 240, 242; and *Lyrics of Earth*, 130; works by: *The Earthly Paradise*, 130; *News from Nowhere*, 240, 242

Muddiman, Bernard, 91

Nesbitt, Bruce, 298n7, 299n17, 328n51
New Frontiers, 21, 300n57
New Masses, 265
Newman, John Henry, 109, 110, 111

O'Hagan, Howard, 267
Olmsted, Frederick Law, 308n20
originality and literary influence. *See* influence, literary
Ottawa Evening Journal, 22
Ottawa Field Naturalists' Club, 202
Ottawa Literary and Scientific Society, 202, 203, 213, 219–20
Ottawa (city), 3, 59–60, 204, 205
Ottawa Valley, 60, 96, 147
Owen, Robert, 199
Ower, John, 80, 309n46
Oxford Book of English Mystical Verse, The, 225–6
Oxford Movement, 109–10. *See also* Keble, John

Pacey, Desmond, 313n8, 315n30
Parker, George L., 311–12n12
Parsons, David, 318n24
Perkins, David, 79–80, 83
Petrarchan sonnet. *See* sonnet form
Pierce, Lorne, 253
Playter, Maud Emma. *See* Lampman, Maud Emma Playter
Poe, Edgar Allan: influence on L, 6–7; and "The City of the End of Things," 246; and "In October," 119
Pollock, Zailig, 312n12
Post-Romanticism. *See under* McLeod, Les
Pre-Raphaelites, 205, 206

Progressive Society of Ottawa, 202, 203, 288
progressivism, 15, 199–217, 265, 288; and "The Better Day," 222; and "The City," 223; and "The City of the End of Things," 238, 247, 248; and "The Clearer Self," 225–7; and "Epitaph on a Rich Man," 253; and "The Land of Pallas," 238, 239–40, 248; and "The Largest Life," 232–5; and "Liberty," 264; and "Man's Future," 219–20; and "The Modern Politician," 254; and "Non Nobis Futura," 236–7; and nostalgia, 218–19, 300n57; and primitivism, 224; Richard Maurice Bucke on, 327n46; Sandford Fleming on, 255; and "Sebastian," 266, 267, 270, 272, 274; and *The Story of an Affinity*, 266, 277, 283, 287; and "The True Life," 258–9
Prometheus Bound (Aeschylus), 115
Protestantism, 110–11, 314–15n22
Pusey, Edward Bouverie, 110, 314n18

Quilter, Roger, 330n18
Quinet, Edgar, 211

Raleigh, Walter, 5, 311n8
Reaney, James, 336n29
Red Tory, 20
Religion. *See* Anglicanism; Catholicism; Protestantism
Ritchie, John A., 6, 274–5, 298n9
Roberts Brothers, 126, 129
Roberts, Charles G.D.: and "Between the Rapids," 86; and "A Dawn on the Lièvre," 93; as editor of the *Week*, 29, 201; influence on L, 6, 93–4; as inspiration to L, 257; and J.E. Collins, 257, 332n60, 332n62; L on writings of, 94; and "Winter Uplands," 193; works by: "An Ode for the Canadian Confederacy," 307n6; *Orion, and Other Poems*, 257; "The Potato Harvest," 93–4, 312n21; *Songs of the Common Day*, 9, 193; "The Sower," 93–4; 312n21; "Tantramar Revisited," 28, 86; "The Winter Fields," 193
Roman Catholic Church. *See* Catholicism
Romanticism: influence on L, 4, 6, 7, 9, 11–12, 20; influence on L waning, 83–4, 93; and progressivism, 198. *See also* Daniells, Roy; Nesbitt, Bruce; Early, L.R
Rose Belford's Canadian Monthly, 201
Ross, A.H.D., 271
Ross, Malcolm, 325n10
Rossetti, Christina, 322n15
Rossetti, Dante Gabriel, 205
Royal Society of Canada, 175, 202, 203, 267
Ryerson Press, 253

St Margaret's Church (Ottawa), 159, 320n47
St Maurice Club, Lake Wayagamack, 182, 188
Scott, Duncan Campbell: and "Among the Timothy," 71, 308n21; and "At the Mermaid Inn" (*Globe* column), 62; on "Between the Rapids," 85, 86; and Christmas cards produced with L, 149; on "A Dawn on the Lièvre," 85; on didacticism in L, 321n5; as Fabian socialist, 328n59; on L and Ottawa, 60; on L and William Dawson LeSueur, 204–5, 234; on L's be-

INDEX

liefs and values, 6, 60, 118, 197, 205, 208, 213; on L's compositional practices, 59; as L's literary executor, 47, 267, 304n24; on L's portrait in *Lyrics of Earth: Sonnets and Ballads*, 288; on "The Land of Pallas," 240; on memorial plaque to L, 320n47; as model for Euktemon in "An Athenian Reverie," 38, 304n24; as model for poet in *The Story of an Affinity*, 280–1; on "The Modern Politician," 258; on "Morning on the Lièvre," 85, 311n9; on Ottawa discussion group, 204; on political poems in *At the Long Sault*, 253; on "Reality," 250; and *The Story of an Affinity*, 276; on "To the Prophetic Soul," 228; on "The True Life," 258, 262; on "Winter Uplands," 194

Scribner's Magazine, 194, 319n39

Scruton, Roger, 33

Scudder, H.E., 126, 127

Seneca: *Hercules Furens*, 32

Shairp, John Campbell, 64–5, 110, 308n20

Shakespeare, William, works by: *As You Like It*, 177, 186; Sonnet 29, 72; Sonnet 65, 108; Sonnet 116, 103

Shakespearian sonnet. *See* sonnet form

Shelley, Percy Bysshe, 6; "Ozymandius," 171

Smith, Goldwin, 200–1, 256, 325n10–11

Smith, A.J.M., 9, 10–11, 298n7

socialism: and "The City," 221–2; and "Epitaph on a Rich Man," 252–3; and L, 14–15, 20, 207–8, 212–13, 262, 300n57; and "The Land of Pallas," 241–2; and "Liberty," 262–5; as link between L and Milton Acorn, 21–2; and "To a Millionaire," 251–2. *See also* Brown, J.H.; Fabian socialism; Lampman, Archibald, prose: untitled essay on socialism; Owen, Robert

Socialist Party of Canada, 15

Somers, Harry: *North Country: Four Movements for String Orchestra*, 318n24

sonnet form: L's approach to, 91–2, 183; L's skill in using, 99, 100; as vehicle for unconventional themes, 22, 122, 249–50; as vehicle for wilderness theme, 183. *See also* philosophical sonnets, L's; wilderness sonnets, L's

Spectator (London), 86, 120

spelling: *Lievre* vs. *Lièvre* vs. *Lièvres*, 311n9; *rapt* vs. *wrapped* vs. *wrapt*, 309–10n52

Spenser, Edmund, 115, 130, 311n8

Stedman, Clarence Edmund, 86, 244

Steele, James, 13, 17

Stevenson, Burton Egbert, 32

Stone and Kimball, 126, 129

Stone, the Axe, the Sword and Other Canadian Poems, The, 21, 300n57

Strong-Boag, Veronica, 311n11

Sutherland, John, 246

Swinburne, Algernon Charles: amorality of, 205; and "Freedom," 68–9; influence on L, 6; and "Sapphics," 163; works by: "The Triumph of Time," 68–9

Tennyson, Alfred: and "The Frogs," 11–12, 79, 80; and "Heat," 115; influence on L, 6; L on Arthur Waugh on, 142–3; and "The Lesson of the Trees," 133;

and progressivism, 224; and "Sapphics," 165; and "The Sweetness of Life," 140, 142–3; works of: *Maud*, 142; *In Memoriam*, 110; "The Lotos-Eaters," 79, 80; "The Oak," 133; *The Princess*, 115; "The Voice and the Peak," 142
Thomson, E.W.: on *Among the Millet*, 3; in correspondence with L on *Lyrics of Earth*, 125–7, 294; as editor of *The Youth's Companion*, 149; as recipient of L's epistolary rants, 253–4; role of in determining design of *Lyrics of Earth*, 124, 127–8, 129–30, 317n1; and non-publication of *The Story of an Affinity*, 275–6
Thomson, James, 130, 246
Thomson, Tom, 18–20, 96, 103, 318n24; *The Jack Pine*, 187
Toronto Evening Telegram, 95
Torrey, Bradford, 6–7
Toye, William, 244
Tractarianism. See Oxford Movement
transcendentalism, 11–12, 14. See also Emerson
Trehearne, Brian, 74–6
Trinity College (Toronto), 59, 110, 280, 314n18, 315n22
Tyler, Moses Coit, 306n3
Tyndall, John, 210
Tyrrell, Henry Grattan, 335n14

Union Station (Toronto), 280
Unitarians, 202–3
United Empire Loyalists, 6, 22, 277
Unwin, G.H., 164
Urquhart, Jane, 336–7n30

Victorian Anthology, A (Stedman), 86, 244
Victorianism: influence on L, 6, 7,
20; influence on L waning, 83–4, 93. See also Daniells, Roy; Early, L.R.: on L's "fissured vision"
Villon, François, 86
Vision Vancouver, 288
Voorhis, Ernest (brother-in-law), 185–6
Voorhis, Isabelle Lampman (sister), 175, 259, 275

Waddell, Katherine: as described in "A Portrait in Six Sonnets," 322n8, 324n38, 334n2; and memorial plaque, 159, 320n47; as recipient of U of T manuscript book, 305n7; as represented in "Kate, these flowers ... (The Lampman Poems)" (Jones), 333n74; and *The Story of an Affinity*, 266, 275–6, 334n2
Walkley, Reverend Albert, 204
War among the Poets, 114–15, 316n35
Ware, Tracy: on L's achievement, 4; on L and fellow Confederation poets as Romantics, 8, 9
Warnock, Mary, 32–3, 36, 54
Watson, John, 14, 15, 200, 202; and "The Largest Life," 234; and "The True Life," 261
Watt, F.W., 15, 250
Waugh, Arthur, 142
Wayne, Joyce, 22
Week (Toronto), 28–9, 201, 221, 255, 267
Western Clarion (Vancouver), 15, 300n58
Wetherell, J.E., 275
Whitaker, George, 110
Whitman, Walt, 63, 307n11
Whitridge, Margaret Coulby, 303n17, 320n47
wilderness sonnets, L's, 48, 163, 180–8

Wilson, Daniel, 200
Wittgenstein, Ludwig, 81
Wordsworth, William: and mind-cure movement, 308n20; and "An Athenian Reverie," 34; and "Between the Rapids," 86; and "The City of the End of Things," 246; and "The Frogs," 80; influence on L, 6; influence on L's memory poems, 28, 34; and "Morning on the Lièvre," 89–90; and progressivism, 219; and *The Story of an Affinity*, 336n29; and "Winter Hues Recalled," 43, 305n2; works by: *The Excursion*, 246; "I wandered lonely as a cloud," 28, 89–90; "Nutting," 336n29; *The Prelude*, 43; "Tintern Abbey," 28, 34, 86

Youth's Companion (Boston), 149